FEMINISM FOR THE AMERICAS

�֎ ✖ ✖

Guided by feminist and antiracist perspectives, this series examines the construction and influence of gender and sexuality within the full range of America's cultures. Investigating in deep context the ways in which gender works with and against such markers as race, class, and region, the series presents outstanding interdisciplinary scholarship, including works in history, literary studies, religion, folklore, and the visual arts. In so doing, Gender and American Culture seeks to reveal how identity and community are shaped by gender and sexuality.

A complete list of books published in
Gender and American Culture is available at
www.uncpress.org.

Feminism

FOR THE AMERICAS

✖ ✖ ✖

THE MAKING OF AN

INTERNATIONAL HUMAN RIGHTS

MOVEMENT

✖ ✖ ✖

KATHERINE M. MARINO

The University of North Carolina Press

Chapel Hill

*This book was published with the
assistance of the Authors Fund of the
University of North Carolina Press.*

© 2019 Katherine M. Marino

Set in Quadraat by Tseng Information Systems, Inc.
Manufactured in the United States of America

The University of North Carolina Press has been a member
of the Green Press Initiative since 2003.

Jacket illustration by Sally Fry Scruggs

Library of Congress Cataloging-in-Publication Data
Names: Marino, Katherine M., author.
Title: Feminism for the Americas : the making of an international
human rights movement / Katherine M. Marino.
Other titles: Gender & American culture.
Description: Chapel Hill : The University of North Carolina Press, [2019] |
Series: Gender and American culture
Identifiers: LCCN 2018031111| ISBN 9781469649696 (cloth : alk. paper) |
ISBN 9781469649702 (ebook)
Subjects: LCSH: Feminism—Latin America—History—20th century. | Feminism—
United States—History—20th century. | Feminism—Social aspects—Latin America. |
Feminism—Social aspects—United States. | Women's rights—Latin America. | Women's rights—
United States. | Anti-imperialist movements—History—20th century. | Luisi, Paulina. |
Lutz, Bertha, 1894-1976. | Vergara, Marta. | Domínguez Navarro, Ofelia, 1894-1976. |
González, Clara, 1900-1990. | Stevens, Doris, 1888-1963.
Classification: LCC HQ1460.5 .M35 2019 | DDC 305.42098/0904—dc23
LC record available at https://lccn.loc.gov/2018031111

Portions of chapters 1 and 4 draw on Katherine M. Marino,
"Transnational Pan-American Feminism: The Friendship of Bertha Lutz and Mary Wilhelmine
Williams, 1926-1944," *Journal of Women's History* 26, no. 2 (Summer 2014): 63–87.

Portions of chapter 5 draw on Katherine M. Marino, "Marta Vergara,
Popular-Front Pan-American Feminism, and the Transnational Struggle for Working Women's
Rights in the 1930s," *Gender and History* 26, no. 3 (© 2014, *Gender and History,*
John Wiley & Sons Ltd.).

For Mary Alice and Joseph, my parents

CONTENTS

✴ ✴ ✴

FIGURES

✕ ✕ ✕

FEMINISM FOR THE AMERICAS

✘ ✘ ✘

Feminismo americano

ЖЖЖ

The intense intellectual work that courses through feminismo
americano reveals . . . women's profound action, completely in tune
with the social reality. The movement . . . is energetic and decisive.
ROSA BORJA DE ICAZA, *Hacia la vida*, 1936

In 1931, a conflict between two prominent women's rights leaders changed the course of feminism in the Americas. From the United States, Doris Stevens wrote to her Cuban colleague Ofelia Domínguez Navarro with instructions to fight for women's suffrage.

Cuba was on the brink of a revolution, and forty-two-year-old Stevens, a veteran of the U.S. suffrage movement, believed that it spelled feminist opportunity. Over the past two years, the worldwide economic crisis had caused political and social tumult in the United States and throughout the Americas, from the Rio Grande to Tierra del Fuego. In Cuba, it fostered the newly repressive dictatorship of President Gerardo Machado, who promised constitutional reforms as window dressing to his undemocratic regime. Stevens viewed it as the perfect time to promote women's political rights and did not hesitate to suggest as much to Domínguez. Failing to do so, Stevens indicated, would set back progress for Cuban women.[1]

Thirty-six-year-old Domínguez bristled at her colleague's unsolicited advice. She too believed this moment heralded women's politicization, but not through the vote, which would be "stale at the source" under a dictatorship. In earlier communication with Stevens, Domínguez had explained Cuba's current "regime of terror," propped up by the U.S. government.[2] Machado had abolished habeas corpus, replaced elected officials with secret police, closed universities, curtailed free speech and free assembly, and jailed political dissidents. Feminists were leading direct action against the dictatorship, alongside students and workers, and were often the targets of violence. Domínguez had just endured two prison sentences. Stevens, however, offered no words of solace or solidarity, only instructions to push for suffrage.

Dominguez fired back with her own letter, telling Stevens there was much she did not understand. In Cuba, Domínguez explained, *feminismo* signified

1

something broader than support for women's political rights. It meant radical transformation—not only women's political and civil equality but also social and economic justice for working women and the political and civil rights of all people—men and women who were suffering under a dictatorship and under U.S. imperialism. Domínguez had recently founded a new feminist group in Cuba that espoused all of these goals.[3]

But now Domínguez was done pleading with Stevens. Her letter was a good-bye.

Stevens's missive was the last straw in the two women's strained relationship. Several years earlier, they had collaborated at the Sixth Pan-American Conference in Havana to found the Inter-American Commission of Women (IACW), a body formed to unite a hemispheric feminist movement and promote international women's rights. Since that time, Stevens chaired the organization unilaterally and focused its efforts solely on women's political and civil rights. She consistently ignored Latin American appeals to expand the commission's agenda.

Dominguez's letter, which brought an end to her collaboration with Stevens, became a call to arms. She reproduced their correspondence on a one-page broadside, front and back, adding only the header "To the Political Conscience of the Latin American Woman," and circulated it widely to Spanish-speaking feminists throughout the Americas.[4]

The way Domínguez framed feminismo spoke powerfully to her many readers. Feminismo was becoming a hemispheric movement—what Domínguez's country-woman Catalina Pozo y Gato described as a "tightly-knit continental network" in which the "Hispanic-American woman" sought the "conquest of her politico-social and proletarian rights."[5] While many of these feministas applauded Stevens's dogged push for women's legal equality, they promoted more expansive goals. They also resented Stevens's unilateral leadership over inter-American feminism, which, as they saw it, was an extension of U.S. imperialism.

Several years later, Domínguez's group called the dissemination of this flyer one of its greatest anti-imperialist acts.[6] It inspired and helped unite feministas across the Americas. Over the following years, they organized as a bloc and asserted their leadership over American feminism. Their legacy of feminismo americano endures today in the global movements for feminism and international human rights.

✼

This book tells the story of the movement that Doris Stevens claimed to lead and that Ofelia Domínguez Navarro and other feministas remade. Over the first half of the twentieth century, feminismo americano galvanized leaders and groups throughout the hemisphere who helped inaugurate what we think of today as global feminism — a fight for women's rights and human rights on a global scale. Working in coordinated campaigns that began after World War I and coincided with a new Pan-Americanism touting the cultural superiority of the Americas, activists moved women's rights beyond the domestic realm. Collaborating and clashing, they ushered in the first intergovernmental organization for women's rights in the world (the IACW); the first international treaty for women's rights; and, in 1945, the inclusion of women's rights in the United Nations Charter and its category of international human rights. In countries throughout the Americas, these innovations sped numerous changes for women — suffrage, equal nationality rights, rights to hold public office, equal pay for equal work, and maternity legislation.

Although U.S. feminists sought credit for this movement, Latin American leaders drove and dramatically expanded it. They assertively promoted a meaning of "feminism" that was broader than the term's definition in the United States at the time. Coined in France in 1880 by suffragist Hubertine Auclert, *feminisme* traveled throughout Europe and the Americas, connoting a modern movement that demanded female emancipation — economic and social justice, women's control over their bodies, and full equality with men in every sphere of life.[7] In the United States, feminism reached a breakthrough in the 1910s, uniting a wide group of reformers and suffragists. However, the mainstream meaning of the term narrowed precipitously in the United States soon after the 1920 passage of the Nineteenth Amendment granting women's suffrage, becoming synonymous with the Equal Rights Amendment. Introduced into Congress in 1923 by the National Woman's Party, the ERA promised to bring women individual rights under the law: rights to independent nationality and to serve on juries, engage in business, serve as witnesses to public documents, and administer property. While supporting many of these rights in theory, wide swaths of progressive reformers in the United States opposed the ERA's sweeping guarantee of "equal rights under the law" for fear it would eliminate hard-fought protective labor legislation necessary to safeguard working women. The Woman's Party's narrowness of vision and explicit resistance to addressing race- or class-based injustices made the group and the ERA anathema to many other movements, as well.[8]

It was, in part, this contraction of the meaning of "feminism" and lack of support for the ERA in the United States that made National Woman's Party leaders like Doris Stevens eager to engage in the inter-American realm in the late 1920s. The single-issue focus on legal equality that they deemed so successful in the U.S. suffrage movement defined their approach to inter-American feminism. Their Equal Rights Treaty, an internationalization of the ERA, provoked concerted resistance from the network of U.S. women's groups opposed to the ERA. As a result, from the 1920s to the 1940s, the inter-American realm became a significant new battleground for U.S. women to play out their domestic ERA debate. Each side believed that it represented the rightful leadership over the Americas, where, aside from the United States and Canada, most countries still had not passed national women's suffrage.

In these years, however, more flexible meanings of *feminismo* flourished in Latin America, where the ERA debate did not exist and where activists of multiple commitments took up the term with far greater ease than their North American counterparts. While Latin American feminisms were heterogeneous, large groups of *feministas* cohered around some common goals for *feminismo americano*.

First, *feminismo americano* demanded not only women's individual rights under the law—for the vote and for civil rights—but also economic and social rights. These rights included equal pay for equal work, extension of labor legislation to rural and domestic workers, and rights of children born out of wedlock and of the mothers of those children. Activists also called for paid maternity leave, day-care facilities, and in some cases health care as "social rights."

Second, *feminismo americano* assertively promoted Latin American leadership and opposition to U.S. imperialism. Many Latin Americans feminists identified U.S. counterparts' presumptions of superiority as imperialist, especially since the United States had long used its perceived preeminence in women's rights as justification for its political and economic ambitions in the region.[9] In inter-American feminism, the questions of who had the authority to speak and to assert common "American" principles became paramount. *Feministas* actively pushed back against a U.S. imperial feminism that often sought to squelch their goals. Their clashes with U.S. leaders helped produce a robust *feminismo americano* that pushed for liberation from multiple and overlapping forms of oppression—against patriarchy, U.S. imperialism, fascism, and often racism.

Debates over U.S. empire fueled the movement's hemispheric goals. The terms "American," "Pan-American," and "inter-American" were important identifiers for these women. But "Latin American" and "Pan-Hispanic," terms that emerged after the U.S. government annexed more than a third of Mexico's territory in 1848, were often more important.[10] Pan-Hispanism was a regional identity based on a common *raza*, language, and shared history of oppression under U.S. economic, cultural, and military imperialism. Profoundly influenced by Pan-Hispanism, early-twentieth-century *feministas* urged each other to take inspiration from their own history and ideas, rather than from Europe and the U.S. Over the first four decades of the twentieth century, Pan-Hispanism also helped shape new forms of multilateral inter-American law that emphasized both international interdependence *and* national sovereignty.[11] This mélange of thought, activism, and dynamism in inter-American jurisprudence facilitated one of *feminismo americano*'s signal innovations and key contributions to international human rights: its push of "women's rights" beyond the purely domestic realm and into international law.

Feminismo americano's demands for international women's rights; its emphasis on social and economic as well as political and civil inequalities; and its calls for a Latin American–led anti-imperialist feminism gained a groundswell of support during the global crises of the 1930s. The economic and political shifts of the Great Depression intensified many *feministas*' attention to social and economic rights. The Chaco War between Bolivia and Paraguay (1932–35) focused new efforts by women on pacifism. Fascism's rise in Europe and Asia, along with the growth of related forms of right-wing authoritarianism in the Americas and the Spanish Civil War (1936–39), helped generate vibrant transnational, antifascist feminist organizing. The global Popular Front movement that declared a "united front" of collaboration between communism and social democracy against fascism had profound national and inter-American iterations throughout the Americas. As *feministas* realized fascism's unique threats to women's rights, and as Popular Front leaders recognized the vital role that women could play in antifascism, the Popular Front gained a dynamic feminist counterpart, as well.[12]

These new developments culminated in what I call Popular Front Pan-American feminism, during which *feminismo americano* peaked. This was a people's movement. It incorporated feminist labor concerns with equal rights demands and knit crucial connections between feminism, socialism, antifascism and anti-imperialism. A dramatic number of new antifascist feminist groups emerged in the Americas in these years that for the first time included meaningful numbers of working women. Popular Front Pan-American feminism also mobilized new campaigns for women's suffrage throughout the region. When in 1939 the famous Spanish Civil War leader Dolores Ibárruri, "La Pasionaria," applauded the vitality of the women's movement in numerous Latin American countries, she was referring to Popular Front Pan-American feminism.[13]

Feminismo americano played a pivotal role in the development of international human rights. It produced a legal innovation in a treaty that sought to surpass national law and grant international women's rights. Groups throughout the Americas rallied around this treaty, as they expanded its meaning. In the late 1930s through the Second World War, Latin American *feministas* joined religious, labor, antiracist, anticolonial, and antifascist groups to demand an interconnected set of "human rights" for all people, defined as rights regardless of race, class, sex, or religion. During the Second World War, *feministas americanas* also looked to Franklin Delano Roosevelt's Atlantic Charter and "Four Freedoms" as promises of *derechos humanos*—international commitments to social justice—that included women's rights.

In 1945, at the San Francisco conference that created the United Nations, inter-American feminists pushed women's rights into the UN Charter, over the express objection of U.S. and British women. Drawing on arguments and experience they had honed over two decades, they internationalized women's rights and proposed what became the UN Commission on the Status of Women. Immediately after the conference, *feministas* demanded a broad meaning for the UN Charter's women's and human rights promises and urged acknowledgment that inter-American thought and activism shaped their formulation. The idea that "women's rights are human rights" emerged not from the United States or Western Europe but from Latin American feminists enmeshed in regional conflicts over imperialism, fascism, and Pan-Americanism.[14]

✳

In spite of the movement's monumental accomplishments, few people know of it.[15] The pantheon of late nineteenth- and early twentieth-century feminist leaders usually include recognizable names from the United States and Western Europe but not from Latin America. The story usually goes that until the 1970s, Latin America produced minimal women's rights organizing because of Catholicism, conservatism, and unstable political climates that would have rendered the vote moot. Where Latin American feminism did exist, it is often characterized as maternalist—privileging women as mothers, wives, and sometimes workers—but not as men's equals.[16] Such interpretations map onto larger narratives that place the United States and Western Europe at the apex of global "progress" and that measure feminist progress through winning the vote. These histories usually portray international feminism of the interwar years as a one-way exportation of ideas from the United States and Western Europe to the "South" and argue that feminism did not truly become "transnational" until after the 1975 International Women's Year Conference in Mexico City. These histories generally fail to recognize how transformative the international sphere was for feminist thought and activism in the interwar years, in part because they limit the scope of the international to the United States and Europe.[17]

If we look south, and explore multidirectional flows of influence, a new hemispheric history of feminism emerges. Given Latin American countries' common histories of U.S. empire and Pan-Hispanic identity, the inter-American realm was a critical site of innovation for new forms of feminism in the early twentieth century. In these years, as the ranks of Latin American *feministas* grew, they envisioned themselves from the start in both regional and national units; transnational interdependence was the hallmark of their thought and activism.

This book argues that Latin American feminisms not only thrived but, in fact, took the lead internationally. It calls for the historical restoration of Latin American feminist leaders as innovators in global feminist thought and activism. In the interwar years, when dominant understandings of feminism in the United States and Western Europe fractured into two increasingly distinct and irreconcilable socialist and "equalitarian" camps, *feminismo americano* called for "equal rights" alongside social and economic rights and saw no incompatibility between these two demands. More than Catholicism or maternalism, Latin American liberalism shaped this supple definition of feminism. Popularized by the 1917 Constitution of Mexico, which became a model for constitutions in Brazil, Uruguay, and other countries in Latin America, this brand of Latin American social democracy upheld *both* the individual *and* the family as fundamental political units.[18]

In the 1930s, communism and the Popular Front also helped to internationalize the social rights claims at the heart of *feminismo americano*. While demanding political and civil rights, *feministas* also acknowledged both the expansion of women's waged labor and the unwaged labor for which women were disproportionately responsible. They blazed new trails, urging international attention to maternity legislation as a "social right" in a way that did not stigmatize working mothers and in a way that did not subvert women's political or economic autonomy or valorize motherhood above all else. Many also called for reproductive rights—including access to birth control and legalized abortion—even if they did not elevate those demands to the status of equal rights treaties. Drawing on an array of tactics, they utilized official inter-American conferences to promote international women's and human rights, while also launching informal, grassroots mobilizations through groups that operated on international, regional, and national scales.[19]

The movement, however, was not monolithic. It was fueled by significant disagreements that often quenched its expansion and above all by a heterogeneous group of feminist leaders. At a time when feminist organizing was structured hierarchically around individual leaders who often became proxies for their nations' ambitions on the international stage, the interpersonal dynamics of *feminismo americano* were critical. This book focuses on the collaborations and conflicts of six remarkable activists who became its dramatis personae: Paulina Luisi from Uruguay, Bertha Lutz from Brazil, Clara González from Panama, Ofelia Domínguez Navarro from Cuba, Doris Stevens from the United States, and Marta Vergara from Chile.

Although history has tended to remember these women for their significant national feminist achievements, they formed a close network and were also well known at the time as among la vanguardia—the modern and avant-garde—for their rebellious international leadership.[20] Luisi, Stevens, Lutz, Domínguez, González, and Vergara shared some key traits: they were all trailblazers who transcended the cultural, social, and professional strictures placed on most women of their era. Significantly, all had the racial and class privilege, the educational pedigrees, and the cosmopolitan connections that facilitated their organizing, as well as their global travel and attendance at elite international gatherings. They were all considered white or mestiza in their national contexts (even if the Latin American women were not considered white by their U.S. counterparts). Most of them were single and none had children, which allowed them to devote considerable time and energy—indeed, most of their adult lives—to their activism.

All six leveraged their prestige to command continental attention to feminist demands and debates, which they publicized in newspaper and magazine articles, pamphlets, books, flyers, and letters that circulated throughout the Americas. They influenced public opinion, and their conflicts with each other took on hemispheric proportions.

Paulina Luisi (b. 1875), the eldest of the six, was the recognized "mother" of Latin American feminism. The first female doctor in Uruguay, Luisi, an obstetrician, also birthed Pan-American feminism. With Argentinian friends she conceived the first Pan-American feminist organization in 1921. Straightforward and capable of blunt judgment, Luisi did not shy from taking U.S. feminists to task. Charismatic, tender, and deeply supportive of other Spanish-speaking leaders, Luisi served as personal mentor to virtually every younger Spanish-speaking feminist who attempted to organize a Pan-Hispanic movement. She nurtured feminismo americano.

Bertha Lutz (b. 1894), a famous biologist, was known internationally as the "brains" of Brazil's suffrage movement. Lutz became a leader of the Pan-American organization that grew out of Luisi's early efforts but embraced very different understandings of Pan-American feminism. Fluent in Portuguese, English, and French, she deemed Spanish-speaking "Latin America" racially backward and believed that Brazil and the United States should lead. Sharp-tongued, quick thinking, and conscientious, Lutz advanced her own idiosyncratic vision at international conferences where the movement took shape. Ironically, her efforts often galvanized even stronger forms of Pan-Hispanic American feminism.

Clara González (b. 1898), the first female lawyer in Panama, championed the leadership of women in Central America and the Caribbean. Known as

8   PROLOGUE

"Panama's Portia" in the United States (after the legally astute heroine of Shakespeare's *The Merchant of Venice*), González drew a connection between the "protection" of protectorates like her own Panama by the United States and the "protection" of women by men. She developed the idea for an international agreement for women's rights and later fought for the Equal Rights Treaty as a representative of the IACW. In spite of her disillusionment with U.S. dominance over this organization, González nonetheless continued to cultivate her original dream — for a Latin American–led, anti-imperialist American feminism.

Cuban Ofelia Domínguez Navarro (b. 1894) collaborated with her good friend González on an American feminism that deemed women's sovereignty and Latin American national sovereignty as mutually constitutive. Also a lawyer, Domínguez traded her faith in law for revolution in the 1930s. She became a passionate leader of the Communist parties in Cuba and in Mexico, where she lived in exile for a number of years during the Machado and Batista regimes and where she organized feminists and workers. Disseminating information throughout the continent about the problematic leadership of the U.S. chair of the IACW, Domínguez was critical to boosting the Latin American resurgence that galvanized *feminismo americano*.

The target of Domínguez's ire, Doris Stevens (b. 1888), was a U.S. suffrage veteran famous for her brief imprisonment for picketing the White House during that campaign. Dubbed the "Apostle of Action" for her aggressive and effective leadership, Stevens garnered admiration throughout the Americas for dramatic acts of defiance often aimed at the U.S. government. But she was also the bête noire of many Latin American feminists. As the chair of the IACW for nearly a decade, Stevens advanced her vision of feminism enshrined in the Equal Rights Treaty, in spite of protest from many Latin American counterparts who sought to expand the agenda beyond demands for civil and political rights. Without her able organizing, savvy media campaigns, and the significant capital she raised from powerful U.S. donors, the commission's international demands would likely not have gained the influence that they did. Yet, without her polarizing personality stoking the resentment of so many feminists in the region, the movement would also not have attracted such a strong Pan-Hispanic rebellion.

Of the five Latin American feminists at the center of this story, Chile's Marta Vergara (b. 1898) came the closest to being Stevens's friend. She would also be one of her most effective opponents, pushing for a broader movement that challenged Stevens's leadership. A well-known journalist, Vergara successfully enlarged the meaning of "equal rights" demands to include social and economic rights for women. She also helped to expand the movement's reach. Like Domínguez, Vergara became a communist; she joined the Communist Party of Chile in the mid-1930s and knit connections with other national, regional, and transnational groups that promoted antifascism, pacifism, and women's rights. She helped create a new Popular Front feminist movement by and for Spanish-speaking women.

Feminist history has long challenged conventional periodizations, and by exploring the movement that these six activists helped create, this book offers yet another one.[21] The period between the "first wave" of feminism and the "second wave," long viewed as the "doldrums," becomes one of great feminist vitality if we shift our geographic focus south. When we do, we find that the historic milestones of the Monroe Doctrine; U.S. military intervention in Nicaragua, Haiti, and the Dominican Republic; the Panama Canal; the Platt Amendment; the Spanish Civil War; and the Atlantic Charter, were all feminist incubators.

These world-historic events formed key backdrops to a series of international conferences that became the staging ground for *feminismo americano* and that provide the backbone of this book. Inter-American conferences were where the book's six protagonists, along with other feminists and statesmen, built and broke alliances, sharpened their arguments, publicized their demands, organized counter-conferences to protest the official ones, and secured their most significant victories. These meetings are as important to feminist history as the 1848 convention in Seneca Falls, New York, often credited for launching the first organized demands for women's rights, and the 1975 International Women's Year Conference in Mexico City, which mobilized new forms of global feminism. They represent key precursors, as well, to the 1993 UN World Conference on Human Rights in Vienna and the 1995 UN Fourth World Conference on Women in Beijing, both tipping points for international recognition of "women's rights as human rights." At these Pan-American conferences, international relations not only shaped feminism, but feminism also influenced diplomacy and Pan-Americanism.[22] From the moment that Cuban and U.S. feminists gatecrashed the 1928 Pan-American conference in Havana, women's rights became a central feature of Pan-American conferences. Years before that conference, male Latin American statesmen had already promoted women's rights in these venues, equating feminism with "civilizational" progress. In the period of the "Good Neighbor," the IACW became a pronounced thorn in the side of the U.S. State Department. At Pan-American conferences, debates over international women's rights treaties produced political showdowns around U.S. empire, national sovereignty, Latin American progress, and, in the 1930s, fascism and antifascism. During the Second World War, when U.S. efforts to solidify its relations with Latin America peaked, the State Department invested more energy and resources into Pan-American feminism than ever before. But it also sought to neutralize the movement. The indomitable persistence of a Latin American–led *feminismo americano*, in opposition to U.S. government resistance to international women's rights demands, unmistakably influenced the emergence of human rights during and after the Second World War.

⚹

Interpersonal dynamics and affect powerfully shaped the movement that, in turn, transformed the lives of the women who propelled it. This book explores the interactions that Luisi, Lutz, González, Domínugez, Stevens, and Vergara had with each other, and with a host of other feminists and statesmen, to recover what global feminism *felt* like. It argues that these feelings and relationships were important to the movement's political outcomes.[23] Competing ideas about empire, language, race, and nation galvanized the movement, and the debates and anger produced by these differences were often productive. *Feministas'* disputes with individual U.S. leaders who, to them, embodied U.S. empire helped to ally otherwise very different Latin American women, who in turn formed tightly cathected relationships with each other. Imperial feminism also prevailed among some Latin American activists, and indeed drove a prominent strain of Pan-American feminism, as well. Bertha Lutz's beliefs in her own racial and cultural superiority, and her insistence that Pan-American feminism should be led by white elites from Brazil and the United States, caused tense relationships with Spanish-speaking feminists. At the same time, some of those Spanish-speaking feminists maintained their senses of racialized and global superiority.[24]

More often, however, Latin American feminists' routine experiences with racism from U.S. counterparts, and the antiracist politics of the Popular Front, caused them to broaden their movement and formulate more indivisible notions of "human rights" based on gender, race, and class. Their experiences and expanding politics influenced the demands Latin American feminists made at the 1945 Inter-American Conference on Problems of War and Peace that women's equal rights be allied with antiracism and explicitly be afforded to "Latin American women, black women, and women of different indigenous races."[25]

Feministas were keenly aware of the affective content of their movement, and it is not a coincidence that a number of them argued that "love" should be the basis of their politics.[26] As Argentinian Popular Front Pan-American feminist Victoria Ocampo explained in the 1930s, women needed to "unite in a solidarity that is not only objective but subjective," by which she meant one focused both on "actions and vested interests" and on "ideas and feelings."[27] *Feministas'* relationships with each other became testing grounds for a *feminismo americano* that combined individual sovereignty with collective forms of justice, including solidarity with people around the world whom they would never meet. This sense of empathy infused their calls for human rights. Clara González understood social democracy as a collective venture akin to friendship, in which people had obligations to each other, as well as individual rights. As she put it, her ideal was a politics "attuned to the real needs of modern life, which is essentially a life of relationships, of interdependence, of solidarity, of mutual aid, of social action, and of love."[28]

The strong networks that *feministas* formed with each other expanded the possibilities of their international engagements and led to material gains at home and abroad. This movement fostered national legislation for political, civil, social, and economic rights throughout the Americas. It also successfully deterred threats to women's rights in many countries—*feministas* drew on international mobilization to block proposed laws that they deemed "fascist." Perhaps most important, it politicized women, awakening many to the connections between global empire and local forms of oppression, and between their roles in their communities, homes, and work and their united political power.

Women's real and imagined bonds with one another constituted the centripetal force of *feminismo americano*. Ofelia Domínguez Navarro knew this. Several years after her conflict with Doris Stevens, she sent a copy of their correspondence to an Argentinean friend as justification for forming a Spanish-speaking confederation of Latin American feminists. Such collective power was as yet untried, Domínguez acknowledged, but together they could be a "force."[29] She urged the same idea to her mentor, Paulina Luisi, who sent Domínguez words of empathy and support during the latter's imprisonment by the Machado regime. Luisi's solidarity gave Domínguez hope that a Latin American–led women's movement would have far-reaching effects. As she wrote to Luisi, "We women will jolt our continent!"[30]

CHAPTER ONE

A New Force in the History of the World

✖   ✖   ✖

In May 1921, twenty-six-year-old Bertha Lutz wrote to forty-five-year-old Paulina Luisi about an issue "that concerns me more and more" — the "question of feminism." The term *feminisme* had been introduced in France and made its way to the Americas in the late nineteenth century but was only now becoming part of the vocabulary of political leaders, socialists, and middle-class women and social reformers like Brazilian Lutz and Uruguayan Luisi. Lutz sought an introduction to some of the international groups with which Luisi, the most famous Latin American feminist, had connections. Apologizing for her "audacity" for writing to Luisi "without having had the honor of meeting you personally," Lutz wrote, "it is well known that in Uruguay, you are at the vanguard."[1]

In Montevideo, Luisi was thrilled to read Lutz's letter. She believed that the time was ripe for a new movement by and for women of the Americas, one free from the dominance of European women, to promote women's suffrage, welfare, and peace in the Western Hemisphere. "Our international correspondence and collaboration ... promise many good things for us," Luisi responded.[2] These two women would help launch what Lutz later called "a new force in the history of the world," Pan-American feminism.

Both women believed that the First World War had shattered the ideal of European cultural superiority. It opened a space for the "new" democratic nations of the Americas, with a common history of European colonialism, to become beacons of progress, social reform, international multilateralism, and peace. The new Pan-Americanism advocated cultural advancement and political sovereignty, and women's rights were central to both.

Luisi and Lutz would find, however, that they maintained distinct and clashing notions of Pan-American feminism. Paulina Luisi privileged a movement organized by Spanish-speaking women of la raza and celebrated a Pan-Hispanic identity over that of a U.S. and Anglo-American empire. Her Pan-Americanism did not always seek to dismantle U.S. hegemony as much as it sought to write the "better constituted" nations of Latin America, such as her own Uruguay, into it. Bertha Lutz, on the other hand, believed that the rightful leaders of Pan-

American feminism were Brazil and the United States, embodied respectively by herself and U.S. suffrage veteran Carrie Chapman Catt. Luisi and Lutz each presumed her country represented continental leadership. Their differences would develop into consequential rifts.

Luisi and Lutz's conflict represented a broader ideological fissure between those who believed Pan-Americanism should celebrate the political culture of the United States as a model for the continent and those who believed that it should explicitly reject such a premise. Discord driven by its participants' divergent views of language, race, and empire proved critical to the origins of Pan-American feminism and would shape the movement for decades to come.

Paulina Luisi and the Origins of Pan-American Feminism

In 1916, five years before her glowing correspondence with Lutz, Paulina Luisi gave the keynote address at the First Pan-American Child Congress in Buenos Aires. In it, she asserted that women's rights should be a Pan-American goal. The term "Pan-American," rather than signifying U.S. economic hegemony or military intervention, was becoming a Latin American–led social movement. Its interrelated goals included democracy, international peace, social improvement, and specifically the growth of welfare states and protection of women and children. While the war in Europe was precluding social welfare advances, Luisi announced that the Americas, whose democratic revolutions had overthrown the shackles of "old Europe," were uniting to do "the work of Life and progress that can only thrive in the shade of the tree of Peace!"[3] Luisi introduced resolutions on sex education and public health, yet her speech emphasized a new demand: the vote for women, then under consideration by her own country as it debated universal suffrage. Women's right to vote would perfect the two critical objectives of Pan-Americanism: political sovereignty and cultural advancement of the Western Hemisphere.[4]

Never before had women's rights been articulated as a Pan-American demand. Still a marginal goal in most Latin American countries in 1916, over the next years it became central to the Pan-American mission.

The 1916 congress marked a turning point for Luisi as well. Soon after her return to Montevideo she created the first national suffrage organization in Uruguay, the Consejo Nacional de Mujeres Uruguayas (CONAMU), an offshoot of the International Council of Women (ICW, 1888) in Europe that already had branches in Argentina and Chile. Luisi also formally connected CONAMU to a new Pan-American women's group established to improve the welfare of women and children in the hemisphere—the U.S.-based Women's Auxiliary to the Second Pan-American Congress. In 1917 in the pages of the CONAMU bulletin *Acción Femenina*, Luisi used the word "feminism" in print for the first time, describing her understanding of the term: "Feminism demonstrates that woman is something more than material created to serve and obey man like a slave; that she is more than a machine to produce children and care for the home; that women have feelings and intellect; that it is their mission to perpetuate the species and this must be done with more than the entrails and the breast; it must be done with a mind and a heart prepared to be a mother and an educator; that she must be man's partner and counselor not his slave."[5]

Such partnership, Luisi explained, necessitated "full rights" related to work, property, and salary and to the care of children. Women required, "in the same form as to the man, the liberties and rights that they have proclaimed as the heritage of the human being." Beyond these individual rights, Luisi envisioned social rights, with implied "responsibilities," tools in the more radical social transformation that feminism could unleash.[6] Over the next several years, Luisi collaborated with friends in Argentina and Chile to push women's rights into the heart of a new movement of Pan-American feminism.

Self-identification with the term "Pan-American" was new for Luisi. Spanish America and Europe were much stronger reference points for her than the United States. She identified with Pan-Hispanism, a movement popularized by early twentieth-century Latin American modernists, which conveyed a shared regional sense of language, raza, and history of independence from Spain and of U.S. hegemony. The U.S. had emerged as an enemy to "Spanish America" as early as the nineteenth century, with annexation of Texas in 1845, the Mexican-American War (1846–48), and U.S. interest in the Isthmus of Panama. But the Spanish-American War in 1898 truly galvanized an oppositional Pan-Hispanism that emphasized "two Americas"—one Hispanoamérica or América Latina, and the other an Anglo-Saxon America. The former was characterized by humanism, idealism, and collectivism and the latter by materialism, utilitarianism, and imperialism. Luisi and many other Latin American elites were influenced by Uruguayan intellectual José Enrique Rodó, who warned in his widely read 1900 book Ariel against U.S. imperial expansion, what was becoming known as el peligro yanqui ("the Yankee danger").[7] Over the next few decades, the term la raza denoted the Spanish-speaking communities on both sides of the Atlantic, and Luisi took up the term with alacrity, declaring herself in 1919 "pro-feminist" and "pro-raza."[8]

Born in Argentina to European immigrants—her mother of Polish descent and her father an Italian citizen—Luisi and her family moved to Paysandú, Uruguay, shortly after she was born and then to the capital, Montevideo, when she was twelve. Her parents were unusually progressive, anticlerical, and supportive of their eight daughters, who excelled in areas traditionally off-limits to women. Paulina, the eldest of her siblings, became a physician, her sister Clotilde the first female lawyer in Uruguay, and her sister Luisa a famous poet.[9] After earning a teaching degree in 1890, Paulina became the first woman in Uruguay to earn a bachelor's degree in 1899 and, in 1908, the first to gain a medical degree, becoming the head of the gynecology clinic of the Faculty of Medicine at the National University in Montevideo. In these years she found her closest friends and professional connections among a coterie of the first generation of female teachers and medical professionals like herself in the Spanish-speaking Southern Cone—Uruguay, Chile, and Argentina.[10]

During the mid- to late nineteenth century of Luisi's youth, industrialization, urbanization, and immigration were altering both political institutions and conditions of everyday life in many Latin American countries, particularly in the Southern Cone, encouraging the rise of democratic constitutions, a middle class, and a move toward secularism. It was within this host of changes that an educated group of women, first as schoolteachers and then, increasingly, as professional doctors, lawyers, and educators, emerged. They led the earliest attempts to create liberal feminist organizations in South America, including the First International Women's Congress, in Buenos Aires, in 1910, one of the first international feminist gatherings in the continent.[11]

This was a critical event for Luisi. Addressing reforms in women's labor, public health, sex education, childcare, and feminism, this regional meeting sought state intervention in support of mothers and children to right the wrongs generated by industrial capitalism, such as child labor and the exploitation of women in the workplace. Participants also introduced resolutions for women's equal access to education and the professions, equal property and custody rights, and equal political rights and called for a "Latin American" feminist movement.[12] Here Luisi met and cemented her relationships with a host of influential female reformers who became lifelong friends—the Chilean educator Amanda Labarca; the Argentine educator Sara Justo, reformer Elvira Rawson de Dellepiane, and physicians Petrona Eyle and Alicia Moreau, the latter of whom became Luisi's closest friend in these years.[13]

These women encouraged Luisi to organize for women's rights in Uruguay, recognized as one of the most progressive countries in the hemisphere. During and after the presidencies of José Batlle y Ordóñez (1903–7 and 1911–15), Uruguay forwarded the most progressive social legislation throughout the Americas— the eight-hour workday, Ministries of Labor and of Industry, and a social security system that was the first not only in Latin America but also in the Western Hemisphere.[14] In part because of these advances and a growing middle class, feminist organizing would thrive there under the leadership of Luisi. By 1918, an article in the popular Argentine magazine *Caras y Caretas* announced that "within South America, the most defined feminist current is to be found in Uruguay."[15]

Paulina Luisi, "la 1a médica uruguaya, 1a doctorada" ("the first female physician in Uruguay, first female doctorate," date unknown). Courtesy of the Biblioteca Nacional de Uruguay, Montevideo, Uruguay, Colleción Paulina Luisi, Iconografía.

Uruguay's reputation for progressivism and feminism encouraged Luisi's eventual turn toward Pan-Americanism. In the early twentieth century, within Luisi's intellectual circles, Latin American jurists, doctors, and experts began to reframe the meaning of Pan-Americanism as a hemispheric union for democracy, liberal internationalism, scientific expertise, and social reform. Luisi attended the 1905 Latin American Scientific Congress where Chilean international jurist Alejandro Álvarez promoted an inter-American synthesis of law and suggested that the following scientific congress become a "Pan-American" event and include the United States.[16]

Álvarez was undoubtedly the most influential mouthpiece for the "new Pan-Americanism" among Spanish American elites. Emphasizing the role of social facts and social justice in international relations, he launched a new definition of the term: a new system of common international law marked by multilateralism and peace rather than by U.S. hegemony.[17] Álvarez applied precepts of European liberal internationalist thought, including arbitration and peaceful settlement of disputes, to the Western Hemisphere. But he argued that Latin America had its own unique and rich history of multilateralism that should be a model for other nations. He drew heavily on the thought of Simón Bolívar, Antonio José de Sucre, José Martí, and other nineteenth-century heroes of liberation who declared the unity of the Spanish-speaking republics. He also incorporated the Pan-Hispanism of Rodó that posited the Latin cultures as superior to Anglo-Saxon culture, asserting that the Spanish-speaking countries of the Americas could lead "civilization." While the Pan-Latin confederation of which Bolívar dreamed had been a utopian fantasy, a Pan-American confederation was not, Álvarez held. Latin America and the United States, he said, shared a history of overthrowing European colonial rule and embracing republican, democratic forms of government. Thus, this Pan-Americanism would look to the United States as an equal partner.[18]

Importantly, while emphasizing equality, Álvarez's new definition of Pan-Americanism reserved a special role for the countries deemed the hegemons in the hemisphere—the South American nations of Argentina, Brazil, and Chile, distinguished as the "A.B.C." countries for their economic and political power, as well as Uruguay, which ranked in cultural and political if not economic status with the A.B.C. nations.[19] Álvarez did not seek to overhaul the Monroe Doctrine but to internationalize it and extend its application to these "better constituted" countries of Latin America, deemed the most advanced.[20] The A.B.C. countries were gaining more of a multilateral relationship with the United States at this time and would play a key role in mediating the U.S. conflict with Mexico in 1916.[21]

Álvarez's vision of Pan-Americanism gained wide purchase, however, because it upheld an "American civilization" that was not defined by U.S. leadership or limited to an arid set of legalist or technical definitions. Drawing from staples in progressive internationalist thought, including the belief in the regenerative power of educating minds and exchanging ideas, he asserted a new Pan-Americanism that would bring the people of the Americas together more meaningfully to secure peace, social welfare, and reform. This collaborative, interpersonal form of Pan-Americanism he envisioned became enormously prominent. In the Americas, advances in communications and transportation sped the exchange of publications and people, promoting the interchange of ideas, person-to-person contact, and influence of public opinion. In 1910 the Commercial Bureau of American Republics became the Pan-American Union, and its *Pan American Bulletin* the clearinghouse for information on a dizzying array of new Pan-American congresses, including the Latin American-led Pan-American scientific and child congresses.[22] Bilingual editions of the bulletin and of other publications like *Inter-America* magazine (founded in 1917) were distributed in major cities throughout the Western Hemisphere.

This new Pan-Americanism rose to unprecedented heights during the First World War, when the U.S. government quickly and opportunistically incorporated Latin American–led meanings of Pan-Americanism in its advocacy for a "union of the Americas." U.S. promotion of Pan-Americanism closely corresponded to the dramatic rise in trade between Latin America and the United States, which increased in magnitude by more than 100 percent in the years after the 1914 completion of the Panama Canal.[23] At the Second Pan-American Scientific Congress in Washington, D.C., President Woodrow Wilson announced a new Pan-American treaty, proposing a union of the Americas to guarantee absolute political independence and territorial integrity and to settle all disputes in the Western Hemisphere by investigation and arbitration. Though the treaty did not pass, it offered a political structure that closely resembled Álvarez's multilateral Monroe Doctrine.[24]

Paulina Luisi recognized the deep contradiction that the same Woodrow Wilson who preached Pan-American equality had also led the 1914 U.S. intervention in Mexico. Even after proposing a Pan-American treaty, Wilson oversaw military interventions in Haiti and the Dominican Republic in flagrant disregard for norms of international law.

But Luisi agreed with the new iteration of Pan-Americanism that promoted continental leadership of the "well-constituted" Latin American countries, above all her own. Uruguay had released a "Decree of American Solidarity" after the United States entered World War I, which inspired similar official messages of "Pan-American" support from a host of other Latin American countries.[25] In 1919, Uruguay elected avid Pan-Americanist Baltasar Brum, who had been

Uruguay's minister of foreign affairs, as president.[26] Brum was a political mentor to Luisi. She would favor his definition of Pan-Americanism, strongly influenced by Álvarez: "not a North American creation nor . . . an exclusive idea of Monroe's" but a synthesis of U.S. and Latin American ideals. Explaining that the "Americas" would be free of "imperialism" and "racial oppression," in contrast to Europe, Brum's Pan-Americanism explicitly reversed the cultural and racial status of Latin Americans, whom many in Anglo-America and Western Europe viewed as racially inferior.[27]

Luisi's support of Pan-Americanism became official in 1915 when she joined the Pan-American Women's Auxiliary created in Washington, D.C. That year, the Pan-American Scientific Congress transformed into a full-dress diplomatic congress because of the war. Female reformers and wives of diplomats gathered separately to form their own Pan-American women's organization, the Comité Internacional Panamericano de Señoras (Pan-American International Women's Committee), dubbed the "Women's Auxiliary." Headed by the wives of the U.S. secretary of state and of a specialist in the U.S. Bureau of Education, the auxiliary was firmly supported by the U.S. State Department and Pan-American Union, though not officially affiliated with them.[28] It sought members from each nation in the Western Hemisphere, culled from the rosters of the Pan-American child and scientific congresses.

The Women's Auxiliary emerged in the context of a broader flourishing of U.S. and European women's internationalism, imbued with progressive beliefs that social justice and world peace required cooperation among the women of the world.[29] Jane Addams, U.S. social settlement reformer and international pacifist, articulated this gendered internationalism at the Pan-American women's meeting in Washington, D.C. Several months earlier, Addams had presided over the 1915 International Congress of Women at The Hague that brought together over 1,200 female delegates from Europe and the United States to denounce war and declare support for women's reform and rights. At the Pan-American meeting, Addams argued that since interactions among people from different nations could help end war, and since "natural intercourse, of social life versus political life, has largely been in the hands of women," women had a particular "obligation" to Pan-Americanism.[30]

A great admirer of Jane Addams, Luisi embraced the Women's Auxiliary and its guiding idea that women's affective relationships could promote international peace. Yet Luisi also saw an omission in the group's goals. While the Women's Auxiliary championed the "social and economic betterment" for women and children, it avoided women's right to vote, still deemed a controversial demand.[31] Internationally, however, including in Latin America, reformers argued that both women's equality and moral superiority necessitated women's full citizenship. International calls for global self-determination and democracy, hastened by the First World War, also made suffrage a more pressing demand. Along with feminist interlocutors and friends in Argentina who also joined the Women's Auxiliary, Luisi began to seek a new Pan-American forum that would formally and unapologetically assert women's political and civil rights.

The strong moves Uruguay was making toward women's suffrage, in contrast to most other countries in the Americas, convinced Luisi that Uruguay could help lead such a movement. In November 1917, Uruguayans supported a constitution that included a mechanism for enacting women's suffrage, promising women voting rights pending ratification by two-thirds of both legislative houses. As historian Francesca Miller has noted, this event made Uruguay, "in theory, the first of all Western Hemisphere nations to recognize female suffrage," even before the United States, where a number of states had granted women suffrage but a federal amendment was not yet in the offing.[32]

In 1919, Luisi founded a new organization, the Alianza Uruguaya para el Sufragio Femenino, to pressure elected officials to enact women's suffrage. As in Europe, where its parent organization, the International Woman Suffrage Alliance (IWSA), broke away from the International Council of Women in 1904 to demand suffrage, in Uruguay, a number of younger, middle-class (rather than elite), and progressive women split from the first organization Luisi founded, CONAMU, to join Luisi's new Alianza.[33] In her Alianza bulletin, and in that of the IWSA, Luisi noted that over the past several years "the name of Uruguay has quickly become known in the feminist circles of the entire world. . . . Uruguay was the first country in South America to initiate a women's suffrage movement."[34]

The vigorous support that now-president Baltasar Brum gave the suffrage movement only strengthened Luisi's desire for a Pan-American feminist movement with Uruguay at the helm. Brum and a number of statesmen from his progressive Colorado Party absorbed the well-worn nineteenth-century socialist idea that civilization could be measured by women's rights. Women's suffrage, they believed, would enhance Uruguay's democracy and power in the world. In 1920 Brum consulted Luisi on a tract for women's political and civil rights that he published and that became famous throughout the continent. In over 200 pages, *Los derechos de la mujer: Reforma a la legislación civil y política del Uruguay* carefully assessed the legal changes that would grant women "equal rights" with men in every sphere except for military service. It specifically argued that women in Uruguay must have these rights when many women already voted in states in the United States and in Britain, Germany, Denmark, Austria, Switzerland, Australia, and Canada.[35]

In 1919 with her Argentine feminist friends Alicia Moreau, Petrona Eyle, and Sara Justo, Luisi began to make concrete plans for a Pan-American conference of women to take place in Buenos Aires two years later, and that would demand women's suffrage. They specifically sought the collaboration of U.S. suffragist Carrie Chapman Catt, with whom the Argentine feminists, especially Moreau, regularly corresponded. Born in 1859, president of the U.S. National American Woman Suffrage Association, and founder and honorary president of the IWSA, Catt was one of the most well-known feminists in the world. Luisi and her Argentine friends believed that Catt's cooperation, as well as that of U.S. director of the Pan-American Union John Barrett, would be strategically important.[36]

The alliance they sought with Catt was instrumental, but it was also bolstered by a sense of the racial and cultural superiority that underwrote Pan-Americanism. Luisi believed that U.S. women like Catt and South American women like herself were connected not only by bonds of womanhood but also by a shared superiority as educated, middle-class, and white female reformers. As historian N. D. B. Connolly has noted, "Much of what lay subtly communicated in Pan-American boosterism included racial arguments about the desired complexion of international brotherhood."[37] This privileging of whiteness was clearly conveyed in the shared history of the Americas that Luisi's Pan-Americanist exemplars Álvarez and Brum promoted. It focused on the continent-wide overthrow of European colonialism and progress toward democracy and avoided any discussion of the genocide of Native American populations during and after colonialism or the violence of slavery of Native American or African-descended people.[38] At the same time that the national histories produced in these countries erased these events from collective memory, their governments were engaged in a process of "whitening" their populations through immigration from Europe as a form of "racial progress."[39] When Brum spoke of a Pan-Americanism "free from [the] partisan hatred and pernicious race prejudice" that riddled Europe, he meant "race" as many did at the time to denote a national or ethnic group.[40] Similarly, when Paulina Luisi celebrated the Hispanic-American la raza, she used the term to refer to Spanish-speaking people.[41] She, Brum, and many Latin American elites participated in a cultural construction of whiteness connected to Pan-Hispanism and the Spanish language. Luisi herself was a eugenicist. While she eventually embraced the Latin-American variant of eugenics that advocated state-led welfare programs and health campaigns, she interpreted the region's socioeconomic problems in terms of heredity and racial degeneration.[42] The common Uruguayan discourse in Luisi's day held that it was a "white" republic in spite of the fact that by 1800 one-quarter of the national population was African and Afro-Uruguayan.[43]

Luisi and her Argentine friends shared not only a European-descended racial identification with Catt but also a Western, teleological history of civilization and progress, whose most recent chapters included the education of women and women's rights. It was the role of educated, middle-class, and typically white reformers like themselves, they believed, to "uplift" their less-educated sisters. Imperialism and colonialism were not counter to but fundamental to the worldviews of international feminists in the predominantly Anglo-American and Western European groups such as the ICW and the IWSA.[44] Even though many of the Spanish-speaking feminists who engaged with these groups, like Luisi and Moreau, opposed U.S. intervention in Latin America, they were nonetheless educated by French-speaking Catholic teachers and steeped in Western, European-looking racial logics. As doctors and scientists, many of them were influenced by social Darwinism, which directly informed their feminism. In an interview published by the organ of the National American Woman Suffrage Association, Moreau explained to a U.S. audience that "two types" of women in Argentina represented two different "stages in . . . evolution." The earlier was the "Hispano-Colonial type": Catholic and backward, "the direct descendant of the woman born in a home formed by the union of the Spaniard and the Indian, a home ruled entirely by the father." The more progressive, enlightened female social reformers, like Moreau herself, were the "Argentine-European[s] . . . from the homes transplanted to this side of the sea by the current of immigration."[45]

This perceived shared evolutionary superiority and elitism were significant to Luisi's expectations for an "equal" Pan-American alliance with U.S. women. Yet she also knew that her U.S. counterparts, including Catt herself, often privileged another racial hierarchy that put Latin American countries on a lower civilizational plane, to be guided by their superior Anglo-American sisters. At a 1919 feminist gathering in Buenos Aires in which Luisi called U.S. women "sisters," she also admonished Catt and Dutch IWSA member Aletta Jacobs for completely overlooking Latin America in their "world suffrage tour." Catt had noted that suffrage associations existed throughout the world, except in "Greece, Spain, Turkey, the black Republic of Liberia and all of South America!" "I demand an exception for Uruguay," Luisi declared, "whose suffrage association I founded in 1916," citing her membership in the ICW and the IWSA. What bothered Luisi most was that Catt had condemned Uruguay and all of Latin America to a lower category than China, India, Egypt, and other countries that, Luisi said, "we consider much less civilized than ours."[46]

These tensions came to a head when Luisi attended the 1920 IWSA meeting in Geneva, Switzerland. At this conference, as historian Leila Rupp has observed, suffrage became the dividing line between the "haves" and the "have nots."[47] Holland and Luxembourg as well as the United States had recently passed female suffrage.[48] Meanwhile, in Uruguay, in spite of an energetic movement and the support of President Brum, conservative political parties had obstructed the passage of the suffrage bill.[49] Luisi and a representative from Alicia Moreau's Argentinian feminist group were the only Latin Americans in Geneva. They felt the distinction keenly, as representatives of what the IWSA termed "non-emancipated" countries (where women still did not have the vote).[50]

In particular, Luisi became outraged when a number of IWSA members sought to disband the international organization since suffrage had already been accomplished in so many places. This demonstrated, Luisi later reported to the Alianza, "the low concept which the international feminist world has of Latin countries! . . . In effect, these are the only countries that, with Eastern countries, keep women in a state of inferiority." Luisi became one of the most vehement opponents of this plan, and her entreaties sparked "very lively and passionate discussions." Although some, she recalled, declared that "emancipated countries had nothing further to do, . . . leaving the most *backward* (Latin) countries to their fate, . . . the International Alliance prevailed and was left standing."[51]

Luisi insisted that instead of disbanding, the IWSA should make more robust connections with Latin American women and organizations. She reiterated what was one of her long-standing demands, that the organization's international bulletin, *Jus Suffragii*, then published in English and French, be made available in Spanish.[52] She also offered herself as the official liaison for Latin American women's groups, to which the IWSA agreed.

Luisi, however, left the conference deeply disillusioned about Carrie Chapman Catt, who had presided over it.[53] Upon returning to Montevideo, Luisi reported to the Alianza Uruguaya that Catt focused too much on "North American methods" and was not sufficiently invested in Latin America. Luisi had not been able to talk with her about the Pan-American women's conference they hoped to plan, nor about anything else, because "International President Carrie Chapman Catt only speaks English," a language that Spanish- and French-speaking Luisi did not.[54]

The following year, Luisi's fears about Catt were confirmed when she learned that Catt's new U.S. organization, the League of Women Voters (LWV), was planning a "Pan-American Conference of Women" in Baltimore, Maryland, yet had not consulted Luisi or her Argentinean friends who had been urging Catt to host such an event since 1919. Luisi, who heard the news from British and Argentinean feminists, from a U.S. member of the Women's Auxiliary, and from Uruguay's State Department before she received a personal invitation from Catt herself, was outraged that Catt had not informed her or sought her advice.[55] Luisi wrote to Catt, expressing disappointment about the delayed contact and regret that she would not be able to attend. She had already been away from her Montevideo medical practice for a long time in Europe and had a medical conference in Paris a few months after the Baltimore meeting. In addition, she noted in Spanish (the language in which she wrote all her letters to Catt), "I don't know English. Remember dear Mrs. Catt that I could not converse with you in Geneva?"[56] She informed Catt, however, that she would send a delegate to the conference, a member of the Alianza, who spoke English.[57]

Although her experiences with Catt shook Luisi's faith in a Pan-American feminist organization based on equality with the United States, they also made her even more determined to assert Uruguay's leadership over whatever new group emerged from the conference. Determined to make her mark, and Uruguay's mark, at the conference, Luisi drafted a proposal for a Pan-American feminist organization that her representative, Celia Paladino de Vitale, would deliver on her behalf. This "Pan-American Association of Women" would "strengthen the ties that should unite the women of our continent" and fight for women's rights. While Luisi's proposal specified that the headquarters of the association should be in the United States, due to the "advanced level of emancipation of the women of North America," she asserted Latin America's active leadership of it. The group would be led by a commission composed of a delegate from each country of the Americas, and after a first meeting in the United States, all future meetings would take place in Latin America.[58] After gaining unanimous endorsement from the Alianza, Luisi explained to Paladino that this new group would be an extension of the Pan-American Women's Auxiliary but would "give it a state of greater prestige and permanence."[59]

Luisi intended to explicitly counter the U.S.-directed Pan-Americanism that she knew was motivated by more imperialist goals, including economic domination. Indeed, Catt had informed Luisi's good friend Alicia Moreau (who, as an English speaker and writer, corresponded with Catt much more than Luisi) that the conference had been initiated by the mayor of Baltimore and governor of Maryland, who sought to enhance trade with Latin America through the Port of Baltimore. They had contacted the Baltimore League of Women Voters to organize it, and the U.S. State Department leaped upon this opportunity, coordinating efforts with the LWV, the Pan-American Union, and ambassadors and chargés d'affaires of various Latin American countries to enlist delegates.[60] The LWV had its own interests in what would be the group's first large event since its founding on the heels of the 1920 suffrage victory—namely, conquering women's rights beyond the borders of the United States.[61] However, the group also sought to promote U.S. investments and economic hegemony in

Latin America. When the executive director of the Maryland LWV proposed the idea to national president Maud Wood Park, she explained its commercial benefits as a primary reason for the conference.[62]

Luisi's proposal for a new Pan-American association of women attempted to push against U.S. hegemony in all forms. She believed that "Uruguay should be the one that does it, the smallest but the first!"[63] Luisi specified that this new group would promote a Pan-Americanism based on "equality" and mutual respect rather than on U.S. superiority and economic imperialism. Before Paladino embarked for Baltimore, Luisi gave her copies of this proposal and Brum's recent publication *Solidaridad americana*, in which he suggested the creation of a Pan-American League of Nations that would refigure the Monroe Doctrine into a multilateral hemispheric policy.[64] Luisi urged Paladino to ensure their proposed organization achieved "the recognition it deserves in the Hearts of all the women of America who fight for solidarity and for friendship of all people of all races."[65] She also instructed her to *not* agree to any other plan without first securing the express approval of the Alianza.[66]

Luisi believed that one of her newest interlocutors, young Brazilian feminist Bertha Lutz, would support her goals for a Pan-American feminism that confronted U.S. hegemony. After Lutz had introduced herself in a letter the year before, Luisi had secured Lutz's membership in the IWSA.[67] Over the following months the two corresponded fairly regularly, exchanging news about women's rights in Brazil and Uruguay and about the IWSA. Now Luisi told Lutz, "I would be really happy to know that you'll be in North America representing the women of South America" at the Baltimore conference. She urged Lutz to consult with her "so that we can come to an agreement" about the conference agenda.[68] No evidence of a response from Lutz exists in either Lutz's or Luisi's archives, and correspondence between the two women waned after this letter. Although Lutz supported Luisi's proposal for a new feminist organization, she embraced a distinctly different Pan-American feminism from Spanish-speaking Luisi. Paulina Luisi's proposal would carry the day, but Bertha Lutz would carry the conference.

Bertha Lutz and the 1922 Pan-American Women's Conference

When she first corresponded with Luisi in 1921, Bertha Lutz was just becoming well-known as the "brains" of Brazil's suffrage movement.[69] Over the next few years, she would become the most visible feminist in Brazil and, ultimately, the recognized leader of the women's movement in that country for nearly a half century. Almost twenty years younger than Luisi, Lutz was born in São Paulo to an English mother and a Swiss-Brazilian father who was a well-known scientist. Educated first in Brazil and then in Europe, Lutz graduated from the

Sorbonne, studying botany, zoology, and biological chemistry.[70] The impact of the feminist movement Lutz witnessed in Britain at the height of suffrage militancy inspired her activism for the vote in Brazil when she returned from Europe. In 1918 Lutz published an article that sparked the formal women's suffrage movement in Brazil. Championing economic independence for women, she called on her Brazilian sisters not to "live parasitically based on their sex" but rather to engage in the nation's political life and "become valuable instruments in the progress of Brazil."[71] In 1920 she formed a small study group for women's rights, the Liga para a Emancipação Intelectual da Mulher (League for the Intellectual Emancipation of Women). The following year her fame grew when she became the second woman in the history of Brazil to win a civil service appointment to a government job, outperforming male competitors on the rigorous science and natural history exams to become secretary of the Museu Nacional in Rio de Janeiro.

Like Luisi, Lutz believed that women and men were equal but biologically distinct; unlike Luisi, Lutz believed that women's anatomy hindered them. As she explained in a 1920 medical journal article, worldwide changes enabled women's intellectual and economic lives outside the home and apart from motherhood. These developments could help them overcome their "biological limitations." As a Brazilian delegate to the 1919 International Labor Conference, she supported policies protecting women's hours and conditions of work. Lutz also believed in equal pay for equal work and equal educational opportunities, though she saw the right to vote and full citizenship as the crux of all of these goals.[72]

Ideas about class and race, similar to those of Luisi, informed Lutz's feminism. Educated white women of the middle and upper classes, she believed, should promote welfare and rights, seek international democracy and peace, and uplift their less fortunate sisters. Unlike Luisi, Lutz never favored socialism, though both women emphasized state-sponsored social welfare guarantees for women and children. Both believed that international efforts such as the ICW and IWSA in Europe and developing Pan-American projects could help fulfill these goals. "At the present moment," Lutz wrote in 1920, "everything depends on collective action."[73]

Yet for this collective action Lutz would turn to English-speaking feminists rather than to Spanish-speaking feminists like Luisi. The Pan-Hispanicism that drove Luisi was not an ideology to which Lutz, who spoke Portuguese, English, French, and German fluently but not Spanish, subscribed.[74] As is evident from Luisi's interactions with Catt, language was critical to international feminist dynamics. Significantly, Lutz wrote to Luisi in French, rather than Portuguese, which seemed to slightly jar Luisi. Though Luisi was also fluent in French and conducted most of her correspondence with British and European feminists in French, she responded to Lutz in Spanish, noting that she hoped that Spanish would be "familiar" to Lutz.[75] While Luisi's letters to Lutz were warm and generous, Lutz's to Luisi were shorter and more formal. Lutz's English-language correspondence with her U.S. and British interlocutors was much warmer and lengthier. Most significantly, when Luisi urged Lutz to promote her plans at the Pan-American Women's Conference in Baltimore, Lutz seems to have ignored this request.

While Lutz acknowledged Luisi was "at the vanguard," she did not seek collaboration with Luisi as much as with the IWSA, which would gain prestige for her Brazilian group. In 1921, when Lutz first wrote to the IWSA about joining the group, its secretary Margery Corbett Ashby recommended she write to Luisi, the designated recruiter of Latin American members, prompting Lutz's first letter to Luisi.[76]

Like many Brazilian elites in the early twentieth century, Lutz upheld Brazil, a former Portuguese colony and monarchy until the nineteenth century, as superior to and separate from what was becoming known in those years as *América Latina*. As she would later explain, Brazil had secured its independence "peacefully," first as a monarchy and then as a nation-state, rather than having undergone the violent revolutions of Spanish republics. Brazil was "young . . . [and] free of preconceptions and the dead weight of traditions." Consequently, Lutz argued, it could "adapt more quickly" than Spanish-speaking nations to "progressive ideas," including feminism.[77]

Lutz used this Brazilian exceptionalism as justification for a particular kind of Pan-Americanism based on shared U.S. and Brazilian hegemony. As Lutz later told U.S. women's groups, Brazil was turning away from "Europe for ideas and ideals" and "realizing now that we can learn far more from" those in the United States "who got their independence from conditions very similar to ours."[78] Both the United States and Brazil had "federated," unlike Spanish-speaking nations that had fragmented into ten republics at the time of independence from Spain, which to Lutz denoted backwardness.[79] Many Brazilian elites at the time espoused a special relationship with the United States. Unlike Spanish-speaking nations in the Americas, Brazil tacitly approved of the Spanish-American War, the Roosevelt Corollary to the Monroe Doctrine, and U.S. interventions in Mexico, Central America, and the Caribbean. Belief in Brazilian/U.S. exceptionalism helped underwrite Brazil's willingness to engage in Pan-American relations with the United States, which grew dramatically during the First World War. Brazil became the only country in the region to fight in the war, after which the Brazilian economy relied more than ever on exports to the United States.[80]

Lutz adhered to these ideas and shared imperial ambitions. As Brazil's delegate to the 1922 Baltimore Pan-American Women's Conference she promoted a Pan-American feminism that, though it celebrated the "Americas" as a whole, clearly elevated Brazil and the United States above all. "For where is there a country more eloquent with freedom, more pregnant with hope [than America]?" she cried out in her speech there. "[In] Africa, which save for its outer fringe of civilization, still slumbers? In Asia, absorbed in assimilating the fruits of Western civilization and amalgamating them with the principles of Oriental wisdom in a harmonious whole? In Europe, engaged in recovering from the horrors of the past war? None of these can help us. It is to America that the world looks."[81]

Reiterating familiar Pan-American tropes of forward-progress of liberty and equality in the Americas over both war-torn Europe and continents of "darker races," Lutz proceeded to reserve special praise for Brazil "with her immense territory, with her traditions of peace which freed slaves and brought about a Republic without shedding a drop of blood," and the United States, "who was called upon to end the war and to make peace." As she concluded, "It is to the United States to lead."[82]

The intensity of Lutz's Anglo-America-philia derived from her personal as well as national racial identity. As the daughter of a British woman, a fluent speaker of English, a lifelong admirer of British and Anglo-American elites, and someone who throughout her life emphatically insisted upon the Anglo spelling of her first name ("Bertha" rather than "Berta"), Lutz believed herself to be unique among and racially superior to Brazilians.[83] Pan-Americanism shifted her keen sense of affinity from Britain to the United States. As Lutz once wrote to Carrie Chapman Catt, with whom she became fast friends in Baltimore, "I am really a North American by temperament."[84]

The special bond Lutz felt with the United States, and above all with the League of Women Voters, was returned by the League, which demonstrated a partiality to Lutz even before the conference began. The strong relationship the United States and Brazil forged during the war, and Lutz's personal connection with a LWV member who had traveled to Brazil, facilitated her receipt of an invitation to the conference well before most other Latin American feminists.[85] The League provided more funding to Lutz, as well. Although the LWV offered each Latin American delegate $500 to help defray costs of transportation and lodging, Leo Rowe, director of the Pan-American Union, emphasized that the group should make every effort to meet Lutz's expenses in recognition of Brazil's importance to the United States. He did not make the same request on behalf of any other Latin American delegates, though other governments similarly expressed concern about the cost. The LWV doubled the amount for Lutz and Lutz alone, giving her $1,000.[86]

Critical to cementing the rapport between Lutz and the LWV was the ex-

Bertha Lutz, 1925, at the Grace Dodge Hotel in Washington, D.C.,
during one of her visits to the United States. Author's collection.

tremely strong friendship that blossomed during the conference between Lutz and League president Carrie Chapman Catt. Their meeting was life-defining for Lutz. Months afterward, Lutz wrote rhapsodically to Catt about their time together, "The days I spent with you were amongst the happiest not only of those spent in this country, but in my life."[87] Over two decades of intimate correspondence, the two women wrote at least once a month until Catt's death in 1946. Catt called Lutz her "Brazilian daughter," and Lutz called Catt her "mother."

From the perspective of the LWV, Lutz's emphatic endorsement of the United States became very important to the optics and success of the event, especially when other Latin American delegates objected to the League's overweening leadership. Indeed, the League's missionary impulse toward Latin American women pervaded the conference. Framed as an opportunity to "bring the women of the United States into friendly relations with the women of South America, Central America, Mexico and Canada," the conference planning excluded input from Latin American feminists, who represented a small fraction of the 2,000 conference attendees.[88] The daily sessions were all held in English and dominated by U.S. speakers from prominent progressive organizations, who urged Latin American women to follow their lead.[89] Even when Latin American delegates challenged U.S. superiority, they had little success. Mexican feminists, for example, were greatly disappointed by Catt's refusal to consider a proposal by educator and communist Elena Torres to discuss oil, land, immigration, the border, and exploitation of Mexican laborers at the hands of U.S. mining companies.[90]

The most heated debates that emerged concerned U.S. women's claims of superiority over their benighted Latin American sisters. In the session "Civil Status of Women," Mabel Walker Willebrandt, the U.S. assistant attorney general, asserted that U.S. Anglo-Saxon common law was preferable to Latin America's Napoleonic Code. In Anglo-American countries like the United States, England, and Canada, Willebrandt remarked, women had gained property rights and rights to their own wages, forms of legal independence still not uniformly achieved in Latin America.[91]

Willebrandt's negative portrayal of Latin American law was part of a longstanding pattern of U.S. elites denigrating the political and legal culture of Latin America, and it prompted a vigorous discussion, in which Celia Paladino de Vitale took the lead. She recounted numerous ways that the Uruguayan women's movement had secured equality for men and women, recognizing women's guardianship rights to children and the hereditary rights of out-of-wedlock children. Paladino pointed to Uruguay's provision of broad social welfare rights to both men and women, still unattained in the United States: the eight-hour workday, old age pensions, and free public education, including textbooks and equipment. Married women in Uruguay, but not the United States, also had independent nationality rights.[92]

The achievement of broad social justice and welfare rights in Uruguay reflected the aspirations that fostered many Latin American variants of feminism. The 1917 constitution of revolutionary Mexico, which espoused social welfare for working women, stood as a continental model for many budding feminist groups throughout the Americas. At the 1922 Baltimore conference, this notion of social rights marked a dividing line between Paladino and the LWV, which understood these social concerns to be of second-tier importance to political and civil rights. Similar tensions had also emerged at the 1920 meeting of the IWSA, which had failed to acknowledge that many of the post-suffrage goals of the alliance were already on the books in Uruguay, much to Luisi's ire.[93] This tendency of U.S. women to privilege individual political and civil rights over social rights and to assume they held a superior legal status persisted within Pan-American organizing for decades.

Another enduring conflict concerned who had the authority to speak and set an agenda. Because the Baltimore conference schedule did not allow time for consideration of Latin American women's own initiatives, a group of Spanish-speaking feminists, led by Paladino, organized separately to protest. As a *Baltimore Sun* article reported, "It is felt by the women who have come here . . . that the time has been too limited for them to go into the problems which they came to the United States to discuss." They demanded an extension of the conference for several days, with Spanish as the official language.[94]

During this extended stay, and in Spanish, Paladino delivered Luisi's proposal for the Pan-American Association of Women. Before an audience of 1,500, she asserted that such an organization would "strengthen the ties that should unite women of our continent" and promote women's social, civil, and political rights.[95] Paladino noted that while U.S. women could help lead the organization, it would not be run by an unchecked U.S. power. "The alarmists tell us that in entering this association with you, we would be absorbed immediately, and that you would exercise your hegemony over us," she acknowledged. "But I do not believe this."[96] Rather, she championed a new Pan-Americanism, quoting Baltasar Brum's *Solidaridad americana*. His words served as a rebuke to the U.S. women dominating the conference and a reminder that his country was a Pan-American leader: "Pan-Americanism implies the equality of all sovereignties, large or small, the assurance that no country will attempt to diminish the possessions of others and that those who have lost any possessions will have them rightly returned to them. It is, in short, an exponent of deep brotherly sentiment, and of a just aspiration for the material and moral aggrandizement of all the peoples of America."[97]

"We hope," Paladino added, that the new association "will benefit our women and will consolidate the American Peace of the peoples speaking English and Spanish . . . a peace that we hope will be permanent for the times to come."[98] Paladino's proposal passed unanimously, creating the Pan-American Association for the Advancement of Women.

Although Paladino's words contained a strong warning against U.S. hegemony, recognition of neither her speech nor her leadership appeared in the U.S. press or LWV accounts, which emphasized the leadership of Catt and Lutz in this new group. The League reported that although "the suggestion had come from Uruguay . . . the enthusiasm came from the Baltimore getting-together and the actual supervision of organization from Mrs. Catt whose wise statesmanship and ripe guidance are . . . essential to such a gathering."[99] Bertha Lutz was quickly appointed chair of the planning committee and with Catt established the new group's priorities: women's rights, the "betterment" of women and children, and peace. Catt would be president and Lutz vice president for South America. They appointed Paulina Luisi the nominal role of honorary vice president.[100]

During the conference, Bertha Lutz's outspoken affinity for the LWV and fluency in English distinguished her from almost all the other Latin American delegates, giving her a wider berth for her platform. The LWV promoted Lutz, facilitating connections for her with the press, which paid her special tribute as young, "very beautiful," and the most progressive of Latin American feminists.[101] When former Pan-American Union director John Barrett commented on her growing fame, he praised her similarity to familiar U.S. female types: she "might easily pass, from her figure, dress, and personality, for a serious college graduate or a gay young flapper."[102]

This media attention and the force of her own personality all redounded to the enormous impression that Lutz made on the U.S. public at large. Representatives from over fifty U.S. organizations, including various state chapters of the American Association of University Women and the National Federation of Business and Professional Women, along with many of the most prominent intellectuals and policy makers in the country, sent Lutz speaking requests and plaudits during and after the conference. Florence Kelley, one of the most influential reformers of the era, invited Lutz to dinner in New York, and Grace Abbott of the Children's Bureau sought a meeting in Washington, D.C.[103] Jane Addams invited her to stay at Hull House in Chicago, where she gave Lutz a special luncheon. Lutz received a personal note from W. E. B. Du Bois, who asked to meet her and inquired about a Brazilian presidential candidate of African descent. Former president Woodrow Wilson conveyed his "personal respects" and "deep interest in everything that affects the welfare and happiness of the women and all the people of Brazil."[104] Lutz's fame grew when the LWV sponsored her three-month post-conference trip around the United States, during which Lutz pronounced the success of the Baltimore conference and praised the United States as the "teacher for all America."[105] At a meeting of the California chapter of the National Federation of Business and Professional Women, she quoted H. G. Wells's hopes for a Pan-American Union. "But he has forgotten one thing," Lutz noted, "the women. Women are a new force in the history of the world."[106] In particular, Lutz believed that the U.S. League of Women Voters was this new force, "a new factor in the heart of America, especially Latin-America."[107]

Imperial Pan-American Feminism

The Pan-American Association for the Advancement of Women that emerged at the 1922 Baltimore conference did become a "new force." The first Pan-American organization to demand women's rights, it introduced and knit together many leaders throughout the Americas, providing a critical institutional apparatus for the movement's later blossoming. A number of the Latin American delegates who attended the 1922 Baltimore conference—from Panama, Chile, Costa Rica, Mexico, and elsewhere—launched new feminist organizations affiliated with the mother association upon their returns home.[108]

Bertha Lutz and Carrie Chapman Catt, however, failed to strongly unite Latin American feminists. Lutz's sense of Brazilian-U.S. exceptionalism made her an inactive correspondent with them. In 1923, Mexican feminist Elena Torres, appointed the "Vice President for North America" of the new group, wrote Lutz a long letter full of hopes for the association. Torres hosted a Pan-American conference in Mexico that gathered hundreds of women, calling for the vote and for a continental organization of women.[109] She explained to Lutz that she and other Baltimore attendees felt very "conscious of the responsibility that we have taken on for the feminist movement of America."[110] Torres urged Lutz to write to her frequently. But Lutz did not respond, nor did she reach out to other Spanish-speaking feminists. Torres wrote to Lutz again exactly a year later, and the latter's eventual brief reply offered little encouragement.[111] Lutz was more interested in bolstering feminism in Brazil and in strengthening her own affiliations with the ICW and IWSA in Europe than in cultivating connections with Spanish-speaking feminists, whom she deemed racially and culturally inferior. In turn, many Spanish-speaking feminists became quickly disenchanted with her and Catt's leadership. Their disappointments peaked in 1923 when, after traveling throughout Latin America, Catt publicized a stream of denigrating views about Latin American feminism.

After the Baltimore conference, Catt embarked on a several-months-long "Latin American tour" of Brazil, Argentina, Uruguay, Chile, Peru, and Panama to assess the status of women and support the Pan-American association. Catt's first stop was Brazil, where she and Lutz helped launch the Federação Brasileira pelo Progresso Feminino. It became the largest women's rights group in Brazil and would define Brazilian feminism for the next two decades.

Nearly every other country Catt visited, however, disappointed her, with the exception of Uruguay, where she found some suffrage momentum. In a private report to the LWV, Catt noted that South America "has the least modern women's organizations of any of the six [continents]." She claimed that she "did not find . . . one woman with the comprehension, the energy and the firm resolve to lead the woman movement," although she drew an exception for Lutz, who she believed did "not really belong to Spanish America."[112] Catt's public speeches in Latin America and published reflections concluded that the women's movement in Latin America was "forty years behind that of the United States." She attributed such "slowness" to a warmer climate and entrenched Catholic traditions. Most damagingly, she questioned Latin American women's readiness for political organization and rights.[113] Spanish-language periodicals reproduced Catt's comments, earning her deep opprobrium and shattering many Latin Americans' hopes for a Pan-American feminism based on equality. When, at a 1925 meeting in New York City of the Pan-American group, Elena Torres resigned from her post, she explained that the widespread condescension of "Anglo-America toward Hispanic-America" made it "impossible" for "Hispanic-American women" to work with U.S. women.[114]

Paulina Luisi was also deeply troubled by the leadership of Catt and Lutz. Although many feminists at the Baltimore conference recognized Luisi as its spiritual leader, neither Lutz nor Catt had informed her of her honorary vice presidency.[115] In 1923, Celia Paladino de Vitale wrote to Lutz to register her and Luisi's alarm over their silence, especially given that the Uruguayans were responsible for the group's creation.[116]

Luisi, however, was no longer relying on Catt and Lutz to forge Pan-American links; she had found an outlet for a different brand of Pan-Hispanic feminism. In 1923, she became the vice president of a new group, the Liga Internacional de Mujeres Ibéricas e Hispanoamericanas, founded by Mexican feminist Elena Arizmendi. Even before the 1922 Baltimore conference, Arizmendi had reached out to Catt and the LWV about affiliating with the new organization, but the outcome of the conference and Catt's subsequent disparaging comments about Latin American women angered Arizmendi, who published a critical appraisal of Catt in the pages of the Liga bulletin.[117] Luisi and Arizmendi galvanized many other feminists in the region around an anti-imperialist, Pan-Hispanic feminism. Although subsequent interpersonal conflicts caused Luisi and Arizmendi to grow apart and Luisi to separate from the Liga, the group provided an important source of Pan-Hispanic feminism for many in Costa Rica, Colombia, Puerto Rico, Ecuador, Peru, Nicaragua, the Dominican Republic, and elsewhere.[118]

Luisi was heartened when she witnessed the inter-American feminism she had envisioned as a counterweight to U.S. empire begin to move into official regional discourse. At the 1923 Fifth International Conference of American States in Santiago, Chile, a group of male delegates from Argentina and Chile unprecedentedly pushed consideration of women's rights into the official proceedings. Until this point women's rights had been discussed only in women's gatherings. Inspired by the growing Pan-American feminist movement and directly pushed by some of the Baltimore conference attendees, male statesmen gained commitments from the Pan-American Union to study and report on women's political and civil rights at future Pan-American conferences. The proposal from Máximo Soto Hall, Guatemalan novelist and delegate for Argentina, emphasized the centrality of the "woman question" to civilizational progress. Official Pan-American conferences already included issues of education, labor, and peace. He argued that women's rights should be among these issues, as a cultural imperative that would help bring democracy to Latin America, especially in light of the suffrage gains in Europe and the United States.[119] Chilean delegate Manuel Rivas Vicuña endorsed this proposal, proclaiming it "a work of social justice exacted by the public opinion of all of the countries of the world."[120] Costa Rican delegate Alejandro Alvarado Quirós called it of "transcendental importance." "The American woman is not, and cannot be[,] inferior to the European woman," he asserted.[121] This proposal, which also emphasized the inclusion of women in government delegations at future conferences, passed unanimously.[122]

Luisi's demands years earlier, at the 1916 Pan-American Child Congress and the 1922 Pan-American Baltimore conference, had made this resolution possible.[123] Her spirit of Pan-Hispanic anti-imperialism had also influenced the resolution. Soto Hall was well known for his writings that openly criticized U.S. imperialism. At the 1923 Pan-American conference, his resolution was part of a broader project Latin American statesmen were making to push against U.S. hegemony in the Americas.[124] This Santiago conference represented a turning point in Pan-American conferences, after which Latin American delegates explicitly utilized them as opportunities to "embarrass Washington," as historian Alan McPherson writes.[125]

Feminists throughout the Americas celebrated the passage of the women's rights resolution.[126] During the conference, Lutz telegrammed her support to Rivas Vicuña in the name of the Pan-American women's organization she led.[127] Afterward she noted that America was entering "the current of modern thought in . . . equalizing the rights between the sexes." She cheered "the auspicious march of equality of civil and political rights of the woman, in all of America," as evidence of an exceptional "American" ethos: "rejection of preconceptions and prejudices of any kind."[128]

Yet preconceptions and prejudices were alive and well in Pan-American feminism. National chauvinism and biases based on geography, race, language, and empire played critical roles in the global feminist designs that saw the bonds between Lutz and Catt grow tighter while theirs with Paulina Luisi frayed. Their conflicts came to a head several months after the Santiago conference, at the 1923 International Woman Suffrage Alliance Congress in Rome. This meeting would be the first and only time that all three women would be in the same room together. Although Lutz and Luisi were polite to each other, they clashed in meeting proceedings when Luisi opposed a proposal to merge the IWSA with its more conservative precursor, the International Council of Women. Luisi had by this time broken all ties with the ICW-linked CONAMU, the first organization she had founded in Uruguay, which now no longer upheld suffrage as a goal. She realized that a union of the two international groups would alienate many in her IWSA-linked Alianza Uruguaya, which continued to push for the right to vote. Immediately after Luisi voiced her dissent, however, Lutz outspokenly supported the merger, explaining that no tension existed between the two groups in Brazil.[129]

Ultimately the IWSA and ICW remained separate, but this debate masked the much deeper fissure between Lutz and Luisi over Pan-American feminism. Paulina Luisi recognized the importance of the 1923 Santiago resolution, yet she doubted that the association led by Lutz and Catt would capitalize on these opportunities. It had not taken up the active, vocal agenda for women's rights that Luisi had hoped, and instead of representing a break with notions of European superiority, it relied mostly upon connections with European groups, especially more conservatives ones attached to the ICW.[130] In Rome, in a conversation with Catt brokered by a translator, Paulina Luisi aired these grievances, also reiterating her irritation that Catt had never notified her of the group's creation or her honorary vice presidency. Catt, informing Lutz about their tête-à-tête, wrote that Luisi was, "I believe, a dangerous woman because she is indiscreet and has very decided notions as to what ought to be done."[131]

Lutz agreed with this characterization. She strongly resented what she viewed as Luisi's jockeying for leadership. Lutz described her antipathy for Luisi starkly when Catt suggested that Luisi might relieve them both of Pan-American feminist duties. By 1923, Catt had grown tired of Pan-American organizing, which she considered ineffectual and requiring more funding than was realistic. Believing Lutz was similarly uninterested, given her lackluster contact with Latin American feminists, Catt proposed that they split the now-titled Inter-American Union of Women into two separate federations: one for Central

Delegates to the Ninth Congress of the International Woman Suffrage Alliance in Rome, 1923. Bertha Lutz marked Carrie Chapman Catt in the back row with a check mark and herself with a short vertical line. Paulina Luisi is standing to the immediate right of Lutz, wearing a large hat. Courtesy of the Arquivo Nacional, Rio de Janeiro, Brazil.

America and Mexico and the other for South America. Paulina Luisi could take over the latter group, and, Catt wrote to Lutz, "you would be released from Pan American cares."[132]

Bertha Lutz protested this plan vehemently. "I was deeply hurt about the suggestion of turning over the leadership to Uruguay," Lutz wrote to Catt. While she reluctantly promised to acquiesce "if you should think it more advantageous for the movement . . . I must say . . . there are some people under whose leadership I will decidedly not serve." Speaking frankly of her dislike of Luisi, she wrote, "I have given up one continent to that lady, and if she must have another then I will drop the whole association and will work on my own for Pan Americanism, not through her organization but through the official channels." Begging forgiveness as a "faulty daughter," she wrote, "I just can't stand her."[133]

Lutz's comments reveal a personality clash with Luisi, but their conflicts were also political. Their discord amounted to a deep-seated rivalry (one felt perhaps more keenly by Lutz than Luisi) over Pan-American feminism. This power

A NEW FORCE IN THE HISTORY OF THE WORLD

struggle reflected, above all, an imperial vision of international feminism—one that divided the world into regions of power and vaunted the role of individual leaders over them. Lutz coveted the prestige that Luisi had achieved in Europe. In 1922, Luisi became the first Latin American woman appointed to the League of Nations, serving as the Uruguayan representative to its International Labor Organization conference and its Advisory Committee on the Traffic of Women and Children.[134] If Luisi had her domain over Europe, Lutz determined that she would have hers over the Americas, where she saw global power consolidating after the First World War. Lutz became fond of saying that "Pax Romana and Pax Britannica had given way to Pax Americana." By Pax Americana she meant both a period of peace in the Western Hemisphere and a continental empire led by the United States and Brazil that would replace the Roman and British Empires.[135] Lutz saw the United States as a missionary leader in the world, with unprecedented global power, and she viewed Brazil its rightful partner. The liberal rights of feminism, which Lutz deemed a distinctly Anglo-American contribution, were vital to this empire, as was her own leadership. Although in 1921 Lutz had flattered Luisi that she was at the "vanguard in Uruguay," when Lutz and Catt had created the Federação Brasileira pelo Progresso Feminino in 1923, Lutz announced to Brazilian audiences that now Brazil would "take the vanguard of the Latin American countries."[136]

Catt responded that she would be happy for Lutz to continue as the president of their Pan-American group and encouraged her to arrange a meeting to bring all the women together. However, she warned Lutz that Luisi might continue to be a thorn in their side: "The lady, whose leadership you spurn and to whom you say you gave up one continent," had returned to Uruguay, Catt informed Lutz. Luisi had "told one of the European women that she had stirred things up in Europe a good deal, but that they would not have any trouble with her now as she was going back to South America and would not be back in Europe for three years. . . . I think, myself, she is rather a difficult one."[137]

Luisi would indeed be a "difficult one" for Catt and Lutz. Back in South America, Luisi would amass correspondents and supporters from throughout the region who actively sought out her mentorship. Her vision for a feminismo americano that challenged U.S. hegemony and privileged Spanish-speaking leadership would spur a resurgent movement in the decades to come. More immediately, her brand of Pan-American feminism would help push forward an unprecedented demand: an international law for women's equal rights.

CHAPTER TWO

The Anti-imperialist Origins of International Women's Rights

In June 1926, at the Congreso Interamericano de Mujeres (Inter-American Congress of Women), twenty-seven-year-old Panamanian Clara González called on women of the Americas to forge a new *feminismo* marked by Hispano-American pride and unity. Before several hundred women and a number of men in the stately *aula máxima* (great hall) of Panama City's Instituto Nacional, she urged "*mujeres americanas*" (American women) to organize "in one group that will enable them, by means of joint action, to obtain political, economic, and social liberation."[1] González then proposed a stunning innovation: she called for an international agreement that would transcend national law and in one fell swoop guarantee equal political and civil rights to women throughout the Western Hemisphere.

González was emboldened to make this demand by the friendship she had forged with young Cuban feminist Ofelia Domínguez Navarro, who would be its greatest champion. González had met thirty-one-year-old Domínguez only a few days before, yet their conversations had already inspired in them great hopes. Both exceptional young female lawyers in their countries, both modern and rebellious, they had each come to the conference with plans to launch a new movement for women's rights and national sovereignty, and against U.S. empire.

Explicitly seeking an inter-American feminist alternative to the group led by Carrie Chapman Catt and Bertha Lutz, Clara González and Ofelia Domínguez Navarro rejected any notion that Latin American women were not ready for the vote. They carried forward the torch of Paulina Luisi, who years earlier had proposed women's suffrage as a Pan-American demand pioneered by Spanish-speaking women. The two women also embraced a hemispheric feminism that, unlike that of their forebears, refused to tout the leadership of the "better constituted" nations—the A.B.C. countries (Argentina, Brazil, and Chile), Uruguay, or the United States. González and Domínguez came from protectorates of the United States—Panama and Cuba—and participated in anti-imperialist movements. They saw women's rights as explicitly linked to their nations' quests for sovereignty. Both believed that organizing collectively for international women's rights would ground a Pan-Hispanic feminism that would challenge U.S. empire in the Americas and would make women's and national "equal rights" mutually constitutive goals.

During a period when U.S. interventions in the Americas and anti-imperialist movements were cresting, their brand of Pan-American feminism would gain profound influence and would shape new activism for international women's rights at the 1928 Pan-American conference in Havana, Cuba. There, Ofelia Domínguez Navarro and hundreds of other Cuban feminists collaborated with U.S. feminists not from Catt's League of Women Voters—which by now had a weak reputation in many parts of Havana—but from the U.S. National Woman's Party (NWP). At the conference, NWP leader Doris Stevens demanded a Pan-American feminism very similar to that which González and Domínguez had urged—one that promised the sovereignty of women and the sovereignty of the Americas—and she insisted on an international Equal Rights Treaty. Later interactions with Stevens would reveal her strategic rather than genuine anti-imperialism. But in 1928 the women's combined efforts for an anti-imperialist Pan-American feminism galvanized hundreds of Cuban women and led to the first intergovernmental organization of women in the world, the Inter-American Commission of Women (IACW). The innovation in international law that González and Domínguez had launched two years earlier in Panama would define Pan-American feminism for the next two decades.

The 1926 Panama Conference:
Sovereignty for Women and Sovereignty for Nations

The 1926 Panama congress, where Ofelia Domínguez Navarro and Clara González announced their bold new goals, grew directly out of the 1922 Baltimore conference dominated by Carrie Chapman Catt and Bertha Lutz. Esther Neira de Calvo, the Panamanian delegate in Baltimore and the vice president of the Inter-American Union of Women (the new name for the Pan-American Association for the Advancement of Women), initiated the congress. When Neira de Calvo learned that Panama would honor the centennial of the 1826 congress of Simón Bolívar, she decided to host a women's congress as part of these events to revive the inactive Inter-American Union of Women.[2] From an elite background, educated in Europe, and fluent in English, Neira de Calvo was closely connected to the Panamanian government and supportive of U.S. institutions and culture. She was deeply disappointed when both Catt and Lutz turned down her invitations to attend.[3]

The absence of Catt and Lutz, however, paved the way for other leaders and new variants of feminism to emerge at the conference. Neira de Calvo gathered a more diverse group of women than had been at the 1922 Baltimore conference. Over 200 from Colombia and Bolivia, countries that had not been represented in Baltimore, as well as from Peru, Cuba, Panama, and elsewhere, came to a conference where Spanish would be the official language.[4]

Clara González became one of their leaders. She had recently gained fame in Panama as the country's first female lawyer and founder of a new feminist organization. Born in the Chiriquí province to a Spanish father and Panamanian mother of indigenous descent who never formally married, González came from a more humble background than the other Pan-American feminist leaders. Her introduction to feminism also came from more traumatic personal experience than that of her counterparts. When González was a young girl, her mother sought paid labor away from home, and her father worked as a traveling carpenter. At age six, she was raped by the son of her godfather, a powerful and wealthy man in Chiriquí, yet her sex and class meant that blame fell on her rather than on the offender. This experience haunted González for much of her life and strengthened her resolve to change patriarchal laws.[5] She gained access to education through scholarships and a burgeoning public education system, then worked as a schoolteacher while taking night courses to finish a law degree at the Instituto Nacional. In 1922, a few months shy of her twenty-fourth birthday, González became the first female lawyer in Panama.[6] The Panamanian Civil Code prevented women from practicing law, but her forthright intercessions to President Belisario Porras resulted in a 1924 law granting women the right to practice law in Panama.[7]

González's law school thesis, "La mujer ante el derecho panameño" (Women under Panamanian law), brought her national and international renown. It was an exhaustive study of the status of women under civil, penal, and political law in her country, the very first of its kind. Its success impelled González to launch a new women's organization, Renovación, to fight for women's juridical equality and suffrage.[8] In 1923 she helped form a separate political party and organization, the Partido Nacional Feminista (PNF), which historians credit with the "birth of feminism" in Panama.[9] Unlike Esther Neira de Calvo's more conservative Sociedad Nacional para el Progreso de la Mujer, which enlisted mostly elite women and focused on the "betterment of women" rather than on the vote, the PNF distinguished itself by its more diverse membership and leadership, including Afro-Panamanian and working women, and its explicit fight for women's equal political and civil rights.[10]

In its first few years, González's PNF successfully changed standards in women's welfare, education, and political rights.[11] The group established a night school for women and pushed for several civil rights enacted into law in

Clara González, date unknown. Courtesy of the Schlesinger Library,
Radcliffe Institute, Harvard University.

1925, including women's rights to administer their property, represent themselves in court, act as witnesses to wills and other legal documents, and be admitted to the bar. Due to the group's activism, Panama revised its marriage law in 1925 so that instead of wives owing their husbands "obedience," husbands and wives now owed each other "mutual protection and consideration" under the law, and divorce was allowed on grounds of mutual consent.[12]

For González, equal rights under the law represented the linchpin of feminist demands but were also a means to greater ends. Though not officially connected to the Socialist Party in these years, González was by intellectual and organizational standards a socialist feminist. Influenced by German philosopher August Bebel's 1910 book, *Woman and Socialism*, she cofounded the Federación de Estudiantes de Panamá in 1922 and joined the Federación Sindical Obrera, Sindicato General de Trabajadores, and Grupo Comunismo, a group inspired by socialism, anarchism, and anti-imperialism. While upholding the vote and civil equality as vital demands, she also sought to promote the rights of all workers, especially women workers, and to address the socioeconomic disparities of Panamanian society. She also recognized these as international goals. Witnessing how World War I and the Russian and Mexican Revolutions impelled vibrant political debates, including feminism, and robust social movements of workers and anarchist varieties, she tethered her feminism to internationalist anarcho-syndicalist ideals.[13]

She also tied her feminism to anti-imperialist ideals. In Panama, the ignominious 1903 Hay-Bunau-Varilla Treaty granted the United States the Panama Canal and "all the rights, power, and authority . . . in perpetuity" to the Panama Canal Zone, the 553-square-mile area bordering it. In 1926, when the terms of the treaty were up for debate, the United States sought to expand its control over the zone.[14] Calls for Panamanian sovereignty persisted in these years, and González's suffrage arguments explicitly drew on the language of national sovereignty.[15]

These ideals inspired González's goals for inter-American feminism. After receiving an invitation from Neira de Calvo to attend the conference, González explained in her PNF organ *Orientación Feminista* that the conference would be "a transcendental event" that would fuse "international" and "local" concerns. She hoped the congress would represent not just affluent women but those of "different backgrounds" and all those engaged in "pursuit of the social ideal, of justice."[16]

González specifically sought a new Pan-Hispanic feminism that celebrated Latin American women of all classes, including poor and working women. Well aware of the groundwork laid by Neira de Calvo, Carrie Chapman Catt, and others, González was troubled by the elitism and U.S. superiority conveyed by their leadership. Comments Catt had made on her 1923 visit to Panama—

accusations that Latin American men were hidebound and that Latin American women were not ready to claim the right to vote—had been widely disseminated and condemned in the Panamanian press.[17] The Panama congress, González noted, would reinforce Bolívar's 1826 dream for Hispano-American unity; there Latin American women could strengthen their bonds with each other and create their own "Hispano-American political unit" to demand their rights.[18]

Asked to speak in the "Women in the Law" portion of the conference, González drafted a resolution for women's equal political rights throughout the continent. She recognized the precedent for such an international law in Máximo Soto Hall's 1923 Santiago resolution and in new trends in inter-American law that sought to make uniform various national codes. González also believed such an international law for women's rights could combat what she called the "prejudice that the Hispanic-American woman is unprepared for the exercise of citizenship," an allusion to the aspersions Catt had cast on Latin American women.[19]

Nearly 1,000 miles north in Havana, Cuba, very similar goals—for the equal rights of women and of nations—focused the mind of Ofelia Domínguez Navarro as she prepared to go to Panama for the congress. Domínguez was born in Las Villas to parents who were active participants in the Cuban War for Independence (1895–98).[20] Domínguez's father had been a revolutionary fighter, and her mother smuggled arms to the rebels with baby Ofelia in her arms. She and her mother lived for a brief time in a *reconcentrado* (reconcentration) camp. A small child in 1898 when the Spanish-American War broke out, Domínguez witnessed Cuba win its putative independence from Spain at the expense of the 1901 Platt Amendment, which granted to the United States not only Guantánamo Bay as a naval base but also the unrestricted authority to intervene in the island. After her mother died when she was fourteen, Domínguez was charged with the care of her siblings, but she managed to finish her high school degree and work as a schoolteacher in rural Jorobada. There she saw U.S. economic and political control over the island and its sugar cane workers grow. As she later explained, "From my preaching parents I knew something of the American pressure, of its exploitation and development of a capital monopoly through the sugar industry. But the presence in living flesh of these realities, in the midst of the rich cane fields that I now had in sight, fueled my sense of human responsibility early on."[21]

After she earned a law degree from the University of Havana, feminism came alive for Domínguez when she worked as a criminal defense lawyer for destitute women and prostitutes. She became aware of the profound sexual and economic disparities that drove women into prostitution. Like González, Domínguez believed that law held a unique promise for more thoroughgoing social

Ofelia Domínguez Navarro, date unknown.
Courtesy of the Archivo Nacional de Cuba, Havana, Cuba.

change. Through her concern for illegitimate children and single mothers, Domínguez gradually came to uphold a *feminismo* that aspired to equal political and civil rights, believing that they could be levers for greater change. In 1923 she attended the First National Congress of Women in Cuba, where she made waves by insisting on paternity testing and the rights of illegitimate children. She joined and became a leader of the feminist organization Club Femenino, which distinguished itself in Cuba for its broad agenda for women workers, unmarried mothers, and illegitimate children and for its challenges to church and family morality. In 1925 it broke away from other feminist groups on the basis of these more radical demands, in part due to the influence of Domínguez, then president of the Santa Clara branch.[22]

When Domínguez received the request from the Club Femenino president that she and fellow member Emma López Seña attend the 1926 Panama congress, she saw it as an opportunity to launch a new kind of *feminismo americano* that directly called for women's rights and asserted Latin American leadership.[23] Domínguez was also no doubt aware of Carrie Chapman Catt's recent disparaging comments and condescension.[24] A 1925 Havana newspaper article explained that Catt's assessment of *feminismo latinoamericano* as "forty years behind" the United States had caused widespread resentment. It likened her insult to "a dart that has struck the heart of the Latin woman" and that Cuban women had been "unable to pull out."[25] Especially in light of such aspersions, Domínguez esteemed Paulina Luisi's vision of feminism—one that actively pushed for women's rights and against U.S. hegemony. Over the past few years Club Femenino had established links with the venerable Luisi. In 1923 members paid homage to her in Havana.[26] Before the 1926 Panama congress, Luisi asked that the Cuban club represent her there and read her speech about the rights of illegitimate children and unmarried mothers in the Americas. Domínguez gladly accepted the honor.[27] The two women later became close friends.

Tasked with the keynote speech of the "Women and Law" panel at the Panama congress, Domínguez understood that her address was a critical opportunity to inspire a broader Pan-Hispanic movement and promote women's political and civil rights. Recognition of the rising movements for women's rights throughout the world and of Máximo Soto Hall's 1923 demands inspired her draft of a resolution calling for equal civil rights for women throughout the Americas. An international measure, Domínguez knew, could pressure presidents and legislatures in various countries, including her own Cuba, where Club Femenino and other groups were fighting for suffrage. Over the course of the previous year, it had become clear that the suffrage support offered by new president Gerardo Machado during his campaign had been lip service. In 1925 he imposed an increasingly restrictive regime, squelching dissent and targeting the newly formed Communist Party in Cuba as well as feminists. "Above all, Ofelia, for Cuba and for women," Club Femenino president wrote to Domínguez before she left for Panama, "it is necessary that this proposal lacks nothing, and there is no one better than you to present it; so make an effort."[28]

Several weeks later, on June 25, 1926, at the podium of the *aula máxima* in Panama's Instituto Nacional, before an audience of several hundred, Domínguez announced her proposal for a new Pan-American feminism based on anti-imperialism and sweeping, continental-wide "equal rights" for women. In her address, she connected an international measure for full civil rights of all women in the Americas with an internationalism based on the interdependence and resurgent sovereignty of all people. Though former U.S. president Woodrow Wilson had famously promoted "self-determination" for all during the First World War, she announced, the war had entrenched U.S. imperialism to the detriment of women, children, and workers in the country's economic and military incursions in Central America and the Caribbean after 1915. That "most generous and noble Nation of the Universe, that gave the clarion call of liberty to all oppressed people," Domínguez said, "emerged as a tyrant when it became strong and victorious."[29]

At the same time, she explained to the crowd, there was one tangible way the war had propelled self-determination: the expansion of women's rights throughout the world. In England, the United States, and many countries in Europe, women had gained the right to vote, which represented a significant step forward for social justice. Women in Latin America were as deserving of rights as those in Europe and the United States, Domínguez averred, and women's self-determination was necessary for the self-determination of all Latin American people. Reviewing gains that Cuban feminists had made in gaining civil equality with men, especially in Cuba's 1917 property law, which granted women authority over their inheritances and rights to custody over their children from previous marriages, and in its 1918 divorce law, Domínguez concluded by urging congress participants to solidify their demands into one goal for all the Americas. She called for "a law which will vest in women all the civil rights that men have . . . a law so simple that it would have only this article: that the woman be considered capable of the exercise of all the civil rights grant[ed] the man, there shall exist no difference between man and woman in the exercise of those rights."[30]

The audience enthusiastically applauded Domínguez's resolution, but its heartiest supporter was her new comrade Clara González, sitting next to the podium where Domínguez spoke. They had met just a few days before and struck up a warm friendship based on their shared political and intellectual goals. The two women, nearly the same age, were both lawyers at a time when female lawyers were anomalies.[31] Both socialist feminists, anti-imperialists, and promoters of a Pan-Hispanic feminism, they identified each other quickly as trusted friends and ideological soul mates. Their relationship would grow over the next two decades.

Although Clara González had planned to promote international political rights, in light of Domínguez's proposal she decided to adjust hers to incorporate Domínguez's demands. After Domínguez's presentation, González ascended the podium and gave a lengthy speech that culminated with her call for an international agreement for women's political as well as civil rights. She framed such an international measure as the crowning achievement in a history of Latin American women questing for autonomy. She traced a long and distinguished feminist tradition in the Americas dating back to seventeenth-century Mexican poet and nun Sor Juana Inés de la Cruz and nineteenth-century Argentinian writer and battlefield nurse in Peru Juana Manuela Gorriti. Her list of *precursoras* included no feminists from the United States. Effectively, she posited a new Pan-Hispanic history of *feminismo* that did not rely upon Western European or U.S. leaders.[32]

González tethered her call for women's political rights to recent calls for the legal equality of the nations of the Americas. There were glimmerings, she said, of more liberal and multilateral Pan-American relations. But the "complete emancipation of women" was essential to putting these much-touted ideals of international equality and justice into action.[33] She called for "a free, uniform and extensive action in the effort to obtain . . . her political rights which are due her" and for "the removal from the legislation of all the American countries judicial discriminations against women."[34] These uniform goals would form the basis of a new, more equal Pan-Americanism. She also insisted upon a new inter-American organization that would unite women around these goals.

While Domínguez's proposal for civil rights sailed through the congress, González's proposal for political rights instigated fierce debate. Delegates and members of the audience rose to discuss the extent to which Latin American women were "ready" for the vote. As in the U.S. suffrage debate, some female reformers argued that the corrupt world of male politics would sully women's moral superiority. At the Panama conference, several people insisted that women would be too conservative and vote with the church, a familiar argument in many Latin American countries. When a delegate from Bolivia suggested that "the average woman would vote for a man on account of his personal appearance," Domínguez rose to retort that it was just as reasonable to oppose male suffrage on the grounds that men frequently sold their votes outright to the highest bidder.[35]

In their defense of the proposal, González and Domínguez both emphasized that claims that Latin American women were not ready for the vote stemmed from a false notion of Latin American inferiority, an idea that helped underwrite U.S. imperialism. The women's arguments were persuasive, particularly when these dynamics came to life in congress itself vis-à-vis its U.S. members. When the proposal came up for a vote, Colombian delegate Claudina Múnera asked that the U.S. women present, including many from the Panama Canal Zone, refrain from voting since they already had their political rights.[36] Yet when Emma Bain Swiggett, representing the League of Women Voters, explained why she was not voting, she stated, "We are not yet convinced Latin American women are prepared to exercise political rights," a comment that Domínguez deemed "ominous."[37] Ultimately, González's resolution for an international measure for women's equal civil and political rights passed.

In addition to her international call for women's suffrage, the following day González also pushed for another contentious proposal—one that asked the inter-American women's congress take a stand for fair negotiations of the Panama Canal Treaty. Having called for equal rights for all Spanish American women, she now sought equal rights for Latin American countries against the Colossus of the North. González knew that U.S. intervention in Panama and elsewhere in Central America and the Caribbean took away sovereignty, not only of nations, but of all men, women, and children in occupied territories. Women's sovereignty, she asserted, was essential to national sovereignty in Latin America. They represented two sides of the same problem of Hispanoamerican freedom.[38]

González's resolution was mildly worded. It called for an "altruistic spirit between the people of a big nation in their co-operation with those of smaller ones, in the interests of human solidarity and international harmony." It expressed hope that negotiations over the canal would demonstrate "American fraternity."[39] Domínguez promised hearty support for the proposal, even though both women recognized that even such benign words would probably not win over a congress populated by many U.S. women from the Canal Zone.[40] Indeed, Domínguez later recalled that González's words had the effect of a "hot coal" that quickly lit a fire. Any proposal regarding the Canal Treaty, with implicit rebuke to the United States, alarmed many of the delegates. Neira de Calvo quickly interjected with a more general resolution that eliminated mention of the canal and promoted "universal peace" and "fraternity among the nations of America."[41] Cuban feminist and Domínguez's fellow Club Femenino member Emma López Seña seconded this muted resolution, insisting that the Canal Treaty was a "purely local" question outside the purview of an inter-American congress.[42]

Ofelia Domínguez Navarro violently disagreed with her compatriot López Seña's characterization, insisting that the treaty was not just a "local" issue. "The fate of the Republic of Panama relates to that of all the American Republics," she explained. "The Panama Canal, this breach in the bowels of the generous and hospitable Isthmus, is a continental problem, rather, a global one, and all issues that relate to it should interest all the people of this New World."[43] In Domínguez's view, the Panama Canal, born of U.S. imperialism, was like an ulcer in the small intestine of the isthmus, disturbing the whole digestive tract of the Americas. She recounted the history of Cuba's status as a protectorate of the United States after the Spanish-American War and subsequent U.S. military occupation. As a Cuban, she explained, she struggled against U.S. imperialism wherever it existed in the Americas. When López Seña challenged Domínguez, insisting that Cubans had much to thank the United States for after the U.S. aided them in their war for independence, Domínguez emphatically denied any notion of indebtedness. The U.S. became involved only "when the fruit was already ripe," Domínguez announced. She found any idea of gratitude for "Yankee aggressions" morally "repugnant to the political consciences of the people of the continent."[44]

In a newspaper article published in Panama after the conference, Clara González amplified these arguments: "Panama is in its relations with the U.S. like a mirror in which all the people of Hispanoamerica can see themselves," she wrote. "An abuse of [U.S.] power and . . . expansion of its imperialism" in Panama, she stated, carried repercussions for "all countries like Cuba, Costa Rica, Nicaragua, Honduras, etc., etc. that also . . . [face] the threat of an expansive . . . force from the homeland of Monroe and Washington."[45] Her proposal simply asked that the United States demonstrate the "justice, altruism, and universal brotherhood" that should govern international relations.[46] As the two women predicted, González's motion was voted down in favor of Neira de Calvo's wording, but the debate that flourished at the conference and in the press afforded Domínguez and González a platform for their anti-imperialist American feminism.

Domínguez and González also fought against the strain of Pan-American feminism represented by Emma López Seña that explicitly saw whiteness and European heritage as part of feminism and forward advancement. López Seña's views on these subjects became crystal clear in a Panamanian newspaper profile of her published after the conference, in which she decried the "backwardness" of Colombian delegate Claudina Múnera, who had not supported Domínguez's suffrage resolution. She blamed Múnera's indigenous background and Catholicism. The Panamanian paper enhanced these racist messages when it compared "[Emma López Seña's] white hands" and blonde hair—calling her "an adorable little doll"—with the "hard, dry, almost ferocious face . . . [and] an asymmetric and obtuse head" of the darker Múnera.[47]

González responded in a newspaper article of her own, criticizing López Seña's "hurtful insults" against one of their *compañeras de labores* as "childish [and] inappropriate" as well as "reckless and offensive." Claudina Múnera inspired the congress, González averred, with her dignity and many noteworthy resolutions—for children's literacy, homes, and juvenile courts.[48] Afterward, González sent her article to Domínguez, noting that she hoped she had not been too harsh in her treatment of López Seña.[49]

During a time when most variants of organized *feminismo* in the Americas were white, González and Domínguez both collaborated with Afro-Panamanian and Afro-Cuban feminists in their countries and called for the vote regardless of race or class.[50] At the Panama congress, they found greater identification with each other than with their fellow countrywomen López Seña and Neira de Calvo. After the congress, they corresponded at length, apprising each other of their national progress on women's rights and communicating their deep affection for each other. In a letter addressed to "my dear and remembered Ofelia," González wrote of the "pleasure" Domínguez's "anxiously awaited letters gave me!" She wrote, "I have read them with true devotion. I have seen and heard you again, so good, so frank, so intelligent, as when you were here among us. You have left indelible memories and a memory of sympathy here in this, your land, too." Cuban feminism was at that time more organized than in Panama, and González urged Domínguez to tell her "all that you can . . . of *feminismo*." In exchange, González pledged Domínguez her loyalty and friendship: "I am at your command. . . . You will always have my good will and my heart [at your disposal] willing to serve you sincerely and decidedly no matter what happens." She signed her letter with "a hug from your sincere friend who wants you to stay well."[51]

Stoking González and Domínguez's friendship was their recognition that they were together launching a new phase of *feminismo americano*, one that sought more radical goals and social justice. Their international resolutions at the Panama congress for women's rights amounted to major innovations in international law and in feminist organizing. The most well-known Euro-American international groups—the IWSA, the ICW, and the Women's International League for Peace and Freedom—had all argued for women's rights and exchanged information across national borders. No group, however, had elevated these demands to an international law for women's rights as Domínguez and González had.

Domínguez and González's 1926 collaboration inspired new activism in the Americas. Domínguez later noted that it furthered "the restlessness of women of the continent [who] . . . initiated in their respective countries women's movements."[52] The president of her Club Femenino brought their resolutions to an International Women's Congress in Santiago, Chile, where she demanded the governments of the Americas "concede political rights to women . . . without privileges or distinctions to those that men exercise" and "the same civil rights as the man, equal before the law for the . . . development of a civilization that is fair and just."[53] In Cuba the following year, Machado agreed to add a proposal for women's suffrage to the constitutional assembly, and feminists felt poised to attain their political rights.[54]

Clara González, meanwhile, was heartened by news that the 1927 International Commission of Jurists in Rio de Janeiro proposed that uniform legislation in the Americas be submitted to the Havana conference, following Máximo Soto

Hall's 1923 decree. Included in that legislation was the complete removal of all legal incapacities of women throughout the continent.[55]

But what really raised González's hope for this legal approach was news of feminist activism at the upcoming Sixth Pan-American Conference in Havana in January 1928. There, feminists from Cuba and the United States, including her friend Domínguez, were preparing to push these demands into inter-American law. On January 18, González carefully typed a letter to two Panamanian delegates to the conference—Ricardo J. Alfaro and Eduardo Chiari, both of whom were her friends and former law school professors at the Instituto Nacional— pressing them to support the international treaty for women's rights that feminists were seeking in Havana. Underscoring the work she had done for a similar measure at the 1926 Congreso Interamericano de Mujeres in Panama, she urged them to invest all of their efforts "toward an agreement on the civil and political rights of women" throughout the Americas, "such . . . that the governments feel really committed to making merit of it."[56]

Anti-imperialism, Women's Rights, and Doris Stevens at the 1928 Havana Conference

By the eve of the 1928 Sixth International Conference of American States in Havana, one journalist asserted that U.S.–Latin American relations were "at the most critical point in the history of this hemisphere."[57] Since December 1926, U.S. Marines had invaded and escalated troops in Nicaragua. In June 1927, U.S. Marines dive-bombed a town to rout the rebel group of Augusto César Sandino, and many described U.S. actions in Nicaragua as the greatest international crime of the day. Delegates from various countries came to the Pan-American conference armed with proposals against U.S. intervention.[58] In this context, associations between the "equal rights" of nations and "equal rights" of women became potent. The anti-imperialist Pan-American feminism that González and Domínguez had articulated in 1926 would be pushed into the Havana conference thanks to the work of Domínguez, hundreds of other Cuban feminists, and, somewhat surprisingly, a group of U.S. feminists from the National Woman's Party who descended upon the diplomatic melee.

Of these NWP members, U.S. feminist Doris Stevens was the leader. Born in Omaha, Nebraska, Stevens had become a suffragist while an undergraduate at Oberlin College. After serving as a full-time organizer with the National American Woman Suffrage Association, she cofounded the militant Congressional Union to promote the federal suffrage amendment. A brilliantly charismatic speaker and canny organizer, Stevens was famous in the United States for her suffrage activism that had landed her in jail, immortalized in her 1920 book, *Jailed for Freedom.*[59]

Section of mass meeting of Cuban feminists in assembly room of the Asociación de Reporteros in Havana, Cuba, January 24, 1928. Standing in front of the window, from left to right: Plintha Woss y Gil (Dominican Republic), Helen Winters (U.S.), Muna Lee de Muñoz Marín (U.S.), Doris Stevens (U.S.), María Montalvo de Soto Navarro (Cuba), Jane Norman Smith (U.S.), Serafina R. de Rosado (Costa Rica), and Julia Martínez (Cuba). Seated at table (without hat): María Collado (Cuba). Courtesy of the Schlesinger Library, Radcliffe Institute, Harvard University.

But on January 24, 1928, she and the other U.S. feminists were bowled over by the nearly 200 women in the packed assembly room of the Asociación de Reporteros in Havana. There, Cuban feminists pronounced the birth of a new movement for women's rights and denounced any notion of U.S. superiority. Club Femenino leader Pilar Jorge de Tella rejected the idea that Latin American women were incapable of exercising political rights. "Implied in that classification is the idea of inferior difference, undeserved and unjustifiable," she stated. The "judgment that the North's civilization is superior and that of the South inferior" was "absurd."[60] Though Jorge de Tella did not say Carrie Chapman Catt's name, the allusion was obvious to everyone in the room. Stevens and the other U.S. National Woman's Party feminists in Havana, however, represented a sharp contrast with Catt. Jorge de Tella assured the audience that the NWP members were united with Cuban women like "twin sisters" in combating any notion of Latin American inferiority. These U.S. feminists had come to Havana "in a gesture of constructive altruism" to support an international resolution for "equal rights" for all and for a more just Pan-America.[61] The entire audience rose and cheered.

"I dam[n] near cracked with sheer triumphant emotion," Doris Stevens wrote in a letter home the next day. "The meeting was electric. . . . The dam[n] press gives no idea of the enthusiasm here. The auditorium . . . was packed to the limit."[62] She later recalled, "I felt as if a great forest fire had swept through me and left me a charred tree. . . . We were supposed to be taking them, [but] they had, as a matter of fact, utterly devoured us."[63]

The feminist movement in Cuba was growing, in part because of the activism of leaders like Ofelia Domínguez. In the wake of Machado's refusal to promote suffrage, these feminists looked to international pressure. Although Machado had promised to defend women's suffrage before the 1927 constitutional assembly, he failed to do so (suffrage would not be achieved in Cuba until 1934).[64] Feminists viewed Domínguez's 1926 work at the Panama congress as an important step toward what they hoped to achieve in the 1928 Pan-American conference in Havana: an inter-American commitment to women's rights that could push Machado to make it a reality.

The 1928 Havana conference was in fact on the radar of the U.S. Woman's Party only because the previous year Domínguez's friend Flora Díaz Parrado, a young lawyer and founder of the Camagüey branch of Club Femenino, had told NWP members about it. In December 1927, Díaz Parrado visited the NWP headquarters while in Washington, D.C., for several professional conferences. She met with president Alice Paul and editor of *Equal Rights* Katharine Ward Fisher and encouraged members of the party to attend the Pan-American conference.

By that point Club Femenino and the NWP enjoyed solid links. In the early 1920s, a U.S. woman who lived in Havana with her businessman husband established contact with Cuban feminists on behalf of the NWP and distributed the party's organ, *Equal Rights*, there.[65] The two groups saw each other as allies in their use of radical tactics that challenged their respective governments. During the First World War, the NWP attacked President Wilson and refused to support the U.S. entry into the war.[66] After suffrage, the organization became considerably more conservative. In 1923, the NWP decided its national goal would be an Equal Rights Amendment: "Men and women shall have equal rights throughout the United States and every place subject to its jurisdiction." This single-issue emphasis on legal equality made the group anathema to industrial women workers and progressive reformers who feared the ERA, with its call for identical laws for men and women, would overturn years of hard-fought special legislation for women workers. It also made the group unpalatable to most African American reformers, particularly since the NWP refused to support anti-lynching legislation or oppose poll tax requirements and other forms of racial discrimination, later allying themselves with southern senators who promised support of the ERA. Yet in Cuba in 1927 and 1928, the NWP still had a reputation for being radical and avant-garde, and certainly more progressive than the other large U.S. group with which Cuban feminists were familiar, the League of Women Voters. In the pages of Equal Rights, the NWP celebrated Cuban feminism and drew parallels between Club Femenino's and its own militancy.[67]

These connections hastened Díaz Parrado's trip to NWP headquarters in late 1927.[68] There she carefully explained to Woman's Party president Alice Paul that in spite of Máximo Soto Hall's 1923 resolution that assured that future Pan-American conferences would include women and study and promote women's civil and political rights, and in spite of continuing pressure by Cuban feminists, women's rights were not on the agenda of the 1928 conference. Though she and others in Club Femenino had asked the Cuban Ministry of Interior to appoint female delegates, their requests had failed.[69] Believing that U.S. women could be politically useful to their national suffrage goals, Díaz Parrado urged the NWP to send representatives to the conference and press for inter-American women's rights.

Just as Club Femenino's desire to have U.S. women in Havana was instrumental, so was Alice Paul's interest in the conference. After her meeting with Díaz Parrado, Paul realized the Pan-American conference would be the perfect way to revive the NWP's national campaign for the ERA — "a very great opportunity . . . [which] we ought not to let . . . go by unutilized."[70] The ERA had been stalled in Congress since its introduction at the end of 1923. After 1925 the Woman's Party sought new international avenues to promote its national amendment. That year, Paul and Alva Belmont, the heiress who provided the NWP most of its financial support, formed an "International Advisory Committee" — a pressure group of prominent female leaders, mostly from England and Western Europe, who would promote "equal rights" in the League of Nations. Paul and several other women from the committee also pushed a resolution demanding "complete equality for men and women in all nations" into the 1925 Washington, D.C. meeting of the Interparliamentary Union, a gathering of representatives from parliaments of various countries.[71]

That success, combined with the news Díaz Parrado brought of the 1923 Santiago resolution, caused Alice Paul to see the Pan-American sphere as a more productive realm for feminism than Western Europe. At the Interparliamentary Union gathering, Latin American delegates, making up a significant proportion of the total delegates, were the most enthusiastic supporters of women's rights.[72] While the League of Nations included some women in the Committee on the Traffic in Women and Children and in the International Labor Organization, it did not provide the formal opening for women's participation or explicit discussion of women's rights that the Pan-American Union did.[73] Furthermore, the international repercussions of the domestic equal rights versus protective legislation debate in the United States were damaging the NWP's chances of gaining a foothold in the Geneva-based groups. Like the ILO and U.S.-European international women's groups, Catt's International Alliance of Women promoted protective labor legislation for women workers, which it feared the ERA would eliminate. Alliance members vehemently opposed the Woman's Party and its ERA. At its 1926 meeting in Paris, Catt's IWSA, now renamed the International Alliance of Women for Suffrage and Equal Citizenship, rejected the NWP's application for membership, leaving the latter group grasping for international consolidation. The U.S.'s unparalleled authority in Latin America, in contrast to its tepid relationship with the League of Nations, of which it was not a member, also made the Pan-American realm seem more propitious to Paul. As she put it, the Havana conference presented "a wonderful opportunity for us to start serious international work, because . . . we would not have the difficulties that confront us . . . at Geneva."[74]

By early January 1928, the Woman's Party had not succeeded in convincing Pan-American Union director Leo Rowe to appoint female delegates to the conference or to change the agenda to include women's rights. Nonetheless, Paul decided she would send an "unofficial delegation," led by Doris Stevens, who had just become chair of the International Relations Committee of the NWP.[75]

The mission of these conference gatecrashers would be to lay groundwork for an international women's rights treaty. Paul, who had begun studying international law after receiving a law degree from Washington College of Law in 1922, believed that an international treaty "would give equal rights to all women on the American continents and much faster than it could ever be won country by country."[76] She was directly influenced in this vision by the inter-American innovations in international law. Paul studied the 1923 Santiago resolution and publications of the American Institute for International Law, the organization created by Pan-American enthusiasts Alejandro Álvarez, the Chilean jurist, and U.S. jurist James Brown Scott, that sought to codify inter-American law. She knew that this group had sponsored the 1927 International Commission of Jurists in Rio de Janeiro, which advanced the use of treaties for private international law, including women's civil status. Díaz Parrado may have also told Paul about González and Domínguez's proposal for a women's rights treaty at the 1926 Panama congress.[77]

On the eve of their trip to Havana, Paul sent Doris Stevens and Jane Norman Smith, chair of the NWP executive body, several legal papers defending the treaty method. They all knew a treaty represented a major departure in feminist strategy. The Tenth Amendment of the U.S. Constitution, guaranteeing the reserved rights of states, made difficult the passage of any international treaty that sought to intervene in national and state jurisdiction. However, Paul found federal legal precedent for an international treaty in *Missouri v. Holland*, a 1920 Supreme Court case designed to protect migratory birds in the United States and Canada. This case concluded that "a treaty applied against the interests of an individual state did not constitute a violation of the Tenth Amendment."[78] As Paul would impress upon Stevens and Smith, in spite of what the U.S. State Department might tell them to the contrary, a treaty for women's rights was constitutional. "It would mean a revolution in thought, perhaps," Paul wrote, but it was not unconstitutional.[79]

Armed with plans for what she called "the first treaty . . . proposed by women on behalf of women," Doris Stevens, along with Jane Norman Smith and Alice Paul, recognized that their success in Havana could not only boost the ERA in the United States but also undermine the international efforts of Carrie Chapman Catt, with whom the NWP had an antagonistic relationship.[80] They were well aware of Latin American vitriol against Catt due to her overweening condescension. Although, like Catt, they believed that U.S. feminism was more advanced than that in Latin America, they determined to not replicate Catt's mistake of asserting leadership over Latin American women. Smith acknowledged that the NWP had "apparently been asleep about the [1923] resolution for the last five years," while Club Femenino members actively galvanized support for it. Thus, "tell[ing] these women what to do" would be "nervy" and possibly even offensive.[81] Katharine Ward Fisher urged Smith to operate on equal terms with Latin American women and "get their point of view. That will mean a great deal, it seems to me, for the future."[82]

Upon their arrival, Stevens, Smith, and the other Woman's Party representatives made a conscious effort to present themselves as sisters to the Cuban women rather than "teachers" or missionaries for uplift.[83] In deliberate contrast to Catt's position of questioning Latin American women's readiness for equality, they asserted that women from Latin America and the United States deserved all the same political and civil rights. They sent a letter to Cuban feminist organizations arguing that women's oppression was worldwide. "In not a single country of North or South America do men and women enjoy equal rights before the law," it explained. Later, they would continue to emphasize that U.S. women "were in the same boat," just as subjugated as, if not more than, Latin American women. Instead of emphasizing U.S. women's rights to suffrage, their letter listed the many states in the United States in which married women's earnings belonged to husbands, in which guardianship and inheritance laws were unequal, and in which a woman could not enter a contract or go into business without her husband's consent. Reversing the standard hierarchy, they emphasized that U.S. women needed the support of Cuban feminists to help *them* attain equal rights.[84] Initially the Woman's Party members received only a tepid response. But as Cuban feminists read and distributed this letter, collaborations blossomed.[85]

In addition to challenging U.S. imperial feminism, NWP members also increasingly portrayed themselves as opponents of U.S. imperialism, more broadly. This strategy was hastened by the opposition of the U.S. State Department to their goals. When Stevens and Smith sought out U.S. envoy and former secretary of state Charles E. Hughes to request a hearing at the conference, Smith recalled, he "treated us more or less like little children."[86] Hughes had come to the Havana conference to defend the status quo in Latin America and to oppose any policy that defied the State Department's narrow definition of international law. These policies included proposals Latin American delegates had brought to push against U.S. intervention and for more multilateral relations. His argument—that women's rights fell under domestic and not international jurisdiction—would become a familiar refrain in future Pan-American debates.[87] It remains a common justification for the United States' resistance to signing international human rights treaties to this day.[88]

In the context of the U.S. armed intervention in Nicaragua, any notion that the U.S. State Department prized Latin American sovereignty seemed a ludicrous contradiction to many. Just before the conference, Nicaraguan revolutionary Augusto César Sandino had scored a series of impressive military victories against the United States, galvanizing official efforts to obtain a U.S. commitment to nonintervention in Latin America.[89] The U.S. banned Sandino from coming to the conference. Increasingly, NWP members in Havana made public that they sided with Sandino, linking this position to their demands for women's rights as a goal for "social justice." One of the NWP delegates, avowed anti-imperialist Alice Park, pointed out the hypocrisy in Hughes's supposed ethical opposition to "dictating to other nations" when he advocated U.S. intervention in Latin America.[90]

Doris Stevens became the key strategist behind these anti-imperialist arguments. Before the conference, she had actually anticipated working with, rather than against, the U.S. State Department, predicting the United States would be "the most advanced country . . . at the Congress" on women's rights as the only country there that had granted women's suffrage.[91] When Hughes and other international jurists, such as U.S. lawyer James Brown Scott and Cuban Antonio Sánchez de Bustamante y Sirvén, questioned the validity of an international treaty, she wrote to Alice Paul. These statesmen granted that migratory birds could be subject to international jurisdiction but questioned that a domestic matter like women's rights could be. In reply, Paul urged Stevens to play the anti-imperialist card. Whether individual rights was a proper subject for international action, Paul advised Stevens, was "of course a matter of opinion—just as it is a matter of opinion as to whether our various acts under the Monroe Doctrine and our present activities in Nicaragua, are proper subjects for international action."[92] Paul and Stevens were not anti-imperialists. (In fact, according to Chilean feminist Marta Vergara, Paul believed that "if an infantry of Marines ever landed in places beyond the Rio Grande, it was for the good of the country thus protected."[93]) Yet, they both knew that anti-imperialism was the keynote of the conference and that many Latin American delegates were pushing for a nonintervention treaty. Both women were shrewd, if somewhat unscrupulous, political chameleons. Paul gave Stevens a strategy that the latter would take up with alacrity for years to come: to use anti-imperialism as an argument for international women's rights.

Paul gave Stevens more ammunition for these arguments when she sent her, several weeks into her trip, a "Proposed Treaty on Equal Rights for Men and Women." The marked enthusiasm of Latin American delegates for the idea prompted Paul to produce a draft of what became "the Equal Rights Treaty." Drawing on language the NWP had pushed at the 1925 Interparliamentary Union meeting and on the ERA, it read, "The Contracting States agree that upon the ratification of this Treaty, men and women shall have equal rights throughout the territory subject to their respective jurisdictions."[94]

When Stevens launched this treaty into public debate in Havana, she cemented her reputation as a Pan-American justice fighter, demanding an international commitment to equal rights from the U.S. government. Havana newspapers praised Stevens as a leader of a new type of feminism and among the "intellectual vanguard of North American women."[95] Through Stevens, the National Woman's Party emerged as an altruistic group, separate from the more inimical forces of U.S. capitalism and imperialism represented by the U.S. State Department.[96] Her history of militant suffrage activism enhanced her credibility for rebelling against the U.S. government. Several articles raved about her book *Jailed for Freedom*, interpreted by one as documenting her efforts in the "campaign for the liberation of women and for peace."[97] A long and detailed profile of Stevens in El País described the NWP headquarters in the Hotel Seville as a sharp departure from the venal activities of the Pan-American conference. The happenings elsewhere in the hotel served as a metaphor for the conference proceedings—foolish, commercial, and above all a reflection of U.S. empire: "waiters running this way and that, carrying enormous . . . bottles of champagne or rum. Laughter, pointless comments, the smoke of Pall Mall or Chesterfield [U.S. cigarette brands] . . . populate this environment where the majesty of the 'dollar' exerts its formidable empire." However, upon taking the elevator up to Stevens's suite, number 312, the author explained, "suddenly everything changes." Stevens's suite served as the NWP campaign "headquarters" where she and other NWP members received Cuban women, the press, and other visitors.[98] With Cuban and U.S. flags next to the door and a purple, white, and gold National Woman's Party flag waving from the balcony, Cuban and U.S. women worked feverishly together, with "enthusiasm," the El País author reported. The article praised the feminists' wide concepts of "liberty and human equality" and bemoaned that they found no counterpart in the rest of the conference proceedings.[99]

Stevens celebrated this press coverage, writing to her romantic partner, New Republic writer Jonathan Mitchell, "It is wonderful to work in a country where women are such tremendous news. . . . Everyday on every one of six Spanish papers we are taking everything from headlines to prominent columns. . . . The Latin American men are so much quicker and so much more sensitive than our fish that we expect results from them but not from ours." Whether or not they supported it, the "Latin American men," she noted, were "captivated by our treaty idea."[100]

Stevens's performance also won over all of the established feminist groups in Havana that rallied in support of the Equal Rights Treaty. A host of women's organizations signed a Spanish translation of it, including Club Femenino, the Federación Nacional de Asociaciones Femeninas de Cuba, the Damas Católicas, the Asociación de Emigradas Revolucionarias, the Partido Nacional Sufragista, and others. A range of political groups, from the more conservative and Machado-supporting to the more progressive, hosted lunches and talks for NWP members. Over lunch, Club Femenino members gave a standing ovation to Stevens, who stood and spoke in English, with a translator, praising the successful efforts of Cuban feminists to promote equal rights. At the large meeting at the Asociación de Reporteros, Stevens portrayed the Equal Rights Treaty as part of a broader effort for inter-American justice: "A new international code is being born here. . . . We wish to make this hemisphere a new world in fact, not theory, for women as well as men." Reiterating her message, she announced that "no nation, no continent has the right to deny us our rights. They are our human rights!"[101]

Ofelia Domínguez, who had moved to Havana from Santa Clara in 1927, was at the heart of these events. She recognized the Equal Rights Treaty as the fulfillment of her and González's 1926 Panama congress resolution, and she lobbied the conference president and delegates to allow the women to represent their demands in a plenary session.[102] Domínguez also rallied support for the NWP feminists, explaining in an editorial that "the serious and reasoned proposals

Doris Stevens, 1928. Courtesy of the Schlesinger Library, Radcliffe Institute, Harvard University.

Lantern slide advertising the "Great Assembly of Women in favor of 'Equality of Rights,' in the Reporters' Association, Tuesday the 24th at 4 pm, Zulueta 5." The advertisement was shown in films played at the Teatro Fausto in Havana, 1928. Courtesy of the Schlesinger Library, Radcliffe Institute, Harvard University.

that Sras Smith and Stevens have presented to the Conference have not been acts of arrogance." They were "a generous group of women," committed to the "liberation of women of the whole continent," she insisted.[103]

The connections between equal rights for women and for nations became undeniably clear on January 28, 1928, an overcast day when over 200 women marched on the anniversary of the birth of José Martí, founder of the Cuban Revolutionary Party, hero of Cuban liberation, and early proponent of an anti-imperialist inter-American solidarity.[104] A Cuban and a U.S. woman, each holding her nation's flag, led the procession to the statue of Martí in Havana's Central Park. Following them, women carried their clubs' banners—the Federación Nacional de Asociaciones Femeninas de Cuba, Club Femenino, Partido Nacional Sufragista, and the Liga Patriótica Sufragista, as well as others. Twenty-one women wore sky-blue bands across their chests with the names of the twenty-one republics of the Americas. After them marched Stevens, the four other NWP members, and a woman holding a banner with a quote from Martí in Spanish: "Women should have the same right to vote as men have." The procession, which spanned several blocks, ended with a huge banner that bore more words by Martí: "Justice admits no delay, and he who delays its fulfillment turns it against himself." After a woman placed an enormous wreath at the foot of the statue, a man hired by the NWP released 2,000 carrier pigeons as symbols of inter-American peace.[105]

This rousing march culminated the women's lobbying efforts and publicized connections between their budding Pan-American feminist movement and Martí's anti-imperialist legacy. Although the U.S. representatives continued to withhold support of the women's hearing, numerous Latin American delegates and, in some cases, entire delegations declared themselves heartily in favor of an unofficial hearing for women at the conference.[106] This support also drew on the groundwork laid over the past several years by Paulina Luisi, Clara González, and Ofelia Domínguez Navarro. Jacobo Varela, president of the Uruguayan delegation and ex-minister of Uruguay in Washington who had promoted Baltasar Brum and Paulina Luisi's vision of Pan-American feminism during the 1922 Baltimore conference, initiated the motion for the women's hearing. One of its most outspoken supporters was Ricardo J. Alfaro, head of the Panamanian delegation, to whom Clara González had sent her appeal.

The charged anti-imperialism at the conference critically hastened Latin American support. Delegates from Argentina, Mexico, Guatemala, Panama, Cuba, El Salvador, Costa Rica, Nicaragua, and Paraguay—many of whom had advocated anti-interventionist policies, only to have their proposals quashed by the U.S. delegation—boosted the feminists' initiatives. Lobbying these statesmen to grant them a hearing, Stevens played upon their shattered illusions; she reinforced the idea that supporting feminism would defy the U.S. government and that the U.S. government's *lack* of support for women's rights was part of its control over Latin America. On February 4, Argentine delegation chief Honorio Pueyrredón boldly protested the United States, calling "diplomatic or armed intervention, whether permanent or temporary . . . an attack against [countries'] independence" that violated those nations' equal rights.[107] This was the sort of challenge to its authority that the U.S. delegation had feared, and Hughes quickly quashed Pueyrredón's non-intervention proposal. Shortly thereafter Pueyrredón personally seconded the motion for the women's hearing, enabling them to speak before the conference a few days later.[108]

A letter from Jonathan Mitchell, Stevens's romantic partner, cheered her success and encouraged her to maximize upon "Pueyrredon's speech attacking the US" by taking "a rap at the US in your speech before the plenary session." She should play on the multiple meanings of "sovereignty," he insisted, and point out how the United States professed "to welcome women as partners" yet denied them many opportunities, similar to how the United States claimed to welcome

Latin Americans as Pan-American partners. If she made the most of "this sovereignty business," he predicted "the temper of the session would be such that the Lats would be ecstatic, and it would be . . . elegant news."[109]

Indeed, in her speech on February 7, 1928, from the stage of the magnificent *aula magna* of the University of Havana, Stevens drew a strong link between Latin American nations rebelling against being told what to do "for their own good" and women rebelling against men for the same reason. In both cases, "protection" meant control, not equality. Flanked by the coat of arms of the twenty-one American republics on the wall behind her, and with a Chilean statesman serving as her translator, Stevens declared, "Enlightened women are in revolt against acts done for their good. We want no more laws written for our good and without our consent. We must have the right to direct our own destiny jointly with you."[110] Stevens also explicitly alluded to Catt's aspersions of Latin American women: "One of our compatriots [has said] that . . . the women of Latin America are not yet ready for [equal rights]. We women resent and disbelieve in any hint of sectional superiority. . . . We do not believe that the men of North America are called upon to be tender protectors of the women of Latin America."[111]

The seven other women who addressed the plenary also united women's equality—under the law and at work—with inter-American equality and justice.[112] Addressing the packed hall of over 2,000 people, Julia Martínez, Cuban doctor and feminist, underscored the connection between women's rights and "Cuban sovereignty." What did it mean for Cuba to be "sovereign" if women did not have equal rights?[113] Muna Lee de Muñoz Marín, a U.S. NWP member who was married to Puerto Rican editor and son of a prominent political family, Luís Muños Marín, explicitly compared the dependent situation of women to the dependency of Puerto Rico. "We have everything done for us and given us but sovereignty. We are treated with every consideration save the one great consideration of being regarded as responsible beings. We, like Porto Rico, are dependents. We are anomalies before the law."[114] Pilar Jorge de Tella furthered a feminism of social justice when she spoke not only on behalf of Club Femenino but also on behalf of the women workers in the Gremio de Despalilladoras (the Tobacco Stemmers' Guild), the largest organization of working women in Cuba, representing 1,500 women, many of whom were Afro-Cuban. El *País* noted that "for the first time a women's organization of a worker character has been represented in a suffrage act" in Cuba.[115]

Also for the first time, women had addressed an intergovernmental conference to speak on behalf of women's rights. Despite their impassioned pleas, only a handful of the delegates at the conference voted for the Equal Rights Treaty, but the conference did vote to establish an intergovernmental organization devoted to the study and promotion of women's rights, the first of its kind.[116] Doris Stevens pressed for its creation in Havana, insisting that Soto Hall's 1923 resolution called for such a body.[117] This Inter-American Commission of Women would consist of one female delegate from every country of the Western Hemisphere, and have an office in the Pan-American Union headquarters in Washington, D.C.

The commission, these feminists hoped, would unite women from throughout the Americas and continue to fight for the Equal Rights Treaty. When Club Femenino hosted a goodbye lunch for the NWP women, Doris Stevens announced that "the women of the Americas will never retreat from the ties made at Havana."[118] She wrote to Alice Paul, "Already we sense the rumblings of excited desire on the part of some of the delegates to hurry back to their respective countries to see that their national laws are improved before the dreaded treaty arrives to bind them."[119]

Back in the United States, members of the National Woman's Party made the most of their Cuban campaign. They promoted themselves as the rebellious force that had invaded the conference and formed the Inter-American Commission of Women (IACW). Muna Lee published an article in The Nation in which she proudly proclaimed that "Sandino was kept out of the Sixth Pan American conference, but the Woman's Party of the United States got in."[120] Doris Stevens announced that "international feminism was born in Havana."[121]

Ofelia Domínguez Navarro also had great expectations for the IACW. Several months after the commission's creation, Domínguez became a leader of a new national group, the Alianza Nacional Feminista, which merged a number of organizations in a broad-based "united front for the vote" and became one of the most influential feminist groups in Cuba. Activism at the Pan-American conference, one member recalled, had provided the catalyst for the group's formation: "It was a milestone in the history of feminism ... contributing perhaps more than any other single event to [Cuban women] realizing all they lacked. Many of us heard the fervent words spoken by women of different countries ... that inspired faith in a future that could only be reached by joint action.... Many of us awoke."[122]

Ofelia Domínguez knew that she and Clara González had helped spark this awakening. At the 1926 Panama congress their call for a supranational lever for women's rights had paved the way for the feminist collaborations in Havana a few years later. In 1929, Domínguez utilized this inter-American momentum to campaign for suffrage. Speaking before the presidential palace in Havana, she declared that bringing women into the political life of the nation would help secure its sovereignty and what she called women's *derechos humanos* (human rights).[123] She hoped that the Inter-American Commission of Women would help make these demands a reality.

CHAPTER THREE

Feminismo práctico

✹ ✹ ✹

In July 1928, six months after the dramatic conclusion of the Havana conference, Clara González and Doris Stevens sat together for a photo shoot orchestrated by the National Woman's Party (NWP). González had just arrived in Washington, D.C., to start work with the new Inter-American Commission of Women (IACW). She and Stevens were the first two constituents of this organization that was to include twenty-one members, one from each Western Hemisphere republic. Under the shade of palm trees in the courtyard of the Pan-American Union, the headquarters of the commission, the women chatted as they attempted several poses. The image the NWP decided upon would be seen by thousands of readers of newspapers in Panama, the United States, Brazil, Chile, Uruguay, Cuba, and elsewhere, often under the headline "Feminismo."[1] With Clara González facing the camera, beaming at Stevens whose mouth was open in conversation, it presented the mise-en-scène the NWP wanted to portray. With their modern hairstyles and clothes, González and Stevens represented new faces of a Pan-Americanism founded on equality and friendship among women of the New World. "For the first time in the history of the world," accompanying promotional text read, "an international group composed of representatives of governments has empowered women to . . . study the status of women and to recommend measures to make men and women equal before the law."[2]

González recognized this organization and her role in it as outgrowths of the goals she and her friend Ofelia Domínguez Navarro had promoted several years before in Panama. There the two women had sponsored resolutions for sweeping international women's rights laws and for a new feminismo americano founded on joint action for women's rights and anti-imperialism. Based on Doris Stevens's leadership in Havana, González had high hopes that the commission would espouse these lofty ideals.

In spite of her initial enthusiasm, however, González would soon find that Stevens ran the IACW unilaterally and excelled at spearheading publicity efforts rather than at fostering inter-American equality or friendship. Over the commis-

Clara González and Doris Stevens sitting in the courtyard of the Pan-American Union, Washington, D.C., Harris & Ewing, 1928. The National Woman's Party distributed this image with news of the IACW's creation to newspapers and magazines throughout the United States and Latin America. Courtesy of the Schlesinger Library, Radcliffe Institute, Harvard University.

sion's first five years, many of the anti-imperialist Spanish-speaking feminists who had fostered its creation, including González, Domínguez, and Paulina Luisi, came to resent Stevens's leadership. They discovered that Stevens's declarations in Havana in favor of "sovereignty" had merely been lip service. As commission chair, Stevens pursued only one goal: women's equal political and civil rights enshrined in international law. She sidelined other objectives that González, Domínguez, and others sought: anti-imperialism, social and economic rights for women, recognition that commission goals would necessarily shift according to local political contexts, and Latin American feminist leadership. Such broader ideals defined *feminismo* for these women and distinguished them from their U.S. counterparts.

These disappointments led to clashes and confrontations, but they also served to strengthen the bonds between González, Domínguez, and Luisi. These women would help create new networks of dissent among Latin American feminists based on anti-imperialism, social justice, Latin American leadership, and unity in opposition to Doris Stevens. Those networks facilitated friendships and created an alternative Pan-American feminism centered on solidarity and support for local struggles, what Domínguez called *feminismo práctico*—"practical feminism."[3] In the early to mid-1930s, the dislocations of the Great Depression impelled new social, economic, and political turmoil in the Americas and created an even greater need for a *feminismo práctico* that Spanish-speaking feminists allied to build. That *feminismo* provided the seedbed for later resistance to Doris Stevens and for the continuing struggle for their goals.

Clara González and the Inter-American Commission of Women

González learned of the successes of the 1928 Havana conference from New York City, where she was studying law and penal institutions for women and delinquent youth at New York University on a scholarship from the Panamanian government. She celebrated this momentum for inter-American feminism that she and her friend Domínguez had helped incite.

A few months later, Latin American and U.S. statesmen on the Governing Board of the Pan-American Union fulfilled the terms of the conference and created the Inter-American Commission of Women. Cuban jurist Antonio Sánchez de Bustamante and Peruvian diplomat Victor Maúrtua, both impressed with Doris Stevens's leadership in Havana, named Stevens chair and U.S. commissioner. The board drew by lottery the six other countries whose governments would choose the first representatives: Argentina, Colombia, Haiti, Panama, El Salvador, and Venezuela. These female delegates would select representatives for the remaining seats.[4] Panamanian diplomat Ricardo Alfaro recommended González as the Panamanian representative, recognizing her role in the commission's creation. González's proximity to Washington, D.C., also made her an ideal candidate for commissioner.

Upon learning of her appointment, Doris Stevens immediately contacted González and urged her to work at the Pan-American Union office. Their first conversation, over lunch in New York City, left each impressed with the other. Stevens wrote to González that it "made me feel that there will be no limits to what the Commission can accomplish, if all its members are as eager, as understanding, and as enlightened a feminist as you are."[5] González agreed to go to Washington, D.C., right away for the summer.

There, González threw herself into the commission's legal work on women's rights. She returned again in the summer of 1929 and for the next two years traveled frequently between New York City and D.C. even during her school term. In Washington she boarded at the Alva Belmont House, the National Woman's Party headquarters prominently located across from the Capitol Building and down the street from the Library of Congress, where Stevens arranged a private carrel for González in the Law Division.[6] Although González initially spoke English with some difficulty, by the end of her time in the United States in 1930 she was fluent in the language. Since Stevens at that time spoke no Spanish, González and Muna Lee de Muñoz Marín, who also volunteered there for a short time, translated correspondence and communiqués into and from Spanish, while Elsie Ross Shields, the commission secretary who was the daughter of a British Foreign Service officer and originally from Brazil, translated to and from Portuguese.[7]

González lent her significant legal expertise to the commission, working long hours at the Library of Congress to create the international compendium of laws that the commission would present to the Hague Codification Conference in 1930 and to the Pan-American conference in Montevideo in 1933. The NWP had for many years compiled discriminatory laws from all of the U.S. states and publicized them in pamphlets and periodicals. Now the party attempted a study of laws throughout the Americas, the first of its size and international scope. The compendium revealed discrimination against women in a wide range of civil, penal, and other forms of law in every country in the Western Hemisphere. Acknowledging the extent of these laws would persuade many statesmen and feminists to support the Equal Rights Treaty. González, who had honed her knowledge of women's rights law in her groundbreaking law school dissertation in Panama, was critical to its production.

González recognized the legal work of the commission for women's civil and political rights as deeply important, but she also expected the group to combat U.S. imperialism, as promised in its founding. In 1927 she had joined the New York chapter of the Federación Latinoamericana de Estudiantes, an anti-imperialist group of Latin American students living in the United States committed to "the liberation of the Latin American people." She attempted to link this group to the commission. A formal statement from the Federación, possibly authored by González, explained that although the commission had been created at one of the Pan-American conferences that served "sinister alliance[s]" and "special interests," the commission itself embodied purer motives: "The vindication of women's rights is really a fight of universal principals . . . [and] just causes cannot be obstructed . . . on account of the circumstances of their origin."[8]

The U.S. government's undisguised aversion to the commission raised González's expectations that it would be an autonomous body for inter-American feminism and justice. Over the commission's first decade, the Pan-American Union and State Department under Presidents Coolidge and Hoover viewed it as either a hindrance or an irrelevance. Internal memos reveal that the State Department considered the commission essentially pointless, since women in the United States had the right to vote.[9] Pan-American Union director Leo Rowe only reluctantly provided its agreed-upon office space in the Pan-American Union after nearly a month of haggling with Doris Stevens, insisting that the commission was not intended to be "official."[10] As Chilean feminist Marta Vergara aptly put it years later, the commission was "a sort of illegitimate child which the [Pan-American Union] had come to recognize in spite of itself."[11]

Always the strategist, Stevens understood the importance of this independence to garnering Latin American support. In press releases and interviews, she emphasized that the IACW was a "non-political" and "non-partisan" group, financially autonomous from the United States. Privately, she celebrated its hybrid intergovernmental/nongovernmental status. As she explained to a friend in 1929, such a "golden situation" would "probably never recur in our lifetime: the chairman a feminist, and we so newly formed that the government paid not the slightest attention to what we did."[12]

In August 1928, Stevens staged a dramatic protest in Rambouillet, France, that emphasized the IACW's independence from the U.S. government. The commission's first large-scale, militant action would disrupt the peace treaty signing of U.S. secretary of state Frank B. Kellogg and French foreign minister Aristide Briand. On the heels of the First World War, many in the United States and Western Europe believed the Kellogg-Briand Treaty, which renounced war as "an instrument of national policy," a serious, near-sacred commitment to world peace.[13] Doris Stevens, however, viewed it as the perfect opportunity to publicize the commission to the world. Since Stevens was going to a League of Nations meeting in Geneva around the same time, she decided to take a detour

Doris Stevens leading members of the IACW in a protest at the Kellogg-Briand Peace Pact Conference outside Château de Rambouillet, France, 1928. Their banner reads in French, "We ask for a treaty giving us equal rights." Courtesy of the Schlesinger Library, Radcliffe Institute, Harvard University.

to France for the signing.[14] In Paris Stevens rallied a group of feminists from Europe and the United States to insist on a joint hearing of the Equal Rights Treaty alongside the peace treaty. When Kellogg demurred, she boldly led nine U.S. and French women to demonstrate outside the French president's private residence, Château de Rambouillet, where Kellogg and other treaty-signers lunched. When asked to leave, Stevens initiated several "flank attacks" in which the women tried to barrel through the guards in front of the palace, landing her and her cohort in a Paris jail. The women spent most of their three hours in custody standing at the jailhouse windows dropping Equal Rights Treaty pamphlets to cheering supporters below. This protest was the first major act of civil disobedience U.S. feminists had engaged in since the suffrage movement, and it made front-page news around the world.[15]

The Kellogg-Briand Peace Pact stunt became a watershed moment in the commission's popularity among Latin American elites. While many in Europe and the United States censured Stevens's actions as scandalous and in bad taste, large numbers of leftists and Latin American statesmen, journalists, and femi-

FEMINISMO PRÁCTICO

nists celebrated them.[16] U.S. secretary of state Kellogg had overseen the violent onslaught of marines in Nicaragua among other interventions in the region. One Puerto Rican feminist writer referred to Kellogg and Briand as "pit[iable] ... buffoons" and their "peace treaty" as a ludicrous contradiction.[17] The International Communist Party had staged anti-imperialist protests in Paris before the peace treaty, and the socialist newspaper the New York Worker claimed Stevens's arrest in France as "the first military victory won by the Kellogg Peace Treaty."[18] Several years later, Senator Pierre Hudicourt of Haiti, who had been imprisoned by U.S. Marines, lauded Stevens as a "fellow political prisoner."[19] Clara González was one of the loudest supporters: "The arrests are unequivocal proof," she told reporters, "that the old world is behind the new in its attitude toward women and their rights."[20]

Latin American support for the Rambouillet action directly aided Stevens in Geneva, where Latin American statesmen helped her propel the IACW's equal rights demands into the League of Nations' upcoming Conference for the Codification of International Law.[21] Orestes Ferrara, Cuban delegate to the League of Nations whom Stevens had impressed in Havana earlier that year, introduced her proposal granting the appointment of women as delegates to the future conference at The Hague, which was accepted. Ferrara "insists on introducing me as 'the young woman who was arrested in Paris for disturbing Mr. Kellogg,'" Stevens reported to the commission. "This seems to delight all the Latin Americans. I gather that Mr. Kellogg is not one of their pets."[22]

In spite of dramatic acts of rebelliousness against the United States, Stevens had no real anti-imperialist investments. Stevens challenged the United States when it was expedient, but she never seriously considered challenging U.S. hegemony as an end it itself. For Stevens, there was one and only one aim for the IACW and for feminism—sex equality. This meant the Equal Rights Treaty, if passed through the International Conferences of American States and other international bodies like the League of Nations, would provide a new lever to change the national laws governing women's lives throughout the world. For Stevens and many others in the National Woman's Party, legal equality in civil and political rights represented the end-all goal of feminism. This narrow commitment to legal equality for women unmoored from other political or social objectives had served the Woman's Party strategically when it fought single-mindedly for the Nineteenth Amendment to the U.S. Constitution. As historian Nancy Cott has assessed the dynamic, it was "forged in the suffrage struggle and applied and misapplied obsessively after that."[23]

After their success in Geneva, Stevens and Alice Paul decided that in addition to an Equal Rights Treaty, the commission should draft an Equal Nationality Treaty that would specifically grant independent nationality rights to married women.[24] They planned to introduce the treaty to the League of Nations, which had been at work since 1924 on a code of law for all nations of the world. The initial attempt to officially inscribe this international code would take place at the Hague Codification Conference in the spring of 1930, where nationality would be one of the first subjects discussed. Due to Stevens's 1928 proposal to include women in these deliberations, this Hague conference would mark the first time women would participate as plenipotentiaries in any League of Nations meeting.[25]

Initially Clara González actively supported this goal.[26] She even defended the commission against some who insisted that focusing on equal nationality rights did not address the needs of Latin American women. Women in many Latin American countries already had nationality rights, while in the United States, despite the Cable Act of 1922, they did not.[27] In Argentina, Chile, Paraguay, and Uruguay, for instance, a woman did not forfeit her nationality upon marrying an alien, and these countries' nationality laws had no distinctions based on sex.[28] Stevens and Paul thought the progressiveness of Latin American law on nationality made it a fitting cause for the IACW. But an article in the Panama newspaper *Gráfico* criticized the commission for focusing on nationality at the expense of other more pressing concerns for Latin American women, such as the vote or economic equality. In a response published in *Diario de Panamá*, González insisted that independent nationality mattered a great deal to all people, especially when immigration was on the rise and female immigrants whose citizenship derived through marriage faced unique problems in national status. The Equal Rights and Equal Nationality Treaties, she announced, would help dismantle all forms of inequality that women of the Americas faced.[29]

While González still maintained faith in the equal rights work of the commission and admired Stevens's international influence, she was increasingly troubled by Stevens's unilateral leadership. In spite of promises of "sisterhood," Stevens integrated little to no input from Latin American feminists. By the end of González's first summer working at IACW headquarters, only the first seven government-appointed commissioners had been named. Other than González, none had been able to spend substantial time in the U.S. headquarters, and most maintained intimate connections to their governments rather than to feminist organizations. They included the wife of a Colombian lawyer who worked closely with the U.S. State Department; the wife of El Salvador's minister of public health; and the sister-in-law of Haiti's president. Of the appointments, Clara González was one of the few who could be called a national feminist leader.[30] Concerned, González wrote to Ofelia Domínguez Navarro that "the governments named many without any value."[31]

González was not the only one frustrated by the selection of commissioners.

Mexican feminist Elena Arizmendi, who with Paulina Luisi co-led the Liga Internacional de Mujeres Ibéricas y Hispanoamericanas, wrote to Stevens and other National Woman's Party members to protest the government sponsorship of commissioners. The "women with whom you have associated, educated as they are, have never struggled in favor of the cause for women," she wrote, "and for this reason they do not mean anything before the eyes of Spanish feminists."[32] She warned that composing the commission with government appointments would take away any power the commission might have in holding the state accountable for violating women's rights: "It will never be the governments who will give guarantees of a strong alliance among us women, but quite the contrary, because such an alliance does not fit in with their plans." She warned that such a strategy would reinforce U.S. dominance over the IACW and harm the "relations between women of the United States and those of Spanish countries."[33]

Stevens brushed aside Arizmendi's concerns, insisting that the commission would draw on the energies of all twenty-one commissioners, who would, sometime in the future, form "local committees" to engage grassroots activism in each country.[34] In truth, however, Stevens determined the commission agenda, and she was most invested in treaties, not grassroots activism.

Although Stevens recognized that the commission had originated from Latin American feminist efforts, she believed that she was the rightful leader of feminism in the Western Hemisphere.[35] Her beliefs rested in part on her sense of racial and national superiority—as an educated, upper-middle-class Anglo-American woman and veteran of a successful suffrage movement. Although Stevens claimed to embrace racial egalitarianism, she, like many members of the NWP, maintained beliefs about white racial superiority over women of color and Latin American women. In her book *Jailed for Freedom*, Stevens made these views explicit when she commented on the "humiliating" insult of being placed in the same jail cell as African American women, whom she referred to as "dusky comrades."[36] Although she called for the "equality" of all "American women" in Havana, Stevens, like many others in the United States, also viewed "Latin Americans," including the women with whom she collaborated, as an inferior race in which ethnic, linguistic, and cultural traits were conflated.[37] She rarely articulated these views outright, realizing the damage it would cause her relationship with Latin American feminists. Her most derogatory comments would only emerge years later, when it was clear that her time as commission chair was at an end.[38]

Stevens's faith in her leadership of Pan-American feminism also rested on her own enormous self-confidence. She believed an individual leader's dogged persistence and transgression of rules were critical to feminist strategy.[39] The events in Havana and Rambouillet in 1928 only intensified Stevens's confidence in herself as the torchbearer for historical change. Letters she received in Havana from her romantic partner, Jonathan Mitchell, compared her to Joan of Arc, Jean-Jacques Rousseau, Woodrow Wilson, Vladimir Lenin, and Martin Luther.[40] In response to Rambouillet, Viscountess Rhondda, president of the British egalitarian Six Point Group, wrote to Stevens with a breathless paean:

> Your powers are only just short of magical. . . . I've never seen any organizing in the world to begin to touch it—it's that capacity for throwing the whole of yourself into one channel, rushing towards one aim; & that there's nothing left of you to see, or hear, or think except towards what you mean to get—& you can exhaust yourself past all human possibility & yet continue to think clearly, & keep your mental & nervous balance. It's almost unbelievable—a kind of absolute self-immolation.[41]

Stevens offered a different sort of imperial Pan-American feminism from that of Carrie Chapman Catt. Unlike Catt, Stevens never questioned whether Latin American women were "ready" for the franchise. However, as Elena Arizmendi wrote to Paulina Luisi, those in the Woman's Party had not "purified their politics," and their Pan-American feminism was no better than that of Catt's League of Women Voters before them. Both the League and the Woman's Party, Arizmendi pointed out, sought to tighten the "domain that they want to have over the Latin woman." Both "fight for supremacy, and this they want to accomplish by doing something that is favorable to the politics of their country."[42] Luisi later hinted to Arizmendi that she agreed: "As respects Sra Stevens, I have known for a long time what can be expected from her and her group."[43]

Indeed, Stevens's sense of leadership was so entrenched that she resisted the appointment of Latin American commissioners whose authority might challenge her own, including early originators of Pan-American feminism Paulina Luisi and Bertha Lutz. Though the Brazilian embassy recommended Lutz's appointment, Stevens ultimately selected Flora de Oliveira Lima, the widow of a former Brazilian ambassador to the United States.[44] The fact that Oliveira Lima lived in Washington influenced this appointment, but Stevens also passed over Lutz because of the latter's support for the League of Women Voters and protective labor legislation.

Paulina Luisi, in contrast, was an "equalitarian" who agreed with the Equal Rights and Equal Nationality treaties, but Stevens refused to support her appointment because she found her possibly threatening to her own leadership. In these years Luisi was based in Geneva, continuing her work in the League of Nations' Committee on the Traffic in Women and Children and with the International Alliance of Women. At the 1928 Havana conference, Uruguayan diplomat

Doris Stevens in the
patio of the Hotel
Sevilla Biltmore
in Havana, Cuba,
during the Sixth
Pan-American
Conference, 1928.
Courtesy of the
Schlesinger Library,
Radcliffe Institute,
Harvard University.

Jacobo Varela had heartily recommended that Stevens appoint Luisi.[45] Stevens did nothing about his suggestion until August 1929, when she met Luisi in Berlin at the founding meeting of the equalitarian group Open Door International, where Stevens announced the IACW's new Equal Nationality Treaty. Since Stevens did not speak Spanish, nor Luisi English, the two spoke to each other in French.[46] While Luisi expressed her desire to collaborate with the group and did join its "nationality committee," which aligned with the Hague Codification Conference, she warned Stevens against replicating, as Luisi put it, "the Monroe Doctrine according to the formula 'All America for the North Americans.'"[47]

For Stevens the defining feature of their interaction was Luisi's unfriendliness. "Her hostility quite overwhelmed me," she later recalled to Alice Paul, and "she quite terrified me in Berlin," Stevens wrote to Chilean feminist Marta Vergara, who was working at The Hague.[48] Luisi's anti-imperialism and lack of friendliness made her engagement in the IACW undesirable to Stevens, and Uruguay's spot long remained vacant. Alice Paul, who worked with Luisi in the League of Nations, informed Stevens that although Luisi was "not friendly" to the commission, she nonetheless wanted to be involved and "seemed exceedingly indignant that she had not been appointed."[49] Stevens's failure to appoint her confirmed Luisi's conviction that the commission occluded the voices of Latin American women, especially those who challenged U.S. authority.[50]

Clara González discovered that Stevens had also sidelined her. The National Woman's Party avidly utilized González in its promotion of the commission—spotlighting the many accomplishments of the thirty-year-old lawyer whom the press called "Panama's Portia."[51] However, Stevens never offered the funding that would make possible González's travels to various international conferences, which provided the key staging grounds for the Equal Rights Treaty. González's exclusion from these venues was significant. The fact that Stevens was parsimonious with González, yet offered some funding to other Latin American commissioners who supported Stevens's vision more than she perceived González did, is also noteworthy. Though Stevens wanted González's legal research work, she definitely did not want her interference if there was a chance that González would champion an agenda different from her own.

González came to identify the issue of funding as critical to the commission's imbalance in power. Although Doris Stevens touted the fact that the U.S. government gave the commission no funding, she raised money for it from wealthy U.S. individuals and institutions, such as longtime Woman's Party patron Alva Belmont and, after 1931, the Carnegie Endowment for International Peace.[52] And Stevens held its purse strings. Stevens used the funding at her own discretion to pay for paper, cables, typewriters, translators, and photographers who assiduously documented the commission's events. Though Stevens worked "without salary," she also used the capital she had raised to pay for her trips to conferences in Europe and Latin America, where she stayed at lavish hotels. However, she did not frequently pay for the travel of Latin American commissioners. She instructed González and most other Latin American delegates to obtain funding from their own governments for these trips. Some did, but many others could not, thus excluding them from these important arenas. Stevens did give salaries to several NWP members who worked with the commission, but González received no salary, even though she was the head of research for the IACW and for the first few years one of the only Latin American women working in D.C.[53] When Stevens invited González to stay at the NWP headquarters, she did not offer free room and board, stipulating a rent of eighteen dollars a month.[54]

For González and other Latin American feminists, these dynamics underscored U.S. economic imperialism over Latin America. Money was always vital to international feminist organizing, which required convening individuals at various worldwide destinations. The work of the affluent U.S., British, and European women in the International Council of Women and the International Alliance of Women had long revealed that women from countries with financial resources generally assumed the positions of power, reproducing hierarchies that placed women from the United States and Western Europe over those from the "global South."[55] These tensions were especially pronounced in Pan-American organizing. A few years earlier, in 1925, when Mexican feminist Elena Torres resigned from Catt and Lutz's Inter-American Union of Women, she had asserted that it would be impossible to collaborate with U.S. women without a "camaraderie born of equal economic situations and with the threat of Anglo-American imperialism."[56]

As two significant international conferences now approached, González recognized how detrimental lack of funding was for Latin American feminists who wanted to raise a truly anti-imperialist *feminismo americano*. Stevens had secured an invitation from the Cuban government to hold the IACW's first plenary meeting in Havana in 1930, and the Hague Codification Conference in Geneva would take place soon after it.[57] González hoped these upcoming conferences could help the commission grow its ranks among feminist leaders from Latin America. The remaining fourteen commissioners were still to be appointed, and protocol stipulated that the first seven commissioners would elect the remaining fourteen. González wanted them to be committed feminists not strictly tied to their governments.

Stevens also believed it a critical time for the commission to grow but, unlike González, supported governmental selection of the remaining fourteen. She viewed these appointments as ways to enhance the IACW's prestige, noting that it "would make the governments feel more responsible for the work undertaken by the Commission" at the upcoming Hague Codification Conference. Thus, Stevens unilaterally decided that rather than being elected by the first seven commission members, as set forth in the charter, the remaining fourteen should be chosen by their governments, as the first seven had been. She began interviewing diplomats from those countries, urging them to appoint delegates before the February 1930 Havana assembly and often suggesting names herself.[58]

This change in procedure dismayed González. She nonetheless advocated the appointment of two feminist friends who shared her own ideals: Ofelia Domínguez Navarro from Cuba and Aída Parada from Chile. Twenty-six-year-old Parada belonged to the feminist group Unión Femenina de Chile. A primary school teacher, Parada had been sent by the Chilean government to Teachers College of Columbia University in 1927. She and González both lived at International House, a lodging for international students in New York City, where they had become fast friends and joined the anti-imperialist Federación Latinoamericana de Estudiantes.[59] If Parada and Domínguez were commissioners or delegates at the Havana conference, González hoped they might effect some changes in the commission and perhaps pass a resolution to loosen Stevens's grip on its funding. González urged Stevens to speak with the Chilean minister in Washington, D.C., regarding appointing Parada as the Chilean commissioner, which Stevens did.[60] Stevens did not, however, seek Domínguez's appointment as Cuban commissioner. In spite of Domínguez's outsized role in the creation of the IACW, Stevens and the Cuban government elected another member of the Alianza Nacional Feminista instead.[61] Meanwhile, Stevens advised González that she should represent both Panama and El Salvador at the Havana conference.

At no point, however, did Stevens offer to pay González's passage to Cuba. In New York, two weeks before the conference, González, still unsure she would receive the necessary funds, wrote to Ofelia Domínguez Navarro, urging her to attend. The two women had not corresponded for some time, although González often recalled their 1926 collaboration. González asked her "dear friend" Domínguez if there was any way she could get herself appointed as a delegate to the upcoming conference or as the official Cuban representative of the commission. Given the fact that so many appointees were not feminists, González wrote, it would be "a comfort to know that there were some people there" like Domínguez who had "knowledge and experience." González expressed her hopes that Panama and El Salvador would provide her the funds so she could "have the pleasure of seeing you and talking with you for a long time."[62]

Ultimately, González was forced to pay her own way to Havana, using her small student allowance and a loan from her friend Ricardo Alfaro.[63] There, with the help of Domínguez and Parada, the problems that González had identified with Doris Stevens's leadership in the IACW—her dominance over the group, sidelining of an anti-imperialist agenda, and fiscal biases—became more widely known during the commission's meeting.

The 1930 Havana Meeting

Although only two years had passed since Doris Stevens had dazzled the Havana public, a great deal had changed. Coinciding with the world economic crisis in 1929, President Machado had begun a new dictatorship with U.S. support, propelling the nation into a protracted period of oligarchic tyranny.[64] Many Cubans were struggling financially, protesting U.S. taxes on sugar and the increasingly violent Machado regime. In this context, Cuban feminists pressed for a broader array of rights than civil and political rights.

Ofelia Domínguez Navarro spoke at a luncheon the Alianza Nacional Feminista hosted for the IACW upon its return to Havana, outlining these broader goals for feminism and explicitly addressing the cause of women workers.[65] Domínguez especially worried about the most vulnerable who worked in tobacco fields and factories, receiving little compensation and gaining no support for motherhood. Not only did these women need social guarantees from the state—maternity legislation and welfare legislation that she called "social rights"—but they, and all Cuban workers, also needed protection from U.S. imperialism. Domínguez recognized the economic problems in Cuba as a global phenomenon throughout the Americas, stemming from Latin American economic dependence on the United States. It was the interconnectedness of these social, economic, and gendered issues that had raised Domínguez's expectations for a Pan-American organization of women in the first place and that now caused her to push for an expansion of the IACW's agenda. Equal civil and political rights were important. But how, she wondered, could these legal treaties make any material difference to the lives of women throughout the Americas who were most in need?

Over the next few days, Domínguez was disappointed when Stevens ignored her pleas for women workers. She was even more dismayed to learn that Stevens was running the organization unilaterally. Domínguez met with González and Parada in the privacy of her own home, where they discussed the proceedings of the commission and shared their grievances about it.

The Havana conference threw Doris Stevens's hierarchical leadership into sharp relief. Some of the commission's meetings were open to the public, but others were limited to the five delegates able to be in Havana. González and

Opening session of the plenary meeting of the IACW in Havana, Cuba, February 17, 1930. From left to right: Aída Parada; Flora de Oliveira Lima; Doris Stevens; Juanita Molina de Fromen; Elena Mederos de González; Clara González. Although this session included only the commission delegates, other sessions in the following days were open to the public. Courtesy of the Schlesinger Library, Radcliffe Institute, Harvard University.

Parada told Domínguez that Stevens abruptly shut down their suggestions to promote greater representation of Latin American feminists. The two called for a resolution that would ask all national governments, as well as the Pan-American Union, to give financial support to the commission. Such monetary help could loosen Stevens's grip on the funds, allowing more Latin American women to stay in the commission's D.C. headquarters and have a greater say in its workings.[66] To expose the problem of the lack of Latin American participation in the commission, Parada also asked Stevens to explain how the original seven commissioners participated in the IACW's work. Stevens was forced to admit that only Clara González, the only delegate living in the United States, had been able to participate.[67]

Resentful of these challenges to her authority and attempts to embarrass her, Stevens rejected González and Parada's resolutions. She insisted that it would be difficult, if not impossible, to get financial support from the Pan-American Union. She denied their request to ask governments for money, advising instead a noncommittal approach where the commission would simply seek funding from different sources as needs arose.[68] Stevens also tried to head off any criticism of the commission, giving the following imperious instructions to the Latin American delegates: "Will you all remember each time you are speaking . . . that you are pleased to be here . . . that you are honored to be appointed [to the first intergovernmental agency for women]?" Stevens instructed them to not even mention the fact that they had secured only eleven of the twenty-one delegates: "Please do not emphasize our faults," she urged, explicitly calling for loyalty. "In other words, say that it is perfectly wonderful—it is." [69]

After Stevens announced the set of rules drawn up for the conference by international lawyer and Stevens's close friend James Brown Scott, González noted that it would be better for a female lawyer to establish their protocol of procedure and suggested Domínguez for the job. Stevens refused, explaining that Domínguez could approve the existing rules but not create new ones. The rules' primary function, Stevens reasoned, was to limit the topic of conversation to feminism, meaning the Equal Rights and Equal Nationality Treaties. She justified the limitations by explaining, "We have had people that wanted . . . to come and talk about various things, to talk about peace, and anything but feminism." [70]

Stevens likely realized that González was trying to bring her friend Domínguez's voice into the proceedings. If Stevens had allowed Domínguez to look at the rules, Domínguez would have likely tried to add women workers to the agenda or achieve more equitable and transparent procedures. Domínguez would probably also have insisted on discussion of U.S.-Cuban relations. A number of Cuban feminists had written to Stevens before the Havana conference requesting that the IACW oppose the rise of U.S. duties on Cuban sugar. [71] The question had become critical after the stock market crash in 1929, when Cuba's single-crop export economy deteriorated. The value of the island's sugar production had been collapsing; it would plummet from nearly $200 million in 1929 to just over $40 million in 1932. [72]

Cuban *feministas'* insistence that the IACW address duties on sugar underscores the centrality that analysis of political economy and U.S. empire had to their definition of feminism. As the Cuban writer and friend of Domínguez Mariblanca Sabas Alomá wrote in her 1930 book *Feminismo*, women of "la América indígeno-hispánica" should fight for women's rights, and also against the "hateful economic . . . and political penetration" of U.S. empire, whether that be U.S. control over Cuban sugar, Brazilian rubber, Peruvian gold, and Chilean salt, or U.S. occupation of the Panama Canal and Nicaragua. [73] In Cuba, the U.S. duties directly affected the livelihoods of many female sugar cane workers and families who suffered from increasing costs of living. Stevens, however, believed the issue of sugar far outside the "feminist" purview.

The conference thus proceeded without even so much as a reference to the new realities wrought by the Great Depression or the political turmoil in Cuba. [74] Stevens even proclaimed Machado, who had sponsored the conference, a "feminist president," which angered feminists who had been persecuted by the dictatorship.[75] This was the first of many times that Stevens allied the commission with dictatorships in Latin America, routinely incensing many who believed she legitimized undemocratic practices. Stevens, however, steadfastly insisted that her principled support for "equal rights" and "feminism" was pure and above politics.[76]

For Domínguez, González, and Parada, however, whose friendship grew during this conference, *feminismo* represented a broader political and social movement that included, yet expanded beyond, women's equal rights under the law. After the conference, Parada wrote to Domínguez that philosophically she believed *feminismo* should be included "together with socialism and democracy, etc. as part of politics." In her view, politics were not distractions from a feminist agenda. Rather, anti-imperialism, economic equity, and social justice were all central goals of feminism.[77]

Immediately following the conference, Domínguez openly expressed these opinions in an interview she gave the Cuban newspaper El País. In an article titled "The Latin Americans Enjoyed the Role of 'Extras' in the Recent Conference of Women," Domínguez explained that Latin American women had been excluded from the conference proceedings and from the constitution of the IACW itself. Latin American delegates, Domínguez told the paper, enjoyed no meaningful leadership or equal participation, in large part because of a lack of financial support: "Governments, because of [troubles in the] economy or indifference respecting these problems," had been "remiss" in failing to "offer . . . financial aid to the commission." Commission delegates Clara González and Aída Parada had confirmed, she continued, that "not a single one of the delegates has been able to stay permanently in Washington D.C. so as to cooperate actively."[78]

The exclusion of Latin American women from the commission stemmed not only from lack of funding, Domínguez wrote, but also from Doris Stevens herself. Any efforts Latin American women had made to address these problems had been unequivocally quashed by Stevens. While Domínguez praised Stevens's tenacity and "unique energy" as a feminist leader, she denounced her "dictatorial character": "Finding herself collaborating with Latin Americans, because of a prejudice deeply rooted in the atmosphere of her people, [Stevens] knows how to smile with cordial superiority as long as no idea that is contrary to her convictions is presented. When this happens, the spirit of her [Anglo-American] race speaks through her mouth and the gentle phrase and ample smile is substituted with the imperious action and arbitrary imposition of her own agenda." Domínguez urged Latin American feminists to resist Stevens's embodiment of Anglo-American superiority. When U.S. women "make . . . their personality stronger and more precise," she argued, "they reaffirm their conviction of superiority the more we diminish our own."[79]

Although Domínguez had vocally supported Stevens in 1928 when the two had worked side by side to create the IACW, Domínguez now felt she understood Stevens's true colors. The commission under Stevens's leadership would not promote real mutual collaboration or recognize the most pressing needs of women suffering in the economic crisis. As Dominguez explained in her interview, "Working under . . . [the] direction" of women from "North America . . . demonstrates once again our condition of being a subject people to the empire of strength, to treaties enforced on us." No organization run on such an unequal dynamic could represent the true "equal rights" of Latin American women. Instead, Domínguez called for the creation of an alternative group of Latin American feminists: "I believe that all efforts carried on as Latin Americans or as women of our country will finally be more useful to our ultimate goals than lending our cooperation to these congresses."[80]

When Doris Stevens learned of this article, she brushed off the criticism, simply saying she "deplored the division of women into North and Latin American women." She also suspected that Domínguez was airing complaints on behalf of Clara González. Stevens believed that she and Alice Paul had perhaps upset González when they reprimanded her for making an error in their nationality report, which, "if it had gone unnoticed in our printed report, would have caused us infinite embarrassment."[81] The archives are silent on the content of this scolding, and it is unclear how significant the incident was to González. However, Stevens's domineering directives to Latin American delegates at the Havana conference suggest that she may have acted with imperious authority in the privacy of commission headquarters, as well.

Grateful for her new bonds with Parada and Domínguez, González left Cuba energized by Domínguez's insurgency against Stevens. As soon as she returned to New York City, González wrote Domínguez, telling her that she "burned with desire" to read her El País interview and asked what impression it had made in Havana. "If she-who-shall-not-be-named has read it," González wrote, "surely she must be burning."[82] González explained that she was waiting for Stevens's "response to a telegram I sent her about El Salvador naming me a delegate to The Hague conference" and that asked for financial help from the commission. "She knows I don't have a penny. . . . She has raised funds in the name of the Commission that I am entitled to since part of those funds are invested in me since I am a named delegate of said Commission." But, González wrote, she had "a better chance of winning the Cuban lottery" than getting money from Stevens. "By the way," she added, "the number I have is 22074 so do me the favor of letting me know how many *thousands* I've won. Don't forget because I think I'm going to The Hague with that money!" She signed off, "A thousand remembrances, your affectionate Clara."[83]

González's humorous words only partially masked her well-placed skepticism about Stevens and her deep disappointment. As she suspected, Stevens offered her no money, and González was unable to travel to the Hague Codification Conference. Although González followed up with Stevens about her recommendation to seek funding from the Pan-American Union, Stevens dodged the question before explaining tersely that upon hearing that commissioners such as González had sought funding from it, the Pan-American Union had decided to give even less support to the IACW.[84] González responded with a short note in English that she "understood perfectly the situation of the Commission. . . . I appreciate your having explained it to me so clearly. I am very sorry of the measures of the Pan-American Union relating [to] the *support* to the Commission."[85]

González probably believed that if Stevens had wanted her to attend the Hague conference, she could have used money from the commission's own coffers or from those of the National Woman's Party. The NWP was paying for four of its own members to travel to the 1930 event with Stevens, and in the summer of 1929, *Equal Rights* reported that the organization had received close to $2 million from contributions, memberships, and rents of rooms that year.[86] Stevens's withholding of funding from González was no doubt retaliation for the article Domínguez had written about Stevens; for the embarrassment that Domínguez, González, and Parada had caused her during the conference; and for the fact that González supported an agenda for Pan-American feminism different from Stevens's own.

Even though González anticipated it, Stevens's refusal of funds was a blow. At the Hague Codification Conference, the IACW would share with the world the Nationality Report, which was the direct result of González's years of energy and research. Being denied the opportunity to attend this conference represented the final nail into the coffin of González's disillusionment with Stevens. A few days after receiving Stevens's message, González sent a letter of resignation to New York University in the middle of her school term, citing poor health.[87] While González did suffer from medical problems after returning to Panama, her desire to end her U.S. work with the commission, given Stevens's lack of financial support, influenced her decision to terminate her studies.[88] Always extremely diplomatic and wanting to preserve her relationship with Stevens given Stevens's prestige, González never publicly aired these problems, telling only close friends about them.[89] Before her return to Panama, González wrote to the Panamanian diplomat Ricardo Alfaro, who had been a booster of the commission and of González's appointment to it, thanking him for lending her money to make her trip to Havana possible. Her letter reflected her ambivalence about the IACW: "In terms of my adventures, there was a little of everything. There was something artificial about ... the Conference, and I found myself, with another delegate [Aída Parada], somewhat in disagreement with the proceedings."[90] She promised him all the details in person soon.

Ofelia Domínguez Navarro and Paulina Luisi's Feminismo práctico

The 1930 Havana conference resulted in a break for Ofelia Domínguez Navarro as well, not only with the IACW but with liberal Pan-American feminist politics more broadly. As she would later explain in her memoirs, her greeting to the commission at the Havana luncheon in February 1930 would be the last words Domínguez uttered on behalf of the Alianza Nacional Feminista, the group she had helped establish.[91] After losing an election to become Alianza president and redirect its efforts toward working women's needs, Domínguez split away from the group. A few months later, Domínguez founded a new radical Cuban feminist organization distinguished by the collaboration of women workers and intellectuals—the Unión Laborista de Mujeres.[92] The group's motto signified its definition of feminism as well as its clear differences with the Inter-American Commission of Women: "Before international law we will fight for peace and for the social rights of working women; before domestic law for the civil equality and the right of suffrage without any restriction or limitation."[93] Rather than allying themselves with the IACW's focus on international goals for civil and political rights, Unión members sought broader international goals of anti-imperialism and "social rights of working women." The latter included equal pay for equal work, maternity legislation and free nurseries for working women, and school breakfasts and lunches for poor children.[94]

In her El País interview criticizing Doris Stevens, Domínguez had called for a group of Latin American women working for feminism on their own behalf, and she now used her new Cuban group as a springboard for such connections. The Uruguayan feminist Paulina Luisi was one of the first people to whom Domínguez turned for support. "Teacher," she addressed Luisi, "my struggle in feminism, although I am young, has been intense." Although they had never met, Domínguez explained in her letter that she had delivered Luisi's speech on the rights of illegitimate children at the 1926 Panama conference and long admired her as a continental feminist leader. Domínguez believed they shared the same Pan-Hispanic feminist vision that opposed U.S. empire, proclaimed the equality of Latin American women, and addressed the needs of women workers during a time of economic turmoil. In her letter, Domínguez outlined the divisions in the Alianza that had arisen because of the Great Depression between wealthier women and those concerned with working women. She said that her own group, the Unión Laborista de Mujeres, was composed of both working women and intellectuals who wanted to "work and interpret feminism in a modern sense."[95]

This letter launched a correspondence between the two women that would last until the end of Luisi's life. Fifty-four-year-old Luisi responded to Domínguez with a long, warm letter that conveyed her praise and enthusiasm for the "beautiful work" Domínguez had undertaken. Luisi was touched by the "almost . . . 'filial' manner" in which thirty-five-year-old Domínguez had addressed her: "You cannot imagine the joy that your letter has brought me, so affectionate, so sincere, so 'fraternal,' written by a young enthusiast like you to an old fighter who is beginning to feel some of the fatigue of thirty-three years of work." Recognizing that Domínguez shared the same goals for a Pan-Hispanic feminism, Luisi hoped their interactions could help advance that movement. "I read in your letter a faith in your Heart, an enthusiasm, a desire for noble struggle, for ideals won. . . . I hope that this first letter of yours . . . starts a happy series of correspondence with my dear sisters of Cuba."[96] Ending her missive with "a long and affectionate hug," Luisi sent a more formal message of support from the Alianza Uruguaya to the Unión Laborista de Mujeres.[97]

In the late 1930s, a grassroots alternative to the rarefied, procedural work of the IACW at international conferences became even more urgent for Domínguez, Luisi, and other Latin American feminists. They sought a *feminismo americano* that embraced anti-imperialism and transnational support for local social, economic, and political struggles. For many, the Great Depression and political revolutions throughout the Americas made the singular commission goals of equal political and civil rights increasingly irrelevant. The growth of socialist and communist organizing in these years and increasing affiliations between feminists and leftist movements heightened these divides. Domínguez, Luisi, and González all moved to the left and increasingly promoted an inter-American feminism based on women's material struggles and shared anti-imperialist solidarity rather than a singular focus on legal equality or international treaties. During a time when failures of liberalism were conspicuous in their own countries, liberal feminism did not hold the answers they needed.

The desire to counteract state violence in their own countries also caused these feminists to seek solidarity with each other, particularly considering the transnational connections between U.S. imperialism and state violence. These connections became palpable in Cuba in these years. For Ofelia Domínguez, inter-American feminism, and her connections with Paulina Luisi specifically, became vital in late 1930, when the Machado dictatorship, supported by the U.S. government, ushered in a new and protracted period of repression and tyranny. Replacing civilian political administrators, provincial governors, and municipal mayors with military supervisors, Machado increasingly relied on secret police to stamp out the mounting opposition throughout Cuba. The resistance included Domínguez and other feminists who were thrown into jail for rebellion against the government. In 1931 Domínguez was arrested and jailed twice, her second term lasting a number of months.[98]

Recognizing that international support could help her organization's cause, Domínguez reached out to Luisi for help. She wrote to Luisi in pencil because it was all that she could find in her jail cell: "If you could know from what place I am answering your letter! I have been in prison from the 4th of March of this year for the second time this year. The fight against the tyrannical government of Gen Machado has turned the old fortress, Castillo del Principe, into a prison, where I have seen much and learned much."[99] Never before had Cuba witnessed such a revolution, Domínguez told Luisi, and "the women are rendering a beautiful effort" of what she called "feminismo práctico." By "practical feminism," Domínguez meant activism that was concerned not only with equal rights for women under the law but also with challenging multiple forms of political, economic, and social oppression and violence. She asked Luisi for help from her group in Uruguay as well as from her connections in Europe.[100]

Luisi received Domínguez's letter while she was in Belgrade for the annual meeting of the International Alliance of Women, with which Luisi maintained a robust involvement and which, in this unusual case, became a source of revolutionary support. Luisi spoke about Domínguez's struggle at the alliance meeting and secured from participants a formal message of support that praised Domínguez's "courageous work and actions" and wished her "success" for her cause. Reporting to Domínguez that "from my lips they heard of your bravery," Luisi assured Domínguez, "I admire and love you more than ever." Luisi also sought to do more for her: "Send me programs, rules, statutes, information about your organization and associated ones, etc. I am so glad to be . . . even more connected to the women of Cuba, and especially to you, my noble friend."[101]

When Domínguez was out of jail but still in hiding, she thanked Luisi for her note, which brought her so much joy, and for the support from the International Alliance, which filled her "with deep emotion." Her second imprisonment of three months, however, had radicalized Domínguez away from liberal feminism and toward communist and Marxist ideologies. As she explained to Luisi, "My struggles have brought with them a marked change to my ideological structure" and the opportunity to identify more closely with "the people." Now, "feminism," she wrote, "with its political and civil aspirations seems to me too narrow a mold to fight for. It seems to me accommodating selfishness. The spirit of the age demands something more just and equitable. I confess I live in a moment when the vision of Russia attracts me. I try to study this phenomenon carefully."[102] While she recognized "the difficulties" of applying communism's "beautiful theories because of the opposition of all the capitalist universe," she urged Luisi to study communism as well. "Pardon my suggestion, but you and I ... who have set ourselves the task of opening new furrows have to drink from all sources."[103]

Domínguez joined the Communist Party of Cuba not long after writing to Luisi, but she never fully abandoned her demands for women's rights. During the revolution she turned away from liberal feminism—which upheld women's civil and political equality—because she believed these goals did not address the needs of working-class women and the broader proletarian struggle against imperialism.[104]

The tension between "bourgeois feminism" and Marxism that Domínguez noted in her letter to Luisi represented a long-standing conflict that arose in different forms wherever sizable Communist Party organizations existed—in China and Russia as well as throughout Latin America. The idea that women's rights had little place in the class struggle prevailed among many communist and Marxist groups that spread throughout Latin America in the 1920s and among the communist opposition groups that arose dramatically in Cuba during the fight against Machado in the 1930s.[105] In Latin America, this debate between bourgeois feminism and Marxist politics also was alive in the anti-imperialist transnational Aprista movement that spread dramatically after the Great Depression.[106] Peruvian political leader Victor Raúl Haya de La Torre had founded the Aprista movement in Mexico City in 1924 and soon after cofounded the Aprista Party of Peru with Magda Portal, who helped lead it for two decades. Upholding the Mexican Revolution, and its promises of agrarian reform and nationalization of foreign property as its lodestars, its motto was "Against Yankee Imperialism, for the unity of the peoples of Latin America, for the realization of social justice." Though Magda Portal vocally supported women's participation in the revolutionary movement, she criticized "feminism" for privileging women's rights above the Latin American class struggle. In 1930 she published an article in *Repertorio Americano* that praised Ofelia Domínguez's new Unión Laborista de Mujeres in Cuba but insisted that in Latin America, "feminism would be untimely" because "the vote is an exercise of democracy, and in America, almost without exception, democracy does not exist."[107] Since the vote could be attached "to the whims of a dictatorial regime," she explained in an article the following year, "the abstract concept of women's suffrage" could never represent "the maximum aspiration of women" in Latin America.[108]

For Portal and Domínguez, a revolution against U.S. imperialism and liberation of women's consciousness represented greater priorities at this moment

FEMINISMO PRÁCTICO

than women's suffrage. Domínguez continued to believe in the transformative power of Latin American women's activism. In her letters to Luisi, Domínguez railed against U.S. support for Machado's "tyranny" and noted it was but one piece of the larger threat of the United States to the "destiny [of] . . . Latin America." In this "moment of intense crisis in America," Domínguez wrote Luisi, they needed "a brave and strong resurgence against the yankee imperialism that depersonalizes us," and Domínguez hoped that a new inter-American women's movement could lead the way: "If we can, we women will jolt our continent!"[109]

Luisi agreed with her young friend's sentiments. Although she was never a member of the Aprista or Communist Parties, Luisi would later become good friends with Magda Portal and join the Socialist Party in Uruguay. In the early 1930s, she continued the fight for women's suffrage in her country. Nonetheless, Luisi found great inspiration in her more leftist friends Portal and Domínguez. She concurred with their belief that women in Latin America needed to unite in their own movement and fight against U.S. dominance and for a broader, insurgent conception of social justice.[110]

This agenda for inter-American feminism clashed sharply with that of Stevens's Inter-American Commission of Women. The simmering conflicts Domínguez had with that group came to a head in what would be Domínguez's final confrontation with Stevens in 1931. In several letters, Stevens criticized Domínguez's group for not fighting for suffrage.[111] Unlike Luisi or women in the International Alliance of Women who had publicly supported the jailed Domínguez and the Cuban revolutionary struggle, Stevens saw the strife in Cuba as little more than a missed opportunity to mobilize around women's suffrage. An article in the Woman's Party organ, Equal Rights, reflected this view, reducing the clashes between the Machado regime and growing revolutionary forces to a "somewhat hysterical civic crisis."[112] This characterization deeply upset even the liberal Cuban feminists friendly to the IACW.[113] After learning of the existence of Domínguez's group, Stevens wrote to the Unión Laborista secretary, pressing the group to fight for suffrage during Cuba's Constitutional Reforms.[114] Ofelia Domínguez answered Stevens that they would not promote suffrage, detailing the many travesties of justice under the Cuban dictatorship that would make women's suffrage meaningless and explaining that feminists were targets of physical violence and imprisonment. In Stevens's terse response, she offered no support and instead implied that they were missing an important opportunity.[115] She also upheld U.S. activists as models, writing, "When we were fighting for suffrage in this country, women had . . . to make demands upon public men to whose policies on most matters they were thoroughly opposed."[116]

This letter was the last straw for Domínguez, who became absolutely incensed. She wrote a long response to Stevens, criticizing her for "lacking . . . frank intelligence [about the situation of] all our sisters of America." She reiterated that "gaining the recognition of our political rights . . . is not the only nor the most urgent of our programs." All feminists in Cuba were fighting for something "far more serious . . . the *restoration of law*, not just ours as women, but of an entire people deprived of liberty . . . and reduced to the worst of slavery." Domínguez pledged her loyalty to the IACW's ideal of equality. But she asserted that she would not follow Stevens's "rules, . . . the current application of which, at this time, would result in disaster." Furthermore, Domínguez "could not stand the idea of lowering oneself to beg for that which she has the right to demand." She quoted Martí: "'Rights should not be begged for.' 'Rights are to be taken.'"[117]

Domínguez's letter was effectively a goodbye to Doris Stevens, to whom she would never write again. But it was also a call to arms. Domínguez utilized this letter to mount significant opposition to Stevens. She reproduced their correspondence in a flyer that reprinted both the letter from Stevens and Domínguez's response on one page, front and back, on Unión Laborista letterhead and under the title "To the Political Conscience of the Latin American Woman."[118] Her group sent the broadside to numerous women's groups throughout the Americas. It was an influential act of resistance that would spur new organizing. Years later, Domínguez's organization ranked it as among its most important "anti-imperialist fights" to date.[119] The flyer's recipients almost certainly included Domínguez's good friends Clara González and Paulina Luisi.

Over the next several years, all three of these women would continue to foster a Pan-Hispanic feminism that supported their broader goals in the midst of dramatic personal and political change. Luisi saw the fruition of the long suffrage battle in Uruguay when full voting rights were granted to women in December 1932.[120] In March 1933, however, a military coup and the resulting rise of a dictatorship under Gabriel Terra destroyed the suffrage euphoria. After Luisi's friend Baltasar Brum, the former president of Uruguay and longtime champion of feminism, failed in his attempts to lead the resistance to Terra's dictatorship, Brum committed suicide by gunshot.

As late as August 1932, Luisi was urging Doris Stevens to appoint her as the IACW delegate for Uruguay so she could attend the 1933 Montevideo conference, hopeful that she could inject her own vision for Pan-American feminism.[121] After the imposition of the Terra dictatorship, however, Luisi believed, as her friend Domínguez had similarly decided, that fighting for women's equal rights was not an appropriate goal. Inciting reprisals against all opposition, Terra arrested Paulina Luisi's sister Luisa Luisi for speaking at the funeral of a slain former deputy and socialist.[122] Paulina Luisi escaped to Argentina and wrote Alice Paul that she and her sisters were fleeing for Europe "as no self-respecting feminist could stay in her country under present circumstances."[123] The following year, Luisi would return to Uruguay and join the resistance against the Terra regime.

Domínguez continued to face a desperate political climate as well. She was jailed again in Cuba in 1932, and in January 1933 she fled for Mexico, where she remained until Machado's overthrow in September 1933. In Mexico, Domínguez tried to rally students and exiled Cubans in favor of the Cuban Revolution and to protest U.S. interventions in determining Machado's successor.[124] When back in Cuba, Domínguez directed the Unión Laborista de Mujeres to oppose the intervention of U.S. assistant secretary of state Sumner Welles and to send missives to the new, temporary revolutionary government of Ramón Grau San Martín, imploring the inclusion of women's equal rights in a new Cuban constitution. Under Grau San Martín a number of reforms were enacted, including women's suffrage.

In the fall of 1933, Domínguez received several requests from friends in Argentina and Guatemala, urging her to appeal to her government to become part of its delegation and represent Latin American women at the upcoming 1933 Pan-American conference in Montevideo. Many feminists throughout the region recognized the Montevideo conference as a key place to make demands for women's rights and for an inter-American feminism that would address the political, social, and economic tumult that was rising throughout the Americas. They also identified Domínguez as the leader to represent that *feminismo americano*. The flyer that Domínguez had distributed widely throughout the hemisphere clearly indicated her different approach from that of IACW chair Doris Stevens.

One appeal came from her friend Máximo Soto Hall, the Guatemalan delegate whose 1923 Santiago resolution had paved the way for the commission's creation. Although Soto Hall had initially been one of the organization's greatest champions, in recent years, he wrote, it had "became a unilateral office, with no other representation than that of the women of the United States."[125] He sent Domínguez a copy of a letter he had written to representatives of the Cuban government outlining these concerns and urging them to send their own female delegates to the conference to wrest leadership away from Doris Stevens.

To his request and to another that she received from a group of Argentinian feminists, Domínguez replied that she could not represent her country at the Montevideo conference. Domínguez believed that all conferences hosted by the Pan-American Union perpetuated "insincerity, lies, demagoguery." However, she did recognize the urgency around developing a counterweight to the U.S. leadership of the IACW. In response to the Argentinian feminists, Domínguez sent the flyer of her earlier correspondence with Stevens in which she challenged Stevens's authority and publicly called her out for not understanding Cuba's political realities. Domínguez noted that it "was written two years ago, but it remains relevant." A real inter-American feminism could not emerge from these Pan-American conferences, but it could arise from a continental congress of Spanish-speaking Latin American women who actively opposed U.S. imperialism. Reiterating the statement that she made after the 1930 conference of the IACW in Havana, she proposed that they should work for a "broad Congress of Latin American women where we can deal broadly with all of the political, social, and economic issues of great interest and influence to humanity today." Such a "broad meeting of female delegates," unattached to their governments, who worked together as "sisters," "women of the continent who share the same language and *raza*," would "have magnificent results for the future of our struggles."[126] Several years later, the Argentinian feminists to whom Domínguez wrote would help form such an organization.

Domínguez and her interlocutors were not the only ones with a low opinion of the IACW on the eve of the 1933 Montevideo conference. Indeed, in spite of some success in pushing nationality rights into the League of Nations conferences, word had spread far and wide of Stevens's dominance over the commission and her narrow, anti-revolutionary objectives. Some commissioners reported being ill or having other commitments that made their presence at the conference impossible. Others insisted their governments would not support them.[127]

Without funding to make the trip to Montevideo possible, Panamanian commissioner Clara González was also unable to attend. In 1931, González had written to Stevens asking her to help sway Panama's president to help appoint her as a delegate to the conference.[128] That year, Panama had experienced a right-wing coup that brought nationalist leader Harmodio Arias Madrid to the presidency; González knew that it would be futile to ask him for money to go to Montevideo but hoped Stevens might be able to help. Despite her efforts, Stevens was unable to secure the president's agreement to send a woman to the conference. Although Stevens had offered the new Chilean commissioner funding to attend, she offered none to González: "Is it not humanly possible for you to get the feminists of your country . . . to get up a mass meeting in your city and contribute sufficient funds to get you to Montevideo and back . . . ? This would seem to be the only way."[129]

Much had changed over the five years since González and Stevens took their promotional photograph together on the sunny Pan-American Union patio. Not only had the commission not lived up to its promises to unite the women of the Americas, but it had alienated, disillusioned, and undermined the hopes of many of the Latin American initiators of Pan-American feminism. Yet it was also galvanizing their assertive opposition to the commission and producing stronger calls for a *feminismo práctico*—one rooted not only in "equal rights" laws but in transnational, inter-American solidarity around local struggles against U.S. imperialism, economic hardship, and gender exploitation, which *feministas* identified as being interconnected forms of oppression. The flyer that Domínguez distributed two years before the Montevideo conference marked a turning point in the movement. It publicized to many just how out of touch the U.S. leadership of the IACW was. Domínguez's resistance would encourage other women throughout Latin America to seize and reinvent *feminismo americano*. It would also dovetail with opposition fomenting against Stevens from other corners—namely, from U.S. women's groups that also objected to the National Woman's Party and wanted Stevens removed as IACW chair. At the 1933 Montevideo conference, Stevens would face real challenges to her authority.

CHAPTER FOUR

The Great Feminist Battle of Montevideo

❌ ❌ ❌

In June 1933, six months before the Seventh International Conference of American States in Montevideo, Uruguay, Doris Stevens had no idea an international coalition was working to unseat her from the Inter-American Commission of Women (IACW). Across the boundaries of country and of feminist principle, Brazilian Bertha Lutz and several representatives of the U.S. Women's and Children's Bureaus in the new Franklin Delano Roosevelt administration began plotting Stevens's demise. Their plans would engage Secretary of State Cordell Hull and Roosevelt himself to appoint to the U.S. delegation at Montevideo a woman sympathetic to their goals. At the conference, Bertha Lutz would join these efforts.

After the IACW's 1928 creation, Stevens had effectively replaced Lutz as the appointed leader of Pan-American feminism. Lutz, like Clara González, Ofelia Domínguez Navarro, and Paulina Luisi, resented Stevens's exclusionary dominance over the movement. Also like them, Lutz recognized that the Great Depression was shifting the social and political landscape in Latin America. Economic turmoil; the loss of jobs for many women; political revolutions in Brazil, Cuba, and Uruguay; and the Chaco War that broke out in 1932 over the border between Bolivia and Paraguay all reinforced her desire for an inter-American feminism that included social and economic goals and commitments to international peace.

However, Lutz was also fighting for her own idiosyncratic vision of Pan-American feminism that differed from that of her anti-imperialist, Spanish-speaking counterparts, one that maintained an unflagging certainty in U.S./ Brazilian—and her own—exceptionalism. Feminist gains in her country, where new president Getulio Vargas had recently promised women's suffrage, enhanced these beliefs and made her more eager to collaborate with U.S. government representatives. Lutz chose as her allies the reformers of the U.S. Women's and Children's Bureaus, who shared her view that the IACW had become "a misbegotten obstacle in the road to women's progress" under Stevens's leadership.[1]

Lutz would also find critical support from other corners. Ofelia Domínguez Navarro's outspoken public challenge to Doris Stevens only a few years before facilitated Lutz's alliance with the Cuban delegation in Montevideo, which agreed that Stevens needed to go. With growing international antipathy for Doris Stevens, Bertha Lutz's sophisticated wrangling, the IACW's contentious Equal Rights Treaty proposal that galvanized opposition from many U.S. women's groups, and the U.S. government's new intervention in international women's rights, Montevideo would change the trajectory of Pan-American feminism.

Bertha Lutz's Continuing Vision

Although the 1928 creation of the IACW usurped Bertha Lutz and Carrie Chapman Catt's tenuous hold over inter-American feminism, Lutz did not relinquish her goals for inter-American leadership without a fight.[2] Even though the League of Women Voters (LWV) informed Lutz in 1929 that her Inter-American Union was "too anemic to be continued," Lutz only agreed to "bury" the group several years later.[3] Early on, she set her sights on removing Doris Stevens from the IACW. In the early 1930s, progress for women's rights in Brazil caused Lutz to believe even more that she was the rightful leader of women in the Americas. At the same time, the turmoil wrought by the Great Depression and perceived failures of capitalism also propelled Lutz's new focus on women's social and economic concerns.[4] Lutz came to believe strongly in the need for an inter-American force to promote women's social and economic rights, peace, and explicit measures guaranteeing women's inclusion in national and international governance, all goals that were absent from Stevens's agenda.

Lutz's star rose in Brazil in the aftermath of the Great Depression and the country's 1930 revolution. After Getulio Vargas swept into power as the new president, he attempted to quell rising dissent and to meet expectations of workers and industrialists by instituting extensive new progressive legislation. He created a federal Ministry of Labor, Industry, and Commerce to regulate industrial relations; established social security, the eight-hour workday, and retirement pensions for a broad range of occupations; and in 1932 granted women suffrage. Brazil became the fourth country in the Western Hemisphere to enact women's voting rights, joining the United States, Canada, and Ecuador, which granted suffrage in 1929.[5] The Vargas government chose Lutz as the women's representative to the committee drafting the country's new constitution.

While Lutz celebrated these feats, she also recognized that Vargas's reforms for women were designed to promote democratic nationalism and quell dissent rather than actively propel women's social and economic rights, which she increasingly believed to be most important. A critical turning point for Lutz came when Vargas signed 1932 Decree-Law 21.417, which curtailed women's work in many occupations between ten at night and five in the morning. This law was in keeping with International Labor Organization conventions on night work, which Lutz had long supported. But now in the context of the Great Depression, Lutz viewed such protective labor legislation as harmful to women's potential as wage earners.[6] Female industrial workers, with few unions to argue for their interests, were being turned out of jobs in the Great Depression and struggled to support their families. Vargas's hours regulations, she believed, harmed women; they satisfied male workers and union leaders who wanted to eliminate female competition and enforce "proper" gender roles.[7]

Given her role in drafting the new constitution, Lutz deemed it a critical time to oppose measures defining women workers in supportive roles to their husbands and children.[8] In 1933, her group, the Federação Brasileira pelo Progresso Feminino (FBPF), inaugurated its journal, *Boletim da* FBPF, which became a pulpit for outlining the organization's bold new priority: equal labor opportunities and pay for women in Brazil, as well as social welfare guarantees such as maternity legislation.[9] FBPF participants called these guarantees "economic rights" and "social rights." As one FBPF member explained in 1932, maternity legislation for women had long been framed in a protective way, to safeguard women and their offspring, but this framing of the issue was wrong: "A woman should be heard to demand that she proclaims the RIGHT (mind you!) the right to maternity assistance."[10] In Cuba, Ofelia Domínguez Navarro's new organization had also identified maternity legislation as a "social right," and Mexican and Chilean feminists were doing the same. In these years, the shift in FBPF's attention toward social and economic rights won it many more adherents. The group flourished beyond middle-class reformers and expanded its class and geographic reach, appealing to working women.

Lutz promoted these views on labor laws and social and economic equality when she helped draft Brazil's new constitution. In 1933, Lutz published her suggestions for the 1934 constitution, *13 princípios básicos*, which included state-supported maternity leave and crèches as well as broad ideals such as "humanization of work," "universalization of social security," "equality of sexes," and "prohibition of violence." They reinforced Lutz's goal of women's equality with men in all arenas of national life (except the military) and also supported Brazil's role as a leader and peacemaker in inter-American politics.[11] Many of Lutz's thirteen points would make it into the constitution, guaranteeing for women the rights to vote, participate in government committees, and hold office in all departments of the civil service as well as rights of equal nationality, citizenship, labor access, and remuneration. It included maternity legislation as a social welfare benefit, alongside old age pensions, unemployment insurance, health and accident insurance, and death benefits, while not forsaking a commitment to "equal rights" for women. The constitution also guaranteed to male and female workers a minimum salary, an eight-hour day, and health insurance.[12]

Lutz's suggestions for the constitution guided her goals for inter-American feminism, which, she hoped, even more in these years could be a countervailing force against political tumult. Although heartened by Vargas's reforms concerning women's rights, Lutz also feared his and other Latin American leaders' usurpation of power. She looked even more to the inter-American realm as a supranational guarantor of rights against undemocratic or recalcitrant states. Even before the IACW existed, Lutz had formulated an idea for an equal nationality treaty, which she continued to defend in these years, on the grounds that international laws that promoted human justice could trump national sovereignty.[13] In the early 1930s Lutz wrote, "I see no advantage in putting the unjust tradition over the fairness to all citizens, regardless of sex or marital status, nor putting the sovereignty of nations over the right of people." Here she made an argument that anticipated those for universal human rights treaties several decades later.[14]

Although this belief in the power of international law was similar to that of Doris Stevens, Lutz increasingly resented Stevens's exclusive leadership over the IACW and narrow goals for feminism. A major point of difference between the two women was that Lutz firmly believed in female moral superiority and responsibility to promote peace. Her ideal inter-American feminism respected diplomatic protocol. Lutz found Stevens's actions in Havana and Rambouillet— militant, flashy, controversial, and oppositional to the U.S. government— morally repugnant and unladylike. Though she was insulted that Stevens did not appoint her as the Brazilian IACW representative, Lutz corresponded with the Brazilian commissioner Flora de Oliveira Lima cordially and explained her differences with Stevens: "The formula for men and women should be less about 'equality' and more about 'equivalence.'" "Woman is a gentler organism ... [who] should be the guard, but never the warrior, always a peacemaker and a pacifist."[15] Global events heightened Lutz's desire for morally superior women in channels of diplomacy. With armed conflict breaking out across Latin America, the recent Japanese invasion of Manchuria, Adolf Hitler's rise to power in Germany, world security and peace seemed at a precipice. Doris Stevens's dramatic antics of at Pan-American conferences, Lutz believed, could make matters worse.

In the early 1930s, Lutz alighted on a new group of U.S. allies to help her enlarge "the scope of the international women's collaboration ... to [include] social and economic questions" and wrest Pan-American feminist leadership away from Doris Stevens.[16] Though her bond with Carrie Chapman Catt remained strong, her connections with the League of Women Voters had frayed. For new

Pan-American feminist allies, Lutz sought out representatives of the Women's and Children's Bureaus, themselves closely connected to Catt and the LWV.

The Children's and Women's Bureaus, established by the U.S. government as agencies of the Department of Labor in 1912 and 1920, respectively, represented the kind of feminism that Lutz embraced. Though women in these bureaus did not self-identify as "feminists," they supported social and economic welfare for women and children and the role of women in national governance.[17] Lutz actively solicited their advice before and during the constitutional reforms in Brazil.[18] Later, she encouraged Brazil to create similar bureaus to study and work on all matters pertaining to the home and child welfare.[19]

Importantly for Lutz, the Women's and Children's Bureaus were part of the large network of U.S. women's groups that opposed the Woman's Party's ERA and its international iteration, the Equal Rights Treaty. Along with Catt's LWV, the Women's Trade Union League, and many other groups, the Women's and Children's Bureaus opposed the ERA and the Equal Rights Treaty on the grounds that they would take away hard-fought special protections for working women, such as maximum hours laws and those prohibiting lifting heavy weights. Such protections were necessary, Women's and Children's Bureau representatives believed, to safeguard women on the lowest rungs of the occupational ladder.[20] These leaders agreed with Catt that the NWP-led Inter-American Commission of Women represented "a new and serious situation" that should be stopped.[21]

Although Lutz herself now opposed protective labor legislation, she nonetheless allied strategically with leaders in the Women's and Children's Bureaus who opposed Doris Stevens. In particular, Lutz found a soul mate in her new friend Katharine Lenroot, a reformer in the Children's Bureau who had, since 1927, become a leader of Pan-American child congresses. Like Lutz, she championed a Pan-Americanism that promoted women's and children's welfare and "world peace," structured by U.S. institutions.[22]

These two women bonded when Lutz stayed in Lenroot's Washington, D.C., home during Lutz's 1932 speaking tour of U.S. natural history museums, a continuation of her work as a biologist at the National Museum of Brazil. After she left, Lenroot wrote, "You've only been gone two days, but it feels like a week." Over the next two months, the two women sent each other at least seven letters, signing off "lovingly" and "with love."[23] Their friendship deepened several months later when Lenroot stayed with Lutz in Rio de Janeiro while on a visit to Brazil, also meeting Lutz's father and brother. During these visits, Lutz narrated the history of Pan-American conferences and women's rights resolutions. Although familiar with some of these wranglings, Lenroot no doubt found Lutz's inside knowledge enlightening.[24]

After Franklin D. Roosevelt became president in 1933, Katharine Lenroot seized the opportunity to push her and Lutz's vision for Pan-American feminism through the new president and U.S. State Department. In June 1933, six months before the Montevideo conference, Lenroot and Grace Abbott, head of the Children's Bureau, asked their friend Frances Perkins, recently appointed secretary of labor under Roosevelt, to help them enlist a woman to the conference. Abbott drafted a letter that Perkins sent to President Roosevelt and to recently appointed Secretary of State Cordell Hull explaining the threat posed by the IACW and urging they send to Montevideo a woman "sympathetic" to the administration's approach to labor and social issues.[25] They recommended Sophonisba Breckinridge, sixty-seven-year-old professor emerita of public welfare administration at the University of Chicago, lawyer, former vice president of the National American Woman Suffrage Association, and longtime member of the League of Women Voters. A social reformer who worked closely with the Women's and Children's Bureaus, Breckinridge was an advocate of protective labor legislation for women and children, fair housing, and rights of immigrants.[26]

Roosevelt, who openly favored protective legislation for women workers, understood the importance of electing a female delegate sympathetic to his administration's goals. On the heels of his New Deal, the NWP was launching a vocal attack on the Roosevelt administration. The NWP insisted that the New Deal did not bring a "fair deal for women," pointing out gender differences in the National Recovery Administration codes that established different minimum wages for men and women.[27] Recognizing the material importance of challenging Doris Stevens and her supporters, Roosevelt quickly complied with Perkins's advice, appointing Breckinridge as one of the five U.S. delegates to the conference.[28]

From Brazil, Lutz rejoiced. Lutz had met Breckinridge at the 1922 Baltimore conference, devoured her legal work on women's status, and corresponded with her several times.[29] A delegate alongside Katharine Lenroot in several Pan-American child congresses, Breckinridge supported mothers' rights, prenatal and postnatal care, education for needy mothers, aid to poor families, and social security as hemispheric goals.[30] In 1929 Breckinridge had written the preface to a League of Women Voters–commissioned book that argued against the IACW and its Equal Rights Treaty.[31] Lutz knew that Breckinridge would champion the type of Pan-American feminism she believed in and help remove Doris Stevens as its leader.

Indeed, while collaborating with Lenroot, Abbott, and Perkins, Breckinridge helped hatch concrete plans to thwart Stevens in Montevideo. The memorandum of instructions that Perkins ultimately sent the State Department opposed both the IACW's women's rights treaties and its continuation. Her directions forwarded the inclusion of protective labor legislation, noting that U.S. delegates should uphold women's "effective equality of opportunity and of protection" while suggesting that the "needs and opportunities for both sexes should be safeguarded by appropriate legislation designed to meet the special problems of each group."[32] Questions of women's civil and political rights should be taken up individually by nations for further study rather than in an international treaty. Final official instructions ordered the U.S. delegation to "abstain" from a vote on even the Equal Nationality Treaty due to the inappropriateness of women's rights as the subject of any international treaty.[33] They also reiterated Perkins's command that if any resolution on the continuation of the IACW was broached, delegates "should refrain from voting," stating they were "without instructions."[34]

Meanwhile, Bertha Lutz used all her connections, even the ones she was covertly working against, to gain appointment as a delegate to the conference. Recognizing Doris Stevens's influence with diplomatic leaders and presidents, she boldly appealed directly to Stevens for help. Wary of Lutz's long-standing support for protective labor laws, Stevens was initially reluctant. However, when a U.S. friend of Lutz who was also a NWP member informed Stevens that Lutz had "recanted" protective labor legislation in Brazil after the Great Depression and "come out strongly for *equal rights*," Stevens agreed to help.[35] Through Stevens's connections to Victor Maúrtua, the Peruvian ambassador to Brazil, Lutz gained appointment as technical adviser to the Brazilian delegation.[36] Lacking full delegate status meant that she would not be able to propose or vote on resolutions. Nevertheless, as a technical adviser Lutz would attend the Montevideo conference on the dime of the Brazilian government, influence its resolutions, and, to Stevens's befuddlement, try to change the course of Pan-American feminism.

Doris Stevens interpreted Lutz's determination to attend Montevideo as indicative of her support of the IACW, which may have boosted Stevens's spirits during an otherwise challenging time. In some respects, Stevens was alone and struggling; several months before the conference, Stevens revealed to Jane Norman Smith that she felt "utterly unequal to the task before us with no money and almost no help."[37] Many commissioners had written to say they would not be going to Montevideo for various reasons—lack of money, revolutionary turmoil, poor health. Some simply no longer supported the IACW.

Stevens was also very likely exhausted. Between 1930 and 1933, she had worked on the IACW campaigns for married women's nationality rights in the League of Nations and built her own pedigree in international law. She traveled to Geneva several times to help with the Women's Consultative Committee report for the League of Nations Assembly, and while in the United States commuted between Washington, D.C., and New York City, taking classes in Spanish, international law, and foreign policy at American University and Columbia University.[38]

In D.C. Stevens labored with other IACW members and NWP volunteers to finish their enormous legal report on women's rights—the report Clara González had toiled on for several years—that they would present at Montevideo. In twenty-one large volumes for the twenty-one Pan-American nations, the report detailed where women did and did not have equal political and nationality rights with men. It also pointed to differences in rights to hold public office, serve on juries, engage in business, marry, serve as witnesses to public documents, administer property, and divorce. In response to Latin American demands, it also took up the questions of parents' joint authority over legitimate and illegitimate children.[39] The *New York Times* announced the report marked "the first time such a search for information on the political and civil rights of women has been made over so large an area."[40] It represented a major achievement, still valuable today.

The afternoon of November 11, 1933, Stevens boarded the SS *American Legion* for Montevideo at the Twenty-Fourth Street pier in New York City along with a research committee member and executive secretary from the National Woman's Party, carrying fifty copies each of the twenty-one-volume report, four boxes of documents, two typewriters, and their summer clothes. As the steamer took off and she waved goodbye to the group of NWP members who had come to wish them bon voyage, Stevens remained upbeat.[41] She focused on the support she expected to receive from Latin American feminists in Montevideo.[42] The Mexican delegation would include as a technical adviser Margarita Robles de Mendoza, Mexico's commissioner since 1930, who had worked in the Washington, D.C., office for several stints in 1931 and 1932.[43] Minerva Bernardino, an alternate for the Dominican commissioner and the secretary of the Acción Feminista Dominicana, would also be a delegate. In addition, Paraguay and Uruguay had enlisted women to their delegations, including Dr. Sofía Álvarez Vignoli de Demicheli, a supporter of women's rights and collaborator with the Terra regime in Uruguay.[44]

Stevens especially looked forward to Bertha Lutz's cooperation. "We are counting without fail upon seeing you in Montevideo to help in every possible way to make our work with the Conference a success," Stevens wrote her. Stevens also told Lutz that the U.S. delegation included "a very superior woman," Sophonisba Breckinridge, who Stevens hoped would "be of great help."[45] Lutz, of course, already knew of Breckinridge's appointment, and Stevens would not be able to count on either woman for support.

Bertha Lutz, Sophonisba Breckinridge, and the
U.S. State Department in Montevideo

Several days into the eighteen-day steamer voyage to Montevideo, Doris Stevens learned from a *Cincinnati Times-Star* article that Sophonisba Breckinridge opposed the Equal Rights Treaty. The article stated that Breckinridge's appointment signified that "the Administration . . . is not enthusiastic over . . . Miss Stevens's views" and "frowned on women's rights as a subject of treaties."[46] In the midst of interviewing delegates from the United States and other countries who were aboard the SS *American Legion*, Stevens sought out Breckinridge. Although Breckinridge exuded "less than warmth," she insisted to Stevens that her "chief interest" at Montevideo would be child welfare.[47] Meanwhile, however, back in her cabin Breckinridge worked on a twenty-two-page memo for the U.S. delegation that detailed the history of the IACW and its contemptible women's rights treaties. She wrote to her friend Edith Abbott, "I think . . . [the U.S. State Department] will clip the wings of the Women's Party [sic]."[48]

On November 24, when the ship stopped in Rio de Janeiro to pick up passengers en route to Montevideo, Bertha Lutz and a group of FBPF members smiled and posed for photographs as they greeted Stevens. Lutz still sought her help to become a full delegate, rather than a technical adviser, to the conference. Privately, Lutz also met with Breckinridge to cement their plans for the conference. The two women resolved to try to stop the IACW, and Breckinridge assured Lutz that they could rely on the U.S. State Department for help.[49]

The Montevideo conference would be the first international conference in which the U.S. State Department actively became involved in battles over women's rights, although initially Secretary of State Cordell Hull deemed the issue of little significance. Amid roiling economic and political tensions in the Americas, the rise of fascism in Germany and Italy, and the Chaco War between Paraguay and Bolivia, the Montevideo conference was the most significant Pan-American conference to date. With lingering U.S. financial control over Haiti and with Roosevelt and Sumner Welles's inept efforts at fostering a pro-U.S. government in Cuba after its revolution, charges of *yanqui imperialismo* rang stronger than ever.[50] As late as October, Cordell Hull had sought to postpone the conference, anxious that Mexico would raise questions of external indebtedness and revision of the Monroe Doctrine.[51] When postponement proved impossible, Hull planned to propose a tariff reduction resolution as well as a "Good Neighbor Policy" that announced a new code of nonintervention by the United States in Latin America. He hoped these accessions to long-standing Latin American demands would promote harmony.

Although women's rights were initially of little importance to Hull, Stevens

Bertha Lutz and FBPF members greeting Doris Stevens and members of the IACW in Rio de Janeiro before the Montevideo conference, November 24, 1933. Left to right: unknown, Mrs. G. Emmons, Orminda Ribeiro Bastos, Bertha Lutz, Doris Stevens, Víctor Maúrtua, unknown, Fanny Bunand-Sevastos, Víctor Andrés Belaúnde, Carmen Velasco Portinho de Lutz, unknown. Courtesy of the Schlesinger Library, Radcliffe Institute, Harvard University.

and her Inter-American Commission of Women made themselves impossible to avoid. Hull had seen Stevens in action at the 1928 Havana conference and understood her to be a scofflaw who surreptitiously appealed to powerful Latin American delegates to push through her resolutions. Her behavior at the Montevideo conference proved particularly disconcerting. On the steamer trip over, Stevens and IACW members foisted themselves into the center of events, lobbying various delegations for their Equal Rights Treaty and attracting the attention of the press.[52] Upon arrival in Montevideo, they secured headquarters directly below those of the U.S. delegation in the Hotel Parque, where IACW members interviewed large numbers of delegates.[53] In the National Assembly, where sessions took place, Stevens even procured an office next to the principal assembly hall. Hull and Breckinridge particularly deplored the "especially close" ties the IACW enjoyed with press correspondents, including the Latin American bureau chief of the *New York Times*, who was Stevens's good friend.[54]

Increasingly, Hull worried that Stevens's unorthodox tactics would jeopardize his efforts to improve U.S.–Latin American relations. He found his fears confirmed by her backstage maneuverings to influence the meetings of the sub-committee to the Third Committee, through which any women's rights treaties and resolutions had to pass in order to be voted on officially. The trouble began when the five subcommittee members from Uruguay, Peru, Cuba, Brazil, and Chile did not unanimously agree on an international treaty giving women abso-lute equal civil and political rights.[55] After studying the commission's lengthy report, a majority of three delegations (Brazil, Peru, and Chile) voted against the Equal Rights Treaty, asserting that such a sweeping international bill would vio-late Latin American national sovereignty.[56] Instead, these statesmen voted for a simple, nonbinding recommendation that states grant political and civil rights to women. Hull and the State Department were likely quite pleased by this de-velopment. Arguments protesting the Equal Rights Treaty on the grounds of national sovereignty had emerged since the beginning of the IACW's efforts, though the United States was usually the most vocal proponent of this argument.

Stevens, however, would not be so easily undone. In clever and clandestine ways, she sought to influence a favorable vote on the last remaining items: the Equal Nationality Treaty and the continuation of the commission. The night be-fore the last subcommittee meeting, she met with its head, Brazilian delegate Francisco Campos. The two co-drafted a proposal that Campos presented the following day. It included three items: adoption of the Equal Nationality Treaty; recommendation to national governments to study and promote women's equal civil and political rights; and promotion of the continuation of the commission, which it lauded for its "unique, notable and unselfish labor."[57] Campos's pro-posal was unanimously adopted. These resolutions proceeded to the Third Com-mittee, in which all countries would be represented.

With so many Latin American delegations—especially those from Haiti, the Dominican Republic, Mexico, and Cuba—chafing against U.S. imperialism, and with some opposing the Equal Rights Treaty on the grounds that it might vio-late national sovereignty, Stevens's covert dealings alarmed Hull. Worried that her underhanded "tactics" to push the nationality treaty and "go over the heads" of Latin American delegates could upset equanimity and possibly spoil passage of his own resolutions, Hull telegrammed William Phillips, the under secre-tary of state in Washington, D.C. and reported that Latin American delegates feared the Equal Rights Treaty would encroach on their national sovereignty. He asked Phillips to consult with Frances Perkins and the president about how to proceed.[58]

Although Hull had previously told Stevens that he "had no instructions for or against continuation" of the IACW, official directions quickly changed.[59] That evening, in response to his telegram, Hull received new orders to abolish the women's organization: "If ... the Conference proceeds to vote on any resolution recommending the continuation of the Inter-American Commission of Women, you should state that your Government does not (repeat not) desire any longer to be represented on the Commission and intends to continue its studies in this field through branches of the Government charged with responsibility in these matters.... The foregoing has been discussed with Miss Perkins who approves."[60]

Phillips later sent a memo explaining that "Miss Perkins emphatically opposes the continuance of the Inter-American Commission of Women. She feels it important from the domestic point of view not to give semi-official standing to an American group of women antagonistic to the Government program with respect to women."[61]

The State Department, fearing its lack of control over the conference proceedings, readily utilized the domestic debate over the NWP's equal rights agenda as a pretext for quashing the IACW. Several days before the vote on the subcommittee resolutions she had coauthored, Doris Stevens heard rumors from Latin American delegates that "the United States ... wanted the Inter American Commission of Women killed."[62] Now when Stevens asked Hull about the U.S. delegation's plans, he said "the matter was entirely out of his hands" and directed her to Alexander Weddell, the chief U.S. member of the Third Committee. When Stevens questioned Weddell, he responded tersely, "Orders."[63] His wife was an avid member of the League of Women Voters, Stevens's rivals, and he heartily supported the plan to thwart the IACW.

If the State Department was using the domestic equal rights debate to fight the commission, Stevens resolved the IACW would use debates over *yanqui* imperialism to fight the State Department. Launching into action the day before the meeting, Stevens and her commission aides Fanny Bunand-Sevastos, Margarita Robles de Mendoza, and Minerva Bernardino canvassed delegations from the afternoon until the early hours of the morning. They alerted statesmen that the United States would speak against the continuation of the IACW and leave its future up to a vote from them.[64] As Stevens had done before in Havana and in Rambouillet, she deliberately contrasted the IACW's mission for "equal rights" with the United States' long violation of countries' rights. Drawing on anti-American sentiments simmering at the conference, Stevens insisted that the IACW was on the same side as Latin American nations beleaguered by U.S. hegemony. They were all fighting the "United States government" together.

In their lobbying, she and her aides also made arguments that statesmen found persuasive—that women's rights meant progress and prestige for Latin American countries. In preceding days Robles de Mendoza and Álvarez Vignoli had given rousing speeches linking women's equality with Latin American advancement and modernity. These were the themes Stevens emphasized in a speech she gave while lobbying Latin American delegates and that the Woman's Party later circulated throughout the Americas:

> Here is a great principle involved. . . . In the long run, the advancement of your women will mean more to the progress of your countries than anything else you do here. If either you or your country cannot afford to defy the United States, tell me and I shall understand. Have you personally anything to lose, or has your country? But if you promise me now to vote for the Inter American Commission of Women in tomorrow morning's session, I shall expect you to stand like a rock with me for equality.[65]

The morning after Stevens and her aides' calls for Latin American support, Alexander Weddell stood before the conference and declared that the U.S. delegation did not support the IACW. The growing representation of women in public office under the Roosevelt administration indicated that women's rights were effectively complete in the United States, he stated. Furthermore, women's legal, civil, and social status should be considered by individual states rather than federal governments and by individual countries rather than international treaties. Thus, Weddell announced, the U.S. government "desired to dissociate itself in the future from the work of the . . . Commission" and would abstain on all votes regarding the commission and its treaties.[66]

From the tiered rows of oak tables and chairs in the assembly room, the Latin American delegates in the Third Committee rose in almost unanimous opposition to Weddell. The U.S. position struck many of them as contrary to the best interests of Latin America, where in most countries, unlike in the United States, women still did not have the right to vote. Peruvian delegate Carlos Neuhaus Ugarteche led the resistance, saying that his country would sign the Equal Nationality Treaty "with pleasure." The Equal Nationality Treaty followed clear precedents of international private law and had received great Latin American support in the Hague Codification Conference. Ugarteche acknowledged that civil and political rights represented "an essentially complex matter in every country" and that those complexities required different solutions, but he believed the IACW had attained a "brilliant conquest" and should continue its work. Tulio M. Cestero from the Dominican Republic declared he, too, would sign the Equal Nationality Treaty. Women's rights, he said, were key to his nation's "moral and intellectual progress."[67] Similar appeals followed from delegates from Mexico, El Salvador, Chile, and elsewhere. The only country to side with the United States was Argentina, whose negative vote Stevens attributed to Weddell. As that country's ambassador, he "dragoon[ed] Argentina into opposing the Inter American Commission of Women."[68] Given the strong, near-unanimous Latin American support, the conference delegates passed the Equal Nationality Treaty, gave warm thanks for the work of the commission, and invited it to continue and report to the Eighth Pan-American Conference to be held in Lima, Peru, in 1938.[69]

As a foreign policy writer observed, "The only important subject at the conference on which the United States opposed majority sentiment was that of equal rights for women."[70] The backlash that the U.S. State Department received in Montevideo on this issue reflected the folly of its attempt to export the United States' polarizing domestic ERA debate to the rest of the Americas. Although U.S. women saw their inter-American work through the lens of this conflict, insisting that their side represented the best interest of Latin American women, the ERA debate did not translate anywhere in Latin America.[71] There, most women still did not have the right to vote, protective labor legislation for women had largely not been guaranteed, and the "rights" in "equal rights" often indicated social as well as individual rights.

Stevens later celebrated that "this is the first and only occasion in Pan American Conferences that Latin America, en bloc, has voted against the United States." Recognizing that "so many [were] not in a mood to follow the lead of the United States," she acknowledged the "hostility [of the U.S. delegation] was . . . our greatest asset."[72] Beleaguered and attacked by the U.S. government, "I became a symbol of repudiation, persecution, an object of pity."[73]

Bertha Lutz, meanwhile, smarted at the success of Stevens's anti-imperialist pandering to Latin American delegates. "Miss Stevens does not represent the women's movement, and . . . all Americans are not business men out to exploit the small republics of Central America," Lutz wrote to Catt.[74] Members of the U.S. delegation who were allied with Lutz shared her resentment. In a confidential memo that described Stevens as "overwrought" and "fanatical," the State Department explained that Lutz had informed them that Haitian delegates, who were "rather in opposition to" the United States, were "on apparently close terms with members of the Women's Commission." Believing Doris Stevens and the IACW would "advanc[e] . . . their country's interests" to greater effect than the U.S. State Department, the Haitian delegates represented just one group that gave its allegiance to Stevens. Weddell and Breckinridge worried that Stevens exerted similar influence on other delegates disgruntled with the U.S. State Department from the Dominican Republic, Paraguay, and Uruguay.[75]

Yet Stevens did not manage to secure the faith of all Latin American delegations protesting U.S. dominance. The Cuban delegates, representatives of the 100-day revolutionary government of Ramón Grau San Martín, were friends with Ofelia Domínguez Navarro. Having just ousted Machado, these men came to the conference ready to oppose the Platt Amendment, which, in spite of the U.S. government's Good Neighbor pronouncements, remained intact, and ready to oppose Doris Stevens's leadership of the IACW.

The Cuban delegation did support international women's rights. The new Grau government promised women's and workers' rights as part of its revolutionary promises, and Cuba would be one of the four countries at the conference that signed the Equal Rights Treaty. But Angel Alberto Giraudy, head of the Cuban delegation and minister of labor, and his fellow delegate Herminio Portell Vilá, opposed Doris Stevens, whose reputation as a strongman among Latin American feminists preceded her. They had likely read Domínguez's El País exposé of the IACW and her widely disseminated correspondence with Stevens, who had essentially dismissed the Cuban Revolution's goals. Before the conference, their friend Máximo Soto Hall had sent the Cuban government a lengthy memo expressing his disappointment with Stevens's "unilateral" leadership and urging the country's delegation to remove her from authority in Montevideo.[76]

When Stevens discovered that the Cubans might oppose the commission's continuation, she boldly threatened them with the reversal of key concessions they had wrested from Cordell Hull on the Platt Amendment. Hull had promised Giraudy that the United States would consider abolishing the Platt Amendment, formulating new trade laws, and recognizing the revolutionary government of Grau (all of which proved later to only be lip service).[77] When Giraudy suggested to Stevens that he would not support the commission's continuation, she reportedly told him that "the Platt amendment changes would not be made" if they did not back her resolutions. Although such a decision was far outside Stevens's influence, her threat infuriated Giraudy.[78]

Outraged, Giraudy and Portell Vilá became somewhat strange bedfellows with Bertha Lutz, who had acted in subtle yet meaningful ways to undermine Stevens since the beginning of the conference. Participating in the subcommittee of the Third Committee as Brazil's technical adviser, Lutz had been the one to propose the simple recommendation for equal civil, political, and nationality rights after the Equal Rights Treaty had failed.[79] She had also proposed that all future Pan-American conferences include female delegates, hoping this would bring in other women not affiliated with the IACW. The subcommittee adopted her proposal, and the Third Committee passed it.[80]

But Lutz's greatest shot across the bow of Doris Stevens came several days after the Third Committee received nearly unanimous Latin American support for the continuation of the IACW. Here, Lutz relied on her collaboration with Cuban delegates. Though the U.S. State Department had failed to remove Doris Stevens, Lutz refused to give up: she drafted a proposal that the chairmanship of the commission rotate among countries. The "Lutz resolution," which Cuban delegate Giraudy brought before the Committee on Initiatives, specified that each Pan-American conference would designate a different country to be the seat of the Inter-American Commission of Women between conferences, and that country's commissioner would act as chairman. Lutz's idea came directly from Latin American nations' suggestions at earlier Pan-American conferences that the leadership of the Pan-American Union itself rotate. Her proposal also required government ratification of any commissioner and stipulated that all commissioners be elected by women who represented "organized feminine opinion" in their countries. Recognizing that the U.S. government would not support Stevens as commissioner, Lutz knew her proposal would remove Doris Stevens from leadership. The subcommittee accepted the plan for rotation, which was then approved by the majority of the Third Committee.[81]

Energized by her success, Lutz took more action. First, she wrote a long memo to Sophonisba Breckinridge and the U.S. delegation, explaining the need to give teeth to her resolution by "indicating the place to which the presidency should rotate." She believed this place should be Brazil and that she should be the new leader. Because the continuation of Doris Stevens's reign "will spell disaster to the latin Americans womens hope [sic]," and because it was necessary that the commission "be used, for and by them," she explained that Brazil was the most rational choice. It was also, she said, one of the few countries in the Western Hemisphere where feminism had been organized for many years and that was "in a position to maintain the Commission." [82]

Then, in the meeting of the Eighth Committee, which considered the management of the Pan-American conferences, Lutz influenced the introduction of another resolution to challenge the IACW. It sought to establish a new group called the "Inter American Labor Institute," to be headquartered in a Latin American capital. Lutz suggested the institute contain a "Women's Department," which would be "responsible for all matters of especial interest to women." Lutz envisioned it as a Pan-American women's bureau, one that would presumably replace the IACW. Directed by women who lived in the capital city where the institute resided, the location must be chosen specifically "where there are resources and women's organizations." Again, Lutz had Rio de Janeiro in mind.[83] Her resolution passed.

Finally, Lutz attempted to reconvene the Third Committee to present her expanded agenda for Pan-American feminism—to broaden its goals to include social and economic rights for women. In a resolution titled "Civil and Political Rights of Women, Minimum Replevin," Lutz advocated not only for equal "juridical, economic and political rights of women" but also for women's authority over the making of laws and public administration "relating to the home, maternity, infancy, and feminine labor." She sought maternity insurance provided by the state in a manner that would safeguard, not hinder, women's work.[84] Again Lutz engaged Giraudy from Cuba as well as Uruguayan delegate Sofía Álvarez Vignoli, who together formally made the proposal.[85]

When Stevens heard Lutz's Third Committee proposals to make a more multilateral and expansive commission, she became alarmed. She fired off an urgent telegram to NWP president Alice Paul asking for help influencing the Cuban delegates: "New Attack on Commission and me has been launched by Lutz and Breckinridge via Cuba and Uruguay. This has driven us desperately day and night.... They have attacked us also in several Committee meetings with maneuvers unbelievable.... They now rely on resolution on floor of Conference. ... Cuba is unmanageable.... Please try to do something on Cuba today from there."[86]

Earlier, Stevens had been dismayed that Lutz, whose conference appointment she had facilitated, was actively hostile to the IACW. In conversations with Brazilian delegates, Stevens learned that Lutz had never spoken with them about supporting the Equal Rights or Equal Nationality Treaties. Stevens also noticed the "close alliance" and "frequent two-some" of Lutz and Breckinridge.[87] To her mind, the only explanation for Lutz's opposition was that Lutz had been dishonest about her support for equal rights. It did not occur to Stevens that Lutz favored a more expansive definition of equal rights, resented Stevens's leadership, and sought domain over Pan-American feminism herself. Regardless, Stevens recognized Lutz as a serious threat and later recalled, "Miss Lutz seemed to become possessed. She tried to reconvene the Third [Committee] to propose various ways to disassociate the Inter American Commission headquarters from the Pan-American Union, that is, remove the seat from Washington; she tried to change the character of the work; she tried by secret petition and various resolutions to change the powers and jurisdiction of the Commission; and finally to kill it outright."[88]

For their part, Stevens and her cohort aggressively interviewed delegates, asking them to absent themselves from the rest of the Third Committee meetings so that Lutz's recommendations, aside from her proposal on the rotation of the commissioner, which had passed, could not be voted on. Stevens had developed a strong enough rapport with most delegates that the majority did not attend the final three meetings of the Third Committee. Without a quorum, the committee could not act on any resolution, thereby thwarting Lutz's proposals.[89] The ultimate plenary session of the conference on December 24 adopted the Third Committee's report, which included no mechanism for rotation of the chairman or definite change to the commission program to include social or economic rights. It included only an "aspiration" that the chairmanship rotate between conferences.[90]

However, Lutz and Breckinridge devised their own plans for the plenary session, which they realized was their last shot at wresting power from Stevens. The day before, they inserted a resolution into the formal list to be announced in the final session, to create a new inter-American women's committee, composed of the women who formed part of their national delegations at Montevideo. They collaborated here again with Cuban delegate Giraudy, who inserted the bill. Because such sessions were usually pro forma, Stevens considered not attending the plenary. But having witnessed Breckinridge and Lutz sharing a "close and animated luncheon conference that day," she suspected they were "up to something" and decided to go to the meeting.[91] Sitting in the audience, Stevens heard, among the other resolutions that were listed in Spanish and adopted, an unfamiliar one that would create a new official group of women. This group would work not only for egalitarian legislation but also to "coordinate and unify the activities of all the women" in the hemisphere "and obtain the support of ... women's organizations and of the governments" in fulfillment of its ends.[92]

Realizing that this "ripper bill" would create a rival inter-American commission of women with Breckinridge and Lutz at its helm, Stevens literally jumped into action.[93] Leaping from her seat, she started scrawling on the only scraps of paper she found available—Western Union Telegraph blanks—messages in English, Spanish, and French to delegates.[94] Conference interpreter José Tercero publicized the scandal to delegates wearing headphones, announcing, "Hell has broken out; the ladies have been double-crossed." When delegates began to protest the new resolution, Giraudy admitted "he had only introduced it by 'request' and that he now wished to withdraw it," drawing applause and laughter from the conference members.[95]

Lutz, Breckinridge, Giraudy, and the U.S. delegation, however, were not laughing.[96] In spite of their best efforts, the IACW remained in the hands of Doris Stevens, who could now celebrate its significant achievements. The Equal Nationality Treaty passed unanimously, as the United States recanted its former position of opposition, and all the countries except Venezuela signed it. Additionally, representatives from four countries—Uruguay, Paraguay, Ecuador, and Cuba—elected to sign the Equal Rights Treaty. Afterward, *The Nation* magazine declared that "the most concrete, as well as the most dramatic, act of the conference" was not U.S. secretary of state Cordell Hull's announcement of the Good Neighbor Policy or his resolution lowering trade tariffs, but rather the passage of an international treaty guaranteeing women's equal nationality rights and the recommendation that all nations grant equal civil and political rights to women.[97] Doris Stevens celebrated this achievement while criticizing the United States: "Where greater powers refused to go, smaller powers led the way."[98]

"It Is a Moral Issue That Is at Stake"

Lutz, whose Pan-American feminism relied upon her deep admiration for the United States, found Stevens's anti-U.S. rhetoric and behavior at the conference morally distasteful. Over the course of the conference, Lutz's feelings for Stevens had evolved from dislike and distrust to, as Alexander Weddell later put it, "a XIVth century, Florentine detestation of Doris Stevens."[99]

As troubling as she found Stevens's successful manipulation of anti-imperialism, Lutz was even more alarmed by what she perceived as Stevens's use of sexual wiles to control men at the conference. In short, Lutz believed Stevens and her cohort had won the support of Latin American delegates because they had seduced them. The Mexican delegate Manuel Sierra "told everyone Miss Stevens had kissed him for shunting off my proposal [to create a rival commission] at the last session," she wrote to Breckinridge.[100] To Catt, Lutz wrote, "Miss Stevens gave a little demonstration of a sex-mad psychopath, calling Miss B and me by zoologic names, of a domestic variety, paying the Mexican delegates in kisses for voting against us, luring the Haitians with a French secretary she has, who lives up to the reputation French women have in South America. The trouble is that men went home with the idea that Miss B and I were sexless puritans in the midst of greek hertairas [sic], in the women's movement. It was a dreadful demonstration."[101] While Lutz's specific charges of Stevens's sexual favors at the conference remain unconfirmed, Stevens may indeed have engaged in romantic relationships with high-powered diplomats. In an unpublished play Stevens later wrote, a Peruvian ambassador tells an international feminist leader that he is "enchanted" with her and "would like to make a son by [her]."[102] The fictional suitor was a thinly veiled fictionalization of Peruvian ambassador Victor Maúrtua, one of Stevens's greatest supporters. More concrete evidence comes from love letters sent her by James Brown Scott, prominent international lawyer and cofounder of the American Institute of International Law. After meeting Stevens at the 1928 Havana conference, Scott quickly became Stevens's most influential advocate. He helped the IACW draft the Equal Nationality Treaty, spoke out publicly in favor of the commission treaties, used his extensive State Department connections to aid the commission, and appointed Stevens to be the first female member of the American Institute of International Law. Critically, he almost single-handedly bankrolled the IACW, helping keep the commission financially afloat in the 1930s through his personal finances and money from the Carnegie Endowment for International Peace, of which he was the secretary.[103] In addition to professional, typewritten letters about commission business, Scott hand-wrote more intimate notes and poems for Stevens, whom he praised as a world-historical, progressive, and beautiful leader who had awakened his "spirit" to women's rights. He signed one of them, "I am, my one and only love, your wholly devoted Jamie."[104] Scott was married and Stevens was in a romantic relationship with Jonathan Mitchell, whom she later married.

Yet the emotional intimacy conveyed in Scott's letters, combined with Stevens and Mitchell's flexible views on monogamy, indicate a likely love affair.[105]

As historian Leila Rupp has demonstrated, Stevens balanced a complicated romantic life of extramarital affairs, divorce, and two marriages with a modern, distinctly heterosocial approach to feminism, embodying the paradox of the New Woman during a time of sexual revolution.[106] She saw no contradiction between sexual adventurousness and her ambitious political goals.

For Lutz, who self-consciously subscribed to a Victorian sexual philosophy that viewed male sexuality as domination, Stevens's sexual politics confirmed that she and the feminism she stood for were reprehensible. Indeed, this conflict revealed one of the thorniest distinctions between the two women. Lutz never married and referred proudly to her status as a "bachelor woman"; she often alluded to Susan B. Anthony's belief that women's rights leaders should be "unmarried and entirely devoted to the cause."[107] Feminism, in her view, should stand for women's purer morality. "Equality," Lutz told a Mexican delegate in Buenos Aires after the conference, was "not desired" if it meant "lowering women's moral standards to those of men," à la Doris Stevens.[108]

After the conference, Lutz fired off letters to Catt, Lenroot, Breckinridge, and other friends in the United States regarding the moral deficiency of the IACW, which she called its greatest failure. "Their morals are atrocious, there [sic] methods are unscrupulous as those of Hitler, whose acute sense of publicity they possess in full," Lutz wrote Catt.[109] To Frieda Miller she wrote that Doris Stevens was "capable of ruining all the achievements that women have obtained until now and of effectively preventing them from getting any further."[110] After narrating Stevens's sexual improprieties to Breckinridge, she concluded, "So now you have the real . . . problem, in the last degree it is a moral issue that is at stake."[111]

In Lutz's opinion, more virtuous and principled women could save Pan-American feminism, but her abiding belief in U.S. and Brazilian superiority caused her to seek out like-minded U.S. rather than Latin American women. She remained convinced of this strategy, even though the Montevideo conference provided Lutz with a rare opportunity to connect with many Spanish-speaking feminists and delegates who also opposed Stevens's leadership.

In a trip to Buenos Aires following the conference, a number of people approached Lutz about deposing Stevens. Lutz met with a group of Argentinian women who sought a new Latin American–only feminist organization. She also spoke with male diplomats—including Angel Giraudy and Máximo Soto Hall—who were so dissatisfied with the commission that they discussed creating a group of women and men to replace it. Lutz found Soto Hall, who had fathered the commission with his 1923 resolution, like "Saturn, anxious to swallow his children."[112]

Lutz also conferred in Buenos Aires with Margarita Robles de Mendoza and Minerva Bernardino, who suggested they might overthrow Stevens in favor of a Latin American feminist or form an alternative group. Even though these two women had officially supported Stevens at the conference as IACW representatives, both had privately hoped that Lutz and Giraudy's proposal to rotate the chairmanship would pass.[113]

In spite of all the support she received in Argentina, Lutz's keen sense of U.S.-Brazilian superiority and faith in her own leadership caused her to naively turn away from these opportunities to collaborate with Spanish-speaking leaders. Lutz rejected the plans offered her in Buenos Aires. Her justifications varied: the Argentine women's proposed confederation of women would give only a small role to the United States, which, Lutz believed, must lead any Pan-American effort, and she personally disliked Margarita Robles de Mendoza.[114] But a profile of Lutz that appeared in Ecuadorian and Cuban magazines after the Montevideo conference underscored the real reason: her steadfast belief in Brazilian pre-eminence. The profile, which celebrated Lutz's focus on pressing economic and social issues for women workers and children and on world peace, quoted her description of her own Brazilian feminist group: "an autonomous group whose intellectual forces are undoubted."[115] While Lutz acknowledged the existence and "coherent ideology" of Spanish-speaking "Latin" feminists, she also did not hide her certainty that Spanish-speaking feminists lacked the "organizational center" or capacity to lead feminism.[116] These views prevented Lutz from capitalizing on her own goal to organize a group that could viably challenge Doris Stevens's leadership.

For her part, Stevens knew that Lutz's Brazilian exceptionalism was her Achilles' heel. In a letter to a NWP member, Stevens mentioned that although Lutz was "very anxious" to create an alternative inter-American women's group and become its "head," "Latin American women have repeatedly told me that [Lutz] works under the very great handicap of being . . . [from] a Portuguese-speaking country, which language Spanish-speaking people do not esteem as highly as they do English and French!"[117]

Some Spanish-speaking men, like Cuban delegate Herminio Portell Vilá, however, voiced strong support for what Bertha Lutz accomplished in Montevideo. When asked in an interview for a Cuban newspaper if "from the point of view of women's issues . . . there [were] some practical results in Montevideo," Portell Vilá replied, "I think so, at least in proving that it's necessary to change the organization and functioning of the Inter-American Commission of Women, so poorly directed by Doris Stevens and her minions." He called the "lack of leadership" of the IACW "most heartbreaking" and distinguished Lutz's efforts: "The Latin American women should be aware that the Conference approved the rotation of the presidency of this Commission."[118]

Indeed, though Lutz's rotation proposal had gained only the status of an "aspiration," feminists did take note and would use this aspiration as the opening they needed for their next effort to overthrow Stevens at the 1938 Lima conference. Though Lutz would not speak for or with Spanish-speaking feminists, her actions at Montevideo had, as Portell Vilá described, provided an opening that had not existed before.

More immediately, and in spite of her lack of interest in Spanish-speaking leadership, Lutz's Montevideo actions also helped push forward a developing Pan-Hispanic feminism. In March 1934, Margarita Robles de Mendoza, the Mexican commissioner who had aided Stevens in Montevideo, latched upon the openings Lutz had forged to create an alternative feminist group, the Unión de Mujeres Americanas (UMA), organized by and for Spanish-speaking women. An elite, educated woman who had taken a central role in her country's suffrage movement, Robles de Mendoza had been the Mexican commissioner since 1930. Like Clara González before her, her chief complaint was that the commission's private U.S. sources of funding made it a "charity by North American women" and ensured "that the complete control of the work would always be under the jurisdiction of Doris Stevens." This control implied "imperialism."[119] Robles de Mendoza had urged Stevens to consider other funding options for Latin American delegates, to little effect.[120] When Lutz's rotation proposal failed to be an official resolution, Robles de Mendoza decided to found the UMA—a Latin American–led group that would unite "all women of the Americas who enlist to fight for their political, civil, social, and economic equality" and promote peace. Its official language would be Spanish.[121]

Just as Ofelia Domínguez Navarro had done years before when she sought support for her new feminist group, Robles de Mendoza enlisted Paulina Luisi, the esteemed "mother" of *feminismo americano*, for advice. Although they had never met, Robles de Mendoza wrote to Luisi, asking her to serve as the organization's president. She emphasized that, as a founding principle, Spanish-speaking feminists must be the leaders of Pan-American feminism. As Robles de Mendoza would later write, "Spanish American women should be the masters of our own destiny and ... it should be our hands and our minds that should mark the route that we are to follow."[122]

Unlike Bertha Lutz, who had dismissed Robles de Mendoza's idea in Buenos Aires, Paulina Luisi embraced it. "My friends have ... painted you as a terrible revolutionary [and] ... a terrible radical," Luisi responded to Robles de Mendoza, and "that's enough to bring you all my sympathies."[123] While Luisi wrote that she could not accept the presidency of the UMA—"it is the initiator who should assume the effective presidency during this early period of organization. No one better than you to carry it out and give it force"—she suggested some additions to the organization's constitution on which Robles de Mendoza had requested advice. Luisi recommended she specifically oppose a Catholic clergy–directed "feminism based on spiritual submission." She also wrote that "it is indispensable to signal in its statutes, that the UMA is independent of all internal political parties, in each country."[124]

All of Luisi's other revisions addressed "avoiding one nation of preference over the others, having supremacy"; she pointed out that "you must anticipate this especially with the United States" and with Doris Stevens. So as not to repeat the mistakes of the IACW, Luisi suggested a rotation apparatus very similar to that which Lutz had advised at the Montevideo conference, with a new president among the American nations every five years. Reiterating her wish that the UMA be efficient and lasting, Luisi wrote, "I repeat, I desire the formation of a group with seriousness/reliability and guarantees of regular work, of a way that it can stand up solidly with the other major world organizations." She recognized that while "the other feminists in the world have a low concept" of Latin American women, "it is necessary to demonstrate . . . that although until today we have not been able to organize ourselves we are just as capable as the others" of doing so. "Your beautiful initiative can do it. . . . We are doing something serious and lasting."[125] Over the years that followed, the UMA would grow and thrive, counting thirty-nine affiliated groups by October 1935.

Although founded as an alternative to the IACW, in the years to come the UMA and many other Latin American feminist groups would continue to ally themselves with the IACW Equal Rights and Equal Nationality Treaties, which went on to have significant juridical effects. Countries throughout the hemisphere, after years of persistence by the commission, passed laws for women's nationality rights. In 1934, after sustained pressure by the NWP, even the U.S. Senate, so opposed to treaty ratification when it impeded states' rights, ratified the treaty, which led to a legislative act granting married women's equal nationality rights.[126] By July 1935, Mexico, Honduras, and Chile had also ratified the treaty, and Latin American delegates helped push the Equal National and Equal Rights Treaties into the Assembly of the League of Nations.[127] That year, a Mexican newspaper article titled "The Great Feminist Battle of Montevideo" celebrated the inter-American feminist movement. It highlighted the Montevideo conference for its passage of a nationality treaty and for gaining signatures from four countries for its Equal Rights Treaty—a feat that many statesmen had formerly believed impossible.[128]

Although many Latin American feminists supported these treaties, they did not believe international law was the only way to measure the achievements of or to advance *feminismo americano*. Grassroots organizing remained a cornerstone, and the UMA was only one of several new engines for activism in the Americas that would emerge in the mid-1930s. Bertha Lutz may have believed they had no "organizational center," but feminists from Spanish-speaking countries were, in fact, taking the lead. These women would embark on a more collaborative movement than in the past, standing for the causes they believed in most strongly. With the rise of fascism throughout the world, the years immediately following the Montevideo conference would reveal great threats to women's rights. Antifascism would prove to be the spark that would mobilize Spanish-speaking feminists, as Luisi predicted, to do something "serious and lasting."

CHAPTER FIVE

The Birth of Popular Front Pan-American Feminism

✼　✼　✼

On New Year's Day 1934, while still in Montevideo, Doris Stevens sent a final cable to Marta Vergara, the Chilean representative of the Inter-American Commission of Women (IACW), insisting that they meet in Santiago.[1] Over the past weeks, Stevens had repeatedly tried to contact Vergara, frantically calling her from telephone booths in the hotel and the city and sending her five telegrams in the heat of conference events, begging her aid.[2] Vergara had responded only once, in Spanish: "Impossible to go, explanation will come by letter."[3] Though flush with the commission's success, Stevens was rattled by Bertha Lutz's and the U.S. State Department's efforts to thwart her. She knew that such challenges to her leadership would only increase at future Pan-American conferences.[4] And she believed that Vergara could help. On January 2, which also happened to be Vergara's thirty-sixth birthday, Stevens flew to Santiago to meet with Vergara before a steamer would take Stevens from Valparaíso back to New York.[5]

Stevens's overtures surprised Marta Vergara, who, months earlier, had not only told Stevens that she could not go to Montevideo but also tendered her resignation from the IACW altogether. Vergara had worked with Stevens for nearly three years on married women's nationality rights in the League of Nations. But, like many other Spanish-speaking feminists, she had grown disenchanted with Stevens's controlling leadership and promotion of a feminism defined exclusively around equal civil and political rights. Vergara, now collaborating with the flourishing Communist Party of Chile, rejected these goals as "anti-revolutionary." Her resolve held over the lunch she had with Stevens in Santiago after the Montevideo conference. Vergara offered Stevens sympathy but no promise to renew her commission work or to become its future chair, an idea that Stevens may have floated as a way to preempt Bertha Lutz's rotation proposal. Nonetheless, when they parted, Stevens pledged her loyalty to Vergara, saying, "If there is any time you are in trouble and the Commission can do something for you, it will."[6]

Almost two years later, Vergara would have cause to remember those words. She would rekindle her work with the IACW as she galvanized new antifascist feminist activism in Chile. Their new collaboration aided both women and the commission itself; Vergara would utilize Stevens's and the commission's help strategically while supporting the IACW and its equal rights treaties. In the process, Vergara, energized by a growing global Popular Front movement, also helped launch a new phase of *feminismo americano* distinguished by the goals that she, Paulina Luisi, Ofelia Domínguez Navarro, and Clara González had long sought.

In the time between 1933, when she broke with the commission, and 1935, when she reunited with it, Vergara's commitments did not alter as much as the world changed. The historical conjuncture of the Great Depression, the inauguration of the Good Neighbor Policy, the rise of fascism in Europe, and the subsequent ascent of the Popular Front focused new inter-American attention on state-led economic development, innovative social policies, workers' rights, and antifascism. The Popular Front, the 1935 Communist International's call to unite with democratic and bourgeois groups in a common front against fascism, resonated profoundly in Latin America. After the Great Depression, numerous right-wing authoritarian populist regimes that resembled European fascism had emerged. Antifascist mobilizations grew in Latin America alongside the swelling ranks of communist and socialist parties in the Americas, the transnational anti-imperialist Aprista movement, and pacifist movements that identified U.S. and British capitalist imperialism as responsible for the bloody Chaco War that had raged for three years and claimed so many lives. Latin American communists, intellectuals, workers, feminists, and pacifists joined the global Popular Front while also forging their own inter-American variants. Perhaps more than any other event, the Spanish Civil War, launched by the overthrow of the Popular Front Spanish government in 1936, activated energetic antifascist mobilizations throughout Latin America around Republican Spain.[7] New groups underscored the connections between U.S. imperialism, global capitalism, and fascism and drew strong parallels between European fascism and Latin American forms of authoritarianism.

The Popular Front had a vital feminist counterpart. Engaging with pacifist and communist women, with workers, and with liberal feminists who were alarmed by the way fascism systematically stripped women's rights, leftist feminists throughout the Americas and Europe began to couple demands for women's equal economic and political rights and social welfare. This new focus on antifascism, peace, and working women's rights paved the way for the emergence of new, robust Popular Front feminist groups in the Americas. In 1935, Marta Vergara cofounded one of these groups in Chile, the Movimiento Pro-

Emancipación de las Mujeres de Chile (MEMCh, or Movement for the Emancipation of Chilean Women). In the context of the Popular Front's effort to reconcile democratic and communist goals, the IACW's Equal Rights and Equal Nationality treaties gained purchase as being compatible with antifascism, world peace, and social and economic justice. Popular Front Latin American feminist groups like MEMCh utilized the commission and its treaties now as part of the fight against fascism. In the process, Latin American feminists forged a new *feminismo americano*—Popular Front Pan-American feminism, an internationalist feminism that combined social democratic labor concerns with international equal rights demands in the context of an antifascist, inter-American solidarity.

Marta Vergara believed that transnational solidarity for women's rights could help defeat fascism and that transnational solidarity against fascism could also promote women's rights. She was pivotal to forging Popular Front Pan-American feminism. The evolution of her international activism, combined with her at-times ambivalent friendship with Doris Stevens, provides critical insight into its development. The two women relied on each other for vital personal as well as organizational support, even though unequal power dynamics structured their relationship. In spite of those power struggles, Vergara cultivated the influence of the commission determinedly. She managed to influence a broad, significant shift in inter-American feminism toward an ideal of social democracy that balanced the needs of the individual with those of the community. Drawing on previous efforts of Clara González, Ofelia Domínguez Navarro, Paulina Luisi, and Bertha Lutz, Vergara effectively widened the liberal "equal rights" agenda of the IACW to support a key demand of leftist feminists: state-sponsored maternity legislation. She helped make the international women's rights movement more inclusive of working-class women. At the same time, the Popular Front Pan-American feminism Vergara also upheld grassroots activism and internationalist antifascist solidarity as just as important to global feminism as women's rights treaties. It was a *feminismo americano* that would become more relevant to wide swaths of women in the Americas.

Marta Vergara's Feminist Evolution

Born in the port city of Valparaíso, Chile, into an aristocratic but impoverished family, Vergara was a young child when the earthquake of 1906 resulted in the loss of her father's merchant job. Her mother died soon after. In the early 1920s, Vergara's brief marriage to an artist ended in divorce, and by the late 1920s she had established a name for herself as a journalist in Santiago. A self-described modernist influenced by avant-garde art, literature, and journalism, Vergara was aware of the 1923 Pan-American conference in Santiago and its women's rights resolutions but initially believed these efforts of a slightly older generation of

Marta Vergara, Chilean representative of the IACW, date unknown. Courtesy of the
Schlesinger Library, Radcliffe Institute, Harvard University.

Chilean feminists were old-fashioned and "unpoetic."[8] When General Carlos Ibáñez del Campo assumed a military dictatorship over Chile in 1927, Vergara fled to Paris, where she worked as a correspondent for El Mercurio, Chile's largest newspaper. Through her political and literary contacts, she landed the opportunity to represent Chile at the Hague Codification Conference in 1930.[9] The Chilean delegation sought an educated female representative, and when Vergara learned that her travel and accommodation expenses would be covered, she decided to go.[10]

This experience changed her life. Upon her arrival at The Hague, Vergara met Alice Paul and Doris Stevens, who introduced her to the Inter-American Commission of Women.[11] This engagement awoke Vergara to feminism. She played a significant role as a delegate in the 1930 conference, especially since Chile was one of the few countries that made no distinction between women's and men's nationality rights.[12] Vergara rose to the occasion, giving her first public speech and lucidly promoting women's legal equality with men.[13] For the next two years, she became a key advocate in the debates on nationality in the League of Nations, working closely with Paul, who lived for periods of time in Geneva in those years, but even more with Doris Stevens.[14]

Stevens served as Vergara's mentor. Vergara initially found Stevens slightly intimidating and immediately recognized the unequal power dynamics structuring their relationship. Stevens, ten years older than Vergara, spoke to her "patiently, as to a child," still "in kindergarten of the feminist school."[15] They communicated in French since Stevens was not fluent in Spanish, nor Vergara in English.

Vergara was also aware of the differences in their politics. Vergara, who immersed herself in leftist circles in Paris, had been studying the Communist Manifesto (1848) and the works of Plejánov, Lenin, and Trotsky, and international events were moving her even more toward the left.[16] The Great Power leadership of the League of Nations disillusioned her; she believed it supported the economic and political hegemony of capitalist countries, marginalized Latin American nations, and did nothing to stop the spread of fascism in Europe or Japan's aggressions against China. She found the Soviet Union's demands for an overthrow of capitalism and universal disarmament the most compelling answers to the world's troubling problems.[17] Socialist thought infused Vergara's feminist politics, which combined a demand for individual women's rights with collectivism and social solidarity. Her notion of feminism held both the individual and the family as "fundamental unit[s] of . . . social and political organization," in keeping with the thought of many Latin American feminists before her.[18]

These views starkly contrasted with the individualism of Stevens and Paul, whose lack of social and economic analysis, Vergara believed, went hand in hand with their denial of the problem of U.S. imperialism. Such views instructed their "concentrated" focus on "equal rights" for women, Vergara wrote, to the exclusion of "other social injustices."[19]

Despite these ideological differences, Vergara admired Stevens's determined promotion of international "equal rights," and Stevens viewed Vergara as central to rallying Latin American feminist support for the IACW.[20] After the ouster of Ibáñez from power in Chile, Vergara returned home in 1932 with plans to organize women for the IACW.[21] She met with Chilean commissioner Aída Parada, who explained to Vergara how Stevens had undermined her, Ofelia Domínguez Navarro, and Clara González at the 1930 IACW conference in Havana. Though Parada officially cited poor health as the reason for her resignation from the IACW, she was concerned about Stevens's rule over the commission.[22] These warnings did not dissuade Vergara, who filled Parada's spot as the commission's Chilean representative and initially immersed herself in this role.

However, Vergara's desire to foster women's equal rights activism at home dissipated as she allied herself more with the Communist Party of Chile. If her socialist consciousness had been stirred in Europe, it became inflamed upon her return to Chile, "totally paralyzed" in economic crisis.[23] Political tumult and grinding poverty characterized the years following Ibáñez's ouster. Struggling with massive problems in public housing, health, and social welfare, Chile became a laboratory of broad-based socialist and communist thought and organizing, into which Vergara threw herself.[24] In 1933, a friend introduced Vergara to Marcos Chamudes, a Communist Party official with whom she became romantically involved and whom she married. Although Vergara did not officially join the party until 1936, she became a heartfelt communist sympathizer.

Given this political and personal history, when Stevens asked Vergara to join her at the 1933 Pan-American conference in Montevideo, Vergara refused. In a letter relinquishing ties with the IACW, Vergara also marked her ideological split from the commission with a linguistic break. After years of communicating with Stevens in French, since Stevens did not speak Spanish, Vergara wrote to Stevens in Spanish. She never wrote to Stevens in French again.

Allying herself with the Chilean Communist Party, Vergara explained that U.S. economic imperialism represented "the highest stage of bourgeois capitalism," against which she and others in the Americas were mobilizing a "global resurgence, and in particular, an American resurgence."[25] Furthermore, Vergara explained, the rights goals the IACW supported were meaningless to the working women with whom she now collaborated. The working woman, she wrote,

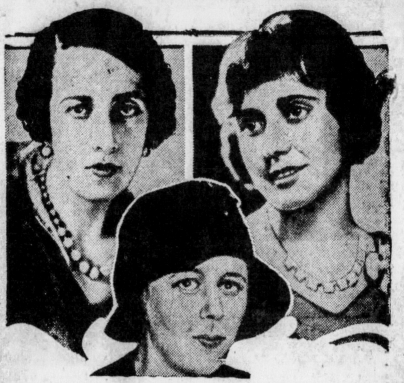

Lead Pan-American Feminists

These women are outstanding at the annual conference of the Inter-American Commission of Women held in conjunction with the Pan-American Conference in Montevideo, Uruguay. Above left, Marta Vergara, Chilean journalist who is on the Consultative Committee on Nationality; right, Carmen Velasco Portinho de Lutz, Brazilia, engineer; below, Doris Stevens of Nebraska, chairman of the commission, who is a militant leader of the feminist cause.

"Lead Pan-American Feminists," Chillicothe (Ohio) Gazette, November 21, 1933, 6.
A number of U.S. newspapers published this image and headline before the Pan-American conference in Montevideo. Stevens anticipated Vergara's help there. Left to right: Marta Vergara, Doris Stevens, Carmen Velasco Portinho de Lutz. Image from newspapers.com.

"understands that . . . she is going to win little with [civil and political rights] if she is also still a slave of the economic system." Women's political rights would have to come in "second place" to the class fight.[26]

Even when Vergara made plaintive appeals to Stevens to recognize their irreconcilable differences, she underscored her continuing personal admiration for Stevens:

> Now you can understand, Doris . . . you and I are in different camps. The aspiration toward a socialist society is not a new one for me. What is more or less new is my actual . . . work toward obtaining it. . . . Thus, Doris, I will continue working for equality, but on the road toward a society without classes. And since this is not your point of view, since you collaborate with the Pan-American Union, and, with you, all the Commission, we become enemies. And this, despite all the personal sympathy I have for you.[27]

The distress Vergara felt upon her break with Stevens was real, but Vergara did not reveal all the reasons behind her decision not to join Stevens in Montevideo. Though Vergara still believed in feminist goals, Chamudes and other Chilean Communist Party officials blocked her attendance at the Pan-American conference. Their disapprobation held in spite of Vergara's insistence that she "could work with feminists and attack imperialism."[28]

Perhaps suspecting that Vergara was not entirely speaking for herself, Stevens did not give up hope that Vergara would join her in Montevideo. In the flurry of telegrams Stevens sent Vergara before and during the conference, she insisted that she, Stevens, did "not represent" the U.S. government. Stevens even offered to wire Vergara money for airfare to Montevideo and lodging at the Parque Hotel there.[29] Given the robust help that Vergara gave the commission in the League of Nations, Stevens viewed her as especially influential. Although Vergara was touched by Stevens's suggestion and her visit to Santiago after the conference, she remained immovable on the question of rejoining the commission.[30]

Over the next few years, however, the rise of fascism caused Vergara to long for the commission's feminist commitments. "The special contempt fascism held for women," Vergara later recalled, was making her "more and more inclined towards a women's organization, organized by the communists" in Chile and globally. Hitler's Germany and Mussolini's Italy were actively "debasing [women] and stripping" them of their rights.[31] On the heels of his 1933 solidification of power in Germany, Hitler launched an aggressive campaign to remove women from all public positions, citing "motherhood" as the number one aim of women's education.[32] Mussolini enacted similar policies.[33] However, Vergara received no help from the Chilean Communist Party, which routinely neglected women's issues. When she broached the subject with militant members, they "either insulted me or simply mocked me."[34]

Popular Front Feminism

Vergara found the inspiration for a women's group organized by both communists and left-liberal feminists in the 1934 Comité Mondial des Femmes contre la Guerre et le Fascisme (World Congress of Women against War and Fascism) in Paris. Although Vergara did not attend the conference, she read with high expectations about this women's congress that united over 1,000 communists, socialist reformers, and women's rights activists. This women's congress had grown out of the Amsterdam-Pleyel movement against war created by Dutch and French intellectuals in 1932 and was one the earliest and most important international meetings to rally women against fascism.[35] It prefigured the official creation of the Popular Front in 1935, when the Communist International formally endorsed alliance between communist and socialist parties in an antifascist struggle.[36]

The congress revealed a distinctly feminist Popular Front politics, concerned with working women's equal rights, social welfare legislation that addressed the needs of mothers and children, and support for democracy and peace. Its resolutions demanded women's "complete civil and political emancipation," equal right to work, equal pay for equal work, and equal access to all social services that male workers received relating to unemployment insurance and family subsidies. Delegates also called for state-sponsored maternity legislation for all working women.[37]

Importantly, this congress was also interracial and included antiracism and anticolonialism as key goals. Attendees included four African American women from the United States, including a sharecropper from Alabama who compared fascism in Europe with Jim Crow in the United States.[38] The conference's final manifesto included a resolution demanding freedom for the Scottsboro Boys unjustly imprisoned on charges of raping white women, one demanding the liberation of all colonial and semi-colonial people, and one rejecting "nationalism, chauvinism, and racism that excite people against each other and throw them into an imperialist war."[39]

This conference raised the consciousness of feminists throughout the world to the need to confront racism, fascism, and imperialism as interconnected struggles, and it proved critical to launching new, broad forms of left and left-liberal feminisms throughout the Americas and the world.[40] The international umbrella group that it created, the World Committee of Women against War and Fascism, formed robust national chapters in England, France, and Spain, where celebrated Spanish Civil War fighter Dolores Ibárruri became its leader, as well as in Mexico, Cuba, Chile, Argentina, Uruguay, and elsewhere.[41]

Paulina Luisi, one of the organizers of the 1934 Paris conference, formed the Unión Femenina contra la Guerra (Women's Union against War) soon after it. This group was a pluralist association of twenty-eight women's organizations in Uruguay. Over the next few years the Unión demanded international women's rights and raised funds for the resistance in the Spanish Civil War and for Ethiopia against Italy's 1935 invasion.[42] In Cuba, Ofelia Domínguez Navarro's organization, the Unión Radical de Mujeres (the new name of the Unión Laborista de Mujeres), learned about the Paris congress from the Mexican Communist feminist Consuelo Uranga, who had represented Mexico and Cuba there and visited Havana afterward. In response, Domínguez's group organized the Frente Único de Mujeres Contra la Guerra, la Intervención, y el Fascismo in Cuba that united over twenty women's organizations and declared their front against fascism, war, U.S. imperialism, and racism. Domínguez and the new group supported the Scottsboro Boys from Cuba.[43]

The vibrant growth of antifascist feminism abroad and in Latin America and the powerful rise of Popular Front ideologies in Chile, specifically, led to a profound growth of antifascist feminism in Chile, with Vergara's help. In the wake of the 1934 Paris conference and the 1935 Comintern support for the Popular Front, Vergara found she could openly rekindle her "equal rights" feminist concerns and fuse them with social justice and antifascist commitments.[44] As she recalled in her memoirs, "The Chilean Communist Party believed . . . that the country's revolution would be bourgeois-democratic in nature," thus paving the way for her to reconnect to feminist organizing: "Why then exclude bourgeois women? Why not help them obtain the benefits enumerated in the platform?"[45]

In 1935 Vergara cofounded a new feminist organization that would uphold these Popular Front feminist ideals in Chile, the Movimiento pro Emancipación de la Mujer Chilena. A cross-class organization, MEMCh soon gained support from the growing Popular Front coalition of Radical, Socialist, and Communist Parties that would control the executive branch of Chile from 1938 to 1947.[46] It became the most important feminist group in the country, including, according to one estimate, several hundred thousand women from throughout Chile.[47] It organized working women with existing unions and organized rural women in their neighborhoods.

MEMCh's manifesto called for women's "economic, juridical, biological, and political emancipation." The group called for legal abortion and birth control access. Significantly, the group connected the goals and women's equal economic rights with antifascism: "Let us fight against fascism, because it tends to

The MEMCh symbol illustrated its Popular Front feminist politics: a woman holding a child in one arm while demanding her autonomy and leading a group of women doing the same. From Diamela Eltit, Crónica del sufragio femenino en Chile (Santiago: Chile Servicio Nacional de la Mujer SERNAM, 1994), 64.

deprive women of her most elementary rights, considering her only qualified to engage in domestic work."[48] But MEMCh urged rights for domestic workers as well, demanding maternity legislation as a "social right" for all workers, including domestic and rural workers. Indeed, MEMCh's blending of "equal rights" demands for the vote, equal civil rights, and social and economic rights would be the hallmark of Popular Front feminist groups throughout the hemisphere.[49]

The 1936 International Labor Organization Conference in Santiago

The Popular Front feminist movement also enabled Vergara to rekindle her connections with the Inter-American Commission of Women, whose equal rights treaties gained new relevance. The 1934 World Congress of Women against War and Fascism in Paris had endorsed the IACW and its treaty as "particularly heartening at this time when the forces of reaction are taking away from women in Europe a large part of their freedom."[50] Vergara knew the inter-American group would also give legitimacy to the budding MEMCh.

Thus, when Doris Stevens wrote to Vergara in November 1935, beseeching her, as the Chilean commissioner, to reconnect with the IACW and be its mouthpiece at the upcoming International Labor Organization (ILO) conference in Santiago in January, Vergara agreed.[51] The ILO had been established in Geneva after the First World War to examine and propose international solutions to labor problems, and the Santiago meeting would be the organization's first regional, Pan-American conference. For Vergara, it was also an opportunity to announce the creation of MEMCh and to unite its goals with an international antifascist feminist movement.

Yet Stevens and Vergara butted heads while forging their agenda, particularly around the question of maternity legislation. The ILO had traditionally supported protective legislation for working women, including its 1919 Maternity Convention, which stipulated benefits for women during a period of maternity leave. Stevens asked Vergara to take a stand against these protective policies. Like others in the U.S. National Woman's Party (NWP), Stevens believed that any asymmetrical provision bearing on sex, including maternity legislation, could violate equality. The NWP deemed the ILO Maternity Convention as coercive and as treating women as a "class" beneath men. Such legislation, the group held, took away a woman's choice, harmed her ability to compete with men, and placed the burden of the pregnancy on the employer.[52] "The state of pregnancy," Stevens wrote to Vergara, was a "special case" that "should be so treated if and when it arises." Upholding "equality" meant that they were "not obliged to advocate a particular method by which the special situation should be handled." But, Stevens explained, when the topic came up at the conference, Vergara should advocate a method by which the state would pay for maternity leave, and demonstrate that "it can be done without penalizing women."[53]

In the United States, maternity legislation did not exist, despite some experiments with state-sponsored maternal aid, including the short-lived 1921 Sheppard-Towner Act and the 1935 Aid to Families with Dependent Children program of the Social Security Act. Mainstream discussions of maternity legislation typically framed it not as a "right" or as compatible with insurance benefits but rather in the more stigmatizing category of "public assistance."[54] Neither Stevens's National Woman's Party nor the influential social reformers and policy makers in the Women's and Children's Bureaus promoted maternity legislation as a "right" in the 1920s or 1930s. In fact, the latter group of women opposed the NWP's ERA in part because it might hamper maternity legislation for working women. However, this group of reformers also did not promote such legislation themselves, due to their deep ambivalence about wage-earning motherhood.[55] Later, during and after the Second World War, it would be working women themselves who demanded national attention to maternity legislation in the United States.

But in the 1930s, Latin American feminists and workers pushed their U.S. counterparts on the issue in regional meetings. Budding labor legislation and welfare states in Latin America were incorporating more explicit provisions for maternity legislation than in the United States. Brazil's revised 1934 constitution, for instance, adopted the 1919 ILO Maternity Convention and included maternity legislation as a social welfare benefit while maintaining a commitment to "equal rights" for women in its new labor codes.[56] In 1934, Chile also ratified the 1919 ILO Maternity Convention.

The 1936 ILO conference would throw into stark relief these differences between Latin American and U.S. attention to maternity legislation. Later, in a confidential report to the U.S. Labor Department, the U.S. delegate and Women's Bureau member Frieda Miller puzzled over the emphasis of Chilean delegates on maternity legislation, calling it "striking evidence of difference of viewpoint and interest from that which would have animated any like committee in the United States ... [where] provision for the family is mainly outside the field that we consider suitable for labor legislation." She pondered to Frances Perkins about "this great difference in focus of interest," wondering if in Latin America "their concept of the position of women in the social and economic scheme of things is different from ours."[57]

Indeed, these differences reflected the more robust notion throughout Latin America that the "family" and the "individual" were fundamental political units, as Vergara had noted years earlier. While Latin American maternity legislation remained poorly enforced and while it also often reflected ideas about the protection of women as a weaker group, growing numbers of Latin American feminists were demanding the inclusion of provision of the family into labor legislation in a way that was pointedly not maternalist. Popular Front feminists increasingly called for maternity legislation as a "social right" so as to not penalize working women. Among this group, the threat that fascism posed to women under the guise of "protection" was helping build consensus against protective labor legislation, with the exception of what they now called "social rights" of maternity legislation.

Thus, while Vergara responded to Stevens that she would happily represent the IACW in Santiago, she explicitly asserted that she would promote both equal rights *and* maternity legislation, framed as a right. MEMCh already planned a robust campaign at the ILO, she told Stevens.[58] Although Chile's labor code, in keeping with the 1919 ILO convention, stipulated a maternity allowance for pregnant women, it asked employers to pay 50 percent, which they usually sidestepped. Vergara explained that she and MEMCh wanted the state to pay for the entirety of maternity benefits and would, thus, explicitly argue for it. Furthermore, her group sought maternity legislation not only for employees in the industrial trades and commerce—those usually considered under ILO codes—but also for domestic, hospital, and agricultural workers.[59] In Chile, domestic workers represented approximately 40 percent of female workers.[60] This attention to household work resonated with the efforts, as well, of black leftist feminists and workers throughout the Americas, who were organizing the first domestic workers' unions in the United States, Uruguay, and Brazil in these years.[61]

Though uneasy about having a commissioner argue aggressively for maternity legislation for any women workers, Stevens did not quibble with Vergara, whose support for "equal rights" she desperately needed. While outside the United States, in both Europe and Latin America, the threat fascism posed to women's rights was helping build consensus *against* protective legislation for working women, in the United States, the Great Depression stoked both the perceived need for protective labor legislation and controversy around the NWP's equal rights agenda.[62] Stevens sent Vergara missives of support and rallied a number of IACW delegates from Panama, Guatemala, Haiti, and Argentina to send Vergara resolutions supporting equal economic rights as fundamental to the Equal Rights Treaty.[63]

Vergara used these missives in a large rally that she organized in December 1935 in Santiago immediately before the ILO conference. In what was MEMCh's first large public meeting, numerous women gave speeches urging delegates from throughout the Americas who had descended on Santiago for the conference to promote "equal rights" for working women. In Vergara's own rousing speech, she included messages of support from the IACW. Contrasting the recent triumphs of the commission at the 1933 Montevideo conference with the growth of fascism in Europe that was stripping women of their rights, she urged Latin American ILO delegates to pass no convention that would put women and men on unequal footing in the economic struggle.[64]

Ultimately, due to the untiring efforts of MEMCh leaders and female workers and their collaboration with Chilean labor delegates, the 1936 ILO conference affirmed values of equal minimum wages, equal hours of work, and work of "equal responsibility" for men and women. It also endorsed MEMCh's proposals for state-sponsored maternity legislation for "all women who work for someone else," thus acceding to demands for inclusion of domestic and agricultural workers, even if not naming them outright.[65] The strong emphasis that Chilean and other Latin American delegates placed on maternity legislation would influence the agenda of the next inter-American ILO conference in 1939 in Havana that took up this issue centrally.[66]

Nonetheless, Vergara deemed the results of the conference to be "superficial."[67] She remained disheartened by the "definite gap" she saw "between the conditions of women presented by laws and reality." Over the course of the year after the ILO conference, Vergara pushed Stevens to expand the IACW's work: "I know that the mission of the Commission is officially . . . juridical, but in order not to separate ourselves from reality, we ought to do other work indirectly."[68] The commission, she wrote several months later, "is in a certain way just a technical organization at the margin of the [national and grassroots feminist] organizations themselves." Vergara suggested collaborating with women workers to "hear from their own lips what they want and to what they are opposed."[69] She urged Stevens to implement "a minimum program of action" that would energize women from various backgrounds throughout the Americas, similar to the one MEMCh had launched to great effect in Chile.[70]

Stevens consistently rebuffed Vergara's class commitments, either not responding to these demands or minimizing them. Stevens also downplayed the work that Vergara had done in favor of maternity legislation. When Vergara wrote a lengthy report on the outcomes of the ILO conference at Stevens's request, the NWP organ *Equal Rights* published an adulterated version of her article, omitting the sections that explained efforts for maternity legislation and keeping intact those relating to women's equal rights.[71]

Vergara nonetheless continued working with Stevens, whom she still admired, in part because she viewed the IACW as an important shield against fascist threats to women's rights. Several months after the ILO conference, when the Chilean government proposed an unequal minimum wage for men and women, Vergara reminded Stevens of the promise of help she had pledged Vergara several years earlier. MEMCh called the Chilean government's proposal "fascist" and in stark contradiction to its commitments at the recent ILO conference.[72] After Vergara appealed to the IACW, Stevens quickly came to Vergara's aid, sending cables to the Chilean legislature against the minimum wage law, and urging commission delegates in other countries to do the same while also sending Vergara words of support and encouragement.[73] Their activism was successful, and months later this proposed change was overturned.

Yet over the next year, Vergara's affection for Stevens would be strained by the growing gulf between their goals. The two women would confront their differences when they met again in Buenos Aires at the end of 1936. There, at two different peace conferences, Vergara and Stevens worked together for the commission's equal rights resolutions, while Vergara simultaneously sought to broaden the IACW's goals. At the same time, Vergara would also work separately from, and to some degree at cross-purposes with, Stevens. Indeed, Vergara found far greater kinship with Argentinian women who were building a pacifist and antifascist movement in their country. With them, she would promote a distinctly antifascist *feminismo americano*.

Popular Front Pan-American Feminism at the Buenos Aires Peace Conferences

Soon after the ILO conference in Santiago, U.S. president Franklin D. Roosevelt announced that the Inter-American Conference for the Maintenance of Peace would take place in Buenos Aires. The growth of fascism and its threat of encroachment into the minds, hearts, and markets of Latin America dramatically influenced the development of his Good Neighbor Policy. The goals of the conference included Pan-American neutrality in the face of the coming war in Europe as well as enhanced trade and social welfare legislation in the Americas.

As a counterpart, immediately preceding this official conference, the Socialist Party of Argentina planned its own "Popular Peace Conference" or "People's Peace Conference." Leading it was Paulina Luisi's old friend Alicia Moreau de

Justo, Argentinean socialist feminist. To challenge as well as influence the Conference for the Maintenance of Peace that followed it, the People's Conference planned to discuss reduction of armaments, free exchange of people and ideas, anti-imperialism, and antifascism. In Spain, Franco had begun his offensive against the Popular Front government in July 1936, and the Spanish Civil War was galvanizing new antifascist activism in the Americas; conference delegates sought to send solidarity to Republican Spain. The conference also supported the Aprista movement, urging the freedom of imprisoned Peruvian leaders Víctor Raúl Haya de la Torre and Magda Portal.

While women's rights were not on the agenda of either conference, despite Stevens and Vergara's lobbying for their inclusion in the official one, Stevens decided to attend both conferences and push women's rights into the agendas.[74] Recognizing her friend's influence among leftists in Latin America, Stevens urged Vergara to join her.[75] Vergara agreed to meet Stevens in Buenos Aires to support equal rights, but she reiterated that the IACW should also advocate antifascism and peace "with new vigor" at these conferences. In the pages of MEMCh's organ, La Mujer Nueva, Vergara was promoting a feminism based on solidarity with Republican Spain and with people around the world oppressed by fascism, noting that "women are the first victims of war, as we have seen with the invasion of Ethiopia." It was imperative, Vergara wrote to Stevens before the conference, for the sake of women around the world that the commission take a definitive stand "before the danger of a world conflagration."[76] Stevens, however, quickly dismissed Vergara's request, explaining that they must prioritize their one single goal in Buenos Aires: "women's rights," not "peace."[77]

In spite of Stevens's dismissal, Vergara resolved to promote her own agenda in Buenos Aires and organize with like-minded women there. She even announced this goal in La Mujer Nueva before the conference. Airing her suspicions about the sincerity behind Roosevelt's benign-sounding "peace conference," Vergara noted that "Yankee imperialism's preferred mode of operating is through . . . penetration without pain." She assured readers that she would promote anti-imperialism, antifascism, and women's rights at both the official and popular conferences.[78]

Although Stevens was uninterested in advocating this broad, Popular Front platform, she did recognize its power. She sought to utilize Vergara's Popular Front credibility in Buenos Aires, urging Vergara that "the Movimiento [MEMCh] and not the Commission should take leadership in piloting the [equal rights] resolutions through" both conferences.[79] Stevens's alliance with Vergara would, she believed, convince like-minded Latin American diplomats to support a women's equal rights agenda. Such backing would also help defend her-

Members of the Confederación Femenina Argentina greet Marta Vergara (center) and Doris Stevens (far right) with flowers upon their arrival in Buenos Aires in November 1936. Courtesy of the Schlesinger Library, Radcliffe Institute, Harvard University.

self from the U.S. State Department, which she knew from the Montevideo conference would be vigilant about quashing Woman's Party activism in Buenos Aires.

Stevens and Vergara's collaborations began as soon as they arrived in Buenos Aires for the first Popular Peace Conference. After getting herself appointed on the Third Commission that would discuss the "free exchange of peoples and ideas," Vergara inserted a statement in support of women's equal rights into the conference resolutions.[80]

When Stevens and Vergara suggested rewording the Third Commission resolution to endorse the Equal Rights Treaty more explicitly, U.S. social reformer Josephine Schain interjected and argued against this plan.[81] A representative of Carrie Chapman Catt's organization the Cause and Cure of War, Schain had arrived to the Popular Peace Conference to denounce the Equal Rights Treaty if and when it was raised. Schain's presence there was in fact due to the dramatic conflict between Stevens and Bertha Lutz in Montevideo and the continuing pressure that Lutz placed on U.S. women to remove Stevens from leadership. On the urging of Katharine Lenroot, Lutz had conferred in Brazil with Frieda Miller, who traveled there after the ILO Santiago conference. Miller resolved to send Schain to the Popular Peace Conference in Buenos Aires. With the help of

Mary "Molly" Dewson, member of Roosevelt's Social Security Board, Miller also secured the appointment of their ally and former Democratic state senator Elise Musser as an official delegate to the governmental Buenos Aires peace conference.[82] Both Schain and Catt urged Bertha Lutz to also go to Buenos Aires, but Lutz refused, saying the 1933 Montevideo conference had traumatized her too much: "I beg of you not to send me to a Conference where Doris Stevens is."[83] Now, at the Popular Peace Conference in Buenos Aires, Josephine Schain acted on behalf of all of these women when she denounced the Equal Rights Treaty. It was too vague, she declared, and "it most certainly would do away with protective legislation for women so badly needed in South America."[84]

However, Stevens immediately and shrewdly framed Schain's comments as reflecting a dangerously far-right agenda. The notes of Stevens's secretary disclosed that when Schain mentioned "protective legislation" for working women, "there were whispers of fascism among delegates. Restriction had no standing at this conference which has devoted hours of debate against restrictions of all kinds.... Many ... delegates here have suffered under ... dictatorships."[85] Stevens capitalized on this moment, making a speech in Spanish. This would mark the first time she gave a speech in Spanish. She furthered the connections between "protection of women" and fascism, defending the Equal Rights Treaty in part by explaining that "Schain represented the extreme right wing of Feminism in the United States."[86] As Stevens acknowledged in a letter to her now-husband Jonathan Mitchell, "That was kind of mean in that left audience but there was nothing else to do."[87] In the United States, of course, the political register was actually reversed—on many social matters, Schain was to the left of the self-proclaimed "classic libertarian" and New Deal–despising Doris Stevens.[88] But Stevens, who coupled her support for equal rights for women with an impassioned plea for freedom of the imprisoned Aprista leader Magda Portal, won the crowd.[89]

In her speech, Stevens insisted that the Equal Rights Treaty was compatible with maternity legislation, reflecting Vergara's influence. Doing so marked the first time Stevens publicly cast the "equal rights" feminism of the IACW as consistent with social democratic goals and centrally concerned with working women and mothers. She also upheld the new constitution of Brazil—which assured equal rights in work, hours, and wages for men and women while also providing maternity legislation for working women—as a model of social democracy and framed Latin America as more progressive than the United States.[90] Her strategy succeeded. Not one vote favored revising the text, and the conference passed the equal rights resolution as drafted, recommending Western Hemisphere–wide adherence to the Equal Rights Treaty.[91]

While Vergara and Stevens were pleased with their victory at the People's

Peace Conference, serious cracks were emerging in their own "united front." At the conference, Vergara spoke out not only for women's rights but also for the free exchange of ideas, freedom of the press, and pacifist networks in the Americas. Stevens thought those efforts were wastes of time.[92] As Stevens later wrote to a colleague in the IACW, "Marta is whole-heartedly a communist now and it is hard to keep her attention on the position of women."[93]

In their personal interactions, Stevens deliberately avoided any discussion of Vergara's newfound communist commitments or personal life. Stevens disapproved of Vergara's recent marriage to Communist Party leader Marcos Chamudes, whom Stevens described to another commissioner as "a Jew, Rumanian by birth ... a communist, black-listed by the government, more or less always on the run, in and out of prison."[94] Their interactions were also somewhat limited since, as Vergara later recalled with some irony, during their month-long stay in Buenos Aires, Stevens used commission funding to stay at the opulent Hotel Alvear, along with Franklin Delano Roosevelt and the U.S. State Department delegates, while Vergara boarded at a small and inexpensive *casa de pensión*.[95]

These power dynamics and inequalities rankled Vergara, as did the fact that Stevens's public advocacy for state-sponsored maternity legislation was more calculated than sincere. Of Steven's speech in Spanish at the People's Peace Conference, Vergara later mused that perhaps for a moment, Stevens had been reliving her younger days of bohemian socialism in Greenwich Village but that, in reality, she was out of place at such a leftist gathering, "like ... a member of the Salvation Army [a group influential in the temperance movement] in a bar."[96]

The tensions between the two women emerged most meaningfully at Roosevelt's governmental conference that took place immediately after the People's Peace Conference. Vergara proposed to Stevens that they boycott the opening session where Roosevelt and other statesmen would speak, but Stevens refused. When, at that plenary, Liborio Justo, the Trotskyist son of Argentinian president Agustín Pedro Justo, called out from the packed rafters *"Abajo el imperialismo!"* (Down with imperialism!) as Roosevelt ascended the rostrum, Vergara raised her fist in the antifascist salute. Embarrassed, Stevens immediately clamped her hand onto Vergara's arm and lowered it.[97]

Although Stevens herself objected to the Roosevelt administration, she deemed working with heads of state critical to carrying their equal rights resolutions. She had hoped that Vergara would provide the lobbying support she had lent the IACW years ago in the League of Nations. Vergara, however, found working with governments "infinitely more" repugnant in Buenos Aires than she had in Geneva, "now that I was a communist."[98] Although Vergara agreed to lobby some Latin American delegates, she refused Stevens's request that she meet with Miguel Cruchaga, the Chilean minister of foreign relations who was the head of Chile's delegation and a noted anticommunist.[99] Stevens, disgruntled by Vergara's recalcitrance, reported to her Commission colleague that "a good deal of [Marta's] time in B.A. was spent conferring with her party colleagues, many of whom were there for the Peoples' Conference."[100]

Vergara was indeed conferring with party colleagues and with leftist feminists outside the halls of the official peace conference. Frustrated by the limitations of the IACW, she sought allies for the broader internationalist goals that she desired in an inter-American feminist movement. At the same time, Vergara did still deem the commission's equal rights treaties as vitally important, and she used her connections in Argentina to aid the IACW in a significant way.

While Stevens knew members of more elite and conservative Argentine women's groups, Vergara later recalled proudly that she connected Stevens with "the best group of women that could be found in Argentina."[101] Vergara introduced Stevens to the Unión Argentina de Mujeres (UAM), led by the famous writer Victoria Ocampo, along with Ana Rosa Schlieper de Martínez Guerrero, Susana Larguía, and communist sympathizer María Rosa Oliver.[102] Formed in 1936 in reaction to a proposed law that would have reduced married women's status to that of minors, the UAM collaborated with other progressive women's groups in Argentina in a broad, antifascist struggle for female suffrage, economic equality, and state-sponsored maternity legislation.[103] When Marta Vergara introduced them to Doris Stevens, these UAM participants eagerly engaged in collaborations on behalf of the Equal Rights Treaty.

As antifascists, some of these Argentine feminists were pleased that the Roosevelt administration assured nonintervention of the United States in the Americas and articulated a common vision for social democracy as a stronghold against fascism. In his speech at the opening plenary, Roosevelt emphasized continental neutrality in the face of war, social justice, and economic welfare, specifically pledging to support higher standards of living "for all our people" in the Americas.[104] This vision corresponded with his popular New Deal policies, as well as with welfare policies throughout the Americas that were establishing new rights to social security, work, unionization, rest and leisure time, food, clothing, housing, health care, and education.

Stevens, Vergara, and their new Argentine feminist allies sought to add "equality for women" to this list of social democratic goals. They knew it would be an uphill battle. The resolutions of the Popular Peace Conference had failed to influence the governmental Buenos Aires conference, and they would have to start from scratch. Early in the conference, Stevens divided the list of diplomats in attendance with Vergara and UAM leader Susana Larguía. Together, they rallied broad support among the Latin American diplomats for including women's rights in the conference's resolutions as part of a broader social justice agenda.

Here, Stevens again positioned herself in support of state-sponsored maternity leave for women.[105] Her explicit endorsement of Brazil's constitution in forwarding both equal rights and social democratic welfare helped influence Oswaldo Aranha, head of the Brazilian delegation at Buenos Aires. He agreed to introduce the topic of women's rights at the Sixth Commission on Intellectual Cooperation and Moral Disarmament.[106]

When members of the U.S. delegation, including female representative Elise Musser, made known their opposition to consideration of women's rights on familiar grounds that it would violate national sovereignty, Stevens and Vergara jointly drafted a statement that called on the Americas to establish international standards in women's rights as a bulwark against fascism. Vergara translated the statement into Spanish and circulated it for signatures.[107] Endorsed by the IACW's representatives from Cuba and Mexico, as well as by a number of women's groups of various political affiliations, the declaration read, "This Conference sets itself up . . . [as a] model . . . for Europe to follow. Women all over Europe at the present time who are suffering under regimes hostile to the full development of the talents of women, look with hope to this Conference for a model of how to treat all women as well as how to treat other bases of friction within and between States. The women of South and Central America insist that this matter has ceased to be of purely national concern."[108]

An international standard for women's rights, they indicated, would serve as a strong measure of democracy and peace against a rise of fascism. Stevens also sent a statement to the *New York Times* explaining that their plea "pointed to the vast number of dictatorships which throttle all domestic efforts to strengthen democracy, not only in Europe, but unhappily on this Continent."[109]

Although Brazil ultimately proposed a weaker version of the resolution than Stevens sought, merely recommending "the adoption of the most adequate legislation in order to recognize fully the rights and duties of citizenship" for women, she believed it was the best they could achieve.[110] Over sixty Argentine women's organizations, spearheaded by UAM and the Argentine Association for Women's Suffrage, petitioned the conference for its signature. While some of them utilized maternalist arguments that women, as mothers, were natural peacemakers, many more argued that fascism's deleterious effects on women demanded women's equal rights in any peace resolutions.[111] Stevens also rallied a number of supporters of the Equal Rights Treaty in the United States and internationally to send cables to the conference and the State Department. In the end, the women's rights resolution passed, even gaining the endorsement of the U.S. delegation.

The Confederación Continental de Mujeres por la Paz

Vergara and Stevens celebrated these accomplishments, seeing them as important milestones in women's hemispheric progress and as an antidote to global fascism. But by the end of the Buenos Aires conferences, their relationship had been irrevocably strained, even if they maintained affection for each other. When they said goodbye to each other in Buenos Aires, Vergara recalled, "Doris, hard Doris, implacable Doris, said goodbye to me with tears in her eyes. Perhaps she felt how much I liked her and admired her, although we were in opposite camps."[112]

They were in opposite camps, indeed. Vergara's fondness for Stevens and collaboration on the IACW's equal rights goals had not stopped her from working separately, outside of the conference halls, to organize a new inter-American feminist group that upheld the broader leftist commitments that Stevens had consistently rebuffed. Antifascist feminist organizing had been flourishing in Buenos Aires for some time before the two women arrived. In November 1936, immediately before both peace conferences, a number of Argentinian women had convened their own peace conference in the city and created a new organization—the Federación Argentina de Mujeres por la Paz. This group would ally with labor, peace, and feminist groups in Argentina to promote peace, antifascism, and feminism.[113] Led by pacifists Adelia di Carlo de Carimati and Susana G. de Lapacó, president and vice president of the Buenos Aires women's peace conference, respectively, the Federación sought connections with European affiliates in the World Congress of Women against War and Fascism, founded by the 1934 Paris congress.

Now they collaborated with Marta Vergara, who, particularly after clashing with Stevens in Buenos Aires, found in these women ideological soul mates. With Vergara's help, the Federación became the seedbed for a larger transnational organization of Latin American women united around these same goals.

Opposition to the narrow goals of the Doris Stevens–led IACW at least partially shaped the new inter-American group that Vergara formed with the Federación. Significantly, the Argentinian leaders of this group did not seek out Stevens's membership, but they did reach out to two of her most well known hemispheric rivals—Ofelia Domínguez Navarro and Bertha Lutz. The journalist Adelia di Carlo de Carimati was the Argentinian feminist to whom Domínguez had only a few years earlier urged the formation of "a broad Congress of Latin American women" and with whom Domínguez had shared her incriminating correspondence with Doris Stevens.[114] When Bertha Lutz had traveled to Buenos Aires after the 1933 Montevideo conference and met Argentinian feminists interested in forming a Latin American women's peace group, they were no doubt part of Carlo and Lapacó's group. They told her they planned to challenge Stevens's leadership by "organiz[ing] . . . a special gathering" of Latin American women only.[115] Later in 1938, Lapacó wrote to Lutz asking her to join their organization.[116]

In December 1936, following the Buenos Aires women's peace conference, Carlo and Lapacó worked with Marta Vergara and other women in Buenos Aires to form what Vergara called the Confederación Continental de Mujeres por la Paz (Continental Confederation of Women for Peace) composed by and for "*mujeres de América*" to promote women's rights, peace, and antifascism. Its name bore striking resemblance to that which Ofelia Domínguez had proposed to Carlo three years before. Domínguez's dream of a confederation of Latin American women was finally being realized.

When she returned to Chile from Buenos Aires, Vergara affiliated this Confederación with her national group, MEMCh, and with a number of other Chilean women's groups. In the same issue of MEMCh organ *La Mujer Nueva* that celebrated the IACW's work at the Buenos Aires conferences, Vergara also published another article announcing the formation of a new inter-American women's group. "This fight of women for peace and for their rights impelled the need to create an inter-American organization that works for the cause of the American woman," Vergara wrote. The Confederación would serve as an alternative to the IACW and promote *feminismo americano*. Significantly, Vergara did not tell Stevens about the formation of this new group.[117]

While Vergara withheld from Stevens information about the Confederación, she continued to write to Stevens about the IACW's international treaty work. Vergara viewed these treaties as influential tools for equality during a time when many governments were seeking to repeal women's rights. Although she did not deem juridical equality a panacea for working women's oppression, Vergara also knew that the moral influence of the commission and its equal rights treaties carried great weight in Latin American countries, including her own. After the Buenos Aires conferences, and after receiving numerous missives from the commission, the Chilean government finally reversed its plans to reduce working women's minimum wages to 20 percent less than men's. This was a huge feat. In *La Mujer Nueva*, Vergara credited the success to support received from UAM in Argentina and from the "prestigious" IACW "that fights for the full recognition of women's political, civil and economic rights ... [and] sent cables to the legislature asking for the removal of this inequality."[118]

Vergara's inclusion of "economic rights" here was significant. Her work in the 1936 ILO and peace conferences shifted the goals of the IACW toward more explicit class concerns. A few years later, in a departure from the NWP line, Stevens again voiced her support for maternity legislation in a memo the IACW distributed widely to feminist groups throughout Latin America titled "Maternity Legislation Not Incompatible with Equal Rights."[119] At the 1938 Pan-American conference in Lima, the IACW confirmed this position by announcing it was undertaking a Western Hemisphere–wide study of maternity legislation for working women.[120] The commission's new explicit goals concerning working women were in line with the expansion of health, welfare, social security, and labor agencies created throughout the Americas in the 1930s and with international concerns over working women demonstrated in ILO conferences. But they had been significantly guided by Marta Vergara and other leftist Popular Front feminists who were forging a new Pan-American feminism. Influenced by these feminists, the IACW was reflecting to a greater extent the brand of social democracy many Latin American feminists favored, one that combined individual sovereignty with social and economic justice.

The events in Buenos Aires — and the movement of the Equal Rights Treaty into economic and social ground — gained the attention of other pivotal inter-American feminists, like Paulina Luisi. In 1936, Luisi announced her firm support for the Equal Rights Treaty. Recanting her earlier belief that the treaty, signed in 1933 by the Terra dictatorship in Montevideo, was meaningless, she now asserted that it could help women's lives by promoting important economic and social change. In the face of retrenchment of women's right to work and denial of state-sponsored support for working women in fascist countries, she stated that "the words 'equal rights'" in the 1933 Montevideo Equal Rights Treaty "imply the equality of *economic rights* that we demand."[121] Directly foreshadowing later twentieth-century arguments for international human rights, Luisi explained that women's rights treaties were critical to overriding the actions of recalcitrant states and setting standards for others. By ratifying these international conventions, she wrote, "the state commits itself necessarily and formally to introducing in its national legislation this equality of rights, to denounce those existing international treaties and conventions that are opposed to this equality, and to modify the national laws contrary to this equality."[122]

Paulina Luisi would also come out in great support for the Confederación Continental that Vergara and Argentinian feminists had hatched. Both this organization and the recently formed UMA were fulfilling Luisi's long-held dream of a Latin American–led feminism. Over the next few years, the Popular Front Pan-American feminism that the Confederación heralded would expand, engaging the vital energies of Ofelia Domínguez Navarro and Clara González, their national groups, and other antifascist *feministas*. Participants of this movement believed that people—women, workers, intellectuals, and activists—and not just statesmen, made peace and democracy. Popular Front Pan-American feminists would continue to promote the Equal Rights Treaty, seeing it as supranational moral lever that could push against dictatorships' threats to women's rights—social and economic as well as civil and political. But they would also insist that advocacy for international law must be coupled with grassroots antifascist and anti-imperialist activism to make those, and a broader array of rights, meaningful. They would assert their leadership over *feminismo americano*.

CHAPTER SIX

United Fronts for Women's Rights and for Human Rights

❊ ❊ ❊

In January 1938, Panamanian feminist Clara González traveled to Mexico City to collaborate with that city's vibrant Popular Front feminist movement. She also sought to escape increasing repression in Panama. Since 1935, González and her group the Partido Nacional Feminista had formed part of the Popular Front in Panama that pushed against the right-wing Acción Comunal in executive power that she and many others deemed "fascist." Acción Comunal leaders, open admirers of European fascism, had incited reprisals against leftists who sought to restore constitutional democracy and secure social rights for workers. They also targeted Clara González personally. Believing her to be a communist, state leaders took away an important governmental post she had been promised and sharply reduced her teaching hours at the National University, effectively halving her salary.[1] Though not a member of the Communist Party of Panama, González was a socialist and unabashed enthusiast of the Popular Front; she dreamed of fighting in the Spanish Civil War, and contacted the Republican government in Valencia through the Spanish foreign minister in Panama about going there. Though she never made it to Spain, in 1938 she did go to Mexico — a haven for political exiles and a hotbed of Popular Front and feminist activism.[2]

Although González officially traveled to Mexico under the auspices of an invitation from the National University of Mexico, she spent much time during her four months there with Popular Front feminist leaders in the Frente Único Pro-Derechos de la Mujer (FUPDM) (the Sole Front for Women's Rights). She called these women "true feminists."[3] The FUPDM, founded in 1935, had quickly become the largest women's group in Mexico and recently obtained President Lázaro Cárdenas's public support for women's suffrage. It had been started by a group of Mexican communist feminists and by González's dear friend Ofelia Domínguez Navarro.[4] Eight years had passed since the two women had last seen each other at the Inter-American Commission of Women (IACW) meeting in Havana, but they had stayed in touch. In 1935, Domínguez had once again fled Cuba for Mexico, where she became an active Popular Front organizer. During

González's time in Mexico City, Domínguez was away, organizing in the southeast of the country. But she was likely responsible for putting González in touch with her FUPDM comrades.[5]

Popular Front feminism was expanding in these years. The Spanish Civil War, development of fascism in Europe, and rise of right-wing powers in many countries in the Americas impelled the exponential growth of Popular Front feminism in Cuba, Panama, Argentina, Uruguay, Chile, Mexico, and elsewhere. A dizzying array of new feminist organizations, national and regional, proliferated. The Movimiento pro Emancipación de la Mujer Chilena (MEMCh), the Unión de Mujeres Americanas (UMA), the Unión Argentina de Mujeres (UAM), the Federación Argentina de Mujeres por la Paz, the Confederación Femenina Argentina, the Unión Femenina contra la Guerra, the Confederación Continental de Mujeres por la Paz, and the Frente Único Pro-Derechos de la Mujer (FUPDM), all emerged in the years between 1934 and 1936 with overlapping goals, names, and members. Self-consciously part of a transnational movement, these groups opposed right-wing powers in the Americas, declared solidarity with Republican Spain in the Spanish Civil War, and called for hemispheric women's rights.

Members of these Popular Front Pan-American feminist groups corresponded across long distances and met at international congresses and conferences, both "popular" and diplomatic. They viewed the international conferences of American states as significant venues to make their demands, to organize extra-official popular demonstrations, and to develop connections with each other. Most deeply supported the IACW's Equal Rights Treaty, even as they recognized that international treaties must be coupled with local and grassroots antifascist activism. The Confederación Continental de Mujeres por la Paz that Marta Vergara had helped create during the 1936 peace conferences in Buenos Aires became a nucleus for uniting antifascist feminists from Argentina, Chile, Panama, Mexico, Cuba, Uruguay, and elsewhere.

Although these feminists mobilized around the IACW's goals, they did not rally around its chair, whose domineering behavior and lack of authentic antifascist commitments led many to sharpen their criticism of her and call her a "fascist" and a "dictator." Organizationally, opposition to Doris Stevens served as a critical bond for Popular Front feminists in the Americas—a common enemy against which to mount a united front.

The Mexican FUPDM feminists with whom Clara González collaborated, along with Marta Vergara and her Argentinian cofounders of the Confederación, would take leading roles in this opposition to Stevens that ultimately bore fruit. Convening at the 1938 Pan-American conference in Lima, FUPDM leader Esperanza Balmaceda de Josefé would work with women allied with the Confederación to promote their own powerful agenda for *feminismo americano*: for international peace, women's rights, and Latin American leadership. In the context of a broader inter-American Popular Front movement that fought fascism and imperialism and that called for the "rights of man" on an international basis, feminists advanced women's rights into the realm of what was becoming known as "human rights." Their influential version of human rights included international commitments to women's economic, social, political, and civil rights regardless of race, religion, or status.

The Inter-American Commission of Women: A "Bulwark for Peace"

In the years after the Montevideo and Buenos Aires conferences, support for the IACW's women's rights platform rose among those who hoped that democracy in the Americas would be a bulwark against fascism. Speaking at the Washington, D.C., headquarters of the IACW in 1938, well-known Irish feminist Hanna Sheehy Skeffington noted that while "fascism and Nazism" were pushing "women not only back to the home but right to the kitchen sink" in Europe, "the center of the women's movement has shifted to . . . the United States and South America."[6] In 1937, at the insistence of both the IACW and Latin American male delegates, the League of Nations formed a group to study the Equal Rights Treaty.[7]

Between 1936 and 1938, growing feminist groups in the Americas looked to the Equal Rights Treaty as a weapon in the fight against fascism. Mexican feminist Margarita Robles de Mendoza's group the Unión de Mujeres Americanas, which she had launched with Paulina Luisi in 1935 as an alternative to the IACW, celebrated the commission's work in Buenos Aires and called the Equal Rights Treaty "a bulwark for peace."[8] UMA grew dramatically after 1936, reporting a membership of over 250,000 members by 1939 and affiliating with feminist groups in Bogotá, Lima, Mexico City, Caracas, Havana, Quito, Managua, Montevideo, San José, and Santo Domingo.[9] In 1936, its New York–based Peruvian president, Evangelina Antey de Vaughan, wrote to Doris Stevens urging close collaboration in a common fight for women's rights against fascism.[10] In Chile and Argentina, feminists credited the IACW's support and its Equal Rights Treaty for preventing proposed changes to a "fascist" civil code in Argentina that would have reduced married women's status to that of minors in that country.[11]

During a time when fascist dictatorships in Europe and the Americas severely threatened women's rights, many leftist and Pan-Hispanic feminists specifically saw the Equal Rights Treaty as a lever for interrelated goals of antifascism and women's full citizenship, including suffrage. Most viewed women's political equality both as an end in itself and as a means to more revolutionary objectives. In spite of recent suffrage gains in Ecuador (1929), Brazil (1932),

Uruguay (1932), and Cuba (1934), Latin American countries still lagged behind the United States and Europe in women's voting rights. While Popular Front feminists saw women's political rights as meaningless under dictatorships, they also believed women's full citizenship could enhance the electoral power of the Popular Front. Between 1934 and 1938, the Popular Front gained power in government and implemented state policies in Chile, Mexico, Spain, and France. In Panama, Argentina, Uruguay, and elsewhere in the Americas, it functioned as a social movement that often turned into an electoral coalition of political parties. Increasingly in these countries, leftist men and women insisted that the triumph of the Popular Front depended on women's suffrage.

While Popular Front feminists frequently drew on maternalist arguments to justify the vote, by emphasizing women as community builders and mothers, many dodged this tactic, stressing women's equality with men in the social struggle. Esther Chapa, Mexican communist feminist and leader in the FUPDM, justified women's electoral rights in 1937 by explaining that women were not only educators and homemakers but also critical to movements against war, imperialism, and fascism. The modern woman, she asserted, favored "the sanctioning of leftist governments to support the proletarian class that has the mission of destroying the capitalist regime under which we live. And [she] ... is denied the vote under the pretext that she is incapable of exercising it!"[12] Afro-Panamanian communist feminist leader Felicia Santizo, who vigorously supported the Equal Rights Treaty as a bulwark against fascism, similarly demanded women's vote on the basis of their equality with men in public and community life.[13]

After 1936, they and other Popular Front Pan-American feminists helped change the political valence of women's suffrage from a goal of liberals into a goal of the left. Throughout Latin America, opponents to women's suffrage had long used the influential argument that women would vote conservatively or with the Catholic Church. Yet as Popular Front feminists now argued, socialism had always inspired feminism, and communist and Popular Front governments were making women's rights a reality. They cited the strong backing of the Soviet Union for women's equal political rights, the vital role that enfranchised women in Spain were playing in the Civil War, and the revitalized support of communist feminists for suffrage in the Americas, especially in Lázaro Cárdenas's Mexico.

In this context, the "equal rights" goals of the IACW gained acute leftist potential. The critical collaboration of leftist Chilean and Argentine feminists with the commission at the 1936 Buenos Aires peace conferences helped cement these connections, as did revolutionary Mexican President Cárdenas's much-publicized support of women's suffrage in Mexico in 1937.[14] Many Popular Front Pan-American feminists believed that the international pressure of the Equal

Rights Treaty could speed the right to vote for women and could also possibly strengthen opposition to right-wing leaders in the Americas.

In spite of these new leftist associations with the IACW and its Equal Rights Treaty, few had any illusions that the leader of the commission, Doris Stevens, was a true antifascist. In these years, Stevens was moving to the right rather than to the left. She and other National Woman's Party members objected to Roosevelt's New Deal, which expanded social democratic rights. Their opposition stemmed in part from discriminations against women in some of the labor codes but also from their perception that such policies took away "individual freedom." In Stevens's case it was further hastened by her belief that the Roosevelt administration personally persecuted her as leader of the IACW. She also vehemently opposed international communism to a greater degree than most in the United States, where a Popular Front movement also flourished. After Stalin's show trials of 1936, she viewed communism as an equal, if not greater threat than Nazi-fascism.[15]

Unlike many Popular Front Pan-American feminists, Stevens did not believe that fascism posed real dangers in Latin America. While she would agree with Latin American feminists who wrote to her about the threats dictatorships posed to women's rights, she wrote more candidly to a fellow Woman's Party member, "I am not one of those who thinks there is any new trend of fascism in South America. They have had dictatorships of varying degrees for so long that there is little Europe can teach them on this front." Her belief that under dictators "women continue to advance on the political rights front" informed the cozy relationships she forged with several dictators in Latin America, including, most notoriously, Rafael Trujillo in the Dominican Republic.[16]

Yet Stevens also recognized, for practical purposes, that most of the feminist vitality in the Americas was coming from the left and that she needed to appeal to leftist feminists. She sought to capitalize on their support for the Equal Rights Treaty, especially with the 1938 Pan-American conference in Lima fast approaching. In late 1936 Stevens and Minerva Bernardino, the Dominican commissioner who now worked in the D.C. office, launched a "Liaison Committee" to bring together feminist groups throughout the Americas, regardless of official connections to the IACW. Using Popular Front vocabulary, Stevens advertised it as a more solid, "closely-knit organ" and a "united front."[17] Such a group would galvanize hemisphere-wide protest or support, creating an instantaneous network to rapidly launch coordinated letter-writing campaigns, a strategy used to great effect during the 1936 ILO and peace conferences.[18] Robles de Mendoza's UMA, the UAM in Argentina, MEMCh in Chile, and a number of women's groups in Panama joined the Liaison Committee, as did affiliates in Peru, Haiti, and Puerto Rico.[19]

At the same time, however, Stevens's eagerness to work for women's rights *with* dictators and her trademark dominance over Latin American women earned her new opprobrium from leftist feminists in the region. In 1936, after Stevens appealed to Honduran dictator Tiburcio Carías Andino to pass women's suffrage, an editorial in the Honduran periodical *Alma Latina* sharply censured her for having the temerity to "speak for the women of Honduras" by asking a dictator for suffrage. The article mocked Stevens for "wondering why they don't do this [push for suffrage] for themselves. Do the Honduran women not have a voice? Do they not have aspirations? Do they not want to enjoy the rights of human and conscious beings? ... No, Doris Stevens, it's not that the Honduran woman lacks aspirations, or doesn't understand the importance of exercising her rights."[20] In Brazil, an editorial in the Rio de Janeiro newspaper *Correio da Manhã* similarly argued that the IACW under Stevens's leadership was out of touch with the reality of women's lives under dictatorships.[21]

Stevens's tensions with Popular Front feminists soon became pronounced in Mexico, where the FUPDM was quickly becoming one of the most powerful feminist groups in the continent. Created mostly by communist feminists in 1935 to unify women's organizations in the country, it included around 800 affiliated organizations and nearly 60,000 members by 1937.[22] Many leftist feminists throughout the Americas looked to the FUPDM as revolutionary regional and global leaders. The conflicts Stevens would have with this group proved consequential.

Initially, the FUPDM welcomed both collaboration with the IACW and its Equal Rights Treaty. In June 1937, the FUPDM organ *La Mujer Nueva* applauded Doris Stevens's protest of a plan by Ecuador's military dictator Federico Páez to revoke women's suffrage from the constitution.[23] Connections between Mexican feminists and the IACW had never been very strong, however. The Mexican commissioner, Margarita Robles de Mendoza, lived primarily in the United States in the 1930s and was not a member of the more leftist FUPDM.[24]

In a series of interactions with Stevens in late 1937 and 1938, FUPDM leaders found her domineering, condescending, and categorically not anti-imperialist or antifascist. Tensions began when Stevens sent to Mexico a U.S. National Woman's Party representative, who essentially instructed FUPDM women to follow the model of U.S. suffragists. Stevens sought to rally Mexican support for the IACW, but this patronizing visit had the opposite effect. In response, María del Refugio "Cuca" García, FUPDM president and member of the Mexican Communist Party, reminded "all the women" of North America that Mexican women had demonstrated their independence and activism long before U.S. women gained suffrage.[25] Only a few months later, Stevens delegated another representative from the IACW, Hazel Moore, to push a suffrage resolution into a Popular Front Inter-American Conference on Education in Mexico City, over the objection of FUPDM leaders there. This 1937 conference, sponsored by the Mexican government and led by Vicente Lombardo Toledano, secretary general of the largest labor union in Mexico, sought to create an inter-American Popular Front movement for antifascist education, education for workers and indigenous people, and the rights and compensation of teachers, many of whom were persecuted by right-wing states. By this time Mexican president Cárdenas had already announced his support for women's suffrage, and FUPDM feminists tactically sought to preserve the conference agenda without reference to suffrage. Moore, however, ignored their desires and insisted that women's suffrage be added to the agenda, to the ire of Cuca García and other FUPDM leaders.[26]

The final and most decisive conflict between the FUPDM and the IACW revolved around Doris Stevens's failure to support Mexican feminists in the U.S.-Mexico oil controversy. After decades of U.S. and British foreign companies dominating Mexican oil production, enforcing repressive labor practices, and paying low wages for workers and a small share of taxes, Cárdenas nationalized the oil industry in March 1938. While Roosevelt and the State Department did not send troops to Mexico because of their nonintervention promises and fears about fascism there, they immediately enforced a range of political and economic sanctions that, in coordination with boycotts by oil companies, damaged the Mexican economy.[27] Mexico's plight became a key cause for the inter-American Popular Front.

Several weeks later, Cuca García reached out to Stevens for help. The nationalization of oil had vital implications for the rights of women workers throughout the Americas, García explained. "The Mexican Government . . . is not only going to create its own economy for the country, but also free the Mexican women from the condition of servitude in which they were placed by the feudal system," García wrote Stevens.[28] She asked Stevens to share the IACW's robust list of feminist contacts throughout the Americas so the FUPDM could seek wide support.

Stevens declined, explaining that the IACW's list of Latin American feminist groups was too long to send. Though Stevens offered to distribute information to others on behalf of García, she also dismissed her concerns. Stevens insisted that U.S. State Department members revealed their "most friendly concern that the Mexican and United States governments will work out a happy solution" and that no official "expresses any desire to put pressure on Mexico on behalf of the oil companies."[29] Stevens's uninformed and unsympathetic response no doubt infuriated García, who never wrote to her again.

Perhaps García was not surprised. She was a close colleague of Ofelia Domínguez Navarro, who had helped found the FUPDM and who viewed disseminating incriminating information about Doris Stevens as a critical act of anti-imperialism. Domínguez almost certainly told FUPDM leaders about her many conflicts with Stevens. Clara González, who was at that very moment in Mexico City spending time with Cuca García and other FUPDM leaders (probably due to introductions from Domínguez), also likely told them about her contretemps with Stevens. González remained the Panamanian commissioner in these years and rallied Popular Front feminists around the Equal Rights Treaty in Panama. But she had left her work with the commission in the United States deeply disillusioned by Stevens's control over it and by Stevens's withholding of funding that would have made it possible for González to attend important conferences. Such information, as well as the FUPDM's own troubling interactions with Stevens, planted the seeds for what would be the group's decisive campaign to depose her.

The FUPDM Unites with the Confederación Continental de Mujeres por la Paz

The FUPDM received much more enthusiastic solidarity around Mexico's oil expropriation from the new coalition of groups that Marta Vergara had dubbed the Confederación Continental de Mujeres por la Paz.[30] This umbrella group, created by Vergara, Susana G. de Lapacó, and a number of Argentinean feminists during the Buenos Aires People's Peace Conference in 1936, advocated the rights of labor—economic and social rights for both male and female workers—and for "peace and democracy through nationalization of war industries; international control of trade in arms; and international commitments to women's political, social, economic, and civil rights."[31] It identified strongly with the broader Popular Front in the Americas that supported revolutionary Mexico in the midst of the oil expropriation crisis, the Aprista movement and its imprisoned leader Haya de la Torre, Puerto Rican nationalism, and Republican Spain. In the years since its founding, the Confederación had grown quickly. By October 1937, its national wing in Argentina, the Federación Argentina de Mujeres por la Paz, had affiliated with over seventy women's organizations in the country.[32] Vergara obtained the backing of numerous Chilean groups, and Lapacó gained adherents from Peru, Uruguay, and Brazil.[33]

To become truly "continental," Confederación leaders set their sights on the 1938 Pan-American conference in Lima, where, as they had done in Buenos Aires, they hoped to organize an alternative, grassroots "Popular Front" gathering of antifascist and anti-imperialist feminists.[34] In preparation, Lapacó sought to bring women together at a large Popular Front conference—the Second World Congress of Youth for Peace—that would take place several months before the Lima conference.[35]

Held in September 1938 at Vassar College in Poughkeepsie, New York, this

World Youth Congress was transformative for the Confederación, further stoking its antifascism and gaining it new affiliates. Organized by the Popular Front International Committee of Youth, it brought together more than 600 young Popular Front delegates and observers from fifty-four countries to organize youth in a proletarian, antifascist, and anti-imperialist internationalism for the "political and economic organization for peace."[36] The largest delegations came from the United States, Great Britain, Canada, and Mexico, but scores of young leaders in national Popular Front struggles, from Argentina, Cuba, and across the Americas, as well as from Asia, Africa, and the Middle East, attended.[37] The conference upheld the equal rights of "all nations, races, and creeds" and supported women's rights.[38]

At the meeting, Lapacó attracted a nucleus of inter-American feminists, including UMA president Evangelina de Vaughan; one of the youngest and most active members of Clara González's Panamanian Partido Nacional Feminista; and several young Mexican feminists, all of whom exchanged information about their own national struggles.[39] They discussed gathering women at the 1938 Lima conference in a separate, independent meeting for "peace and democracy."[40] In addition, they decided to organize a future feminist assembly—an "Inter-American Congress of Women for Peace and Democracy" in Mexico the following year—to bring together even more women of the continent. After the youth congress, Lapacó traveled to Brazil, Uruguay, and France to share this information with feminist pacifists, including French members of the World Committee of Women against War and Fascism created by the 1934 Paris congress.[41]

This Confederación group at Vassar included one U.S. woman, Frances Benedict Stewart, a member of the Women's International League for Peace and Freedom (WILPF). A daughter of Bahá'í missionaries, Stewart had grown up in Chile and spoke fluent Spanish.[42] Popular Front Pan-American feminism came alive for her at the 1936 Buenos Aires People's Peace Conference, which she attended as a WILPF representative. There she met Marta Vergara and Lapacó and helped them organize the Confederación Continental.[43] Afterward she lived for some time in Argentina with a Marxist Argentinian feminist who was also a key Confederación member.[44] Stewart's connections with Popular Front feminists grew when she went to the 1937 Inter-American Conference on Education in Mexico. She was enlisted by Doris Stevens to be an IACW representative there but found herself engaged much more by Mexico's vibrant antifascist activism than by the commission's suffrage resolution. Instead of taking orders from Stevens and Hazel Moore, Stewart allied herself with FUPDM feminists such as Cuca García, with whom she struck up a lasting friendship.[45]

Stewart was notable for being the only U.S. member of the Confederación.[46]

While not a communist, she was a fellow traveler. Because of her leftist politics and her fluency in Spanish, she managed much better than other U.S. feminists to forge mutual friendships with anti-imperialist Latin American women. Living in Mexico for much of 1938, Stewart helped to connect the Confederación Continental with the FUPDM there.[47]

Soon after the World Youth Congress, FUPDM leaders developed a set of plans to inject their brand of feminism into the upcoming official Pan-American conference in Lima. Their plans included removing Stevens as IACW chair. At a large rally and dinner in Mexico City that FUPDM leaders had organized for Margarita Nelken, Spanish president of her country's Antifascist League and leader in the World Committee of Women against War and Fascism, Cuca García and others seem to have worked on these plans with Margarita Robles de Mendoza, the Mexican representative of the IACW and the UMA leader who had long criticized Stevens's ideological and financial control over the commission as representing "imperialism."[48]

Days after this meeting, FUPDM leaders helped secure the appointment of one of their own members, Esperanza Balmaceda de Josefé, as a technical adviser to the Mexican delegation to Lima.[49] A leader of the FUPDM, a professor of social reform at the University of Mexico, and member of the Communist Party, Balmaceda would be the only female representative in the Mexican delegation. At the Lima conference, she would sit on the Fourth Committee on Political and Civil Rights of Women, which handled all matters related to women's rights. With other FUPDM members, Balmaceda drew up a number of proposals to reorganize the Inter-American Commission of Women.[50]

Their plans reflected most of the demands that Ofelia Domínguez Navarro, Clara González, Paulina Luisi, and Bertha Lutz had made over the past decade and a half. They included the proposal González and Domínguez argued for in Havana in 1930, for the IACW to receive funding from the Pan-American Union; the resolution that Lutz had made at Montevideo in 1933, that the chairmanship of the commission rotate; and the principle for which Luisi had always fought—that individual governments should have less control over the appointment of feminists. They also proposed that the commission operate primarily through national subcommissions, organized democratically and elected by women themselves, rather than under the sole direction of the chairman or government-appointed delegates.[51]

Balmaceda and FUPDM allies also drew up a number of proposals that would reorient Pan-American feminism around grassroots Popular Front mobilization as much as around international law. They incorporated the Confederación's plans to form an inter-American congress of women that, unlike the IACW, would be independent from governments. Many of these goals were clearly

NUESTRA DELEGADA A LA VIII CONFERENCIA EN LIMA

Por la Srta. Profesora Carlota de Gortari Carbajal

Para VIDA FEMENINA

La Sra. Profesora Esperanza Balmaceda de Josefé, designada por el señor Presidente Cárdenas para llevar a la VIII Conferencia en Lima la voz de la mujer mexicana, es una revolucionaria convencida; una luchadora que desde niña tuvo privaciones y vió la vida frente a frente, y recibió las enseñanzas de revolucionarios internacionales. Por su talento y méritos

Drawing of Esperanza Balmaceda in her profile by Carlota de Gortari Carbajal, "Nuestra delegada a la VIII conferencia en Lima," Vida Femenina, December 15, 1938, 10.

spelled out in a December 1938 profile of Balmaceda by a Mexican feminist that appeared in *Vida Femenina*, an Argentinean socialist magazine. Titled "Our Delegate to the VIII Conference in Lima," the "our" referred not only to Mexican women but the leftist international, Latin American readers of *Vida Femenina*.[52]

Calling Balmaceda "a convinced revolutionary" and "one of the champions" of the women's movement in Mexico, the article outlined her agenda for Lima. Women, Balmaceda argued, should be "incorporated into democracy" economically and socially, specifically with "rights . . . to maternity and to maternity protection," which had to be secured in the context of a broader antifascist front to promote "peace and democracy." Referring to a recent formation of an antifascist Latin American labor union, she also resolved that at Lima she would try to bolster the cause of "Pan-American workers."[53]

Although Balmaceda did not spell out her specific plans to depose Doris Stevens in the article, her silence about the IACW would have spoken volumes, given the centrality of the commission to the discussion of women's rights in every Pan-American gathering since the 1928 Havana conference. Balmaceda's actions at the conference would become legendary. Several years later, a group of women in Mexico from Argentina, Uruguay, and Chile would celebrate Balmaceda's efforts to create a large "*Federación de mujeres latinoamericanas* ... to openly oppose the Inter-American Commission of Women," with "all the force that the mass of the Continent's women could have."[54]

Meanwhile, Doris Stevens made her lack of Popular Front commitments starkly clear when she allied herself with one of the most notorious dictators in the Americas. In August 1938, Stevens and Minerva Bernardino took a well-publicized trip to the Dominican Republic to secure support from General Rafael Trujillo. The previous year, Trujillo, an open admirer of Franco's Spain, had overseen the slaughter of between 15,000 and 20,000 Haitians and black Dominicans in the Dominican Republic, in what historian Margaret Stevens has called "the single most important act of fascist aggression in the hemisphere ... enacted upon black laborers during this period."[55] Doris Stevens, well aware that Trujillo had invited the IACW to improve his image, agreed to go on the promise that he would endorse the Equal Rights Treaty and women's suffrage.[56] While there, Stevens praised Trujillo lavishly for his "already immensely impressive list of brilliant and integral achievements."[57]

Stevens received widespread public condemnation for this trip. The Junta Revolucionaria Dominicana, a New York–based group of Dominican exiles, castigated her in a telegram for selling herself "to Trujillo who was using her influence to secure the women's vote ... to strengthen his regime."[58] Stevens shrugged off the criticism, unaware of how appalling her visit was to many influential feminists in the region.[59] She saw her Dominican visit as great publicity for announcing a new treaty that the IACW would present in Lima—one that would focus solely on women's suffrage.[60]

As she prepared for the Lima conference, Stevens was blithely oblivious to the transnational opposition rising against her from a large group of Popular Front Pan-American feminists. She had little idea that Latin American feminists were organizing their own inter-American group to challenge the IACW. The commissioners with whom she corresponded, including Clara González and Marta Vergara, did not tell her. Both women did, however, tell Stevens that they were unable to attend the Lima conference because of health reasons. González, in addition to not having the money to go to Lima, had become so ill from stress due to the political and personal sabotage of the Panamanian government that she had to be hospitalized. Vergara reported to Stevens that she also was too ill to attend, and she sent another MEMCh feminist in her place.[61]

In spite of their absence, Stevens looked forward to what she believed would be key support from two Argentinian feminists from the UAM with whom she had worked in Buenos Aires in 1936.[62] After visiting Clara González in the hospital en route to Lima, Stevens wrote to her husband, Jonathan Mitchell, "Principal thing is I'm riding high. Four speeches in Panama. Spirits good."[63] But her spirits would soon flag as she realized that forces from Latin America and the United States were uniting to oppose her.

The Roosevelt Administration in the "United Front"

Ever since the 1933 Montevideo conference, the network of women from the Roosevelt administration, the League of Women Voters, and the National Women's Trade Union League had ratcheted up efforts to oppose Doris Stevens yet were stymied time and again. In December 1937, a full year before the Lima conference, Elise Musser advised leaders of these groups that Stevens had "women lined up in practically every country to lobby for the Equal Rights Resolutions" in Lima and encouraged them to take action.[64] At the 1936 Buenos Aires conferences, Musser and her colleague Josephine Schain had been baffled by Stevens's success rallying leftist Latin American feminists around the IACW's treaty while portraying protective legislation as fascist. Reversing this association—affiliating *Stevens* with fascism—would be central to their strategy at Lima.[65]

They relied upon the State Department to carry out their plan. As early as March 1938, Molly Dewson wrote to Sumner Welles, the under secretary of state and Latin American specialist, outlining their desire to remove Stevens as chair. In August, Dewson sent Welles a *Washington Post* article detailing Stevens's visit with Trujillo and explained that "clearing up this situation lies in the hands of the State Department."[66] Predictably, Brazilian feminist Bertha Lutz helped formulate this plan, reaching out to U.S. women and the U.S. State Department to set in motion her Montevideo proposal to rotate the IACW chairmanship.[67] In these years, Lutz bolstered her bonds with Adolf A. Berle, a key member of Franklin D. Roosevelt's "Brain Trust" who shared her distaste for Stevens.[68]

The U.S. government had always viewed the IACW as a thorn in its side, but these men in Roosevelt's State Department particularly opposed Doris Stevens for being dangerously right-wing and anti-Rooseveltian. Berle, who in 1938 became assistant secretary of state for Latin American affairs, most boldly articulated this view when at the official 1936 Buenos Aires conference he told Stevens point-blank that she was "fascist." Her dogmatic commitment to "equal rights," he told her, meant she did not "care about the difficulties which flowed from [her] principles."[69] Berle, Welles, and Laurence Duggan, chief of the Division of American Republics, found Stevens's visit to the Dominican Republic particularly repugnant. Even though the U.S. State Department implicitly condoned Trujillo's dictatorship in order to secure compliance with U.S. strategic demands, and even though Secretary of State Cordell Hull had given Stevens approval to go, Welles, Berle, and Duggan, twenty to thirty years younger than Hull, were of a different diplomatic school than he.[70] They celebrated the social democratic goals Roosevelt espoused, the welfare policies supported by the U.S. Women's and Children's Bureaus, and, to some degree, the antifascist sensibilities of the Popular Front. Doris Stevens represented a threat to all of these ideals.

Thus, Berle, Welles, and Duggan launched a formal State Department investigation of the IACW in order to find a way to remove Stevens. The report noted that "the work of the Inter-American Commission of Women has been the cause of considerable discussion and embarrassment to the American delegation at both the Montevideo and the Buenos Aires Conferences." In order to avoid a "similar situation" in Lima, they must take steps to reorganize it and replace Stevens as chair.[71] Berle, Welles, and Duggan drew on the help of Leo Rowe, head of the Pan-American Union, to locate the technical loophole that would remove Stevens: she had been appointed in 1928 by the governing board of the Pan-American Union but never by the U.S. government itself. Thus, they proposed that the IACW be recast as an "official" body composed only of representatives appointed by respective governments. Since the Roosevelt administration did not support Stevens, she would be removed, and the work of the commission would be subsumed more securely under the direction of the U.S. State Department.[72] This proposal was very similar to that which Lutz had made in Montevideo several years before.

After gaining Roosevelt's endorsement of these plans, the State Department collaborated with Molly Dewson and Mary Winslow to appoint Elise Musser as a full U.S. delegate to Lima.[73] To counter the IACW's equal rights goals, Mary Anderson, head of the Women's Bureau, drafted a new resolution on "women's rights and duties." To avoid any taint of "fascism," this statement took a more positive approach, rather than the previous tactic of shunning the Equal Rights Treaty. It called for women's political and civil equality as well as "elimination of discrimination because of sex, injurious to women." Although it included promotion of protective legislation, it avoided the word "protection," instead supporting "legislation against economic exploitation and physically harmful conditions of employment including the safeguarding of motherhood."[74]

Immediately before the conference, confidential State Department instructions to the U.S. delegation spelled out clear mandates to replace any mention of an Equal Rights Treaty with these nonbinding resolutions and to reorganize the commission. "For your confidential information," it read, "this Government believes that the manner in which the question of the problems of . . . women has been handled at various Conferences of American States since the Conference at Habana ... has served to bring before each Conference a highly controversial issue which has caused irritation and annoyance and has retarded the general progress of Pan American conferences."[75] The State Department hired a League of Women Voters member to be Musser's assistant. Anderson and Winslow also hired a representative from the Children's Bureau to join the U.S. delegation and write newspaper articles about women's issues in Lima to counteract Stevens's extensive press connections and seize the narrative.[76]

In order to inform their conversations with Latin American affiliates of the IACW, U.S. delegates began to gather evidence as soon as the steamer left for Lima that Stevens identified with the far right. "Berle followed me around like a spy," Stevens wrote to her husband; Duggan asked her in an "almost belligerent" manner why she had gone to the Dominican Republic when she knew that Trujillo was a dictator.[77] "To whom would you speak in Latin America, Larry, if you had no commerce with dictators?" Stevens shot back.[78] Meanwhile, Musser's assistant goaded Stevens on her opinions about the Soviet Union, suggesting that the United States could learn something from the Soviets on women's rights "as a model for our reforms." Stevens retorted, "We can evolve something indigenous to this continent ... more suitable than anything the Soviet has done."[79]

As the steamer approached Lima, Stevens learned of the U.S. delegation's plans to remove her as chair. She quickly understood that these people were accumulating evidence that she was "not radical enough" for her Latin American affiliates.[80] Upon their arrival, Stevens overheard Berle tell the two Argentinean representatives of the IACW, Ana Rosa Schlieper de Martínez Guerrero and Susana Larguía, that the Roosevelt administration did "not approve of Miss Stevens ... and ... are not in sympathy with her ideas."[81]

Schlieper and Larguía, who had helped cofound the UAM, had collaborated with Stevens at the 1936 Buenos Aires conferences. But Berle's charges of Stevens's "fascism" rattled them and Graciela Mandujano, the Chilean MEMCh representative who was joining them in lieu of Marta Vergara.[82] As antifascists allied with the Confederación Continental, all had come to Lima to promote women's rights, to fight fascism, and to help develop the alternative inter-American congress that Lapacó and others sought. Earlier in 1938, Schlieper had announced her beliefs, in Spanish over an inter-American radio address, that the "purpose" of "the feminist movement throughout the Americas" was not only for women's "complete civil and political rights" but also for "the welfare of all Humanity."[83] Just before the Lima conference, the Chilean feminist with whom Vergara had cofounded MEMCh wrote an article in a Chilean newspaper underscoring how "extraordinarily important" the women's rights resolutions at Lima were to antifascism. Over the past few years, she wrote, women in the Americas had made "the most serious attempt so far to stop the material and moral invasion of fascism [and] to protect and promote democratic regimes among the American countries." In Lima they would make their demands for "peace and democracy" heard.[84] These women also believed that the Lima conference represented a break with a long past of U.S. imperialism in a new common goal of antifascism. Now, under Roosevelt's Good Neighbor Policy, the U.S. government was not beholden to Wall Street, MEMCh's *La Mujer Nueva* proclaimed: "A new fact has arisen in which the interests of both Americas coincide—the fight against fascism."[85] These women took seriously the charges made by U.S. State Department members that Doris Stevens tilted toward "fascism," especially when Stevens's close relationship with the Peruvian dictatorship only seemed to confirm these accusations.

Upon their arrival in Lima, Stevens informed Larguía, Schlieper, Mandujano, and Minerva Bernardino, much to their dismay, that she had worked with the Peruvian government to secure their lodging in a private home far from the main hotel and conference center. The Popular Front, however, deemed Peru the seat of Nazi-fascism in the Americas; since 1935 the Benavides regime had outlawed and imprisoned Apristas and communists. At the Lima conference, as the *New York Times* later reported, Benavides's government not only tried to control the newspaper correspondents but also spied on the delegates, imposing a "regime of censorship, intimidation, and spying such as we have never before seen in any Pan American assembly."[86] Schlieper and the others told Stevens they would not be housed in a remote, isolated place offered them by a "fascist dictatorship" and where they "would be under . . . police surveillance."[87]

Stevens, who deemed her relationships with state leaders, even dictators, as critical leverage for her diplomatic maneuverings, took their opposition as a deep personal affront. She told these women that she found their fears preposterous and their resistance to "accept[ing] the hospitality" of the Peruvian government "exceedingly rude" and "ungracious." When Bernardino insisted that the housing scheme was a government plot, Stevens told her to "shut up!" Stevens also ignored Mandujano's request for financial help to stay with the others at the Hotel Bolívar in the center of Lima.[88] Ultimately, Stevens helped Mandujano pay for the hotel, but only after receiving an urgent missive from Marta Vergara (who must have received a cable from Mandujano about her conflicts with Stevens) to not convey the "bad impression . . . that you are a dictator within the Commission." Explicitly reminding Stevens of the problems that Aída Parada had with Stevens at the 1930 Havana meeting, Vergara emphasized that "it is necessary that all have the impression that the Commission is a *democratic organization*."[89] Stevens herself stayed in the opulent home that the government had offered her. The Peruvian government also put at her disposal a personal driver and a maid.[90]

Minerva Bernardino, Susana Larguía, Ana Rosa Schlieper de Martínez Guerrero, and
Doris Stevens (left to right) having lunch together during the Lima conference, 1938.
Courtesy of the Schlesinger Library, Radcliffe Institute, Harvard University.

Back in 1930, Ofelia Domínguez Navarro had identified Stevens's "dictato-
rial character" toward Latin American feminists who disagreed with her as an
Anglo-American trait that was part and parcel of U.S. imperialism.[91] To these
women in Lima, the pattern may have become clear. Although Stevens had
long been careful to use a language of egalitarianism in her dealings with Latin
American feminists, her private correspondence with her husband, Jonathan
Mitchell, during the Lima conference reflects clearly racist assumptions. After
Stevens conveyed the lack of support she was receiving from IACW representatives and the U.S. delegation, Mitchell advised her to "behave like one of Rud-
yard Kipling's pukha sahibs," the aloof administrators of the British Empire.
"There must be some good reason why the British behave as they do in the presence of colored races," he wrote. "Don't let the Latin Americans see you are
worried or disappointed, no matter what happens.... As far as that goes, Elise
[Musser] was born and raised in Switzerland until she was 17, which makes her
practically a member of the colored races.... What I mean is ... that you are
more beautiful, gifted, cleaner, sweeter person than your opponents. Act as if
you were. Act as if you knew they were dirt beneath your feet."[92]

Mitchell's likening of Stevens's leadership of the IACW to a British imperial
overseer of colonial subjects and his placing her Anglo-American whiteness
over her Latin American (and Swiss) counterparts reveal how deeply her sense

of racial, cultural, and national superiority shaped Stevens's sense of entitlement to leadership over the commission. Stevens later wrote him that his advice to "play the white man was excellent."[93] Her mask of racial egalitarianism seemed to fall when she was embattled, and in Lima, her racism was laid bare.[94]

The U.S. State Department was keenly aware of Stevens's diminishing popularity among Latin American delegates. An internal memo noted that although a number of "militant" and "radical" Latin American feminists who were "in disfavor with existing governments" acknowledged the strength of Stevens's leadership, "even her staunchest supporter, Miss Bernardino of the Dominican Republic[,] said definitely there must be an end of one woman rule in the Women's Commission."[95] Outside the conference halls, Elise Musser forged connections around this goal with Schlieper, Larguía, Mandujano, Bernardino, and Esperanza Balmaceda.

Esperanza Balmaceda at Lima

As technical adviser to the Mexican delegation, Esperanza Balmaceda emerged as a pivotal leader at Lima. About a month before the conference, she had stationed herself at the Mexican embassy in the city, researching women's status in Mexico and elsewhere in the Americas.[96] During the conference, she organized large and informal "people's conferences" of women that intentionally excluded Doris Stevens. These meetings, held in the lobby of the Hotel Bolívar, where most delegates stayed (aside from Stevens, who stayed in the house the Peruvian government provided her), and in parks and restaurants in Lima, gathered women who were there in both official and unofficial capacities.[97] At these meetings, Balmaceda insisted that "controversial issues be forgotten" and that they "concentrate on three subjects of interest to all of them, namely, peace, democracy, and solidarity."[98] These goals united women of different political stripes — liberal pacifists; reformers invested in the social welfare of women and children; feminists engaged in women's political, civil, and economic rights; and communist feminists. Balmaceda expressed her hope that they would launch a new and more far-reaching Pan-American feminism, and she called for a continental conference of women.[99] She downplayed her communist commitments in part to avoid the censure of the Peruvian government and in part to appeal to this broad array of women, including some in the U.S. delegation. Balmaceda had met Elise Musser and her Lima press correspondent, Elisabeth Enochs, several years earlier at the 1935 Pan-American Child Conference, and they now collaborated to defenestrate Doris Stevens.[100]

Balmaceda and Musser had inordinate influence over the conference proceedings concerning women's rights. Both were appointed to the Fourth Committee on Political and Civil Rights of Women, with Musser as vice chair, later as chair. At past Pan-American conferences Stevens had lined up prominent male supporters in the committees, but she failed to do so at Lima.[101] Together, Balmaceda and Musser handily defeated Stevens and her proposals. The committee quashed the IACW's treaty proclaiming suffrage, passing instead the U.S. resolution on "rights and duties" of women that Mary Anderson had drafted.[102] While the Fourth Committee thanked the IACW for its work, it also placed the organization "on an official and permanent status" as an advisory body to the governing board of the Pan-American Union. As the State Department officials had planned, this meant that each commissioner had to be appointed by her government. Stevens recognized that such a change would effectively remove her as chair.

While Stevens and commissioners were able to speak before the committee, they did not have any real influence over it. When none of the other feminists who were presumably allied with the commission rose to her defense, Stevens felt betrayed and angry. Of Susana Larguía and Ana Rosa Schlieper's lack of support, she later told her husband, "The Argentines behaved like rats."[103]

Unbeknownst to Stevens, however, other Latin American feminists were also backing Balmaceda from great distances. From Santiago, Marta Vergara actively aided the Mexican feminist. Although Vergara had told Stevens that illness prevented her from going to the Lima conference, Vergara was not too ill to lead a large delegation of feminists to the Mexican embassy in Santiago to promote Balmaceda's proposals there. When Vergara heard that the Chilean delegation was not supporting Balmaceda in Lima, she and this group of MEMCh feminists asked Mexican diplomats in Santiago to utilize their suasion and urge the Chilean delegation to vote for all of Balmaceda's recommendations.[104]

Balmaceda used her powerful position on the committee to assert an expansive definition of *feminismo americano* and international women's rights that included support for working women, defined broadly, and antifascism. Her role as spokesperson gained stature given President Cárdenas's recent promise of Mexican women's suffrage. On the first day of the conference, Balmaceda noted that it was "a little anachronistic that in 1938 we should have to come humbly to ask for what we have already earned with our efforts," not only through fighting for the independence of their countries alongside men but also through their economic contributions. Injecting a Marxist feminist perspective into the proceedings, she pointed out that both before and since the Industrial Revolution, women provided the "base of the economy" through their domestic, agricultural, and increasingly industrial work.[105]

She emphasized that the Fourth Committee should consider women's rights, but "not only from the legal, strictly juridical point of view." A treaty for civil and political rights would be meaningless, she pointed out, without also ad-

Esperanza Balmaceda speaking at the final session of the Fourth Committee at the Lima conference, December 22, 1938. Author's collection.

dressing "the problem of the woman in all her roles, as a worker, as a fighter, and above all . . . as a mother."[106] Here Balmaceda supported resolutions that Pan-American feminists had made at earlier conferences that endorsed rights to maternity legislation and that sought to expand labor rights to domestic and agricultural women, including indigenous women.

In order to effectively fight for these rights, Balmaceda argued in the Fourth Committee for a new women's alliance "that is a true Pan-American front that fights for peace, for justice, and for liberty." The "Inter-American Congress of Women for Peace and Democracy" she proposed would be a grassroots counterpart to the official, inter-governmental Inter-American Commission of Women. Unlike the IACW, the autonomous congress of women would address women's issues "in an independent form, with absolute liberty."[107] When a Peruvian delegate pointed out that Balmaceda's proposal surpassed the conference agenda, which was limited to resolutions for women's civil and political rights, Balmaceda spoke out against censorship. She explained she sought "dynamic results out of this conference, not merely static results!"[108]

Balmaceda's objection to censorship would have resonated with the many Latin American feminists long silenced by Doris Stevens, who increasingly appeared to many as the fascist "dictator" of the commission. Connections between Stevens and "fascism" became stronger when the only vocal support Stevens received in Lima came from Dominican dictator Rafael Trujillo, whose formal endorsement of Stevens was read aloud in the Fourth Committee, and from the far-right Brazilian delegate Rosalina Coelho Lisboa, a key diplomat in Getulio Vargas's regime.[109] Coelho Lisboa, part of Ação Integralista Brasileira, a right-wing Brazilian nationalist group inspired by Italian fascism, vehemently opposed all proposals to reorganize the commission in the Fourth Committee sessions. She also opposed Balmaceda's Inter-American Congress of Women for Peace and Democracy, which she suggested was a communist front.[110] Trujillo's and Coelho Lisboa's ringing endorsements of Stevens only contributed to the already deteriorating relationships Stevens had with Popular Front feminists at the meeting. Stevens, however, celebrated this forthright challenge to Balmaceda, writing to her husband that Coelho Lisboa "is a fascist, and she doesn't care who knows it!"[111]

In response, Balmaceda contrasted the collaborative, antifascist ethos of Popular Front feminism with the cult of personality propagated by Stevens. Now they were no longer working under "an individualist spirit, but rather with one . . . truly of the collective interest." The form and content of feminism were vitally interconnected, Balmaceda stated: "We have not only advanced the woman in her conquests" of rights "but . . . in the expression of her organized movement." She said to a prolonged applause, "Now we just need to have a tactic: that of the united front." The conference ultimately voted in favor of the creation of the Congress that Balmaceda suggested.[112]

Inter-American Human Rights

This Lima conference represented a victory not only for Popular Front Pan-American feminists but also for the Popular Front in the Americas. While tensions at Lima revealed the Americas were far from politically or ideologically unified, the "Declaration of Lima" that resulted from the conference announced to the world an inter-American commitment to security in the face of Nazi-fascism. In addition to its statement of continental solidarity for the people of America against foreign interventions, it also contained a strong commitment to individual rights under international law. Leftist Popular Front delegates from Cuba and Mexico had brought to the conference demands for workers' rights, freedom of speech, and racial and religious freedoms. Initially the resolutions were sidetracked due to lack of support from delegates from countries that supported dictatorships and from the United States, in an effort to assuage Peru and roiled by Argentina's pro-Axis position.[113] Esperanza Balmaceda had been one of the greatest defenders of these proposals. She initiated her plan for the Inter-American Congress of Women for Peace and Democracy the same day the Mexican and Cuban rights resolutions were foundering in session and urged their discussion in the Fourth Committee.[114] Ultimately the conference passed the resolutions in a slightly weakened form, stating that "any persecution on account of racial or religious motives . . . is contrary to the political and juridical systems of the Americas."[115] Significantly, the Lima Declaration also pronounced "respect for the rights of all nations and of all individuals regardless of race or religion."[116]

These 1938 Lima resolutions represented a critical turning point in the articulation of "human rights." Only during the Second World War would that term become tantamount with an international commitment to rights of "all people regardless of race, class, sex, and religion." But the Lima conference's resolution on "Freedom of Association and Freedom of Expression for Workers," the "Lima Declaration in Favor of Women's Rights," and especially the "Declaration in the Defense of Human Rights" deserve to be recognized as marking the first time "human rights" was the subject of a resolution in an international conference.[117]

These Lima resolutions gained broad traction among the Latin American left, including the newly legalized Communist Party of Cuba, which considered them "a testimony of continental solidarity against Nazi-fascism that would assure the peace in America."[118] Antiracism had a long tradition in Cuba and was a key ideology behind labor and communist organizing there; in 1939 the Communist Party of Cuba explicitly applauded the Lima resolutions "in defense of the woman and against discrimination of the oppressed races and exploited of the world (Jews and blacks)."[119]

Popular Front Pan-American feminism's adherence to "rights for all regardless of race, class, or sex," attested to a growing intersectional form of inter-American feminism—one that addressed racial equality as well as class and gender equality. For many leftist *feministas*, antiracism had been part of their anti-imperialism; a number of them decried Jim Crow segregation and racism in their attacks against U.S. empire.[120] Now, the movement was unmistakably influenced by the organizing of black feminists in both Pan-Africanist and Popular Front movements committed to a global politics of antiracism and antifascism. Latin American *feministas* openly decried fascist violence in Ethiopia against "our dark-skinned brothers and sisters in Africa" and others drew attention to the rights of indigenous women in the Americas.[121] In 1939, thanks to long-standing efforts by Afro-Cuban women and the influence of the Communist Party, the Third National Women's Congress in Cuba explicitly upheld antiracism as a feminist goal. The congress included detailed resolutions on "the woman and racial prejudices," including "situation of the black woman in Cuba," specifically "her social, cultural, and economic problems"; "legal and real equality for black and white women in Cuban life"; and "the racial prejudices

and their manifestations in the world: fight against them."[122] Ofelia Domínguez, who had by now returned to Cuba, attended this congress and supported
these resolutions. The previous year, she had spoken out about the "triple aggression" that black women experienced based on gender, race, and class and
under "the weight of capitalist exploitation."[123]

Also attending this 1939 Third National Women's Congress in Havana was
Esperanza Balmaceda. Emboldened by her success at Lima, Balmaceda embarked on a long tour of Latin American countries to organize, meet with feminist allies, and promote the new Inter-American Congress of Women for Peace
and Democracy. In addition to traveling to Havana, she went to Buenos Aires,
where she met with Susana Lapacó and with Frances Stewart, who was visiting.
The women made plans to promote an inter-American congress of women in
Mexico in 1939 as well as a world congress of women in Cuba that would also
include Popular Front activists from other parts of the world.[124] Their goal was
a *feminismo americano* that supported, yet transcended, international treaties and
that actively drove grassroots organizing around a range of goals.

In addition, Balmaceda traveled to Chile, where she met with Marta Vergara
and members of MEMCh, who also supported these new plans. Vergara continued to be selective about what she told Stevens. She wrote to Stevens that
Balmaceda had visited her at the hospital in Santiago where Balmaceda had indicated that she had changed the IACW's "spirit and composition" but not provided Vergara with details about Lima. Vergara knew more than she let on, but
she valued her friendship with Stevens enough not to openly defy her.[125] Though
Vergara did deem Stevens a friend, she had also long viewed Stevens's leadership over the commission as domineering and its program too narrow. Vergara
was heartened by the seeming explosion of a Latin American–led Popular Front
feminism that she had herself helped set into motion; she believed it was time
for the IACW to be led by a Latin American Popular Front feminist.

For her part, Stevens remained in the dark about Vergara's active support of
Balmaceda. Although Stevens resented the lack of Latin American feminist loyalty in Lima, her real anger was directed at the U.S. State Department and specifically at Eleanor Roosevelt, whom she believed to be personally responsible
for her ousting.[126] For the next year, Stevens, along with a group of National
Woman's Party members and male diplomats, would campaign to reinstall herself as the chair, but to no avail. Her removal deeply embittered Stevens, who
later amassed evidence of the Roosevelt administration's machinations that she
hoped to publish. She would reflect on her decade as the chair of the IACW as
the "best working years of my life."[127]

Meanwhile, word of the Inter-American and World Congresses of Women
in Mexico and Cuba spread to Clara González and Partido Nacional Feminista

members in Panama, the UMA in New York City, and Paulina Luisi in Montevideo, who wrote to Balmaceda in hearty support.[128] Luisi allied her Popular Front feminist group in Uruguay with these plans; disseminated the news to her friends in the World Committee of Women against War and Fascism in England, Spain, and France; and threw her energies into helping organize the congresses in Mexico and in Cuba. In 1938, Luisi also cofounded a new group in Uruguay, the Instituto Uruguayo de Investigación y Lucha Contra el Fascismo, el Racismo, y el Antisemitismo (the Uruguayan Institute of Investigation and Fight against Fascism, Racism, and Anti-Semitism).[129] Luisi gave a broad platform to all of these goals at the Congreso de las Democracias (Congress of Democracies) in Montevideo in March 1939.

In what contemporaries described as the "largest popular Pan-American conference" in history, the Congreso de las Democracias gathered hundreds of antifascist students, intellectuals, workers, and feminists from the Americas. Luisi was one of the forum's organizers and key speakers. She urged its attendees to support both the 1933 Montevideo Equal Rights Treaty and the formation of the new Inter-American Congress that Balmaceda had sponsored in Lima. Both of Luisi's resolutions passed, along with others that promoted antiracism, anti–U.S. imperialism, Puerto Rican nationalism, and support of Spain against the global rise of fascism. Luisi collaborated at this Congreso with a number of Argentinian and Chilean feminists from the UAM, the Federación Argentina de Mujeres por la Paz, and the Confederación who had come to Montevideo, including Susana Larguía and Frances Stewart, who became a close friend of Luisi.[130]

Although in April 1939 the Nazi-Soviet pact temporarily shattered the Popular Front, and the Inter-American and World Congresses of Women for Peace and Democracy in Mexico and Cuba never materialized, leftist feminists continued to push for their goals.[131] Later that year, Dolores Ibárruri, Spanish communist feminist and leader of the World Committee of Women against War and Fascism, distinguished the work of "the Latin American women" in the fight against fascism. "With the development during recent years of the Popular Front movement in Latin American republics," she wrote, "the woman's movement there has also gained in vigor."[132] The national groups to which she referred, in Argentina, Chile, Mexico, Cuba, Panama, and elsewhere, were themselves connected in an inter-American movement. Popular Front Pan-American feminism played a key though, until now, overlooked role in the history of international feminism. These Latin American activists not only shifted the organization of the Inter-American Commission of Women but also broadened the meanings of international women's rights and global feminism.

In October 1939, Luisi distinguished their work on the radio: "In this time of concerns and anxieties when men seem driven by a diabolical desire for conquests and settling their differences by barbarous methods of war," she announced, "a group of women of different nationalities and different ideologies — but united by the powerful bond of a common and ardent love for freedom and an inflexible repudiation against brutal . . . wars of aggression — direct to all women a call to come together in a common action in defense of the Peace and Freedom that are threatened."[133] While underscoring what she believed to be women's inherent pacifism, she also asserted calls for women's equal political, civil, economic, and social rights with men. In words that reflected the human rights resolutions of Lima and the 1939 Montevideo Popular Front conference, Luisi asserted that democracies around the globe must secure the rights of all people "without distinction of sex nor of race, of fortune, of class, of beliefs."[134] This broad definition of women's and human rights as being indivisible — social and economic as well as political and civil rights for all, regardless of race, class, or sex — would become even more influential during the Second World War.

CHAPTER SEVEN

Mobilizing Women's
Rights as Human Rights

⚒   ⚒   ⚒

In October 1942, Paulina Luisi received a letter from her *compañera* Ofelia Domín-guez Navarro. Domínguez, now forty-seven, was writing to Luisi in an official capacity, as the director of the Office of War Propaganda of the Cuban Ministry of Defense. Aiming to mobilize women and men in civilian defense in Cuba, Domínguez wanted to exchange information with the corresponding depart-ment in Uruguay and sought the address from Luisi, to whom she sent a "warm and loving hug" and a request for her news.[1] Many years had passed since they had been in touch, and sixty-seven-year-old Luisi was overjoyed to hear from Domínguez. She returned "a big and rejoicing embrace" with "all the mater-nal affection of this old friend." Luisi affirmed that they shared the same goal: "to give everything we can to win the war! Destroy . . . ruthless Nazi-fascism and see the flag of democracies fly throughout the world." Luisi similarly urged Domínguez to send a long personal letter "telling me of your adventures, your heroisms, your admirable struggles." "I have great desires to know what you have done," Luisi added, "above all because once you called me 'mother' and 'mothers' always want to know.'"[2]

The intervening years had seen dramatic changes in both women's lives, al-though both had continued to advance their commitments to Popular Front feminism. In spite of her declining health, Luisi had become a radio personality known as *la Abuela*, "the Grandmother," to her many Uruguayan listeners who heard her call out for women's rights and against fascism over the airwaves.[3] Meanwhile, Domínguez, who had returned to Havana from Mexico in 1938 after Fulgencio Batista legalized the Communist Party of Cuba, had thrown her-self into antiracist, labor, feminist, and antifascist organizing with the Partido Unión Revolucionaria Comunista.[4]

After the December 1941 attack on Pearl Harbor and subsequent entry of Cuba and Uruguay into the Second World War, Domínguez and Luisi redoubled their antifascist efforts and allied with the United States in the hemispheric fight against fascism.[5] For two anti-imperialist women, this new solidarity with the

Paulina Luisi, date unknown. She used this photograph on her campaign posters in 1942 when she ran as a candidate for the House of Representatives for the Socialist Party. Author's collection.

Ofelia Domínguez Navarro. In 1940, Domínguez served as a representative of the Partido Unión Revolucionaria Comunista in the province of Las Villas, Cuba. Courtesy of the Archivo Nacional de Cuba, Havana, Cuba.

United States represented a marked shift. But, as Luisi explained in 1942, "in these moments when the Peace of America is threatened, the strongest bonds that we [women] can establish among us, from the north to the south, will be the best response to those who try to bring their . . . desires for domination to our Continent."[6]

Indeed, women throughout the Americas were forming new alliances around what Franklin D. Roosevelt referred to as "fundamental freedoms" and what people throughout the world were now calling "human rights." For Pan-American feminists, "human rights"—which drew on the 1938 Lima resolutions, earlier concepts of the "universal rights of man," global antifascism, antiracism, the Atlantic Charter, and Roosevelt's "Four Freedoms"—also included women's rights. World War II moved Pan-American *feministas* of different political stripes to a similar position, one that sought inter-American solidarity against totalitarianism while upholding international commitments to women's rights as human rights. Growing numbers of *feministas* in the region were recognizing Luisi, the *abuela*, and other longtime leaders Domínguez, Bertha Lutz, Marta Vergara, and Clara González as progenitors of this international movement that deemed women's rights as imperative to sustaining democracy and fighting fascism.

Luisi and other Pan-American feminists saw the still-existing Inter-American Commission of Women (IACW) as a potentially vital engine for this advocacy, but they were increasingly disappointed by the U.S. leadership that had replaced the deposed Doris Stevens. These new leaders, representatives of the U.S. Women's and Children's Bureaus, fiercely opposed the ERA and explicitly attempted to move Pan-American feminism away from the Equal Rights Treaty long promoted by the IACW and from "women's rights" overall. Instead, their inter-American priorities included women's engagement in civilian defense, the study and regulation of women's labor and welfare reform in the Americas, and the geopolitical imperatives of the U.S. State Department, which funded most of their initiatives.

The goals of these U.S. women contrasted sharply with those of growing numbers of self-described *feministas*. Although civilian defense—the role that civilians and women, specifically, played in the war, administering first aid, educating the public about health and nutrition, selling war bonds and raising funds, among other activities—was vital to many of these feminists, it was important in large part because it was connected to the political rights of citizenship that women still lacked in many countries in Latin America. *Feministas* also continued to push for state-sponsored maternity legislation and now argued for this as a "human right."

Toward the end of the war, Paulina Luisi, Ofelia Domínguez Navarro, and other *feministas* realized that it would not be women from the United States but rather a new group of Latin American advocates in the IACW who would actually make women's rights part of the postwar human rights promises. As in the past, opposition to U.S. hegemony fostered more tightly knit transnational connections among a growing group of Latin American feminists who now sought international women's rights in the postwar world. These *feministas* would utilize inter-American conferences, and especially the Inter-American Conference on Problems of War and Peace in Mexico City in 1945, to insist that women had demonstrated their citizenship through their war work and thus deserved full political and legal equality, as well as social and economic rights. They connected their calls for international women's rights to the new global demands for "human rights."

Women as the Basis of Pan-Americanism

The 1938 Pan-American conference in Lima represented a triumph for Popular Front Pan-American feminists. It paved the way for Latin American leadership of the IACW, with Argentinian Popular Front leader Ana Rosa Schlieper de Martínez Guerrero named as its new chair.

Yet when they ousted Doris Stevens, Popular Front feminists had struck a Faustian bargain with the U.S. State Department. The requirement that governments approve their respective IACW commissioners connected the group far more intimately with both the U.S. State Department and state power than ever before. The U.S. State Department now provided most of the commission's limited funding and could meaningfully call the shots. Thanks to her close relationship with the State Department, the new U.S. representative, Mary Winslow, based in D.C., unofficially chaired the commission. On the eve of the Second World War, when the U.S. government enhanced its Latin American initiatives in anticipation of war in Europe, the State Department became increasingly involved in the commission, seeing Pan-American women's organizing as a key tool for its Good Neighbor agenda.

The U.S. State Department had hand-chosen Schlieper de Martínez Guerrero, with whom some of its members had collaborated in Lima, as official chairman of the commission because she appeared politically anodyne. The U.S. ambassador to Argentina's assurance that Schlieper was primarily involved in "philanthropic and charity work" clinched the department's decision.[7] Such a characterization was in fact inaccurate. Though she was not a communist, Schlieper was a leftist feminist who led a radical feminist group. A leader of the Unión Argentina de Mujeres in Argentina, she would also cofound in 1941 the Junta de la Victoria, a significant Popular Front feminist group that supported the Allied effort to win the war and upheld women's rights and antifascism.[8] Her appointment was intended to provide a pro forma appeal to Argentina, long a thorn in the side of the U.S. hemispheric policies.

Schlieper's appearance and race and the fact that she was not a devotee of Doris Stevens played significant roles in her appointment as well. The U.S. State Department opposed Minerva Bernardino, who also desired this position, on the grounds that she was a close ally of Stevens, a charge that Bernardino denied.[9] Perhaps more meaningfully, Bernardino was described by contemporaries as "mulatto" or "colored," and Schlieper was blonde, blue-eyed, and praised by many for her "beauty."[10] News outlets in the United States touted a distinctly white notion of Pan-American feminism in the promotion of Schlieper's appointment. The *Pan American* magazine announced her chairmanship of the IACW with a full-page portrait of Schlieper as "the 'new woman' of Latin America," contrasting her image with that of an elderly indigenous woman "representing an age that is passing."[11] Such a characterization of Schlieper was at odds with the arguments that many leftist feminists in the Americas like Schlieper were making against discrimination based on race, class, sex, and religion.

Schlieper's relocation of the commission's headquarters to Buenos Aires and the important transnational work that her Junta de la Victoria initiated with feminists in Uruguay and elsewhere were significant. However, the new relationship between the IACW and the State Department meant that the Pan-American Union in Washington, D.C., would remain its unofficial headquarters and the locus of yearly gatherings. After 1941, funding came from the office of the Coordinator of Inter-American Affairs (CIAA), an agency established by the U.S. State Department to promote cultural and economic ties with Latin America. Under the leadership of Assistant Secretary of State Nelson Rockefeller, the CIAA—what *Pan American* magazine called "a new phase of the New Deal"—mounted an unprecedented effort to promote the consumption of goods and cultural exchange throughout the Americas.[12] It did so in order to preserve Cordell Hull's reciprocal trade agreements and bolster "continental solidarity" in the face of economic penetration from fascist Europe.[13]

Nelson Rockefeller believed women were critical to Pan-Americanism, and he knit close connections between the IACW and the CIAA, calling the commission "an excellent medium through which the women of the various countries could coordinate their work."[14] In 1941 Rockefeller helped appoint to the CIAA Mary Winslow, who was already U.S. representative to the commission. At a meeting of twenty-nine national women's groups, cochairs Rockefeller and Winslow attempted to synchronize inter-American activities with the CIAA, placing the commission at the helm of these efforts.[15] In December 1941, on Eleanor Roosevelt's recommendation, Winslow also became part of the Office of Civilian Defense in order to develop programs of volunteer defense activities

REPRESENTING AN AGE THAT IS PASSING—This smiling grandmother of Tehuautepec, Mexico, is giving way to the vibrant Latin-American woman of a new era. (See photograph of a of a woman of the new era on Page 30.)

THE "NEW WOMAN"—Of Latin America is exemplified by Senora Ana Martinez Guerra of Buenos Aires. She flies her own plane, battles for women's rights and is chairman of the Inter-American Commission of Women. (See Who's Who on Page 55.)

The text under these images reads: (left) "REPRESENTING AN AGE THAT IS PASSING — This smiling grandmother of Tehuautepec, Mexico, is giving way to the vibrant Latin-American woman of a new era. (See photograph of a woman of the new era on Page 30.)" and (right) "THE 'NEW WOMAN' — Of Latin America is exemplified by Senora Ana Martinez Guerrero of Buenos Aires. She flies her own plane, battles for women's rights and is chairman of the Inter-American Commission of Women." Pan American: Magazine of the Americas, November–December 1940.

by women in Central and South America, which quickly became a primary focus of the IACW.[16]

A former social worker, Winslow had been a legislative executive in the National Women's Trade Union League and had worked in the Women's Bureau for a decade. The chair of a conglomeration of women's groups that opposed the Equal Rights Amendment, Winslow had been the first choice to replace Doris Stevens among the anti-ERA reformers close to Eleanor Roosevelt.[17] In Winslow's first public speech as U.S. commissioner, she made clear that the inter-American group would no longer support "equal rights" for women, which she characterized, erroneously, as a "northern import" that held little meaning for "Latin American women." The goals of the commission would now be inter-American solidarity, social reform for women and children, and "friendship," an agenda that dovetailed, not coincidentally, with that of the State Department.[18]

While Winslow was not the "chairman" of the IACW, her close connections to the State Department meant that she essentially assumed that role. These connections only increased after Rockefeller named her the "coordinator of women's efforts" of the CIAA.[19] Winslow used CIAA funds to bring Schlieper and other Latin American commissioners to Washington, D.C., each year for annual meetings and "goodwill tours" in the United States that promoted Pan-American education and exchange.[20]

The new direction of the U.S. IACW leadership is perhaps best illustrated by Eleanor Roosevelt herself, who promoted the connections between women and Pan-Americanism but not women's rights. As host of a new weekly radio program in 1941 sponsored by the Pan-American Coffee Bureau and geared toward homemakers, Eleanor Roosevelt interviewed Pan-American leaders like Nelson Rockefeller and Leo Rowe. In addition, she hosted receptions, press conferences, dinners, and luncheons attended by Latin American visitors, diplomats, and feminists. As she stated at a 1941 event at Russell Sage College, which conferred honorary degrees to Schlieper and five other female visitors from Latin America, "The roots of friendship between the Americas will grow deep and strong if the women of the various countries come to understand each other." The broader goal, she made clear, was to "lay the foundations for . . . better commercial relationships and firmer ties which make us a stronger group of nations."[21]

Eleanor Roosevelt never promoted a Pan-American fight for women's rights. She proclaimed the passing of what she called "militant feminism" and stressed the cooperative labor of women.[22] Her continuing animus for the ERA's threat to protective labor legislation, along with what she believed to be U.S. women's progress in political and civil status over the past two decades, made "feminism" passé to Roosevelt.[23]

Yet the many self-described *feministas* who looked to Roosevelt in admiration would vehemently disagree. For the longtime activists in Latin America and rising numbers of new ones, "feminism" was neither passé nor the "northern import" that Winslow had described. "Militant feminism" was in fact growing in many parts of Latin America, where most women still did not have the right to vote and suffered other material forms of oppression under reactionary dictatorships.

The 1938 Lima resolutions that knit together women's rights, antifascism, and defense of democracy were helping spur new, vibrant feminist organizing, especially for women's suffrage. In direct response to the Lima declarations, new national Acción Femenina (Women's Action) groups sprouted in major cities throughout the Americas, including teachers, workers, nurses, and university students. The Acción Femenina Venezuela helped launch a vital suffrage

Eleanor Roosevelt meeting with the Inter-American Commission of Women in the White House in Washington, D.C., November 1941. Standing, left to right: Mary Winslow (U.S.), Carmen B. de Lozada (Bolivia), Amalia González Caballero de Castillo Ledón (Mexico), Esther Neira de Calvo (Panama), Mariana de Cáceres (Honduras), Graciela Mandujano (Chile), María Piedad Castillo de Leví (Ecuador), Eloise Davison (assistant director in charge of group activities of the Office of Civilian Defense). Sitting, left to right: María Currea de Aya (Colombia), Ana Rosa Schlieper de Martínez Guerrero (Argentina), Eleanor Roosevelt (U.S.), Minerva Bernardino (Dominican Republic), Angela Acuña de Chacón (Costa Rica). Esther Neira de Calvo Papers, box 2a, folder 35, Georgetown University Library Booth Family Center for Special Collections, Georgetown University, Washington, D.C.

campaign in that country between 1943 and 1944. In Peru, the Acción Femenina Peruana also fought for suffrage. In Nicaragua, feminist groups drew on the 1938 Lima resolutions to push for women's suffrage. In Colombia, the women's movement grew to include new organizations of working-class women who pushed for suffrage as well. These groups, and many others, allied themselves with the IACW, the Liga Internacional de Mujeres Ibéricas e Hispanoamericanas, the Unión de Mujeres Americanas, and other regional groups. They explicitly connected international women's rights with the defeat of Nazi-fascism.[24]

In light of these new, dramatic feminist mobilizations throughout the Americas, the IACW's shift away from women's rights goals deeply disappointed Paulina Luisi and many other Latin American feminists.[25] Even Bertha

Lutz, who never went so far as wishing for Stevens's return, bemoaned the new State Department–led vision of Pan-American organizing.[26] As she explained in a 1940 letter to Carrie Chapman Catt, Lutz hoped the IACW would rededicate itself soon to a "code of laws for women" and embrace an agenda "from a world perspective and not just from the perspective of women from the USA."[27] She wrote to Mary Winslow and to her old friends in the League of Women Voters that while "we feel that Latin American women alone could not influence events, . . . a united effort of all American women for the rights of women will certainly have a repercussion far and wide."[28] Yet she received unenthusiastic responses to her pleas. At a time when, as she put it, her own "feminist convictions grow stronger and stronger," she noted that feminism seemed to be dying among her U.S. allies.[29] In an interview with the *New York Times*, Lutz stated, "I can't help but feel that Pan-Americanism, as a weapon against totalitarianism, is on a very flimsy basis right now."[30]

The War for "Freedom from Fear and Want" and the IACW

Several months after Lutz uttered these words, on December 7, 1941, Japanese bombers and fighter planes attacked the U.S. naval base at Pearl Harbor, and the United States declared war on Japan and soon after on Germany and Italy. Roosevelt's bold new "Four Freedoms"—freedom of speech, freedom of worship, freedom from want, and freedom from fear—reproduced in newspapers and on the radio throughout the Americas, became central to building Pan-American solidarity against fascism.[31] A few months earlier, in June 1941, Nazi forces had invaded Russia, which caused communist groups to rededicate themselves to the fight against fascism and ally with the war effort. Pan-Americanism became more popular than ever before, as various groups—statesmen, feminists, students, and workers—found a common goal in fighting Nazi totalitarianism and promoting new international rights they called "human rights." Roosevelt had averred in his "Four Freedoms" address that these individual and social rights meant "the supremacy of human rights everywhere."[32] Lutz, Luisi, Vergara, Domínguez, González, and others would endorse these human rights while they continued to insist upon the inclusion of "women's rights" within them. During the war, they and new groups of feminists drove international women's rights back into the official channels of Pan-Americanism.

These feminists eagerly looked to the January 15, 1942, Pan-American conference in Rio de Janeiro, where statesmen upheld human rights as part of the continental front against fascism. Roosevelt called the conference in order to solidify Allied support against the Axis powers; urge Latin American countries to sever diplomatic, commercial, and financial relations with Germany and Japan; and coordinate hemispheric defense. Significantly, the conference also upheld the Declaration of the United Nations. Established at a New Year's Day summit of twenty-six Allied nations in Washington, D.C., in 1942, the Declaration of the United Nations articulated the Allied war aims and reaffirmed connections between individual and international security established in the Atlantic Charter and in Roosevelt's "Four Freedoms."[33] All of these resolutions affirmed international "social rights," which linked individual security (realized through domestic social welfare programs) with international security and peace and sought to promote what *Nation* journalist Freda Kirchwey called a "new deal for the world."[34] New nongovernmental organizations and movements in the United States and in Latin America now utilized the term "human rights" broadly to describe these interrelated international commitments to welfare and individual rights, as well as to anticolonialism, antiracism, and international economic justice.

The 1942 Pan-American conference in Rio de Janeiro pledged international commitments to self-determination, restoration of self-government to those deprived of it, and global cooperation to secure better socioeconomic conditions for all. It extended promises for a restored balance of economic and political power in the world alongside the rights of groups and of individuals in the Americas where these commitments spoke to wide swaths of people. The idea the United States promoted, that the Second World War was a "people's war," gained valence not only in the United States but in Latin America as well.[35] After the Rio conference, Latin American countries that had not already broken diplomatic relations with Germany and Japan quickly did so, except for Argentina and Chile, and many also declared war on the Axis over the next years. The U.S. built military bases in Panama, Cuba, and Brazil; Brazil and Mexico sent troops to war; and increased industrialization in Latin American drove expanding numbers of people and women into factory work.

In Latin America, the Second World War hastened a process that had begun after the Great Depression: the shift from an economy based on U.S. and European exports to one based on industrial production and, during the war, Latin American exportation of food and goods to the United States. Wartime needs resulted in escalated production in mines, farms, and fields. Progressives, labor, and the organized left in Latin America allied with new economic initiatives driven by the Board of Economic Warfare. The government agency led by U.S. vice president Henry Wallace from 1941 to 1943, the Board of Economic Warfare carried out foreign economic policy in Latin America as it related to the war.[36] Wallace, whom some have called "the spiritual and political leader of the international New Deal," focused the Roosevelt administration's wartime foreign economic relations on public capital and alliances with Latin American labor. He upheld that a new world order would follow the war, one in which there would be an end to imperialism, abolition of cartels, and freedom from want.

The Atlantic Charter, which contained universal promises of self-determination, human dignity, and equal access to trade and raw materials, raised the hopes that the United States would fulfill these promises after the war.[37]

The Atlantic Charter and Four Freedoms spoke to Latin American progressives, labor groups, and the organized left, which allied in an unprecedented way with the United States in the fight against fascism. As historian Joshua Frens-String writes, these groups believed "the persistence of economic and social inequities in their own countries were, at least in part, inspiring declarations like the Four Freedoms and the Atlantic Charter."[38] These wartime commitments to international democratic and social rights also confirmed many of the antifascist goals that the transnational Popular Front had demanded in the mid- to late 1930s in inter-American venues: democratic freedoms for all people, "regardless of race, class, religion, or sex."[39]

Pan-American feminists like Marta Vergara and Bertha Lutz rallied to this effort. They interpreted the Atlantic Charter as fulfilling their long-standing demands for international women's rights. In 1941, Vergara and her husband moved to the United States, where she taught Spanish at several colleges and her husband gained U.S. citizenship and enrolled in the army.[40] Though no longer a member of the Communist Party or a leader of the Movimiento pro Emancipación de la Mujer Chilena, Vergara retained her role as the Chilean delegate to the IACW.

Vergara attended the first meeting of the IACW after Pearl Harbor in November 1942, where she and others restored "women's rights" as a central Pan-American aim, over the resistance of U.S. commissioner Mary Winslow. One of Vergara's allies in this effort was the new Brazilian commissioner and member of Bertha Lutz's Federação Brasileira pelo Progresso Feminino (FBPF), Anna Amélia Querioz Carneiro de Mendonça. Sent by Lutz to the United States with a list of proposals demanding international commitments for women's political, social, economic, and civil rights, Carneiro met with Marta Vergara, Ana Rosa Schlieper de Martínez Guerrero, Minerva Bernardino, and other delegates who came with similar goals to reinstate women's rights.[41] They heartily agreed with Winslow's promotion of civil defense, an area in which many had leadership roles in their countries.[42] But they explicitly connected women's work in civil defense to women's citizenship and called for the IACW to focus on promoting international equal rights. Marta Vergara and the Peruvian commissioner explained that women in Chile and Peru did not have national voting rights and that, above all, "women needed equal rights more than ever to help in the new fight for democracy." In the tradition of many Popular Front Pan-American feminists before them, they connected these democratic rights to the antifascist fight, since, as Vergara explained, "fascism destroyed women's rights."[43]

The commissioners also demanded that women be integral members of the peace conferences that would follow the war. As Carneiro explained, women's participation in postwar planning was essential to ensuring a "just and democratic peace."[44] The IACW delegates embraced maternalist notions that women would promote pacifism in whatever multilateral body replaced the League of Nations, but they also believed that women must be at these conferences to make "women's rights" an explicit part of the postwar world. The commission resolved, in accordance with the set of FBPF resolutions that Carneiro brought with her, to give "an endorsement of the Atlantic Charter as a declaration of principles ... and appeal to every government to name a woman as Plenipotentiary Delegate at the coming Peace Conference."[45]

Although they unanimously agreed on the inclusion of women and of international women's rights in the agenda for postwar planning, Latin American feminists did not entirely form a united front at the 1942 commission meeting. Their gathering occurred when the United States was mobilizing an embargo and blockade against Argentina, which opposed joining the Allied fight. Minerva Bernardino—who resented the appointment of Argentinian Schlieper as chair of the IACW over herself—forwarded a resolution that urged the governments of Chile and Argentina to break with the Axis and consolidate a hemispheric front. She received support on this proposal from Amalia González Caballero de Castillo Ledón, the new Mexican commissioner in the government of Manuel Ávila Camacho.[46] Although Schlieper deeply supported the Allied fight, she relied upon the Argentine government to continue her position in the IACW, and Bernardino's resolution would have been damaging to her personally and politically. This resolution was voted down in favor of one that called on all Latin American countries to support the Allied fight, but the debate over it revealed new alliances and fractures within the commission.[47]

These Pan-American women did make significant collective progress by agreeing that women's social rights be included alongside individual rights and reinstated into the IACW and plans for the postwar peace. Over the resistance of Mary Winslow and other U.S. women, Vergara collaborated with Bernardino, Schlieper, and other Latin American commissioners to reestablish "equal rights" as a primary goal of the commission. Winslow acceded as much when she wrote to Eleanor Roosevelt that the IACW had agreed to include many parts of the FBPF platform that Lutz had sent them and that Carneiro had reinforced, including "extension of political and civil rights for women, full opportunity and equal pay for equal work," and a commitment to "social rights" such as maternity legislation.[48]

Vergara and other Pan-American feminists saw these rights as intimately connected to the Atlantic Charter and Declaration of the United Nations, which genuinely inspired them. They believed that international commitments to women's individual and collective rights must be part of the fight against fascism and the promises of the postwar world.[49] These rights were taking on new importance with millions of women entering the paid workforce to support the war effort in the United States and many urbanizing parts of Latin America. For working women, they concurred, commitments like the Atlantic Charter would be revolutionary, leading to meaningful changes in their lives and a new, more equal balance of power in the Americas.

Maternity Legislation as a "Human Right"

In securing these rights, many Latin American feminists looked with hope to the U.S. Women's Bureau, which was becoming more active both in inter-American affairs and in promoting women workers during the war years. The Latin American press took note when, just after Pearl Harbor, Women's Bureau director Mary Anderson encouraged the mobilization of women into war production and protested discrimination against women workers on the basis of sex, marriage, "race, age, or residence."[50] Marta Vergara celebrated the dramatic entry of more than 2 million U.S. women into the workforce as part of the war effort, crediting Anderson for U.S. women's newfound "rights to wear pants" and "rights to work."[51] Stepping up its Pan-American activities, the Women's Bureau also positioned itself and the Children's Bureau as models for welfare state development throughout the Americas. Through a new inter-American division supported by the U.S. State Department, the Women's Bureau exchanged information about women's labor with Latin American government policy makers and feminist groups.[52]

Since the mid-1930s, the Women's Bureau had sent representatives to inter-American meetings, including the Pan-American child congresses, led by Children's Bureau director Katharine Lenroot. During the war, State Department support for its efforts in Latin America gave the members of the Women's and Children's Bureaus hope that they could bring a "New Deal" for the Americas to benefit women and children. Like Winslow, Roosevelt, and others, however, they resisted international commitments to women's rights.

In these years, Latin American feminists were leading calls for women's rights to work and to maternity legislation as "human rights." Their interactions with U.S. Women's Bureau members threw into sharp relief that Latin American commitments to these rights were much stronger than in the United States. The long-standing Popular Front Pan-American feminist articulation of maternity legislation as an international "right" challenged the conceptions of U.S. Women's and Children's Bureau members who, when they discussed maternity legislation at all, spoke of it as a "protection" rather than a "right." At each Pan-

American labor conference during the 1930s, however, leftist Pan-American feminists pushed maternity legislation as a "right." Their resolutions had influenced the International Labor Organization and allowed grassroots groups of working women in both rural and urban areas to demand enforcement of existing maternity laws and expand them to cover farm and domestic workers.[53] By the late 1930s, Brazil, Argentina, Cuba, and Venezuela had federally supported maternity leave and day care, joining the ranks of a number of European countries.[54] By 1942, Chilean labor codes covered the installation of nurseries in factories, leave for working women six weeks before and after birth, and state-funded half pay during leave and job security upon return.[55] In stark contrast, no national maternity legislation existed in the United States.

In practice, many Latin American businesses failed to implement these broad maternity policies, but their passage alone points to salient differences in political cultures between the United States and Latin America.[56] In the United States, where federalism and states' and individual rights prevailed, the power to legislate labor fell more often to the states than to the national government. In Latin America, which conceived of the "family" as a more suitable realm for national legislation, labor worked closely with government to promote social welfare policies that encompassed the family, including maternity legislation. In addition, many Latin American countries saw the incorporation of maternity legislation as part of an expanding welfare state that would help further their economic development.

Also significantly, while in the United States the conflict generated by the ERA between equal rights and protectionist legislative strategies precluded a united front, Latin American feminist arguments and mobilizations had critically advanced these laws for maternity legislation. Many of the most visible national feminist groups in Brazil, Chile, Cuba, Mexico, Panama, Venezuela, and elsewhere viewed maternity legislation as part of the state's social security schemes and as connected to women's citizenship and "right to work," so they argued for it as a "right." In contrast, neither the National Woman's Party, which claimed the mantle of "feminism" in the United States in these years, nor the progressive women leaders in the Women's Bureau called for maternity legislation as a "right." Only after the Second World War, when U.S. women workers themselves began to vociferously push for maternity leave, did the Women's Bureau promote it.[57] Before the war, the Women's Bureau remained ambivalent about wage-earning mothers and aware of the broad opposition in the United States to any public legislation on "private" family matters.[58] Beliefs that women who were mothers belonged at home with their children, along with race- and class-based notions of women's work, perpetuated the fiction that women who were mothers (at least if white) stayed at home with their children.[59]

The disparities with Latin American feminists had become more meaningful when U.S. Women's Bureau members took over the reins of the IACW in 1939. That year, during a regional ILO conference in Havana, where she chaired the group drafting reports for women and children, the new U.S. IACW representative Mary Winslow officially supported policies for maternity legislation promoted by Latin American feminists. Yet she confessed to "a certain feeling of impatience" that so much time had been "spent on setting up protective principles for the employment of pregnant women and mothers who are nursing their babies." "To my mind," she continued, "no satisfactory solution of this situation will ever be accomplished until the families of workers have sufficient economic security so that women who are bearing children and who are nursing little babies are not obliged by necessity to go to work to supplement the family income."[60]

Winslow's words did not satisfy the Latin American delegates who had been the most vocal proponents of international commitments to maternity legislation as an "international right." Leftist feminists Rosa María Otero Gama de Lombardo Toledano, wife of labor leader Lombardo Toledano from Mexico, and Pilar Jorge de Tella from Cuba (the same feminist who had in 1928 rallied with Doris Stevens and Ofelia Domínguez Navarro for the creation of the Inter-American Commission of Women in Havana) insisted on the "rights" of women and mothers in the workforce. They both saw these demands as part of the long movements of Pan-American feminism and of the Popular Front. Jorge de Tella responded directly to Winslow's comments by connecting maternity legislation to women's right to work as a "human and essential right." Jorge de Tella affirmed the series of rights they had established—the right of pregnant women to continue to work and to receive an allowance, the right to receive "equal pay for equal work," and the right of married women to work. She and other Popular Front feminists at the 1939 ILO conference argued that these social rights were part of the antifascist promotion of democracy in the world.[61]

Over the next few years, Latin American feminists continued to insist that maternity legislation was a "human right," especially after the Women's Bureau created its International Division and appointed Mary Cannon as its chief Women's Bureau member. A former representative from the Young Women's Christian Association who coordinated the international YWCA in Buenos Aires from 1931 to 1937, Cannon was fluent in Spanish and in Portuguese. Between 1941 and 1943, she traveled extensively in Latin America to Argentina, Chile, Brazil, Ecuador, Paraguay, Uruguay, and Peru, supported by Nelson Rockefeller's CIAA. Cannon met with trade union organizers and women leaders, studying labor legislation, learning about government bureaucracies that set policies on women and children, and suggesting the creation of women's bureaus in other countries.[62] Cannon's stature among Latin American feminists and among the Women's Bureau grew on these trips, and in 1943 she replaced Mary Winslow as the U.S. delegate of the IACW.

Cannon managed to gain the trust of many she met in Latin America in part because they saw her as separate from U.S. imperial interests. The Women's Bureau viewed her trips as part of the U.S. Good Neighbor Policy, to bring the "New Deal to the world," and to promote U.S. trade interests in Latin America. Cannon, herself more skeptical of U.S. trade interests in the region, revealed her own doubts about the U.S. Good Neighbor efforts.[63] As she wrote to Anderson from Argentina in 1941, "There is a very real fear among some people that the United States is entering into a policy of economic and commercial imperialism, and that all these missions coming down are part of that policy." "Frenzied interest in inter-American solidarity" was not as pronounced in Argentina as it was in the United States, she wrote, noting the meaninglessness of Rockefeller sending "second rate pianists" down to Latin America. Cannon realized later that part of her mission was to sell the American way; she explained, "We wanted to know what they [the Latin Americans] were thinking. . . . We wanted them on our side."[64]

Cannon recognized that the greatest threat to inter-American understanding and solidarity was the vast economic disparity between the United States and Latin America.[65] Thus, in her well-attended talks and articles that she published during her travels, she took pains to underscore that U.S. women were not as they appeared in the movies, with cars and lavish houses. Like women in Latin America, she emphasized, they too had economic hardships and cared for and worried about their children and homes.[66]

Though somewhat critical of inter-American trade interests in the region, Cannon generally upheld the view that the United States represented a beacon of democratic progress and modernity, of which women's labor was an important part. She saw her role as promoting the New Deal in the Americas as well as forming new and more equal partnerships through social welfare bureaucracies. In speeches back home to U.S. audiences, she remarked that Latin American women were "catching up" to U.S. women and "looking to us for not only political democracy but democracy more broadly."[67] When traveling to Latin American countries, Cannon played the role of a U.S. "inspector" to whom the various government bodies in Latin America had to prove their standards in women's rights and budding social welfare programs.[68]

Even as Cannon played the role of purveyor of "American democracy," she increasingly learned that many of these labor laws in Latin America were in fact more progressive than those for working women in the United States, challenging her notion that Latin American women were trying to "catch up" to those in the United States. Over the course of her extensive travels in Latin America, Cannon shifted from being a teacher to being a student, particularly on maternity legislation, a subject that had not even been on Cannon's radar until she traveled to Chile and Argentina in 1941.[69]

After learning from these groups about the 1939 ILO convention on maternity rights, Cannon wrote to Mary Anderson inquiring what the United States was doing in terms of "maternity legislation," which she had to define for Anderson: "i.e. giving expectant mothers time off with salary and some medical assistance." She knew of only two U.S. states with any provisions and asked, "Has there ever been any movement towards such legislation? What stand does the Bureau take?"[70] After not receiving a response from Anderson, Cannon wrote to her again a month later with a flurry of imperatives and questions:

> I need some enlightenment—and as soon as possible! What has the U.S. Department of Labor or the State Departments of Labor done about the recommendations of the I.L.O. conferences—on maternity legislation—especially those of Havana. If nothing has been done—what is the explanation[?] . . . What happens to women workers—factory and otherwise during pregnancy—are they given the necessary time away from their jobs—is there any provision in any way for compensation for wages—do they get their jobs back. Has anything *official* been done about day nurseries[?] . . . Do Public Health agencies or others . . . give free medical care?[71]

Cannon attached a document outlining the series of ways that the Chilean labor law accounted for maternity and noted her awareness of other Latin American countries that had similar laws. People were asking her what the United States was doing for maternity, she told Anderson: "Newspaper reporters want to cover the whole field—and people here are especially interested in social legislation." She needed answers.[72]

The response that Anderson ultimately sent to Cannon came in the form of a memo from the assistant director of the Women's Bureau, with the indirect but unequivocal answer, "There has been strong objection to women with small children being employed in this country."[73] Cannon learned that no legislation for maternity existed on a national basis in the United States and that only six states had maternity laws. She also learned that federal employees could use their sick leave with pay for a period of confinement but that these laws reserved no funding for pregnant women nor required any paid benefits. The memo also explained that motherhood was not the concern of employers: "No employer is bothering to determine whether the woman has children so that we have no ideas as to the extent of employment of women with small children. As far as we know, where wives and husbands are both working, they work on different shifts, one being responsible for the household while the other is at work."[74] At the very least, these words demonstrate a remarkably ambivalent attitude at a time when large numbers of increasingly married women had begun working in defense jobs in the United States, with a total of 13 million women employed nationally.[75]

The Women's Bureau's ambivalence over maternity legislation continued even during the Second World War, when the mass entry of U.S. women into work became one of the most visible social changes the war wrought.[76] As of May 1942, the employment of women in war industries had reached around 1 million, double the number of women who had started working in defense right after Pearl Harbor. Although these numbers would force the United States to pay greater attention to maternity leave, day care, and maternal policies, the two key wartime maternity legislation measures produced came from the Children's Bureau rather than from the Women's Bureau, which deemed "maternity" an issue of child care and thus outside its remit.[77] The Emergency Maternity and Infant Care Act, passed in 1943, provided maternity aid and health care to women whose husbands were soldiers in the four lowest pay grades, in support of "babies and soldiers."[78] The Lanham Act, which initially passed in 1941, "funded community facilities in 'war impact areas,' but it was not until early 1943 that these provisions were interpreted as being applicable to child care centers."[79] These acts were framed in the context of patriotism, need, or aid to children rather than of "women's rights," and they did not generate feminist mobilization or broader support for maternity legislation beyond these specific programs. Furthermore, both were ultimately marred by unwieldy apparatuses, lack of enforcement, and racial barriers that prevented access to minorities.[80]

The exigencies of the war drove these policies, but it is important to recognize that the policy makers in the Children's and Women's Bureaus were keenly aware of Latin American legislation on this score. Mary Cannon vocally promoted the social legislation of Latin American countries around maternity, and Children's Bureau director Katharine Lenroot had extensive contacts with Latin American feminists through the Pan-American child congresses. In December 1943, Lenroot proudly wrote to her longtime friend Bertha Lutz about the Emergency Maternity and Infant Care program, emphasizing that "we now have enough money to carry on a nation-wide program of free maternity and infant care, provided as a right and not a charity."[81] Lenroot did not tell Lutz that the "rights" provided in the emergency act applied only to the wives and children of enlisted men rather than to all women.

Mary Cannon was also keenly aware that, in contrast to the United States, countries such as Brazil, Chile, and Argentina viewed maternity legislation as a fundamental right of citizenship for women, and she began to uphold this as a model of social democracy from which the United States could learn.[82] Increasingly, in speeches and interviews in the United States, she criticized the absence of maternity legislation in the United States and upheld Latin America as a model.[83] After returning from Ecuador, Brazil, Peru, and Paraguay, she explained in a *New York Times* interview that federal labor law in these countries followed ILO recommendations and was "in many cases . . . more comprehensive and advanced than in the United States." In most of these countries, women workers got a rest period of a few weeks to several months before and after pregnancy, did not lose their jobs, and were provided "crèches" or day-care centers in their factories.[84]

At the yearly gathering of the IACW in D.C. in 1944, Cannon in her new role as U.S. commissioner explained that "social security in some South American nations provide wider benefits for women workers than does our system. . . . Several nations have established plans whereby maternity leaves are given to the women workers . . . and money from the social security fund is paid to women during the period that they are out of work." She also noted that "equal pay" laws were stronger in Latin America than in the United States, where "'equal pay for equal work' is still a controversial issue in several States."[85] Cannon's statements, which were reproduced in the *New York Times*, may not have significantly changed U.S. policies regarding maternity legislation, but they did influence public opinion to some degree, and they also altered U.S. engagement in Pan-American feminism.

Mary Cannon became the first U.S. commissioner who did not impose her own agenda over Latin American feminist leaders and who, instead, looked to them for direction. Cannon was also the first U.S. commissioner who was fluent in Spanish and the only one who had lived in Latin America for any significant amount of time. Still, it would be the Latin American members of the commission who proactively pushed their vision for individual and social rights for women into a broader agenda for human rights in the postwar world.

"The Imperialist Ghost . . . Darkens the Future of America"

As the Allied victory seemed more secure, inter-American calls for women's "individual and collective rights" became overlaid with concerns over the economic and political makeup of the Americas following the war. Pan-American feminists had long drawn connections between inter-American trade, economic order, and women's rights, particularly for working women in the hemisphere. In the 1930s, Paulina Luisi had decried the domination of the U.S. and British oil companies capitalizing on the Chaco War to seize more oil reserves and continue to keep Latin America in a state of underdevelopment.[86] Luisi shared the view with many other Popular Front feminists in the region that Latin America's economic underdevelopment hurt women as much as, if not more than, men, severely limiting their opportunities for work and income.[87] She and many others looked to the Atlantic Charter and the Declaration of the United Nations as promises to level imperial powers and economic hegemony. When it became clear that the United States would abandon many of these promises after the war, Luisi and other Spanish-speaking feminists began to rekindle their ideas for an anti-imperialist, antifascist movement, which they would lead.

During the war, the United States had made two significant economic promises in exchange for Latin American wartime support: first, large-scale governmental loans that would help Latin American countries diversify their development and become more self-sufficient by stimulating native-owned businesses along with national economic planning; and second, price stabilization for the primary products and commodities those countries exported. As the war began to wind down, however, the United States moved away from both of these promises. Representatives of the United States urged Latin American governments to accept new priorities, including free-market trade and private foreign enterprise and investment. Most Latin American governments did not believe these new goals would bring prosperity and resented the United States' betrayal of its promises.[88] Yet most also recognized their limited power against the United States, which was emerging from the war with unprecedented industrial and political might.

Paulina Luisi registered these concerns in a March 1943 questionnaire she filled out from the CIAA's Latin American Research Bureau polling Latin American intellectuals on "what role the social question and the economic situation of working classes should play in the postwar world." Her answer emphasized rights for women, for workers, and for Latin American countries in the emerging social and economic order as interrelated issues. After the First World War, she wrote, the distribution of raw materials from Latin America to the United States had been a "Gordian knot" that had caused major economic imbalances in the Americas. The social and economic work of the United Nations, or of a similar postwar economic body, must, she explained, take up equal and proportional distribution of primary materials and food supplies. She argued for a multilateral organization that would regulate trade, control world production, and allow for equitable distribution of primary materials and food supplies. As part of this vision for social justice, Luisi called for the explicit inclusion of women's rights in any postwar body, citing millions of women's wartime work as justification and foreseeing the unfair unemployment of these female workers during demobilization. "This war has demonstrated categorically . . . that an inescapable interdependence exists among all the people of the universe," she insisted. Luisi argued that the broader social and economic structures could not be separated from the realities of the lives of laborers, many of whom were women.[89] "If the democratic principles the governments proclaim are really sincere," she wrote, they would address these issues. The war was being won, she underscored, "with the effort and sacrifice of *both men and women*. In the movement of the reconstruction of the world, *it is necessary that this be remembered*."[90]

At the April 1944 meeting of the IACW in Washington, D.C., Latin American feminists, who once again formed a mostly united bloc, similarly connected their hopes for women's rights with desires for equitable trade policies, protective tariffs to secure fair commodity prices, and a multilateral international body to enforce such provisions. Tensions over the United States' turning its back on these economic promises loomed over this meeting. Minerva Bernardino, who had now replaced Schlieper as the chair, and Amalia de Castillo Ledón from Mexico, the newly appointed vice president, announced their concerns before 500 representatives of U.S. women's groups who had come to the meeting.[91] This was a time "of undeniable uneasiness, almost apprehension, with regard to the future of the Good Neighbor policy," Bernardino announced.[92] Castillo Ledón asked "when victory [is] . . . achieved and the U.S. [finds] . . . itself with armed forces and unprecedented industrial capacity . . . what will be the fate of the Spanish and Portuguese speaking countries of the Americas?"[93] The Colombian commissioner told the group that the free-market trade that the United States promoted hurt working women in Latin America.[94]

Several months later, the July 1944 Bretton Woods conference on monetary and trade issues, and the Dumbarton Oaks meeting that followed it, confirmed Pan-American feminists' fears of U.S. hegemony in the postwar world. Bretton Woods, which sought to stabilize international financial and economic development through the establishment of the World Bank and International Monetary Fund, promoted the institutionalization of commitments to free trade and opposition to protectionism, despite the opposition of Latin American governments.[95] It also gave veto power to the three major powers, the United States, Great Britain, and the Soviet Union.[96] The Dumbarton Oaks conference, which took place between the summer and autumn of 1944 in Washington, D.C., and charted out the postwar plans for the United Nations, reflected Great Power hegemony as well, involving only the "Big Four"—China, Great Britain, the United States, and the USSR. These powers decreed that the future United Nations would be dominated by a security council that included those four powers alone. The only Latin American governments consulted in these plans were Venezuela, Brazil, and Mexico, and that consultation had been perfunctory.[97]

The Bretton Woods and Dumbarton Oaks agreements did not reflect the "New Deal for the world" enshrined in the Four Freedoms or Atlantic Charter:

an integrated system of global safeguards through political, judicial, and economic means that would preserve individual and international security. It was clear to many Latin American statesmen, jurists, feminists, and journalists that the United States would preserve U.S. interests above Latin American ones and abandon the inter-American system of regional security.[98]

Many Latin American feminists also objected to the fact that the Dumbarton Oaks agreement included almost nothing regarding human rights or women's rights. While the "purposes" of Dumbarton Oaks incorporated the broad phrase "promoting respect for human rights and fundamental freedoms," the text made no specific statement that such rights and freedoms should be enjoyed by all "without distinction as to race, sex, language, or religion," an important commitment authored by the Mexican and Cuban Pan-American representatives at earlier inter-American conferences.[99]

The absence of these guarantees became a new reason and rallying point for a revitalized anti-imperialist, antifascist, inter-American feminism. In December 1944, the Peruvian Aprista leader Magda Portal, who had over the past few years become an outspoken feminist, wrote to her friend Paulina Luisi, "I have not only skepticism but certainty that the postwar period will be much more terrible than the war itself. We are already seeing the imperialist struggles to preserve and enlarge the domain of those who do not want to lose their spheres of influence." Noting that "the semi-colonial continents and the colonials don't count for anything in the conferences" dominated by the "Great Powers," Portal wrote, "We live in a world of shameless predators who don't even wait for the end of the war to bring out their steely claws." She predicted, "America's destiny is at stake.... If we don't unite—those from Mexico down—we will be devoured. We are no longer masters of ourselves, Paulina, we depend totally and absolutely on the United States.... The imperialist ghost more than ever darkens the future of America. And this ... should be our fight.... It will no longer be the threat of nazi-type-fascism, but of the great captains of war."[100]

Longtime friends Paulina Luisi and Ofelia Domínguez Navarro also reconnected around Portal's idea that they should "unite—those from Mexico down." Just two years earlier, the two women had written to each other about their hopes for a continental fight for democracy. As the minister of defense, Domínguez had rallied Cubans around the fight alongside the United States and all the Allied powers for the Four Freedoms. But now, in January 1945, after Bretton Woods and Dumbarton Oaks, Domínguez and Luisi were disappointed and fearful. Yet in their correspondence, they turned their shared fears into action. Now was the time, they believed, to rekindle their anti-imperialist and antifascist front of feminists in Latin America. Luisi wrote to Domínguez about creating new formal bonds between their Cuban and Uruguayan feminist groups, and Domínguez responded with enthusiasm and a sense of urgency: "We are living through the most dramatic moment in history," Domínguez responded. "The women of the continent ... cannot, nor should not, remain ... at the margins of these events. Within each of our countries, and throughout the American territory, we must unite." She explained that their fight would maintain women's rights as central to their demands—"as something in common to defend." Women throughout the Americas, she reasoned, "should be disposed to militant action."[101]

Feministas at *Chapultepec*

In this shifting international context, Luisi, Domínguez, and other Latin American feminists set their sights on the Pan-American Chapultepec Conference on War and Peace, where grievances with the Dumbarton Oaks resolutions would be aired. On the initiative of Mexican foreign minister Ezequiel Padilla, a number of representatives of Latin American countries had called for an inter-American conference in Mexico City at the Chapultepec Castle in late February 1945. While not an official Pan-American conference, it would gather statesmen from all of the Latin American countries except Argentina, which had still refused to join the Allied effort, to revise the Dumbarton Oaks decrees and formulate their own resolutions for the social and economic cooperation of the Americas. They planned to bring resolutions from Chapultepec to the upcoming San Francisco meeting that would create the United Nations.

Minerva Bernardino and Amalia de Castillo Ledón, who would attend the conference as president and vice president of the IACW, reached out to feminists throughout the Americas, seeking suggestions for resolutions and support. Castillo Ledón wrote to Marta Vergara as a *compañera* in "this feminist work that interests us all," urging her attendance as well. Although Vergara could not travel with Bernardino and Castillo Ledón to the conference, she redoubled her commitments to their goals: to ensure that women—and women's rights—be included in what would become the United Nations Charter.[102]

Bernardino and Castillo Ledón were not leftists—both were liberal feminists who emphasized legal equality and cooperation with their nation states, which in Bernardino's case was the Trujillo dictatorship. Yet, they were committed to promoting women's social rights and the rights of Latin American nations. They knew these demands would find favor with Latin American statesmen seeking to preserve the Pan-American system and human rights agenda.

Popular Front Pan-American feminists in turn looked to them as allies and in 1945 sent numerous suggestions to Castillo Ledón before Chapultepec to try to influence their goals there. One list of demands from an unknown group of Popular Front feminists presented in stunning detail and depth the high expectations these feminists had of the IACW. They asked the commission to promote resolutions for international women's individual political and social rights and to take decided stands against imperialism, fascism, and "secret treaties" made by powerful governments without public support. They insisted that international guarantees for women's rights should include social rights in the form of a "Charter for Women and Children." Upholding Soviet legislation as a model, they called for women's full independence as well as recognition of the social function of maternity. They also included demands such as the following:

> To salute women combatants and enrolled in armed bodies in the US, England, China, Soviet Union, and France.
> To adopt a resolution that asks Roosevelt, Churchill, Stalin, and Chiang Kai-shek, commit that in the deliberations on peace, there is the voice of a female delegate from this commission.
> A strict resolution that should consider racial prejudice a crime against antifascist unity in general.
> That the democratic countries of this hemisphere make every possible effort by diplomatic and economic means to eliminate the danger of a new totalitarian penetration in Latin America.[103]

These leftist feminists influenced the action taken at Chapultepec. Although Castillo Ledón did not act on many of these suggestions, she did incorporate a number of them for presentation at Chapultepec, namely the insistence that women be at the peace table in San Francisco (a resolution the IACW had itself already voted upon), a resolution opposing racial prejudice, and a women's and children's charter that strongly asserted women's social rights.

Although Bernardino, who was based in D.C., also sought out recommendations from Mary Cannon and Frieda Miller, she and Castillo Ledón authored their proposals for Chapultepec, influenced by these Popular Front Pan-American feminist demands and by their own long-standing calls for women's rights. Cannon and Miller's suggestions on "economic, political, and civil rights" for women were broad, and only their second draft included state-sponsored maternity legislation as something of an afterthought.[104] The "Women's and Children Charter" and the other resolutions that Bernardino and Castillo Ledón announced at Chapultepec were far more detailed than what Cannon and Miller provided. They called much more unequivocally for women's individual and social rights as matters of human justice and retained the Popular Front's specific call for ending racial prejudice.

Significantly, Bernardino and Castillo Ledón's resolution for women's civil and political rights emphasized the need for social rights, and their "Women's and Children's Charter" for women's social rights emphasized the need for civil and political rights, revealing how interdependent they believed all of these rights were. In their proposal calling for an international commitment to women's "civil and political rights," they explained that women's labor during the war justified their full citizenship. Their "Women's and Children's Charter" called for social rights for working women, including maternity legislation, as well as women's political citizenship. It also exhorted countries to give women the vote, emphasizing that maternity legislation would be meaningless without full citizenship. The charter promoted as well equal rights for women to collective bargaining and to legislative systems that decided social welfare more broadly.[105] Finally, the charter emphasized that proactive steps must be taken in the face of the "chaotic avalanche of unemployment" for women that would follow the war. They urged each country in the Americas to establish a committee "to study the problem of unemployment of women in the post-war period."[106]

Significantly, influenced by Popular Front antiracism, the two women also connected all of these "equal rights" for women with racial equality. They explicitly asserted the rights that Latin American women and women of color throughout the Americas needed and linked these as connected antiracist struggles. "In the return to peace and the return to normal life," their resolution averred, "it would be absurd, humiliatingly unfair, and even unpatriotic, to leave the Latin American women, black women, and women of different indigenous races in such a notorious situation."[107] In so doing, Castillo Ledón and Bernardino coupled women's rights arguments with growing calls during the war and at the Chapultepec conference itself for racial equality as a fundamental human right.[108] Their resolutions gained great support from various women's and worker's groups in Mexico that cabled their support to the Mexican delegation and State Department.[109]

Their resolutions, which also connected women's equal rights with the equal rights of nations, gained support from many male Latin American delegates who had brought their own human rights resolutions. The "Project of Resolution of the Cuban Delegation on the Declaration of the International Duties and Rights of the Individual" and Cuba's proposed resolution on "the Rights and Duties of the Nations" called for "social and economic rights" for both individuals and nations. These declarations as well as the "Project of the Resolution of the Mexican Delegation on the International Protection of the Essential Rights of Man" framed a series of human rights as inter-American contributions. They called for "equality in sovereignty of the States and of the individual liberty [of peoples] without religious or racial prejudices."[110]

While Bernardino and Castillo Ledón's resolution on women's civil and political rights sailed through the conference, their "Charter on Women and Children" met with greater resistance, and with especially heavy criticism from

Children's Bureau director Katharine Lenroot, longtime friend of Bertha Lutz who was a "technical adviser" to the U.S. delegation.[111] Lenroot found the charter "defective in style and material" and collaborated with male delegates on the Committee on Social Rights to strip away any mention of women's rights, including political rights, or women's equality.[112] Lenroot, as a *Washington Post* article noted, was more interested in "social problems as a whole than the spread of women's suffrage."[113] Part of Lenroot's resistance to women's rights demands no doubt came from her opposition to the ERA in the United States and perhaps also from her belief that improvements to human welfare came less from organized social movements than from welfare policies and a class of educated professionals and social reformers who would develop juvenile courts and justice systems. The revisions Lenroot made also deemphasized the problems surrounding women's right to work after the war and the question of committees studying women's unemployment. Her efforts reflected the goals she had long pursued in Pan-American children's conferences—the "rights of the child" and establishment of homes for child refugees during the war.

Lenroot justified her suggested changes by attributing some of them to recommendations that her friend Bertha Lutz and the FBPF in Brazil had sent to the conference, although her attribution occluded the robust women's rights demands that the FBPF also made. Lutz and her FBPF colleagues had organized a meeting in Rio de Janeiro before the Chapultepec conference in which they strongly asserted women's rights goals, emphasizing the contributions of Latin American women to the war effort and arguing for the interdependence of women's social, economic, political, and civil rights. Several of the FBPF resolutions did stress expertise and institutional solutions to social and economic problems, and those resolutions were the only ones that Lenroot latched onto.[114] Lenroot's changes to the Charter on Women and Children diluted the interdependence between women's social rights and individual rights that Lutz, Bernardino, Castillo Ledón, and many other Pan-American feminists had long sought to assert.

At Chapultepec, Bernardino and Castillo Ledón did, however, successfully advance two other important resolutions to secure women's rights in the postwar world. The first recognized the importance of the IACW as a fundamental part of Pan-Americanism and called for its continuation. The second argued that in order to gain full democratic cooperation in the creation of the postwar world, women must be included in the governmental delegations to the upcoming conference in San Francisco that would form the United Nations. The Second World War, it averred, had demonstrated that women were "a factor of prime importance for the moral elevation and material progress of all nations."[115]

This resolution would pave the way for a dramatic representation of Latin American women in their delegations to the San Francisco conference the following month, where they would vociferously push for women's rights. It reflected the nearly unanimous opinion of Pan-American feminists, from Lutz's FBPF to the Popular Front Pan-American feminists who had rallied around an Inter-American Congress of Women against war and fascism in the mid-1930s. Late in 1944 a new mass organization of women founded in Panama by Clara González demanded not only women's suffrage but also "the greater union of women of the continent and the world in an effort to consolidate a permanent peace . . . in the United Nations."[116] Early in 1939, González had been replaced as IACW Panamanian commissioner under that country's "interpretation of the Lima Resolution," but, nonetheless, she continued to mobilize Popular Front feminism in the country.[117] In 1944 in Chile, a national congress representing 213 women's organizations called on the Chilean government to support the United Nations and "to nominate women as delegates at the International Peace Conferences."[118] Chilean Pan-American feminist leader Amanda Labarca believed that for "justice, liberty, democracy, and well-being" to prevail at the UN peace table, "women needed to work with men."[119] Women in the United States also demanded a presence at the UN conference, but not in order to advance women's rights, since, they believed, those rights had been largely achieved.[120]

The accomplishments that Bernardino and Castillo Ledón brokered at the Chapultepec conference were crucial to pushing women's rights and human rights into the postwar firmament. With a few exceptions, U.S. press coverage overlooked these achievements, focusing instead on fears expressed by Latin American delegates that the forthcoming UN conference in San Francisco would dismantle the inter-American system.[121] But an article in the *Bulletin of the Department of State* captured the lasting import of the Chapultepec conference in defining both human rights and women's rights. The author credited "inter-American conferences held during the past half-century" for "leading toward the establishment of the ideal of social justice as a cardinal objective of international relations." In this account, the emphasis on women's rights at Chapultepec represented the most meaningful part of this commitment to social justice.[122]

Bernardino and Castillo Ledón recognized their work as part of an even longer history of inter-American feminism. Before making one of her proposals before the conference, Castillo Ledón had gained strength by seeing on the wall of Chapultepec Castle the large portrait of seventeenth-century Mexican nun and feminist *precursora* Sor Juana Inés de la Cruz. This image had given her the strength to make the women's rights arguments that she and Bernardino now looked forward to advancing in San Francisco.[123]

A month later at the founding of the United Nations, Pan-American feminists would continue this work and deploy their inter-American experience on the world stage. They would insist on the interdependence of individual and social rights and on the interdependence of women's rights and human rights. *Feminismo americano* would shape the mission of the fledgling United Nations.

CHAPTER EIGHT

The Latin American Contribution
to the Constitution of the World

❌ ❌ ❌

On April 21, 1945, Bertha Lutz gazed from her window in the Pan American clipper to see vapors of sulfur smoke and ashes wafting from an active volcano in Costa Rica. Thrilled by the sight, she alerted the others on the plane to this "once in a lifetime vision."[1] Her fellow passengers were male statesmen, members of the Brazilian, Uruguayan, and Ecuadorean delegations to the United Nations Conference on International Organization (UNCIO) in San Francisco.[2] They represented only a handful of the 2,000 delegates, experts, advisers, and secretaries from fifty countries, in addition to 2,400 correspondents and radio reporters and close to 200 members of U.S. nongovernmental organizations, who were making their way to what would be the largest diplomatic conference in history.

The sight of the smoking crater turned Lutz's thoughts to aerial bombardment in distant lands and to her own special duty as the only woman in the Brazilian delegation to a conference that would draft the postwar peace. Admittedly, Lutz would have preferred to stay at home with her tree frogs than go to a conference that would last over two months.[3] But 40 million people had been killed, and the war was not yet over. Lutz blamed the war on the "excessive masculinism" that bred greed and fascism. Only by establishing a strong role for women in the new peacekeeping body and women's rights in its charter, she believed, would war be eliminated.[4]

Lutz had some doubts about how to accomplish these goals in the UN Charter. The basic framework hashed out the previous autumn by the "Big Four" at Dumbarton Oaks contained not a word about women's rights or the inclusion of women in the organization. Worse, it established dominance over the UN by a Security Council made up of those four powers — the United States, Great Britain, China, and the USSR — alone.

Weeks later, in the heat of conference proceedings, Lutz would remember the "bubbling cauldron" in the mountains of Costa Rica. The conference had become a "living hell," she wrote friends back home in Brazil, in large part because, to her deep disappointment, the female British and U.S. delegates refused to support the inclusion of women's rights in the charter. Lutz, however, connected with a number of female delegates from Latin America with whom she shared Pan-American feminist goals. In particular, Minerva Bernardino and Amalia de Castillo Ledón, president and vice president of the Inter-American Commission of Women (IACW), had come to promote women's rights, as they had done in Chapultepec the month before. A number of other Latin American feminists had arrived with similar intentions. Lutz would find engaged collaborators in them and in Jessie Street, the female delegate from Australia. Together, these women pushed women's rights into the UN Charter and into the framework of international human rights. Their proposals, which rested on several decades of sustained Pan-American feminist activism, helped establish "equal rights for men and women" in the preamble and in the "purposes" of the charter and a statement ensuring women equal representation in United Nations bodies. Their efforts also led to the inclusion of "human rights" in the UN Charter.

Joining a group of nongovernmental representatives, unofficial observers, and delegates from the "smaller and medium powers," and above all from Latin America, these feminists pushed to secure "human rights and fundamental freedoms" that were largely absent from the Great Powers' Dumbarton Oaks proposal into the UN Charter. These principles for "human rights and fundamental freedoms" — for justice as well as for peace — were unprecedented in international treaties. Diverse actors at the UNCIO gave the term "human rights" multiple meanings — from anticolonialism, civil rights, and racial equality, to antifascism and opposition to anti-Semitism, to the social democratic rights of the Atlantic Charter and Franklin D. Roosevelt's Four Freedoms. In the hands of Bertha Lutz and other Pan-American feminists, they also meant international commitments to women's social, economic, political, and civil rights. The successful inclusion of these rights in the UN Charter was momentous. Everything that the United Nations would go on to do rested on this international treaty. Without Pan-American feminist activism, the UN Charter likely would have contained little to nothing about women's rights.

The success of the Pan-American women's rights agenda at this conference relied on several recent developments that came together in San Francisco. For many, women's contributions to the war effort justified their full citizenship, while antifascist promotion of women's rights connected with a broader human rights agenda. The pervasive language of human rights, mobilized by all nongovernmental groups and by "smaller powers" against the "Great Powers," served as a lever that helped these women further their goals. To oppose Great Power hegemony in the Security Council that would effectively control the new organization, Latin American nations and other countries pressed to expand the other organs of the new UN—the General Assembly, the Economic and Social Council—as countervailing weights. Advocating human rights and women's rights in these organs became a key part of this effort.

While demands for human rights advanced women's rights, demands for women's rights helped advance human rights. The joint proposal that Lutz, Bernardino, and Castillo Ledón made for the inclusion of "promotion of respect for human rights and fundamental freedoms regardless of race, sex, condition, or creed" was the first public amendment proposed for human rights at the conference and helped ensure its inclusion in the preamble and statement of purposes. For these Pan-American feminists, the enshrining of human rights in the UN Charter represented a long-sought goal. In ways that often directly challenged the authority of the nation-state, and that of the United States in particular, Pan-American feminists had long called for international women's rights, deeming them vital to global peace and security.

These earlier calls for an international, universal feminism had always been marked by tensions over race, class, and nation, and this 1945 moment was no less contested. Lutz, Bernardino, and Castillo Ledón, all appointed to the conference by their national governments, together represented only one side of a multivalent movement that had fought not only for words in international charters but also for grassroots mobilizations, meaningful social change in women's lives, and structural change in inter-American relations. Lutz, Bernardino, and Castillo Ledón were not Popular Front Pan-American feminists. Unlike some of their Popular Front counterparts, they were allied with their governments and privileged working within diplomatic processes. At the UN conference in San Francisco they focused on narrower, though no less challenging, goals— pushing "equal rights" for women into as many resolutions as they could. Yet their activism at the 1945 meeting drew on the sustained visions and work of Popular Front Pan-American feminists.

At the San Francisco conference, as at the Pan-American conferences leading up to it, their affective experience deeply informed their work. In San Francisco, the dogged opposition of the United States and other Great Powers to Lutz's feminist demands and their treatment of Latin American delegates as racial others moved Lutz to embrace a new self-identification as "Latin American." Her coalition with Pan-American feminists in turn galvanized Latin American support for a women's rights agenda that included the creation of a UN organ that would study and recommend changes on women's rights—the Commission on the Status of Women. Their promotion of women's rights meaningfully embedded human rights in the United Nations at its formation.

Bertha Lutz, "Anglo-Brazilian"

Ever since the 1922 Pan-American Conference of Women in Baltimore, Bertha Lutz had dreamed of an international group of women from the Western Hemisphere collaborating for women's rights and world peace. Her notions of Pan-American feminism had always been shaped by her ideal of shared leadership from "Brazil" (by which she meant herself) and the "United States" (by which she meant other white women in the League of Women Voters, Women's Bureau, or Children's Bureau). But toward the end of the Second World War, she was disappointed by what she perceived as the failures of U.S. women. In spite of her work to reinstate a women's rights agenda into the IACW, she perceived a real lack of U.S. leadership on international commitments to women's rights.

Along with this setback, the rise of nationalist and proletarian influences abroad and in Brazil caused Lutz to turn her sense of identification away from the United States and toward Great Britain. Her beliefs in white racial superiority and in the British Empire undergirded this identification. During the war, she wrote to a British correspondent at the BBC, drawing connections between Gandhi's nationalism in India and political gains by communist politicians at home. "This is not a Christian and civilised form of communism, at all," she wrote of Brazilian communism in 1945, "but one that is deeply intermingled with a race and colour feeling, which cannot be unfamiliar to Britons, who are used to dealing with backward peoples in the Empire."[5]

Toward the end of the war Lutz predicted the erosion of the prevailing Pan-American system, which further diminished her faith in U.S. world leadership. At the Chapultepec conference, Latin American delegates had made their protests known, but given their economic reliance on the United States, they had little leverage. During the war Roosevelt had suggested that Brazil, with which the United States had long enjoyed a special relationship, might have a seat in the Security Council of the United Nations, the peace-enforcing organ that would give the UN its teeth. But when Roosevelt died right before the UNCIO, these possibilities became null and void.[6] Before the San Francisco conference, Lutz wrote to her BBC correspondent that she had "a feeling of greater allegiance to Britain [than to the United States], as an Anglo-Brazilian," and explained that Britain should beware of a U.S.-led Pan-American bloc at the San Francisco conference:

The Conference at Chapultepec, Mexico, has brought one aspect of the San Francisco Conference very much to the foreground of my mind. . . . I hope Britain realizes that . . . the U.S.A. is going to that conference as a big man of war with a large flottila (sp) of small countries in attendance.

America always pretends to express disapproval of the British Empire but she has a group of satellite nations too. They are not so well-behaved as the Dominions and they do not rally to her like the dominions do to Britain. They may occasionally have to be bribed like ill bred children but—she can always count on the support of the majority of them, especially if it is put as a question of continental importance and they are made to feel important. She will always be able to choose a few among them who will stand by her if they are on a council with her.[7]

If anything gave Lutz a glimmer of hope for the San Francisco conference, it was that due to her own work and that of the IACW, women would be included at the conference. Though Lutz had not attended the Chapultepec conference, she made the women's rights demands of her group, the Federação Brasileira pelo Progresso Feminino (FBPF), known through Leão Veloso, the Brazilian foreign minister, who promoted them there. Lutz's resolutions resonated with those of commission president Minerva Bernardino and vice president Amalia de Castillo Ledón.

Their Chapultepec resolution that demanded that delegations appoint women to the San Francisco conference directly led to a large number of Latin American women in their countries' delegations. Of the only six women to be named full delegates to the UNCIO, three were from Latin America: Bertha Lutz from Brazil; Minerva Bernardino from the Dominican Republic; and Isabel Pinto de Vidal from Uruguay. Pinto de Vidal was a senator in Montevideo who was a longtime colleague of Paulina Luisi and member of her Alianza Uruguaya.[8] The other three female delegates came from the United States, China, and Canada— Virginia Gildersleeve, dean of Barnard College; Wu Yi-Fang, president of Ginling College, a Christian women's college, and member of the People's Political Council; and Cora Casselman, a member of the Canadian Parliament. Several other Latin American countries sent women as technical advisers, including Amalia de Castillo Ledón and Adela Formoso de Obregón Santacilia from Mexico, Isabel Sánchez de Urdaneta from Venezuela, and María Piedad Castillo de Leví from Ecuador. All of these Latin American women, educators, and administrators at the conference were Pan-American feminists.[9]

Lutz initially invested her highest hopes in U.S. delegate Virginia Gildersleeve and the two British female advisers to their delegations, Labor MP Ellen Wilkinson and Conservative MP Frances Horsbrugh.[10] However, her expectations for Anglo-American feminist collaboration were quickly dashed. Lutz had scarcely arrived in San Francisco when she received an invitation to attend a reception in Gildersleeve's sitting room at the Fairmont Hotel. That tea, Lutz later recalled, was an ominous "prelude to subsequent happenings."[11] One of only a

Bertha Lutz and the entire Brazilian delegation to the United Nations Conference on
International Organization in front of San Francisco City Hall, 1945.
Courtesy of the Arquivo Nacional, Rio de Janeiro, Brazil.

few delegates to attend, Lutz immediately felt condescended to by Gildersleeve
and the two British women. Wilkinson "did not deign to take an interest in Latin
Americans," Lutz concluded, while Gildersleeve peppered Lutz with questions
about her qualifications, trying to "place her."[12] "Try Percy B. Martin's *Who's Who
in Latin America*," Lutz responded.[13]

Most disappointing was the primary aim of Gildersleeve, Horsbrugh, and
Wilkinson: to dissuade the other female delegates from promoting women's
rights. When Lutz announced her feminist goals, Gildersleeve warned that
"urg[ing] any special measures for women in the Charter" would be "very vul-
gar" and "unlady-like."[14] Wilkinson explained to Lutz that she herself was "on
the King's Privy Council," which meant that "women had arrived." "I'm afraid
not," Lutz retorted; "it only means that *you* have arrived."[15]

Lutz marveled that Gildersleeve, Horsbrugh, and Wilkinson, who had all
benefited from the feminist movement and were part of women's associations
in their countries, were so eager to disassociate themselves from women's rights
demands. They reflected a broader trend in women's organizational politics in
both the United States and Great Britain. In the United States, with women's
suffrage and expanded roles in the Roosevelt government serving as proof that

women's citizenship was secured, liberal women's groups embraced what they called the "new humanism" at a series of 1944 White House conferences on postwar planning. Defined as an ethos "dedicated to humanity, to solving the world's problems in terms of human rights and human needs," the new humanism would replace "feminism."[16] These women believed that women's inherent pacifism justified their participation in postwar planning. They focused on getting women included in policy-making positions, particularly in the peacekeeping instruments that would emerge after the war, but not on women's rights.[17] Feminism, Eleanor Roosevelt announced in 1944, "almost no longer exists" in the United States. It was anachronistic, unnecessarily antagonistic, and distracting from more pressing humanitarian goals that should take precedence — humanitarianism, international cooperation, and peace.[18]

Their aversion to "feminism" was deeply informed by their long-standing opposition to the Equal Rights Amendment, which had for the past two decades defined feminism in the United States and now loomed anew as a threat. After Doris Stevens's removal as head of the IACW, the National Woman's Party (NWP) had created a new international spin-off, the World Woman's Party, that, in the lead-up to the San Francisco conference, vocally advocated equality measures in the UN Charter as a lever for the ERA. The ERA gained new adherents in these years, when many viewed it as consistent with the Allied fight against totalitarianism and for the Four Freedoms. In 1944 both the Democratic and Republican Party platforms supported the ERA, and the next year the House of Representatives considered the amendment. This momentum alarmed long-standing ERA opponents, including Eleanor Roosevelt, who influenced Gildersleeve's appointment to the San Francisco conference as a proponent of "new humanism" rather than of women's rights.[19]

Founder and president of the International Federation of University Women, the sixty-eight-year-old Gildersleeve had long sought to advance broad "internationalist" goals involving the cosmopolitan education of youth and women. A self-described "progressive conservative" — identified by one journalist as "a little right of the Rooseveltian 'slightly left of center'" — she was fond of saying, "There is no conflict between true internationalism and true patriotism."[20] Along with Wilkinson and Horsbrugh, Gildersleeve believed that the broader priorities of the U.S. and British governments should take precedence over women's rights at the UNCIO. The three women upheld a common belief in Anglo-American exceptionalism and trusted that other nations and newly emancipating colonies would benefit from their countries' aid and leadership. They assumed they would help women through the example of their own exalted diplomatic positions, but not by imposing women's rights onto a conference otherwise focused on security and peace.[21] When reporters asked Horsbrugh and Wilkinson "how it felt to be women delegates," the two women "replied indignantly: 'We are *not* "women delegates." We are delegates of our country and ministers of our government.'"[22]

Gildersleeve described Bertha Lutz as "a militant feminist in favor of what seemed to me segregation of women." Greatly surprised to encounter delegates who upheld "that old militant feminism which I thought had passed away," she objected that they "felt it necessary to call attention frequently to women and their problems and to rub in the fact that they were women."[23] Along with the Venezuelan and Ecuadorean representatives who belonged to the IACW, these militant feminists included Minerva Bernardino, Amalia de Castillo Ledón, Isabel Pinto de Vidal, and Lutz. Gildersleeve later mused that "perhaps in the backward countries, where women have no vote and few rights of any kind, spectacular feminism may still be necessary."[24]

But Lutz considered Gildersleeve the backward one, calling her a "very old fashioned anti-feminist."[25] The condescension and antifeminism of these U.S. and British delegates severely challenged Lutz's faith in the English-speaking women she had long upheld as role models. After that tea, Lutz wrote to her friends in Rio recognizing that the "Latin American women are going to be the most helpful" to advancing women's rights at the conference.[26]

Pan-American Feminism in San Francisco

Desire for full citizenship drove the goals of the Pan-American feminists who gathered in San Francisco. They brought this agenda to the UN conference, explicitly seeing their efforts as levers not only for individual rights but also for social rights for women, including state-sponsored maternity legislation. In addition, they sought greater multilateralism and global equality for Latin American countries in the face of rising Great Power hegemony.[27] Before the conference split into four commissions to outline the general provisions of the UN Charter and the structure of the General Assembly, Security Council, and Judicial Organization, all of the delegates proposed amendments to the Dumbarton Oaks plans that would shape those discussions. Several days after her tea in Gildersleeve's hotel room, Lutz gathered all of the female delegates and advisers, with the exception of Gildersleeve, Horsbrugh, and Wilkinson, at the St. Francis Hotel, where all of the Latin American delegations were staying, to formulate their own women's rights amendments.[28]

Lutz's collaboration with Minerva Bernardino represented something of a rapprochement between the two women, who had worked at cross-purposes twelve years before at the Pan-American conference in Montevideo. There Lutz had tried to remove Doris Stevens as the IACW chairman, while Bernardino had defended Stevens.[29] For Lutz, racism mingled with personal jealousy in her disparaging view of Bernardino, whom Lutz described as "the mulatto president of the Inter American Commission of Women."[30] Yet during the war Lutz and Bernardino had seen their Pan-American feminist goals align, and they even collaborated with each other.[31]

In addition to their support for international women's rights, the two shared similar, uncomfortably close relationships with dictatorships. Presidents Getulio Vargas and Rafael Trujillo used the international renown of feminists like Lutz and Bernardino to demonstrate their "democracy" to the world. Lutz and Bernardino knew such claims were spurious, but they curried favor with these dictators in order to enhance their own careers, gain personal autonomy, and assert their women's rights agendas, which they convinced themselves would be acts of resistance and moral weights toward democracy.[32] Rather than fighting to overthrow dictatorships, both women promoted women's rights within them; they believed such rights would be fulfilled when democratic rule was eventually restored, while ignoring other human rights violations.[33]

The unexpected opposition that Lutz and Bernardino both faced from U.S. and British women caused them to work more closely together than ever before at the UN conference. This opposition became apparent when the two women presided with Castillo Ledón over the St. Francis Hotel meeting that Lutz called. In addition to delegates and technical advisers, the meeting also included U.S. representatives from the League of Women Voters, the American Association of University Women, the General Federation of Women's Clubs, and the National Federation of Business and Professional Women (NFBPW) who had come to the conference with "consultant" status and representatives from the Women's International League for Peace and Freedom, the NWP, and the People's Mandate who attended as "unofficial observers."[34] By and large, with the exception of some women from the NWP and the NFBPW, few of these U.S. women supported the women's rights agenda that the Latin American cohort sought because of the continuing ERA debate in the United States. Many U.S. women warned that any explicit mention of "women's rights" in the UN Charter would, like the ERA itself, threaten social welfare measures for working women, such as maternity legislation, and be unnecessarily divisive. For Pan-American feminists, this was a stale debate. Lutz, Bernardino, and Castillo Ledón all insisted, as they had earlier, that "equal rights" could include commitments to social rights for women and provisions for maternity, explaining the series of resolutions they had just passed at the Chapultepec conference and measures passed in their own countries' constitutions as evidence of this.[35] But as Isabel Pinto de Vidal, who did not speak English, told Bertha Lutz, with these U.S. women, "No se saca nada" (We will gain nothing).[36]

Only a handful of the non–Latin American women in attendance actively supported demands for women's rights in the charter. One of them was Margaret A. Hickey, president of the NFBPW Clubs.[37] Her experience as chair of the Women's Advisory Committee of the War Manpower Commission during the war had led Hickey to be a strong advocate for women's political, professional, and economic equality. She believed that the UN Charter needed firm guarantees for women's rights.[38] Hickey and several other U.S. women who collaborated with the Pan-American group agreed that Gildersleeve represented an "insurmountable obstacle" to this goal.[39] Their other key supporter was Australian delegate Jessie Street, who gave robust help to the women's rights claims.[40] As Edith Goode, representative of the NWP and supporter of these initiatives, noted, "We have at San Francisco this surprising situation: . . . women delegates from South America [and] Australia . . . favoring full civil, political, and economic equality for women, while women of the United States are so divided among themselves that there is no effective demand at this moment."[41]

Lutz, Bernardino, Castillo Ledón, Pinto de Vidal, Urdaneta, Street, Hickey, and Lucy Jennings Dickinson, U.S. president of the General Federation of Women's Clubs, formed a drafting committee to articulate their proposals.[42] Here the Latin American feminists drew on decades of experience at previous Pan-American conferences in Montevideo, Buenos Aires, Lima, and Chapultepec, which had given them essential skills and actual drafts of resolutions. The resolutions that Lutz, Bernardino, and Castillo Ledón had launched at Chapultepec for equal rights for women and for the inclusion of women in international conferences served as their blueprints. They began to draw up amendments to incorporate equal rights for men and women into the purposes of the organization, assert women's rights as human rights, and ensure the representation of women in all integral bodies of the UN.

The "Gulf Stream" for Human Rights

As this feminist cohort decided on the precise wording for their amendments, they turned to the vocabulary of "human rights" pervading the conference. During the Second World War, the terms "human rights" and "rights of man," sometimes used interchangeably, had become key to the political vocabulary of many intellectuals, activists, statesmen, reformers, and workers in the Americas. These terms grew out of the social democratic promises of the Atlantic Charter and Four Freedoms and from transnational antifascist and anticolonial movements that protested racism, anti-Semitism, and imperialism. At Pan-American conferences, Latin American jurists and statesmen had long fused these strains of thought with a longer tradition of inter-American liberal multilateralism and calls for individual rights to be guaranteed by international law. In the United States, advocates—including numerous U.S. faith-based, civic, and civil rights groups, all consultants to the UNCIO — banded together prior to the conference to formulate their demands for stronger human rights provisions in the charter. While they had different priorities — opposing anti-Semitism, racism, and colonialism — all believed human rights and protection from discrimination had to be included more strongly in the framework of the United Nations.[43]

A number of Latin American delegations also brought specific human rights resolutions to San Francisco. Ricardo J. Alfaro from Panama, secretary general of the American Institute of International Law and longtime friend of Clara González, argued that the charter must include an explicit statement of both political and social rights: "right to work," "right to education," "right to participate in government," "individual freedom," "right to social security," and "right to equality before the law."[44] Representatives from Cuba, Uruguay, and Mexico also proposed detailed antiracist human rights resolutions with the backing of delegates from Haiti and other Latin American republics, explicitly drawing on inter-American principles of racial and religious nondiscrimination.[45] At Chapultepec, many Latin American jurists and statesmen disappointed by the United States' backing out of the Atlantic Charter promises of economic aid to and protective trade policies for Latin America had organized as a bloc to pass resolutions on the rights of man, the rights and duties of nations, freedom from racial discrimination, and women's rights.[46] At the San Francisco conference, human rights became critical to the project of chipping away at Great Power hegemony. As a newspaper editorial in Havana asserted, the UN must recognize "the wellbeing, the dignity, and the inviolability of the human being" and not only rely on the maintenance of "peace" by the four Great Powers.[47]

All of these groups pushing for human rights formed what Lutz called a "gulf stream" of demands for justice as well as peace: like the "gulf stream that flows through the cold waters of the Atlantic and tempers the climate of sundry lands," she noted, there was a persistent stream of demands for "human rights and fundamental freedoms without distinction of race, sex, and religion."[48] In addition to Latin American delegations, the greatest push for human rights was coming from U.S. "consultants" — members of U.S. civil society groups to whom the State Department had conferred access to meetings with U.S. delegates — who were pressuring the State Department to recognize "human rights" more fully in the charter.

The same day that Lutz gathered all the women in a meeting together, consultants Margaret Hickey and Lucy Jennings Dickinson joined a group of other consultants — including Walter White of the NAACP and James Shotwell of the Commission to Study the Organization of Peace — to make their demands face to face with Secretary of State Edward Reilly Stettinius Jr. After this meeting, Stettinius agreed that the United States would include a statement on human rights in its proposed amendments.[49] Lutz and her Pan-American cohort were heartened by the U.S. acceptance of a human rights provision, seeing it as a way to push women's rights more broadly. They also cheered the announcement of Jan Smuts, the premier of South Africa, in the May 1 plenary session in the stately War Memorial Opera House, that the preamble would include the words "the equal rights of men and women and of nations large and small."

Still, they believed that the charter needed to spell out the rights of women in more concrete terms. Drawing on both the proposals of the nongovernmental consultants and the formulations of human rights at Chapultepec, Lutz, Bernardino, Street, Castillo Ledón, Hickey, and Dickinson collaborated to propose four different amendments. The first was that "Chapter I, Purposes" of the UN Charter should include the following sentence: "To ensure respect for human rights and fundamental freedoms, without discrimination against race, sex, condition, or creed."[50] In another amendment for "Chapter IX, Arrangements for International Economic and Social Cooperation," they sought to include the phrase "and promote respect for human rights and fundamental freedoms and foster the democratic principle of equality of status, opportunity, and responsibility for men and women." Their other two amendments called for representation in the United Nations and positions in the secretariat being "open to men and women under equal conditions."[51] Together, these four amendments sought to establish equal rights for men and women in the purposes of the organization, in the section of the charter that outlined the social and economic work of the General Assembly, and in the structure of the organization itself.[52]

On May 5, Lutz, Bernardino, and Castillo Ledón proposed these four amendments jointly with the Brazilian, Dominican, and Mexican delegations. In addition, Isabel Pinto de Vidal introduced her own amendment from Uruguay that explicitly called for inclusion of women in all organs of the UN. Lutz and Bernardino became the pivotal voices supporting her amendment in committee meetings after Pinto de Vidal had to leave the conference early.[53]

The joint amendments that Lutz, Bernardino, and Castillo Ledón submitted were the first public proposals for human rights at the conference.[54] Their wording for the "Purposes" of the charter was later credited with influencing the wording of the Great Powers' amendment that was written into the charter: "promotion and encouragement of respect for human rights and fundamental freedoms for all without distinction as to race, language, religion, or sex."[55]

Latin American delegations cheered these proposals in a show of Pan-American solidarity. As one newspaper article reported, Pan-Americanism was the "hottest potato" at the UN conference.[56] With the Great Powers threatening to totally eclipse decades of multilateral inter-American treaties and institutions, most Latin American countries sought to preserve a regional security system. Tensions were further inflamed when the USSR pushed for the exclusion of Argentina from the conference because of its fascist alliances and Latin American delegations then threatened to leave the conference en masse, ultimately seeing the admission of Argentina.[57] These delegates saw these women's rights proposals as part of their project to save Pan-Americanism and gave robust support to the amendments of Lutz, Bernardino, and Castillo Ledón. Hours after the women made their resolutions, the president of Argentina cabled congratulations to Lutz, Bernardino, Castillo Ledón, and Urdaneta, lauding their work and their "demonstration of unity . . . of the American nations."[58]

The women's rights resolutions also gained the favor of U.S. human rights advocates, who were still angling to get even more specific and enforceable human rights provisions into the charter. The variety of coalitions supporting the women's rights proposals reveal the diversity of meaning that the term "human rights" had at this moment. For instance, civil rights activist and lawyer Alonso Perales, cofounder of the League of United Latin American Citizens (LULAC) and legal counsel to the Nicaraguan delegation in San Francisco, believed that "human rights" should be harnessed to oppose discrimination against Mexican immigrants and U.S.-born Mexican Americans. He congratulated Lutz for her human rights proposals, explaining that they promoted "mutual respect on the basis of equality."[59] The NAACP, which promoted a definition of "human rights" that included civil and social rights for African Americans and anticolonialism, also supported the feminists' proposals, seeing their statements for equality based on "race, sex, condition, or creed" as inclusive of its own goals. Although NAACP representatives Walter White and W. E. B. Du Bois did not focus on sexual inequality, NWP representatives Edith Goode and Alice Morgan Wright, recognizing that "sex goes in along with race and creed," brought the amendments directly to White to gain his support.[60]

While Goode, Wright, and all the female delegates spoke about racial equality in the same breath as sexual equality, few female representatives at the conference assertively pushed explicitly for racial equality and anticolonialism. Two exceptions were Mary McLeod Bethune, a consultant with the NAACP and president of the National Council of Negro Women, and Vijaya Lakshmi Pandit, sister of Jawaharlal Nehru, member of the Legislative Assembly of the United Provinces, minister for local self-government and public health, and president of the All-India Women's Conference. She came to the conference to protest the British-chosen Indian delegation and speak out against imperialism. While both women, who befriended each other during the conference, were leaders of women's groups, neither self-identified as a "feminist," and their goals at this moment focused less on women's rights than on anticolonialism and antiracism.[61] Bethune was connected to the Pan-American feminist group through her membership in the Committee on the Participation of Women in Post War Planning, and though neither she nor Pandit were delegates or spoke at conference proceedings themselves, Bethune supported the women's rights efforts from the sidelines.[62]

The leftist Popular Front Pan-American feminists who explicitly promoted anticolonialism and antiracism were also not among the delegates representing their governments in San Francisco. Before the San Francisco conference, the executive committee of the Bloque Nacional de Mujeres Revolucionarias, the outgrowth of the Frente Único Pro-Derechos de la Mujer in Mexico, composed of 300 women's groups, wrote to Castillo Ledón, urging her and the other "patriotic and antifascist women of America . . . that go as Delegates to the Conference" to pass certain resolutions in San Francisco, including one to demand democratic governments break relations with Franco's Spain.[63] Yet Castillo Ledón, Bernardino, and Lutz did not make any proposals that would counter their own governments' plans. These feminists were diplomats. While they did insist on the inclusion of "equality of race, religion, and sex" in the UN Charter, they did not position themselves in any meaningful way against colonialism.[64]

Although in public speeches at the conference Lutz asserted widespread opposition to prejudice based on race and color, her private views on race and the British Empire in fact put her in the opposite camp from Bethune, Pandit, and the NAACP. Her definition of "human rights" aligned more with that of Jan Smuts, South African prime minister and author of "equal rights of men and women" in the UN Charter preamble, whose segregationist policies later laid the groundwork for apartheid in South Africa. The two became friends over the course of the conference, bonding over their shared interests in the flora and fauna of the San Francisco Botanical Gardens, and Lutz praised Smuts for his "liberalism." Like him, Lutz saw no contradiction between "human rights" and what she believed was the superiority of white British civilization.[65]

Lutz had always resolved this paradox with her brand of imperial feminism. She believed that white, educated, more "civilized" women like herself were the rightful leaders of feminism and that the "uncivilized" populations of the world that mistreated women would be aided by women's rights laws. Lutz's colonialist beliefs demonstrate the real limitations of her "human rights" work in San Francisco. Yet at the conference Lutz would also be challenged by her realization that representatives of the British and U.S. "Great Powers" saw her as a Brazilian, and thus a racial other, rather than as one of them. In an ironic twist, Lutz's own racial logic—that people of the "lower races" were unfit for world leadership—was turned against her. This opposition only made her more determined to push universal demands for women's rights into the charter.

In spite of their congruence with many different definitions of "human rights," women's rights were not so mainstream in 1945 that support for them was a foregone conclusion. A large part of the struggle of Pan-American feminists at the conference would be in explaining why women's rights could not be taken for granted as already included under the rubric of "human rights." Amalia de Castillo Ledón's own delegation had mocked her feminist ambitions before they left for San Francisco until she had explained that women's rights were part of Mexico's revolutionary promise and key to the welfare of all people.[66] Recognizing that they would face an uphill battle, Castillo Ledón, Lutz, Bernardino, Street, and Pinto de Vidal conducted what Street later called "a special campaign ... to ensure that women were accorded universal respect and that human rights and fundamental freedoms applied to them" specifically.[67]

The argument that women's rights were already implied in human rights (and thus did not merit special mention) became the key argument against them in their first battle over the explicit statement that women would be eligible to serve in any capacity equally in the UN. Debating Isabel Pinto de Vidal's amendment that "representation and participation in the organs of the Organization shall be open both to men and women under the same conditions," delegates from the United States, Britain, and Cuba contended that explicit inclusion of equal rights for women was unnecessary, since it was understood that women were not excluded from participation in any international body.[68] Lutz pointed out that although women had not been excluded from participation in the UN conference, they nonetheless composed only 1 percent of the delegates.[69] Street argued that "in many countries women are excluded from occupying various positions just because the law does not specifically state they are eligible." She also noted that "there was nothing specific in the law which excluded women from voting and yet in practically every country the women had to carry on a long agitation before they were given the vote."[70] Such exclusion had long been the case in Latin American countries where "*ciudadanos*" was interpreted as male-only when applied to suffrage.[71] Citing major constitutional declarations from the Magna Carta to the Preamble of the U.S. Constitution, Lutz pointed out that "men have never found it unnecessary to make a statement of their rights. Why, then, should it be unnecessary to make a statement of the rights of women?"[72]

Street and Lutz also drew connections between women's rights and human rights in order to underscore the weakness of U.S. commitments to human rights. Although the Great Powers had agreed that they would include mention of universal human rights in the preamble and purposes of the charter, the

United States had eviscerated these principles by resolutely foreclosing discussion of extending the jurisdiction on human rights beyond the domestic sphere. The U.S.'s objections to international application of human rights largely came from its unwillingness to hold itself accountable to rights promises for African Americans in the Jim Crow South, particularly when the delegation would have to appeal to southern Democrats for Senate ratification of the UN Charter. One of the U.S. delegates to the UNCIO, Texas senator Tom Connally, had scuttled three anti-lynching bills in Congress. John Foster Dulles, adviser to the U.S. delegation, inserted a "domestic jurisdiction" clause into the charter that would limit the enforcement of human rights that included the following phrase: "Nothing contained in the Charter shall authorize the United Nations to intervene in matters which are essentially within the domestic jurisdiction of any state."[73]

This domestic jurisdiction clause dissatisfied every group that had come to San Francisco to fight for human rights. Capitalizing on this disappointment, Lutz and Street argued that including women in the UN would serve as a way to counter the weakness of the U.S. commitments to human rights. Street stressed that "the expression of this principle [antidiscrimination on account of sex]" was essential "because in all these places in the Charter no action can be taken to put it [human rights] into effect. The Charter specifically states that we shall not interfere with the domestic affairs of any country." But if their provision was placed in the charter—applying the concept of nondiscrimination to women in the UN itself—"it actually means that a status has been given to women which shall be carried out in practice by the International Organisation" and would thus be a victory for human rights.[74]

Lutz agreed that their resolution, explicitly asserting women's equal inclusion in the organization of the United Nations, would provide "teeth" to the human rights proposals. In a note to the Dutch delegate in the session, Lutz wrote, "The four sponsoring powers have agreed to mention the principle of equal rights of all regardless of race, sex, and creed. This formula is perfectly reasonable but we should like it in a precise form such as Uruguay's amendment."[75] In letters to the U.S. delegates Charles A. Eaton and Sol Bloom, chairman of the House Foreign Affairs Committee, she sharply urged the United States, which had recommended "human rights and freedoms," to practice what it preached: "If one advocates something in principle, one should practice what one advocates."[76]

Lutz, Street, and many others at the conference knew that the human rights rider the United States had suggested with the other Great Powers had been lip service to appease those clamoring for universal human rights. As a result, Lutz and Street's advocacy of the women's rights resolution as a way to make "human rights" meaningful persuaded many delegates who wanted to hold the United

States accountable. Nearly all the delegates who were not from the United States or Great Britain backed the women's proposals in supporting speeches that lasted one and a half hours. As Street recalled, "I have never heard so many panegyrics about women before—pretty well every country spoke."[77] Although the United States and Cuba voted against it and the United Kingdom abstained, all other delegates gave the women's provision hearty support. Thanks to their efforts, Article 8 of the UN Charter called for women's participation in the UN.

The final wording of the resolution was slightly different from Pinto de Vidal's proposal: the UN "shall place no restrictions on the eligibility of men and women to participate in any capacity and under conditions of equality in the principal and subsidiary organs." Though the wording was less powerful than what the feminists had originally sought, the conference participants knew that this accomplishment was the result of an intense battle that also was wrapped up in larger battles over human rights and Pan-Americanism. The San Francisco News touted this "victory" for the "senoras from Latin American nations battling for advancement of women's rights" with headlines "Charter Grants Sex Equality" and "Latins Win Feminine Rights."[78]

While Lutz celebrated this win, she was deeply dismayed by the lack of support from U.S. women. Harried and drained, she described the conference to FBPF friends as a "living hell."[79] Often in three committee meetings a day, she spent "about fifteen hours [a day] listening to men talking, talking, talking endlessly."[80] NWP members Alice Morgan Wright and Edith Goode sent Lutz encouraging missives, assuring her that "you are more likely than anyone else to bring about the fulfillment of the hope [for women's rights].... We want you to get all the rest you can. We want you to stay alive."[81] Indeed, most of the actual work of canvassing and lobbying delegates had been done by Lutz, Bernardino, Castillo Ledón, Urdaneta, and Street, who as full delegates also had the power to speak at meetings.

Frustrated by the lack of U.S. support, Lutz indirectly called out U.S. women groups in a live NBC radio broadcast on May 19, in the midst of the battle over the resolution, about a month into the conference. In a "United Women's Conference" organized by the San Francisco chapter of the NFBPW, Lutz credited "Latin American women delegates, with the help of the woman from Australia, who is quite a legion of women in herself," with attempts "to put in some amendments ... that will secure for them [women] a legal footing in the international organization." Although they had "been able to do a good deal," Lutz noted, "we are only a very few women working at it." She let her absence of praise for U.S. women speak for itself. "Above all we must practice unity," she urged.[82]

Her words had some effect. Two days later, a number of U.S. women at the conference sent Edward Stettinius a cosigned letter supporting the amendment the Latin American feminists were proposing.[83] Lutz wrote to Catt, "Your American women's associations here gave us very luke warm support until I told them straight that we expected more than that from them." She continued,

> Your Brazilian daughter and the Latin [A]merican women with Australia have been doing great battle to get an article into the Charter giving women representation and participation on equal terms. Contrary to all expectation we have had no support at all from Britain and America, but good support from the Latins and some of the Orientals. The Russians are also standing by us. . . . I can assure you that we . . . have been sick at heart but we stood the fire and will stand it to the end.[84]

But, Lutz concluded, "I believe your mantle is falling off the shoulder of the Anglo-Saxons and that we [Latin American women] shall have to do the next stage of the battle for women. We shall do so."[85]

The "Grand Slam" for the Commission on the Status of Women

As Lutz predicted, it would not be the support of U.S. and British women but the alliance that she would forge with men and women from Latin America and other "smaller powers" that would ultimately lead to one of the largest achievements of the Pan-American feminist delegates—the creation of the Commission on the Status of Women. Such alliances were very new for longtime Anglophile Bertha Lutz, who never more palpably than at this conference felt the second-class status of being a "Latin American." The arrogance of the Great Powers combined with the lack of support of U.S. women's groups was causing her to shift her allegiance toward Latin America, if not her fundamental ideas about race. In a letter to Catt, Lutz complained that the British and American delegates "make one feel one is being patronized" and that Secretary of State Stettinius "has been so inconsiderate of the Latin Americans that they are all feeling humiliated and sore."[86] Both casual and explicit discrimination toward Latin American delegates marked the Great Powers' attitude at the conference. One British delegate wrote to his wife that "I generally sit next to the American. . . . I tell him he's our heavy artillery and I am the sniper. . . . We wiped the floor with a Mexican last night."[87] At the beginning of the conference, the chairman of the Russian delegation publicly mocked the Mexican foreign minister for parroting the U.S. position on the host nation serving as chair, sarcastically applauding him for delivering so well a speech written by the U.S. State Department.[88] In a particularly tense interaction Lutz had with Sol Bloom, he told her, "'I don't care a dam[n] about Brasil or Latin America, we have done enough for you.'" Lutz retorted, "'Are you sure you don't mean 'enough to us'?"[89]

The anti-imperialist implications of Lutz's comments to Sol Bloom were also new; until the 1940s, Lutz had only praise for U.S. engagement in the world.[90] Yet her experiences at the UNCIO affected her profoundly. In spite of her long disassociation from Latin America and the racial inferiority she believed that category implied, the conference made her feel personally subjugated in a new way. Sharing a similar plight with other representatives from the "smaller and medium" countries, Lutz began to self-identify as a "Latin American" under U.S. hegemony. She collaborated more than ever before with other Latin American feminists and with male delegates from the "smaller and medium powers" who were pushing against the hegemony that the Great Powers would have in the Security Council. Though she sought support from those who opposed discrimination based on "race and color" and publicly spoke out against these discriminations at the conference, privately she maintained her personal sense of the "white man's burden."[91] Her new alliances, however, did spark a keen sense of separation from her beloved United States and a new allegiance to Latin America, both of which were central to promoting women's rights and human rights at the UNCIO conference.

This identitarian political activism emerged strongly in Lutz's appointment to Commission II that discussed the voting and veto system of the Security Council. Like many delegates from Latin American countries and from other "smaller powers," Lutz, who served on the committee discussing the veto, was disillusioned by the Great Powers' control over the Security Council, the organ responsible for keeping the peace. She wrote to Catt, "Without justice and democracy this thing will never work. It will only perpetuate tyranny."[92] According to the Dumbarton Oaks plans, the "Great Five" countries (which had expanded from the four to include France) alone would hold exclusive jurisdiction in the Security Council. Delegates from other countries, including Brazil, which was still smarting from its recent rejection as the sixth member of the Security Council, searched for loopholes to undermine this absolute authority and made proposals for revisions to the veto power.[93] Uniting in opposition, they also redoubled efforts to enhance the powers of the General Assembly and commitments to human rights and the rights of colonial people. They did this in part to undermine the veto power.[94] While they did not succeed in altering the undemocratic nature of Great Power leadership of the United Nations, they had greater success in pushing human rights resolutions into the General Assembly and into the economic and social functions of the United Nations. They hoped these resolutions would chip away at the significance of the Security Council.[95]

Viewing the Great Powers as arrogant and power-hungry, Lutz identified with these medium-sized and "small nations" that she viewed as "very eager for progress on social, economic, and cultural lines." "What has pleased and comforted me most is the progressive attitude of the delegations from Ethiopia,

India, Lebanon, and Latin America," Lutz wrote to Catt.[96] These countries had all backed the Latin American feminists' resolutions for inclusion in the United Nations. They were also pushing for human rights and for an expansion of the Economic and Social Council (ECOSOC).

These smaller and medium powers would engage in what became the greatest battle concerning women's rights at the conference: the debate over Lutz's proposal for establishing a Commission on the Status of Women as part of the newly created ECOSOC. Due to the lobbying pressure from Latin American and other nations at the conference, ECOSOC grew from a tangential organ to a "principal organ" of the UN.[97] Australian foreign minister Herbert V. Evatt, who became one of its most vocal supporters, emphasized that the body would promote social and economic rights, a dearth of which had contributed to the rise of totalitarian governments.[98] ECOSOC would contain a cluster of specialized agencies, including labor, health, trade, banking, and food and agriculture, as well as a separate commission on human rights.

Lutz wanted an agency added to this list that dealt specifically with women's rights. She had developed this idea early on at the conference with Arcot Ramaswami Mudaliar, British-chosen head of the Indian delegation. A member of the Justice Party in India, Mudaliar had in 1939 been appointed member of the viceroy's executive council and in 1942 to Prime Minister Winston Churchill's War Cabinet. He was the prime target of Lakshmi Pandit's criticisms about the British-appointed Indian delegation that bolstered the British Empire. Mudaliar had asserted his beliefs in the rights of men and women in the plenary session and worked closely with Lutz on plans to propose a separate commission. He and Lutz believed it should function centrally, not tangentially, in the organ that dealt with human rights in the UN. Such a group could apply moral pressure on the various nations of the world, they believed, and assert international legislation for women's civil, political, economic, and social equality. Lutz wrote to him, "I know that you—who are a great liberal—feel like I do, that we must do something for the women of some countries and that the war-effort of women deserves recognition."[99] Both Lutz and Mudaliar were also vocal opponents of the veto provisions. Although Mudaliar was appointed by the British delegation, he also sought to counteract Great Power hegemony and believed that expanding the human rights functions of ECOSOC was one way to do that.[100]

As the chair of the commission tasked with organizing ECOSOC, Mudaliar helped Lutz draft a proposal for the Commission on the Status of Women's Rights, which they renamed the Commission on the Status of Women, emphasizing that the contributions women had made to the war justified their rights and that human rights were coterminous with women's rights. So far, the amendments for human rights had all been "good words," Lutz believed, but she wanted something "more than platonic wishes." She did not want women's rights to get lost in the "fundamental freedoms."[101] Lutz believed the Commission on the Status of Women would be something lasting that could come out of the UN conference.[102]

When Lutz sought support for her and Mudaliar's proposal from her feminist cohort, she found that U.S. women were even less supportive of this proposal than of her other initiatives. Many feared it would undermine the influence of the existing international network of women, specifically the Commission on the Status of Women created in the League of Nations in 1938.[103] Led by Dorothy Kenyon, the commission had not been in existence for a month before it was shut down because of the war. Lutz dismissed its import out of hand, writing to Mudaliar that it was "2 women, 10 men, and no work."[104] Plus, she wrote, the Soviets would oppose "the revival of any organ of the ancient League."[105]

Once again, Lutz gained important support from her Pan-American cohort and from Jessie Street. Although Minerva Bernardino also initially resisted the proposal, fearing it would eliminate the need for the IACW, Lutz ultimately convinced her to agree, explaining that the two commissions could work with and help each other. Soon, Bernardino was "very keen" on the idea of the Commission on the Status of Women.[106] Street hailed it as a way to increase ECOSOC's power and give both the women's rights and human rights resolutions more teeth.

After these three women canvassed widely for support among the male delegates, Lutz introduced the proposed amendment, later called the "Brazilian Declaration":

> Whereas the status of women in different countries has to be radically improved and their rights have to be extended to attain the objectives of the Economic and Social Council to promote human rights and fundamental freedoms for all without distinction of sex;
>
> And whereas the part that women have played in the war makes the consideration of their status and rights an urgent problem requiring solution:
>
> The Delegation of Brazil recommends that the Economic and Social Council should set up a special commission of women to study conditions and prepare reports on the political, civil, and economic status and opportunity of women with special reference to discrimination and limitations placed upon them on account of their sex.[107]

In her speech defending this proposal, Lutz argued that women's rights were part of the Four Freedoms. Women's rights, she said, were particularly limited in Japan, Italy, and Germany, yet even in the most democratic nations in the

Bertha Lutz addressing Commission I/Committee 2, UNCIO, June 15, 1945. UN Photo/Milli.

world women did not enjoy complete equality with men. Bernardino spoke out in support, asserting that the IACW, long working along these lines, would collaborate with the Commission on the Status of Women.[108]

As in the debates over whether or not the UN Charter should explicitly call for women's inclusion in UN bodies, the debates over the Brazilian proposal revolved around whether or not women's rights should be discussed separately from human rights. The greatest opposition to this idea came from the Great

Powers. Although Frances Horsbrugh and Ellen Wilkinson had returned to England, much to Lutz's relief, Virginia Gildersleeve served as a delegate on the committee that considered the proposal.[109] Gildersleeve lobbied behind the scenes, arguing that, as she later put it, "women should be regarded as human beings as men were and ... the Commission on Human Rights would adequately care for their interests."[110]

On the day that the commission was debated in session, Gildersleeve sent Esther Brunauer, a technician for the State Department and adviser to the U.S. delegation, to oppose the proposal. Brunauer explained that the charter's opposition to discrimination on the basis of sex in its preamble and purposes was enough of a safeguard for women's equality and that the addition of a separate women's commission might ultimately lead to the exclusion of women from other UN commissions.[111]

Yet nearly every smaller and medium power on the committee backed the Commission on the Status of Women, seeing it as a way to promote both human rights and the rights of small nations. A number of delegates argued that women's participation in the Commission on the Status of Women and their participation in other UN commissions were not mutually exclusive. Significant to their support was the fact that fights over the Security Council and veto power were still very much alive, and many delegates saw the women's rights resolution as a way to enlarge the scope and function of ECOSOC, which they believed could push back against Great Power hegemony and hold the Great Powers at least minimally accountable. Carlos Romulo, the Philippine delegate who was actively pushing for anticolonialism and independence as a "human right," spoke out in favor of the commission, as did delegates from Brazil, Peru, Panama, Mexico, Chile, Honduras, Haiti, Nicaragua, Venezuela, New Zealand, Australia, Ethiopia, Iran, France, Greece, Turkey, and Luxembourg.[112] Alonso Perales of LULAC also supported the proposal, writing to Lutz that he was proud to collaborate with her for the "elimination of economic and social discrimination, by reason of race, color or creed."[113]

When the question was put to a vote, a large majority of the committee, thirty-five delegations, voted in favor of setting up a Commission on the Status of Women.[114] In the end, even Britain supported the proposal, leaving only the United States in opposition. Mudaliar sent Lutz a note: "You must be congratulated on having a field day for your proposition. But I think it is only right as it concerns half the population of the world."[115] The Guatemalan delegate who was the "rapporteur" for the committee sessions wrote to her afterward, "Warmly support[ing] your declaration, not only as rapporteur, but mainly as a delegate of Guatemala."[116] The Mexican delegate commended Lutz on "a grand slam."[117]

Even Virginia Gildersleeve, who opposed the creation of the Commission on the Status of Women, acknowledged that Lutz had gained the support of many delegates from the smaller and medium powers. In her memoirs, Gildersleeve mocked Lutz for the nickname that "British and American men" gave her for her persistent women's rights entreaties — "Lutzwaffe," after the German air force Luftwaffe that had bombed Britain. Yet, she wrote, "some of the men of other nationalities felt differently . . . [and] spoke to me with admiration of the feminists, especially of Dr. Lutz."[118]

Over the last days of the conference, some Latin American delegates left feeling satisfied that they had expanded both the powers of the General Assembly and the ECOSOC and pushed human rights to the fore. As Panamanian delegate Octavio Méndez Pereira asserted in a report to the Panamanian delegation, Latin Americans had advanced "certain fundamental principles that . . . could not at bottom be ignored."[119]

In particular, Latin American feminists had helped achieve significant accomplishments: human rights in the charter's preamble and purposes, the equal eligibility of men and women to participate in the UN, and the establishment of the Commission on the Status of Women. In her detailed report about the UNCIO to Brazilian foreign minister Leão Veloso, Bertha Lutz asked him to make sure the Commission on the Status of Women was in fact created and that the leadership of it remained "in Latin American hands since our republics . . . are currently in the vanguard of feminist demands."[120] In San Francisco, delegates and the press viewed all of these accomplishments as specifically *Latin American* contributions. At the concluding plenary meetings of the conference, Peter Fraser of New Zealand offered hearty congratulations to the female delegates from Latin America for their work on the charter.[121]

Lutz underscored this point when she spoke in these closing sessions, which marked the first time a woman spoke in the UNCIO Plenary Assembly.[122] The *San Francisco News* reported that "a small riot" broke out "amongst the cameramen" to capture the historic occasion "as [Lutz] . . . walked to the rostrum." They referred to Lutz's dramatic entrée on the U.S. stage at the 1922 Pan-American conference.[123] Now, over two decades later, Lutz called the article including women and men on equal terms in the United Nations "a Latin American contribution to the constitution of the world."[124]

Lutz credited feminists not only with securing the Commission on the Status of Women and inclusion of women in the UN but also with establishing human rights in the Charter. "The women delegates from the other Latin American countries with the help of the heads of our delegations were . . . instrumental in bringing before this great assembly the statement that there should be recognition of the fundamental rights of human beings, irrespective of sex, creed, or race." Yet these successes, she explained, did not "mere[ly]" represent "the

*Bertha Lutz signing the United Nations Charter in the Veterans' War
Memorial Building, June 26, 1945. UN Photo/Mclain.*

rights of women. Though I am a firm believer in such rights." They represented
"more than this. . . . There will never be unbreakable peace in the world until the
women help to make it."[125] Now, the success of the UN, Lutz explained, "will
depend on how much real effort, how much good intentions, and how much
hard work we put into the implementing of what has been resolved upon."[126]

To Catt she gave a more unvarnished opinion: "The real truth, and to you I
can tell it, is that the United Nations have written beautifully sounding words
into the Charter . . . but have no intentions of carrying them out."[127] To some de-

gree, the following years bore out Lutz's prediction. In June 1946, the UN made good on the "Brazilian resolution" by formally creating the Commission on the Status of Women under ECOSOC as a separate body from the Commission on Human Rights, in spite of the fact that U.S. women, including Dorothy Kenyon, Mary Anderson, and Frieda Miller, as well as Lutz's former British friends in the International Alliance of Women, had opposed its creation. They and other U.S. and British women argued that "women's rights" and equality with men should not be siphoned off from the broader cause of "human rights" and from the Commission on Human Rights. U.S. women also opposed the Commission on the Status of Women because they feared the Equal Rights Amendment. Indeed, as Edith Goode reported from the UNCIO to a fellow NWP member, "Foreign delegates tell us that the disagreement among our own women is an obstacle . . . and therefore obstructs the advancement of the status of women all over the world."[128] The domestic debate over the ERA would continue to stymie U.S. women's engagement in international women's rights. U.S. leadership dominated the formation of the Commission on the Status of Women, which became a body devoted to studying laws and proposing recommendations to the UN General Assembly rather than the locus of action that could potentially launch international rights resolutions that Lutz, Bernardino, and Castillo Ledón had all sought in San Francisco. Bernardino and Castillo Ledón took active roles in the Commission on the Status of Women in which they persisted in lobbying for these goals, even though continuing splits over the ERA in the United States and emerging tensions over the Cold War prevented the commission from demanding "equal rights" for women.

These conflicts also stopped robust notions of women's rights from being written into the UN Universal Declaration of Human Rights, a document urged by the Commission on Human Rights, although here too Pan-American feminists made their mark. Drafted between 1946 and 1948 almost entirely by a number of male delegates in a commission led by Eleanor Roosevelt, the declaration generally referred to "human beings" rather than to women in particular. Roosevelt largely opposed explicit attention to women's rights in the declaration, insisting that "human beings" already included women.[129] Yet, Pan-American feminists, with allies from other nations, did manage to push some of their demands into the Declaration of Human Rights. Here, in deliberations over the declaration, the network they had built at the San Francisco conference proved critical.[130] Minerva Bernardino, Amalia de Castillo Ledón, and Jessie Street, as well as Chilean feminist Amanda Labarca, who had an active role in the UN in these years, all worked closely with Indian reformer, educator, and activist Hansa Mehta, one of the two women who helped draft the declaration, to revise statements of equality for "all men" to "all human beings."[131]

While legal scholar Mary Ann Glendon has acknowledged this work of Mehta, the power of Pan-American feminists behind her and the singular work of Amalia de Castillo Ledón in influencing the declaration have gone overlooked. Though Castillo Ledón was not herself a delegate, she was a participant in the third session of the Commission on Human Rights, in May 1948 in Lake Success, New York, where delegates deliberated and voted on the draft of the declaration. Representing the UN Commission on the Status of Women, and having just worked with Bernardino to push women's rights resolutions into the 1948 Pan-American conference in Bogotá, Colombia, that also embraced an International Declaration on the Rights of Man, Castillo Ledón brought these goals to the 1948 Lake Success meeting. Here, thanks to resolutions she had drawn up with Bernardino, Street, Labarca, and others, Castillo Ledón was responsible for a firmer declaration that men and women had "equal rights" under marriage. She also expanded the definition of "family" so that it was not defined by marriage only. She noted that the statement that began, "The family *deriving from marriage* is the natural and fundamental group unit of society" (and went on to aver rights for men and women) would exclude illegitimate children and their mothers. The alternative that she urged—"The family is the natural and fundamental group unit of society and shall be entitled to protection"—and that was accepted would encompass the rights of those children as well as of working women seeking support for maternity. Her work demonstrated the long-standing efforts of Latin American feminists to incorporate consideration of illegitimate children and their mothers and maternity legislation into Pan-American feminist definitions of the capacious terms "women's rights" and "human rights."[132]

Although the Universal Declaration of Human Rights is recognized as the foundational human rights document of the United Nations, in the late 1940s the rights declarations of the UN Charter inspired even greater expectations among feminists throughout the Americas and other parts of the world. Though Lutz's words to Catt may have revealed her lack of faith in the United Nations itself, they should not be taken as a lack of faith in the words of its charter. She and many other feminists believed the charter itself was separable from the United Nations and could be taken as an international promise. Other Pan-American feminists would build on the work that Lutz and others had done, even when U.S. dominance over UN proceedings and ideological divisions of the Cold War hindered their efforts. In the process, they continued to expand the meaning of "women's rights" and "human rights"—often calling for a broader array of rights than their proponents in San Francisco had anticipated.

EPILOGUE

History and Human Rights

The United Nations Charter, to a greater extent than the Universal Declaration of Human Rights, wrote women's rights into international human rights. It called for equal rights for men and women and, unlike the declaration, emerged at a time before it was clear how much the Cold War would limit the meaning of both documents. Ofelia Domínguez Navarro later explained that what was utterly original about the UN Charter, and cause for true celebration, was its establishment of a new world order "in the name of *we the people*," rather than "in the hands of . . . governments."[1]

Many others shared her high expectations. Feminists throughout the world immediately translated the charter into broad goals for women's and human rights that far transcended those of Bertha Lutz, Minerva Bernardino, and Amalia de Castillo Ledón. In Paris in September 1945, when a group of mostly Soviet and eastern European feminists formed the new transnational feminist group the Women's International Democratic Federation (WIDF), they upheld the UN Charter as a testament to women's and human rights ideals. The WIDF, which became the most significant transnational feminist group over the next three decades, demanded anticolonialism, antiracism, and antifascism alongside women's political, civil, economic, and social rights.[2]

Pan-American feminists recognized the charter as the fruition of their own movement begun only several decades before. Margarita Robles de Mendoza, UMA founder, wrote to Doris Stevens that the IACW had "planted the seed" that led to the UN Charter.[3] In September 1945, old friends Clara González and Ofelia Domínguez Navarro applauded the charter when they met in Havana for the first meeting of the Federación Internacional de Abogadas, a new group of Latin American female lawyers committed to women's rights.[4] At this gathering, the first time the two women had seen each other since the 1930 Havana conference, Domínguez gave a speech connecting the women's rights "pacts of Lima and San Francisco" to her and González's early efforts at the 1926 Congreso Interamericano de Mujeres in Panama and to the 1928 Havana conference. She called all of these achievements for "human rights."[5]

The San Francisco conference filled Marta Vergara with new hope as well. Vergara and her husband moved to Washington, D.C., in September 1945 so she could continue working as the IACW Chilean commissioner from its Pan-American Union headquarters. There, she would do much of the legal research for the women's rights resolutions the IACW secured at the 1948 Pan-American conference in Bogotá that promoted both social and individual rights. She credited these resolutions combined with the work of Chilean feminists on the ground as responsible for the 1949 women's suffrage victory in Chile.[6]

Yet, Vergara continued to desire a more grassroots form of *feminismo americano*. Alarmed by the U.S. atomic bombings of Hiroshima and Nagasaki, she worried about a "return to the era of the big stick."[7] In 1947 she collaborated with a group of U.S. and Latin American women—Women's International League for Peace and Freedom (WILPF) leaders Heloise Brainerd and Frances Stewart; Paulina Luisi; Isabel Pinto de Vidal; Victoria Ocampo; Chilean educator and recent Nobel Peace Prize winner Gabriela Mistral; and a group of Guatemalan feminists—to organize a gathering to launch a new inter-American organization that, unlike the IACW, would be nongovernmental.[8]

The resulting 1947 Primer Congreso Interamericano de Mujeres (First Inter-American Women's Conference) in Guatemala City drew on the past three decades of Pan-American feminism and the UN Charter's human rights promises while also distinguishing itself from the past.[9] The conference gathered several hundred women from nineteen countries to Guatemala, where only a few years before, a popular uprising had ushered in the first democratically elected president, Juan José Arévalo. The clouds of the Cold War were already looming. The U.S. State Department opposed Arévalo and kept close tabs on the conference, which it deemed communist.[10] These tensions, however, did not stop conference participants from drafting a new agenda for *feminismo americano* that embraced internationalism, women's rights, and human rights, as well as peace in the face of nuclear weapons and escalation of armaments around the world.

Notably, the conference asserted racial equality as a primary goal. It brought together indigenous women, U.S. women from the National Congress of Negro Women, and more Afro-Latin American feminists than in the past, including Afro-Panamanian feminist Gumersinda Páez as the conference president. Páez perhaps best represented their new, more expansive vision. She had been elected to the Panamanian legislature in 1941 after decades of working with Clara González's Partido Nacional Feminista and fighting for the rights of women and of all races. She upheld a truly progressive version of American feminism. The conference itself passed numerous resolutions that opposed racism, imperialism, colonialism, and militarism.[11]

For these feminists, the power of the UN Charter did not come from the United Nations but from themselves and their ability to translate its human rights guarantees to their own ends. They connected these accomplishments to the long inter-American feminist movement in which many of them had taken part. This was the case for Bolivian feminist Ana Rosa Tornero, who chaired the committee "Struggle for Human Rights." Over twenty years before, Tornero had scarcely been nineteen years old when she participated in the 1926 Congreso Inter-Americano de Mujeres in Panama where she witnessed Clara González and Ofelia Domínguez Navarro demand international women's rights and anti-imperialism. Later, as the Bolivian commissioner of the IACW, Tornero had attended the 1933 Montevideo conference, where she supported the Equal Rights and Equal Nationality treaties. A journalist who had reported from the front lines of the Chaco War, Tornero had long desired an expansion of an American feminist agenda toward peace and meaningful improvement in the lives of women and families. Now in Guatemala, she defined "human rights" as embracing a wide range of women's rights—not only political and civil equality but also "the social inequities [that we] believe to be obstacles to democracy," including the eradication of racism, equal pay for equal work, health care, the elimination of illegitimacy as a social indicator, and freedom of expression.[12] To Tornero, these interdependent *derechos humanos* represented the true goals of American feminism.

The 1947 Guatemala conference concluded by paying tribute to Paulina Luisi, whom participants recognized as the mother of inter-American feminism. Luisi was at that time in Montevideo, too frail to attend the conference, but she later read its resolutions from home, as well as its cable calling her "the great fighter for women's rights."[13] She no doubt felt immense pride in this accolade. The Guatemala conference embodied the kind of inter-American feminism for which she had spent the past three decades fighting: one that embraced broad understandings of women's and human rights, inter-American interdependence, and a transnational activism outside of governmental channels and not dominated by the United States.

After the 1945 UN conference in San Francisco, Luisi harbored no illusions about the looming threat of U.S. hegemony on the world stage yet still hoped that women's collective activism could make meaningful the broad social rights aspirations of the war years. Her dream of an interdependent world relied upon the actual and imagined links that *feministas americanas* forged with each other, connections that now seemed more urgent than ever. As her like-minded friend Frances Stewart wrote to her in Spanish, "Surely, seeing the sorry situation at San Francisco," where the United States had thrown in its lot with imperial powers, "one must realize" that only through "the channels of MUTUAL FRIENDSHIP, DEEPENED INTO THE DEGREE OF MUTUAL CONFIDENCE AND TRUST," could real change happen.[14]

If Luisi reflected on the mutual confidence and trust in her own life, she would likely have thought of her longtime friend Ofelia Domínguez Navarro. The two women had never met in person but, since their first letters in 1930, had shared an exhilarating intellectual friendship based on common ideas, arguments, and hard-won victories. They viewed each other as true *compañeras* and, as Domínguez put it in letters to Luisi, *correligionarias*—people who share the same religious, political, or ideological beliefs. Neither of these words has a good English synonym. *Correligionaria* indicates a reciprocal affective bond that keeps faith alive, especially in difficult times. *Compañera* means "companion," "friend," "equal," or "ally," but it refers to a truly affective relationship in a way that the English terms do not. Luisi and Domínguez used both forms of address to describe their relationship that was intensely dynamic, political, and intimate.

Almost twenty years older than Domínguez, Luisi would die several decades before her, on July 16, 1950, at the age of seventy-five. Their last extant correspondence is from 1945, right before the Chapultepec conference. Domínguez viewed this exchange as significant enough to reproduce in her memoirs, published in 1971. Their words convey great affection and optimism about rekindling contact with each other and about, in Luisi's words, strengthening "the ties of the democratic women of our countries already so often linked in the defense of our . . . humanistic ideals." Domínguez responded in kind, sending Luisi her "love and sincere admiration always" and voicing her strong support for *feminismo americano*. She offered Luisi a "warm, tight hug" from "your sister the Cuban woman, and from this *compañera* who follows with devotion and care the ascent of the women's movement that at every moment expands in meaning."[15]

In spite of the new activism that the UN Charter helped spur, soon after the charter went into effect in October 1945, the Cold War quickly contracted the expansive meanings of feminism and human rights and cast a long, dark shadow over the history of Pan-American feminism. The worldwide pitched ideological battle between communism and liberal democracy redefined the latter to mean "individual rights." The far-reaching movement for "human rights" ushered in by the Popular Front gradually withered away. Anticommunism brought with it a growing suspicion of "social rights," which dampened the efforts of Pan-American feminists who rallied around the UN Charter.[16] "Feminism" in this period also became defined more narrowly, meaning individual political and civil rights.[17] These interrelated phenomena played a critical role in the collective amnesia about Pan-American feminism.

Although the Cuban Revolution in 1959 definitively triggered U.S. government fears about communism in Latin America, the Cold War announced itself in Pan-American relations a decade earlier at the 1948 Ninth International Conference of American States in Bogotá, Colombia. At this conference, Latin American delegates passed the International Declaration on the Rights of Man that would influence the 1948 UN Universal Declaration of Human Rights, and Minerva Bernardino successfully pushed for what became the Inter-American Convention on the Granting of Political Rights to Women.[18] Yet, at this same meeting that defined a Pan-American agenda for human rights, the United States overturned resolutions against colonialism and against anticommunist repression promoted by Venezuelan delegate Rómulo Betancourt and others. Thereafter the U.S. government used the newly created Organization of American States (OAS) that replaced the Pan-American Union as a tool to fight perceived communist threats in the hemisphere and justify intervention against left-wing movements or governments that challenged U.S. capitalism's hegemony.[19]

After the Cuban Revolution, "Pan-Americanism" came to mean the militarization of the hemisphere.[20] The IACW, now better known by its Spanish name and acronym, Comisión Interamericana de Mujeres (CIM), and part of the OAS, continued its work.[21] Yet the U.S. government largely controlled the meaning of the term "human rights" in the region, using a defense of individual rights to justify CIA- and U.S. military–led coups against democratically elected leaders in Guatemala, Brazil, Argentina, Chile, and elsewhere. In reality, these actions resulted in human rights violations and countless deaths of civilians.[22]

The Cold War unmistakably shaped the lives of the six Pan-American feminist leaders in this book, with the possible exception of Paulina Luisi, who died in Montevideo in 1950. All the others—Ofelia Domínguez Navarro, Marta Vergara, Doris Stevens, Bertha Lutz, and Clara González—continued to engage for many years in national and international conversations about the welfare of women and children. However, the Cold War prevented them from calling for the broad, interdependent meanings of "human rights" around which they had collectively organized in the 1920s through the 1940s. None of them were widely recognized for their work in American feminism at the time of their deaths.

Each, however, attempted in different ways to preserve the movement in the historical record, starting with Paulina Luisi, who saved many of her papers, which now sit in three different archives in Montevideo, Uruguay. They attest to her conflicts and her passionate friendships and activism with feminists throughout the Americas and the world.[23]

Ofelia Domínguez Navarro's political trajectory shifted in the 1940s and 1950s as the Communist Party in Cuba, renamed the Partido Socialista Popular, declined in size and power. In 1946 she became the secretary of the Cuban Association of the United Nations, a group that sought to connect everyday people to the UN. Yet, U.S. anticommunism severely tested her faith in the power of "human rights" and in the UN itself. The FBI had kept close tabs on Domínguez since the 1940s, and in 1950 U.S. authorities arrested and detained her for several days after she arrived at the Miami airport on a trip for a United Nations meeting.[24] An article in the Cuban magazine *Bohemia* titled "Derechos humanos" pointed out the contradictions between U.S.-supported "human rights" resolutions and the treatment of Domínguez at the hands of "G-men" who had torn her luggage and invasively searched her clothing and person: "The multiple diplomatic representations before the State Department were not sufficient" to afford "Ofelia Domínguez... her fundamental human rights as enshrined at the Ninth conference [in Bogotá in 1948]. Article 1 ... states everyone has the right to life, liberty, and security of person.... Article 5 reads 'everyone has the right to protection of law against abusive attacks upon his honor, his reputation, and his private life.'"[25]

In her memoirs, Domínguez related this interrogation about her communist commitments: "When you returned to Mexico in 1933, did you not lecture against the oil companies? *It's true, I would have done the same if they were exploiters of Cuban nationality.* Are you not an advocate of violence? *No!* But you are not in favor of capitalism? *I am not, in its current form. Neither were Roosevelt or Churchill.*"[26]

In the 1950s, Domínguez supported the Cuban Revolution and in 1974 applied for admission to the Communist Party of Cuba. Though she was accepted into it, her old left feminist politics were not entirely legible to the Castro government or to the new group of women in the Federación de Mujeres Cubanas, which supported women's education, health, and social rights but deemed bourgeois and Western the rights-based feminism Domínguez and other old-left feminists had supported.[27] In 1975, the year before she died, Domínguez donated many of her papers to archives in the Instituto de Historia and the Archivo Nacional in Havana, Cuba. She also wrote her memoirs, in which she detailed the history of her activism in Cuba and Mexico, and her collaborations with Clara González, Paulina Luisi, and Doris Stevens. She also formally revised the aspersion she had cast upon the IACW when Stevens led it. She credited the commission with a sizable accomplishment: the dramatic expansion of women's suffrage in Latin America after the 1945 UN Charter—in Guatemala and Panama in 1945; Argentina and Venezuela in 1947; Chile and Costa Rica in 1949; Haiti in 1950; Bolivia in 1952; Mexico in 1953; Honduras, Nicaragua, and Peru in 1955; Colombia in 1957; and Paraguay in 1961.[28]

Domínguez and Clara González remained in touch throughout the 1940s and 1950s, when the Cold War and shifting political climate in Panama shaped González's career as well. In 1948, González ran for vice president of Panama but lost the election.[29] She continued to push against the government of Arnulfo Arias and participated actively in the movement that led to his deposition in 1951 for having eliminated the constitution. Later that year, González helped create the first juvenile court in Panama and became its judge, a position she held for many years. In this role, she collaborated with child welfare leader Katharine Lenroot in UNESCO on social work and juvenile delinquency.[30] She also maintained a prominent position in the Federación Internacional de Abogadas that pushed for international women's rights treaties well into the 1960s and remained allied with the IACW.[31]

In these years González married a former U.S. engineer from the Canal Zone, and a sojourn she took with him to California in the 1960s led to her interrogation by U.S. government officials for suspected communist commitments. In a long report that González wrote defending herself against such charges, she outlined her history, downplaying her leftist pursuits and emphasizing that she had always been in favor of "*liberal ideals*" such as women's rights. Privately, she was also deeply critical of anticommunism and bemoaned U.S. interventions in the Americas.[32]

Clara González also lamented that Pan-American feminism had been lost to history. In 1960, when an old friend asked her about the 1927 Chilean congress that reinforced the international women's rights resolutions she and Domínguez had made at the 1926 Congreso Interamericano de Mujeres in Panama, she shared with him some correspondence. Yet González noted "these papers undoubtedly only have a sentimental value for me now, because there remains no record of the pioneering work to which all the world witnessed at this time in favor of women's rights. . . . There are other people who have received the credit for it."[33] Indeed, when Pan-American feminism was mentioned at all, credit was given to U.S. feminists. Simone de Beauvoir's groundbreaking 1949 tome on the historical treatment of women, *The Second Sex*, mentioned the early work of the IACW and its "treaties [that] elevated women's status by international convention" but portrayed them as outgrowths of the U.S. suffrage movement. The book said nothing about Latin American feminists.[34] The Cold War and the resulting division of the world into "first," "second," and "third," with most of Latin America grouped in the last, entrenched an understanding of liberal feminism as a distinctly a "first world" product of the United States and Western Europe.

Clara González left a large archive of papers to her nephew, with whom she was close, and her papers remain with her family in Panama City. She died in 1990, soon after witnessing U.S. forces invade Panama in "Operation Just Cause" (which Panamanians renamed "Operation Just Because") that resulted in the death of between 500 and 1,000 Panamanians. In the decades before her death, a new generation of feminists in Panama began to restore González's life to national historical memory. Upon her death, *La Prensa* reprinted an interview conducted with her on the cusp of the 1975 United Nations International

Women's Year Conference in Mexico City. In it, Gonázlez exhorted women to take action: "There is great work to do. . . . We are not emancipated. . . . The equality of opportunities does not prevail. An awareness of women is needed. . . . In the new generation there should be constant belligerence. . . . Offer systematic seminars and . . . form . . . groups [that will do] serious and profound work on national and international problems. . . . Demand to be heard. . . . There should be a resurgence of the feminist movement."[35]

Marta Vergara also sought to write *feminismo americano* into the historical record. After she and her husband returned to Chile in 1951, Vergara wrote several books. Her autobiography, *Memorias de una mujer irreverente*, published in Chile in 1961, would be her most famous, winning the Premio Municipal de Literatura Santiago. It recounted her work with the IACW and Chilean feminist activism. The following year, after a long lapse in communication with Doris Stevens, Vergara wrote to her, announcing herself as "a ghost" and asking Stevens if she would like a copy of her memoirs: "You are in it. . . . I express in the book my admiration for your personality." After these many years, their friendship remained of signal importance to Vergara, who signed off, "Your friend always."[36] Her book reflected on the 1930s as a time of vital activism and revealed her deep disappointments in the Cold War Pan-Americanism that set back so many of the goals she had supported.[37] One can only guess at the despair with which Vergara lived through the U.S.-backed coup that overthrew democratically elected socialist president Salvador Allende in 1973. She spent the last years of her life in the Israelita Nursing Home in Santiago, where she died in 1995.[38]

Doris Stevens also spent the last years of her life trying to write herself and the IACW into history, although her politics were far to the right of the aforementioned feminists. After a lawsuit that she filed against Alice Paul and Paul's successor as president of the National Woman's Party ended in defeat in 1948, Stevens withdrew from the organization. In the years that followed, she and her husband, Jonathan Mitchell, still an editor for the *New Republic*, engaged intimately with McCarthyism and red-baiting. They provided information on the House Un-American Activities Committee to their friend the British journalist Rebecca West, who became a significant anticommunist mouthpiece.

Stevens and Mitchell also devoted a great deal of time researching and writing a memoir about Stevens's time as head of the IACW. After her ouster as chair in 1938, she had defiantly taken the enormous archive of the commission with her. She and Mitchell studied this vast collection as well as research that Mitchell did in State Department archives to learn about the role the Roosevelt administration had played in her expulsion. The memoir focused on Stevens's leadership and diplomatic skills, her tenacious championing of the Equal Rights Treaty, her support from Latin American feminists, and suspected communist affiliations of key members of the Roosevelt administration.[39] Although the account was never published, Stevens's legacy did live on after her death in 1963. Her husband had the resources to help endow one of the first chairs in the new field of "women's studies" at Princeton University—the "Doris Stevens Chair of Women's Studies"—and donated her vast papers to the recently created Schlesinger Library at Radcliffe College.[40] When scholars in the 1970s and 1980s began to write the first histories of feminism, they uncovered Stevens's life and national activism, though very few wrote about her international feminism.[41] It only became possible to fully appreciate that work in 2007 when the Schlesinger Library opened to the public her capacious papers that related to the commission.

Bertha Lutz, who worked with the IACW until the 1960s, also hardened into an anticommunist position in these years. She too suffered the ignominy of not being remembered in history. When the U.S.-backed coup launched a new period of dictatorship in Brazil in 1964, Lutz focused most of her energies on her scientific work at the Museu Nacional and published a posthumous book of her father's scientific work, a source of great pride for her.[42] Before she died in 1976, Lutz left an archive of her papers to the Museu Nacional and an even larger archive of Federação Brasileira pelo Progresso Feminino papers to the Arquivo Nacional in Rio de Janeiro. In 2018, a fire tragically destroyed the Museu Nacional's enormous holdings, including Lutz's papers. Both repositories contained an extensive cache of information about the San Francisco conference and as much about her international and Pan-American activities as about her national activism. Her engagement in Pan-American feminism from the 1920s to the 1940s represented the highlight of her life.

When a U.S. woman from the Society of Women Geographers traveled to Rio de Janeiro in 1974 to interview the elderly Lutz, a longtime member of the group, the conversation focused on Lutz's scientific work on tree frogs. Upon being asked what had given her the "most satisfaction" in her life, Lutz distinguished the work she had done at the San Francisco UN conference. When the interviewer credited Lutz with the inclusion of women's rights in the UN Charter, Lutz added, "Yes, and the Commission on the Status of Women was proposed by me! And now nobody ever thinks I really did that, I get no credit for it."[43]

Lutz was right. Those who were writing the first histories of the United Nations never mentioned the role Lutz or other Latin American delegates played, let alone considered what "human rights" meant to them. These omissions may have been facilitated by an untruthful account written by the U.S. female delegate to the San Francisco conference, Virginia Gildersleeve. In her 1954 book *Many a Good Crusade*, Gildersleeve not only diminished the role of Latin American feminists there but also fallaciously wrote that the conference had voted down the Commission on the Status of Women. Bertha Lutz wrote in the margins of Gildersleeve's narrative, "*muita informação tendenciosa e errata*" (much biased and wrong information) and "liar!"[44] Yet many scholars of human rights have continued to use Gildersleeve's book as a definitive account of the San Francisco conference, of women's work there, and of the meaning of human rights at the time.[45] U.S. and English-language sources have held disproportionate power over the meanings of human rights and our historical narratives about them.

Some, however, did remember Lutz. The year before her death, Lutz was gratified to be an honored guest at the 1975 UN International Women's Year (IWY) Conference in Mexico City, that gave her an award, acknowledging her work at the 1945 San Francisco UNCIO that had paved the way for the Mexico City conference.[46]

The IWY conference had been suggested by both the UN Commission on the Status of Women and the WIDF, and included 6,000 participants from all over the world. It marked a new generation of feminists on the international stage. Activists from Latin America and from newly decolonizing parts of Asia and Africa pushed international agendas alongside those from Western Europe and the United States and called for a feminism that addressed geopolitical inequality, economic marginalization, and racial discrimination. This conference, and the UN Decade for Women (1975–85) it launched, fostered unprecedented new grassroots and global feminist organizing. Coinciding with a new field of international relations and development studies that focused on women and gender inequality in the third world, topics concerning women — maternal mortality, female infanticide, sexual trafficking and forced prostitution, rape and violence against women — increasingly became legitimate areas of study and international policy discussions. In 1979, the UN General Assembly also passed the Convention on the Elimination of All Forms of Discrimination against Women (CEDAW).[47]

During this period of feminist ferment in the 1970s, new nongovernmental organizations like Amnesty International and transnational protest against human rights violations by Latin American dictatorships also spurred what historians have called the "breakthrough" moment of human rights activism. U.S. president Jimmy Carter shaped international diplomacy around human rights more than any U.S. president before or after, promoting a particular definition — political and civil rights, and freedom from torture — that typically did not include women's rights.[48]

In the late 1980s and 1990s, feminists pushed to make "women's rights" "human rights." Latin American feminists were at the forefront of these efforts. At the first Encuentro Feminista Latinoamericano y del Caribe (Latin America and Caribbean Feminist Encounter) in Bogotá, Colombia in 1981, groups called for an "International Day against Violence against Women," in honor of the Maribal sisters who were violently assassinated by the dictatorship of Rafael Trujillo in the Dominican Republic, to bring attention to gender-based violence and state violence as interrelated harms.[49] U.S. feminist activists Charlotte Bunch and Catharine MacKinnon promoted use of international human rights law to confront women's rights, and in the Americas the IACW, after having suffered major budget cuts, revived itself in the late 1980s and began to focus on sexual violence in an unprecedented way. In 1988, the IACW drafted the first international convention that defined gender-based violence as a violation of human rights in the Convention of Belém do Para, adopted by the Organization of American States in 1994. The IACW situated this convention within a legacy of its own advocacy for the Equal Rights Treaty in the 1920s and 1930s and of the human rights regime dating to the 1945 UN Charter.[50] The following year, Hillary Clinton brought the greatest international attention to this movement at the 1995 UN Beijing conference for women in her famous speech that announced that "women's rights are human rights and human rights are women's rights."[51]

While Clinton's speech has been celebrated as the apotheosis of this idea, it is important to remember that the meanings of "women's rights as human rights" were just as contested in 1995 as they had been decades earlier. At the same 1995 Beijing conference, Afro–Latin American feminists pushed for an intersectional notion of "women's rights as human rights" and demanded that antiracism measures be included in women's human rights conventions. Later, at the United Nations Conference against Racism, Racial Discrimination, Xenophobia, and Related Intolerances, held in Durban in September 2001, Afro–Latin American feminists successfully pushed for human rights resolutions that were both antiracist and feminist.[52] Latin American groups have also been at the forefront of pushing for the rights of lesbian, gay, bi, and transgender people to be considered "human rights." The landmark 2011 United Nations Resolution on Human Rights, Sexual Orientation, and Gender Identity stemmed from a 2004 "Brazilian Resolution," the first international effort to include the LGBT community in human rights protections.[53]

When activists from the late twentieth to the early twenty-first centuries announced that "women's rights" are "human rights" and pushed for broad, international meanings of these terms, they were standing on the shoulders of Pan-American feminists. Numerous scholars have been critical of this slogan and exposed the hypocrisy of U.S.-led efforts in which white U.S. and Western European women position themselves as the harbingers of human rights to oppressed third world sisters, sometimes while using them as justification for military interventions. Others point out the continuing paradox of the United

States proclaiming leadership in human rights while resisting signing international treaties that promise women's and human rights, including CEDAW, which has been signed by every government in the world except the United States, Iran, Somalia, South Sudan, Sudan, and the Pacific Island nations of Tonga and Palau.[54]

The history of *feminismo americano* shows us that the idea that "women's rights are human rights" is not a product of only, or even predominantly, U.S. or Western European activism, thought, or state power. Its history illustrates the transnational, collective, and social movement–driven origins of human rights as well as the tensions surrounding it today. From the 1920s through the 1940s, *feministas americanas* were in the vanguard in their calls for a broad array of international women's rights. Many of them were also forerunners in understanding the complexity of power relations in international affairs and developing a feminism that embraced an analysis of political economy and that was sensitive to multiple forms of oppression. These *feministas* recognized the interdependence of women's rights, antifascism, antiracism, and anti-imperialism. Many knew that equal rights for women and men were connected not only to national sovereignty but also to equal rights for the most oppressed and impoverished members of their communities. Unpacking their politics and relationships and the limitations of their visions can help restore full meaning to the notion they imparted that lives on today—that "women's rights are human rights."

The six feminists who helped drive this ideal knew that history is about authority and about who has the power to tell the story. Their racial, class, and educational privilege enabled their sense of historical importance and made it possible for them to create their archives and write books. They were able to attend Pan-American conferences and write themselves into their national histories, even if their combined transnational efforts are only now being recognized. Yet the many more who made *feminismo americano* the vital movement it was rarely had the resources at their disposal to create their own archives or publications. It is important to more fully recover the histories of these activists—those who marched, who protested, who worked, who struck, who petitioned, who lobbied, who organized clandestinely, and who looked to collective international solidarity as a way to propel their own local agendas. Their voices and actions will help us better appreciate diverse, expansive notions of women's rights, human rights, social interdependence, and the various forms of oppression—local, national, and global—that make them necessary. Their ideals broaden our understandings of feminism in the past and point us to new possibilities in the future.

ACKNOWLEDGMENTS

✷ ✷ ✷

Researching and writing this book has been a collective venture, and my profuse thanks go to numerous colleagues, historians, archivists, friends, and *compañeras* who have generously helped me.

I would like to Diana Carey, Jenny Gotwals, Sarah Hutcheon, Ellen Shea, and Amanda Strauss at the Schlesinger Library; Virginia Freidman at the Biblioteca Nacional in Montevideo; Daniela Eugenia Schüte González, coordinator of Memoria Chilena at the Biblioteca Nacional de Chile in Santiago; Iris Lorena Navarro de Castillo at the Archivo Ricardo J. Alfaro in Panama City; Ana Lucia Jatahy Messeder at the Arquivo Nacional and Ubirajara Mendes at the Museu Nacional in Rio de Janeiro; and the archivists at the Archivo Nacional in Havana and at the Archivo General de la Nación and the Archivo del Centro Republicano Español in Montevideo.

I am extremely grateful to Laura González de Lombana and Ricardo Lombana for opening their home to me and for sharing Clara González's personal papers and their memories of her with me. Special thanks to Yolanda Marco Serra who made that introduction and also shared her own research and invaluable insights about Clara González as well. Many other historians and friends helped me immeasurably before and during my research trips—with tips, conversation, connections to their own academic communities, and friendship. I especially thank Yolanda Marco Serra, Gladys Marel Garcia-Pérez, Graciela Sapriza, Daniela Hirschfeld, Cecilia Azevedo, Glaucia Fraccaro, Nelly de Freitas, Alexandre Luís Moreli Rocha, Alex Borucki, Vannie Arrocha, Ana Tipa, and Corinne Pernet. My thanks go to Christine Ehrick for helpful advice before my first research trip to Montevideo and to K. Lynn Stoner, without whose help my research in Cuba would not have been possible. For research assistance I am extremely grateful to Nelly de Freitas, Aisnara and María de los Ángeles, Lucía Arroyo, Danae Brugiati, Catherine Tracy Goode, Andrea Mary Binder, and Isadora Fernandes. Special thanks to Eileen Boris, Michelle Chase, Glaucia Fraccaro, Max Paul Friedman, Eric Gettig, Cristina Teresa de Novaes Marques, Jocelyn Olcott, and Karin Rosemblatt who generously shared their own archival findings with me.

My travels, research, and writing were enabled by a number of grants and fellowships. At Stanford University, the Michelle R. Clayman Institute for Gender Research Dissertation Fellowship and the Andrew W. Mellon Dissertation Fellowship, as well as grants from the Society of Historians of Foreign Relations, the Schlesinger Library, the OSU WGSS Department's Coca-Cola Critical Difference for Women Program, and the OSU Mershon Center for International Security Studies, made my research possible. My visiting scholar fellowship at the American Academy of Arts and Sciences in Cambridge, Massachusetts, and the mentorship and community I gained there, were vital to finishing the book. I am grateful to Nancy Cott for offering generous hospitality and support during my time in Cambridge.

I benefited enormously from presenting my work at Stanford University's Modern U.S. History and Women's and Gender History workshops; the Fundação Getúlio Vargas in Rio de Janeiro, Brazil; the "Núcleo de Pesquisas em História Cultura" at Universidade Federal Fluminense in Niterói, Brazil; the Massachusetts Historical Society and Schlesinger Library's Boston Seminar in the History of Women and Gender; the American Political History Seminar at Boston University; OSU's Space and Sovereignty workshop; and the U.S. after the Global workshop at the University of York, and am grateful for all of those opportunities.

Thanks are due to the many colleagues who read sections or earlier versions of my work and gave me helpful feedback, insights, and criticism: Les Beldo, Susan Besse, Megan Black, Thaddeus Blanchette, Eileen Boris, Laurence Buell, Lisa Bhungalia, Celso Castilho, Sueann Caulfield, Gordon Chang, Genevieve Clutario, Dorothy Sue Cobble, Melissa Curley, Ellen DuBois, Merve Emer, Lori Flores, Glaucia Fraccaro, Zephyr Frank, Nelly de Freitas, Max Paul Friedman, Brenda Frink, Manu Goswami, Rachel Guberman, Donna Guy, Annelise Heinz, Rebecca Herman, Allyson Hobbs, Clayton Howard, David Huyssen, Jill Jensen, Jane Kamensky, Patrick William Kelly, Asunción Lavrin, Lisa Levenstein, Becky Mansfield, Natalie Marine-Street, Laura Jean Martin, Thomas McDow, Caroline Merithew, Joanne Meyerowitz, Francesca Miller, Michele Mitchell, Alexandre Luís Moreli Rocha, Rachel Nolan, Cristina Teresa de Novaes, Emily Owens, Juno Parreñas, Joy Rankin, Lukas Rieppel, Emily Remus, Andrew Robichaud, Karin Rosemblatt, Leila Rupp, Sarah Seidman, Kathryn Sikkink, Noah Tamarkin, Dawn Teele, Inés Valdez, Marcela Vignoli, Kirsten Weld, Leigh Ann Wheeler, Richard White, Rachel Wise, Judy Tzu-Chun Wu, Leandra Zarnow, and Kari Zimmerman.

Enormous thanks go to Estelle Freedman, Alice Conklin, Nancy Cott, Sandra McGee Deutsch, Susan Hartmann, Mary Alice Marino, Anton Matytsin, Jocelyn Olcott, Mytheli Sreenivas, Susan Ware, and the anonymous University of North Carolina Press readers for reading the entire book manuscript (sometimes multiple times) and giving me such critical advice.

ACKNOWLEDGMENTS

I am especially grateful to the mentors who have shaped my intellectual development since my undergraduate days. Jonathan Fortescue and Timothy McCarthy encouraged and inspired me early on. Susan Ware has been a pivotal mentor since I took her class on feminist biography in college. Her class and scholarship made feminist history come alive to me and cultivated my own interests in biographical writing. Since then, she has become a dear friend and guide.

At Stanford, Estelle Freedman, Gordon Chang, and Zephyr Frank gave me invaluable advice and support. I am forever indebted to Estelle. She continues to be a wise, rigorous, thoughtful, and generous mentor. She has profoundly influenced the way I think and write, not only through her feminist scholarship and her incisive feedback on my writing, but also through the deep commitments that she brings to every aspect of her life.

I am also especially indebted to Nancy Cott, who has given me inspiration and support every step of the way. Early on, her encouragement to pursue multinational archival research gave me the confidence and sense of direction I needed. Her generous mentorship was indispensable to this book.

Over the past two years, my work has been enriched by the brilliant mind and thoughtful attention of Jocelyn Olcott, who has offered me extraordinarily incisive advice as well as unwavering encouragement.

My thanks go to Jin Auh at the Wylie Agency for believing in me and to Jessica Freidman and everyone at the Wylie Agency for their great support and help.

I am grateful for Mark Simpson-Vos's belief and interest in this project and tremendous help, particularly his editorial wisdom, quick feedback, and keen insight. Cate Hodorowicz gave incredible editorial feedback and helped me tell a story. Jessica Newman, Jay Mazzocchi, and Dino Battista also provided astute and wonderful help. My thanks go to everyone at UNC Press.

Many dear friends and colleagues at Ohio State University, in Columbus, and beyond have sustained me over the past five years: Anton Matytsin, Judy Tzu-Chun Wu, Koritha Mitchell, Birgitte Søland, Susan Hartmann, Alice Conklin, Clayton Howard, Juno Parreñas, Noah Tamarkin, Ying Zhang, Mytheli Sreenivas, Margot Kaminski, Annelise Heinz, Katie Krummeck, Genevieve Clutario, Leila Janah, David Plunkett, Konstantin Kakaes, Stephanie Smith, Thomas McDow, Jennifer Eaglin, Elizabeth Bond, Jennifer Suchland, Shannon Winnubst, Mary Thomas, Laura Jean Martin, Ezra Feldman, and many others. The History and Women's, Gender, and Sexuality Studies departments have made OSU a warm and wonderful home. I am also grateful to my students who have taught me so much.

Finally, my heartfelt thanks go to my family—Mary Alice Marino, Joseph Marino (dad), Joseph Marino (brother), Marilyn Evans, Jeannette Marino, Valentina Gissen, and Nikolai Gissen Marino—for their constant support. My parents are responsible for my becoming a historian. A 1996 trip my mom took me on to the archives of San Francisco suffragist Maud Younger at the Bancroft Library sparked my interest in history. Subsequent years of her coaching me on History Day papers cultivated my passion for it. Since then she has read, edited, offered keen insight on, and praised everything I have written (including terrible first drafts). My dad has been my steadfast supporter and always encourages me to "tell a story." Their engagement and love mean the world to me. I dedicate this book to them.

NOTES

ABBREVIATIONS

ACG	Archivo Personal de Clara González, Panama City
AFBPF	Fundo Federação Brasileira pelo Progresso Feminino, Arquivo Nacional, Rio de Janeiro
AGC-SRE	Archivo Particular Amalia González Caballero de Castillo Ledón, Secretaría de Relaciones Exteriores, Mexico City
APH	Alice Park Papers, Hoover Institution, Stanford University, Stanford, Calif.
ARA	Archivo Ricardo J. Alfaro, Panama City
BLMN	Fundo Bertha Lutz, Museu Nacional, Rio de Janeiro, Brazil
DSP	Doris Stevens Papers, Schlesinger Library, Radcliffe Institute, Harvard University, Cambridge, Mass.
ENC	Esther Neira de Calvo Papers, Georgetown University Library Booth Family Center for Special Collections, Georgetown University, Washington, D.C.
GE-SRE	Archivo Histórico Genaro Estrada, Secretaría de Relaciones Exteriores, Mexico City
JBSP	James Brown Scott Papers, Georgetown University Library Booth Family Center for Special Collections, Georgetown University, Washington, D.C.
JSP	Josephine Schain Papers, Sophia Smith Collection, Smith College, Northampton, Mass.
LAT	*Los Angeles Times*
LWV	Records of the League of Women Voters (U.S.), Library of Congress, Manuscripts Division, Washington, D.C.
MMB	Mary McLeod Bethune Papers: The Bethune Foundation Collection, microfilm collection
NAWSA	National American Woman Suffrage Association Records, Library of Congress, Washington, D.C., microfilm collection
NWP	National Woman's Party Records, Library of Congress, Washington, D.C., microfilm collection
NYT	*New York Times*
ODN-AN	Archivo Ofelia Domínguez Navarro, Donativos y Remisiones, Archivo Nacional de Cuba, Havana
ODN-IH	Fondo Ofelia Domínguez Navarro, Archivo Instituto de Historia de Cuba, Havana
PL-ACRE	Fondo Paulina Luisi, Archivo del Centro Republicano Español, Facultad de Humanidades y Ciencias de la Educación, Montevideo
PL-AGN	Archivo Paulina Luisi, Archivo General de la Nación, Montevideo
PL-BN	Archivo Paulina Luisi, Biblioteca Nacional de Uruguay, Montevideo
RG 59	Record Group 59, General Records of the Department of State, National Archives and Records Administration, College Park, Md.
RG 86	Record Group 86, Records of the Women's Bureau, International Division,

General Records, 1919–52, National Archives and Records Administration, College Park, Md.

RG 174   Record Group 174, General Records of the Department of Labor, National Archives and Records Administration, College Park, Md.

SBP   Sophonisba Preston Breckinridge Papers, Library of Congress, Washington, D.C., microfilm collection

WILPF   Women's International League for Peace and Freedom Records (DG043), Swarthmore College Peace Collection, Swarthmore, Pa.

WP   *Washington Post*

PROLOGUE

1. Doris Stevens to Margarita de Aragón, September 18, 1931, and Stevens to Ofelia Domínguez Navarro, undated, box 65, folder 6, DSP.

2. Domínguez and de Aragón to Stevens, October 3, 1931, box 65, folder 6, DSP.

3. Domínguez to Stevens, November 23, 1931, box 65, folder 6, DSP.

4. "Union Laborista de Mujeres, A la Conciencia Política de la Mujer Latino Americana, Carta de la Srta. Doris Stevens, Presidenta de la Inter American Commission of Woman a la Unión Laborista de Mujeres," caja 675, no. 8, ODN-AN.

5. Catalina Pozo y Gato, "Reflexiones," 1930, ODN-AN.

6. Domínguez to "Compañeras," letter attached to "Informe," September 8, 1933, caja 675, no. 11, ODN-AN.

7. Cott, *Grounding of Modern Feminism*, 14–16; E. Freedman, *No Turning Back*, 6–7.

8. This period is often called the "doldrums" of U.S. feminist history. See Rupp and Taylor, *Survival in the Doldrums*. Many historians have explored the diverse array of activism for and by women that continued in these years, in spite of the limited usage of the term "feminism" itself. See for example Cott, *Grounding of Modern Feminism*; Ware, *Beyond Suffrage*; Cobble, *Other Women's Movement*; McDuffie, *Sojourning for Freedom*; Gore, *Radicalism at the Crossroads*; Blain, *Set the World on Fire*; Weigand, *Red Feminism*; Storrs, *Civilizing Capitalism and Second Red Scare*; Levenstein, *Movement without Marches*; Zhao, *Holding Up More Than Half the Sky*; Ruiz, *Cannery Women*; Orleck, *Rethinking American Women's Activism*; and Cobble, Gordon, and Henry, *Feminism Unfinished*, among others.

9. The U.S. government and U.S. female reformers often justified interventions or imperial pursuits by arguing they would advance women's progress as part of a "civilizational" mission. On connections between U.S. empire and promotion of women's rights from the late nineteenth to early twentieth centuries, see Hoganson, *Fighting for American Manhood*, 191–94; Briggs, *Reproducing Empire*; McPherson, *Invaded*, 116–17; Sneider, *Suffragists in an Imperial Age*; and Tyrrell, *Woman's World, Woman's Empire*.

10. Gobat, "Invention of Latin America."

11. Grandin, "The Liberal Traditions in the Americas."

12. I capitalize the "Popular Front" to denote the "democratic social movement." Denning, *The Cultural Front*, xviii.

13. Ibárruri, *Women Want a People's Peace*, 58.

14. My interpretation challenges that of Samuel Moyn and others that "human rights" did not emerge until the late twentieth century. While Moyn's work has deeply influenced my thinking and tremendously advanced scholarship on the history of human rights, it overlooks the importance of both feminism and Latin America as producers of thought and activism. On the lack of influence early feminist organizing had on human rights, he writes, "Insofar as a generally rights-based movement like the women's movement took on international form, its internationalism was about sharing techniques and building

confidence for national agitation, not making the global forum itself a scene of invention or reform, participation in the international quest for peace aside." Moyn, *Last Utopia*, 39. This characterization is not true of inter-American feminists, who indeed made "the global forum itself a scene of invention" and reform. Moyn's work, highlighting the unprecedented "breakthrough" moment of human rights in the 1970s, helps us critique its mainstream and U.S.-led meanings and its complicity with neoliberal projects. But understanding earlier feminist forms of human rights, particularly from Latin America, is deeply important to this project, as well. Moyn's latest book acknowledges the distributive justice ideals that helped forge human rights in the 1930s but fails to acknowledge that feminism or Latin American forms of social democracy also internationalized economic and social rights in these years. Moyn, *Not Enough*. My work has been enriched by scholarship that has explored the influence of Latin American social movements and diplomacy, as well as decolonization movements, in the formulation of international human rights. Sikkink, "Latin American Countries as Norm Protagonists," *Evidence for Hope*, and "Reconceptualizing Sovereignty in the Americas"; Kelly, *Sovereign Emergencies*; Grandin, "Liberal Traditions in the Americas"; Grandin, "Human Rights and Empire's Embrace"; Glendon, "Forgotten Crucible" and *World Made New*; Carozza, "From Conquest to Constitutions"; Dubois, "Enslaved Enlightenment"; Jensen, *The Making of International Human Rights*; Burke, *Decolonization and the Evolution of International Human Rights*; Encarnación, *Out in the Periphery*.

15. Until now there have been no book-length, transnational histories of Pan-American feminism, although my work relies upon the insights of many scholars who have explored important parts of its history. See Miller's works *Latin American Women*, chapters 4 and 5, "Feminisms and Transnationalism," "International Relations of Women," and "Latin American Feminism"; Towns, "The Inter-American Commission of Women." On Pan-American activism of different national Latin American feminist movements or figures, see Stoner, "In Four Languages"; Antezana-Pernet, "Peace in the World and Democracy at Home"; Pernet, "Chilean Feminists"; Ehrick, "Madrinas and Missionaries"; Ehrick, "Il femminismi ispanici"; DuBois and Derby, "Strange Case of Minerva Bernardino"; Lavrin, "International Feminisms"; Lau Javien, "Entre ambas fronteras"; Rodríguez de Ita, "La Comisión Interamericana de Mujeres durante la presidencia de Amalia de Castillo Ledón"; Novaes Marques, "Entre o igualitarismo e a reforma dos direitos das mulheres"; Manley, *The Paradox of Paternalism*, chapter 1. Gabriela Cano's work has explored the leadership of Mexican feminists in inter-American feminisms: Se *llamaba Elena Arizmendi*, "El 'feminismo de estado' e Amalia de Castillo Ledón," "México 1923." Sandra McGuee Deutsch's work has explored the antifascist Junta de la Victoria in Argentina as an important site of Latin American women's transnational activism: "Argentine Women against Fascism," "Hands across the Río de la Plata." "New School Lecture 'An Army of Women.'" Donna Guy's work has underscored the importance of women's transnational activism in Pan-American Child congresses: "Politics of Pan-American Cooperation" and "Pan American Child Congresses." Most works exploring Pan-American women's collaboration from U.S. perspectives and sources have concluded that U.S. imperial feminism made Latin American leadership impossible. See Threlkeld, *Pan American Women*; Hill, "International Law for Women's Rights"; and Wamsley, "Hemisphere of Women."

16. On maternalist interpretations of Latin American feminisms, see Chaney, *Supermadre*; Miller, *Latin American Women*, xiv, 68–109; González and Kampwirth, *Radical Women in Latin America*, 11–13; Nari, *Políticas de maternidad*; Lavrin, *Women, Feminism, and Social Change*. Maternalism indeed was significant to many Latin American iterations of feminism, but as Sandy McGee Deutsch has also recently explained, there are limits to how much "ma-

ternalism" explains the wide range of Latin American feminisms in this period, and especially the strong antifascist feminism of the 1930s. Deutsch, "New School Lecture 'An Army of Women.'" These interpretations that Latin America experienced minimal feminist activism in contrast to the U.S. and Western Europe have persisted in spite of the rich historical work on different national feminist movements. See, for example, Miller, *Latin American Women*; Lavrin, *Women, Feminism, and Social Change*; Guy, *Sex and Danger in Buenos Aires* and *Women Build the Welfare State*; Ehrick, *Shield of the Weak*; Marco Serra, *Clara González de Behringer*; Lavrin, *Women, Feminism, and Social Change*; Olcott, *Revolutionary Women* and "The Center Cannot Hold"; Rosenblatt, *Gendered Compromises*; Stoner, *From the House to the Streets*; Antezana-Pernet, "Mobilizing Women"; Caulfield, *In Defense of Honor*; Besse, *Restructuring Patriarchy*; Hahner, *Emancipating the Female Sex*; Deutsch, *Crossing Borders*; Sapriza, "Clivajes de la memoria"; S. Smith, *Gender and the Mexican Revolution*; Macías, *Against All Odds*; and Fraccaro, *Os direitos das mulheres* and "Uma história social do feminismo."

17. The tendency to privilege Western Europe and especially the U.S. as centers of feminist leadership dates back at least to the efforts of Susan B. Anthony and Elizabeth Cady Stanton in their two-volume *History of American Suffrage*, and their founding of the International Council of Women, to position themselves as originators of the women's rights movement nationally and internationally. Tetrault, *The Myth of Seneca Falls*, chapter 5. For an example of feminist history that privileges suffrage as the metric for achievement, see Evans, *Feminists*. Pioneering scholarship that has explored predominantly U.S. and Western European transnational and comparative feminist organizing include Rupp, *Worlds of Women* and "Constructing Internationalism"; Alonso, *Peace as a Woman's Issue*; Foster, *Women and the Warriors*; Schott, *Reconstructing Women's Thoughts*; Offen, *European Feminisms*; Tyrrell, *Woman's World*; B. Anderson, *Joyous Greetings*; McFadden, *Golden Cables of Sympathy*; Teele, *Forging the Franchise*; and Delap, *The Feminist Avant-Garde*.

18. Grandin, "Liberal Tradition in the Americas," 75–76. Other works that trace the deeper roots of liberalism, modernity, republicanism, and democracy in Latin America include J. Sanders, *Vanguard of the Atlantic World*; and Schwartz, *All Can Be Saved*.

19. My understanding of Popular Front Pan-American feminism has been enhanced by scholarship that illuminates the often mutually constitutive relationships between feminism and international socialism and communism in the early twentieth century. Francisca de Haan has argued that the effects of the Cold War occluded the leftist feminism of the Women's International Democratic Federation and its multipronged, socialist-inspired feminism. De Haan, "Eugénie Cotton, Pak Chong-ae, and Claudia Jones." See DuBois, "Woman Suffrage and the Left" and "Woman Suffrage"; DuBois and Oliviero, "Circling the Globe"; McDuffie, *Sojourning for Freedom*; Weigand, *Red Feminism*; Valobra and Yusta, *Queridas camaradas*; Valobra, "Formación de cuadros y frentes populares." Dorothy Sue Cobble, Eileen Boris, Jill Jensen, and Vicki Ruiz are shedding light on women's transnational labor organizing. Cobble, "Higher 'Standard of Life'"; Boris and Jensen, "ILO."

20. Given the strong influence of communism and the Popular Front on *feminismo americano*, I also use this term in a nod to its Marxist-Leninist usage. The revolutionary "vanguard" was the select group of individuals imbued with and entitled to an unchallenged authority to lead.

21. Kelly-Gadol, "Did Women Have a Renaissance?"; Shepard and Walker, "Gender, Change, and Periodisation."

22. Scholars have explored how gendered concerns and women shaped foreign policy in these interwar years when women were still excluded from the foreign service. McCarthy, *Women of the World*; Gottlieb, "Guilty Women"; Threlked, *Pan American Women*.

Most, however, do not find feminism and women's rights as fundamentally shaping foreign policy until the 1970s and 1980s.

23. Feminist scholars have long emphasized the importance of affect, intimacy, and emotion. Berlant, "Intimacy" and *Intimacy*; Hennessy, *Fires on the Border*; Gould, *Moving Politics*. On the role of lesbian desire and affection in the U.S. solidarity movement with Nicaragua, see Hobson, *Lavendar and Red*. Historians of international relations have also recently turned their attention to emotion as an area of analysis. Costigliola, "Reading for Emotion" and *Roosevelt's Lost Alliances*; Eustace et al., "AHR Conversation."

24. On positioning Latin American anti-imperialism against a range of anticolonial movements, Michael Goebbel writes, "Imperialism emerges as a variegated landscape of many shades of gray, not as clear-cut opposition between colonizer and colonized." Goebbel, *Anti-imperial Metropolis*, 8.

25. *Diario de la Conferencia Interamericana*, February 27, 1945, 84. Although the movement incorporated antiracism and included feminists of African descent from the Dominican Republic, Haiti, Cuba, and Panama, Pan-American conferences were elite spaces that privileged whiteness and largely excluded women of color. Those spaces, combined with the whiteness of many self-proclaimed *feministas* produced significant limitations in the movement, which gave minimal attention to racial violence and failed to actively include indigenous and Afro-descended women until the late 1930s and 1940s. Ofelia Domínguez Navarro and Clara González, however, both organized actively with women of color in Cuba and Panama and embraced antiracist politics. Black women forged their own dynamic and powerful transnational connections from the Latin America and Caribbean to the United States that also influenced inter-American feminism. On black women's internationalism and transnationalism in these years, see Blain, *Set the World on Fire*; McDuffie, *Sojourning for Freedom*; Henry, "Promoting Historical Consciousness"; G. Sanders, "La Voix des Femmes"; Rief, "Thinking Locally, Acting Globally"; and Wells, "'She Pieced and Stitched and Quilted,'" among others.

26. Marta Vergara explained that her ideal of socialism was guided by Barbusse's notion of "the love of man, the desire to dignify him." Vergara, *Memorias*, 53.

27. Ocampo, "Woman and Her Experience," in Ocampo and Steiner, *Victoria Ocampo*, 171. As Deutsch explains, Ocampo was referring to Spanish diplomat and writer Salvador de Madariaga's term "subjective solidarity," quoted in Deutsch, "New School Lecture, 'An Army of Women,'" 116.

28. González drew on Aristotle's notion of friendship to support this idea. Clara González, "Fundamentos de organización política" (unpublished essay), ACG. Quote from Marco Serra, *Clara González de Behringer*, 109.

29. Domínguez to Adelia di Carlo, November 5, 1933, caja 673, no. 9, ODN-AN. Years later, this Argentinian feminist would help lead a "Confederación Continental de Mujeres por la Paz," specifically aimed at uniting "*mujeres de América*" against war, fascism, and imperialism. See chapter 5.

30. Domínguez to Luisi, June 10, 1931, carpeta "D," PL-BN.

CHAPTER 1

1. Bertha Lutz to Paulina Luisi, May 14, 1921, Qo.ADM, COR.1921.11, pp. 11, 43, AFBPF. The Brazilian press had long followed Luisi, and copies of Luisi's Alianza publication *Acción Femenina* had found their way to Lutz through friends in the scientific world.

2. Luisi to Lutz, July 14, 1921, Qo.ADM, COR.1921, pp. 12–16, AFBPF.

3. Paulina Luisi, "Sesión de apertura del 1° Congreso americano del Niño," 1916,

doc. 7, sección 3, serie 3.2, PL-ACRE. Also attending the First Pan-American Child Congress in Buenos Aires was her close friend Argentine feminist and doctor Alicia Moreau.

4. Luisi, "Sesión de aperture del 1° Congreso americano del Niño."

5. Paulina Luisi, [untitled], *Acción Femenina* 1, no. 1 (1917): 1–2. Also cited in Lavrin, *Women, Feminism, and Social Change*, 34, 372, and "Paulina Luisi," 161. This was not the first time "feminism" was mentioned in print in Latin America. In 1901, for instance, Argentinian Elvira López published an influential work, *El movimiento feminista*. In 1913, when Uruguayan president Batlle sent Luisi to Europe to study sexual hygiene, she also absorbed lessons from the French feminist movement and became friends with French leaders. Sapriza, "Clivajes de la memoria," 257.

6. Luisi, *Acción Femenina* 1, no. 1 (1917): 1–2.

7. Ehrick, "Il femminismi ispanici"; Rodó, *Ariel*; Capello, *City at the Center of the World*, 65–66. "El peligro yanqui" was popularized by Argentinian Manuel Ugarte's eponymous article and writings. Manuel Ugarte, "El peligro yanqui," *El País* (Buenos Aires), October 19, 1901.

8. Paulina Luisi to Hermila Galindo, December 23, 1919, correspondence, carpeta "G," PL-BN.

9. Ehrick, *Shield of the Weak*, 95; Parker, *Uruguayans of Today*, 307–8; Andrade Coelle, "Esthetic Education," 393. Both of these sisters would join Paulina in feminist activism and would participate in Pan-American initiatives.

10. Sapriza, *Memorias de rebeldia*, 85–87.

11. Miller, *Latin American Women*, 52, 73–75; Lavrin, *Women, Feminism, and Social Change*, 29–32. The 1910 Buenos Aires Congress was organized by the Asociación de Universitarias Argentinas president, Julieta Lanteri Renshaw. It had been preceded by the first convention of the International Council of Women in Washington, D.C., in 1888 organized by Susan B. Anthony and others in the National Woman Suffrage Association.

12. López, "Keynote Speech."

13. Ehrick, "Madrinas and Missionaries," 407; Miller, *Latin American Women*, 73.

14. Between 1880 and 1900, Uruguay experienced immigration from Europe, urban development, slower population growth, growth of industrial labor, and economic development based on booming exports in meat and wool. By 1913, Uruguay boasted the highest per capita gross domestic product and the highest per capita tax receipts in Latin America. Markaria, *Left in Transformation*, 10; Andrews, *Blackness in a White Nation*, 2.

15. "El feminismo en marcha," *Caras y Caretas* (Buenos Aires), December 1918, 12; Ehrick, "Madrinas and Missionaries," 407.

16. He introduced this resolution in the Committee on Social and Juridical Sciences. The next Latin American Scientific Congress would be in 1908–9 in Santiago, Chile, and was the first "Pan-American" scientific congress. Álvarez, "Latin America and International Law," 353. More on Álvarez can be found in Koskenniemi, *Gentle Civilizer of Nations*, 302–22; and in Burnett, "Contingent Constitutions," chapter 4.

17. Álvarez, "Latin America and International Law," 327; Koskenniemi, *Gentle Civilizer of Nations*, 302.

18. Donna Guy has also emphasized a Latin American–led Pan-Americanism in the Pan-American Child Congresses that began in 1916. See Guy, "Pan American Child Congresses," and "Politics of Pan-American Cooperation."

19. Esquirol, "Alejandro Álvarez's Latin American Law," 932.

20. Álvarez, "Latin America and International Law," 339.

21. Representatives from these nations and Uruguay were also among the most avid proponents of Pan-Americanism. Chilean minister to Great Britain Augustín Edwards

deemed his own country at the "vanguard of Pan-Americanism," while those in Uruguay, Brazil, and Argentina would claim similar mantles. Petersen, "'Vanguard of Pan-Americanism,'" 111. Juan Pablo Scarfi has pointed out the pro-U.S. positions of Alejandro Álvarez, who defended the Monroe Doctrine and collaborated with U.S. international lawyer James Brown Scott in 1912 to create the American Institute of International Law. Scarfi, *Hidden History of International Law*, 32–36.

22. These new initiatives, spearheaded by both U.S. and Latin American elites, included the Pan-American Sanitary Commission, Pan-American Journalist Conferences, Pan-American Conferences of International Law, and Pan-American Eugenics Conferences.

23. Gilderhaus, *Pan American Visions*, 37; Rosenberg, "World War I and 'Continental Solidarity'"; McPherson, "World War I and U.S. Empire."

24. Gilderhaus, *Pan American Visions*, 49.

25. These countries included Bolivia, Chile, Brazil, Mexico, Peru, and Guatemala, among others. Uruguay, Ministerio de Relaciones Exteriores, *Memoria del Ministerio de relaciones exteriores*, 438–40. The decree proclaimed that "an offense inflicted on the rights of one country of the continent should be accepted as such by all, and should provoke in them a uniform and common reaction." Dr. Baltasar Brum, "Uruguay's President Defends Monroe Doctrine," *South American* 8, no. 8 (June 1920): 8.

26. Karr, *Uruguay and the United States*, 88, 90, 98–99, 110.

27. Brum, *La paz de América*.

28. John Barrett to E. B. Swiggett, November 19, 1919, container 3, Records of the Pan American International Women's Committee, Library of Congress, Manuscripts Division, Washington, D.C.; "Latin American Women Greeted," *WP*, June 15, 1918, 7.

29. Addams, Balch, and Hamilton, *Women at The Hague*. See Rupp, *Worlds of Women*, esp. 26–29, 84–85; Dawley, *Changing the World*, 7, 16–18, 93–96.

30. Swiggett, *Report on the Women's Auxiliary Conference*, 60.

31. Mrs. Robert Lansing to Julia C. Lathrop, December 16, 1916, container 1, folder 1, Records of the Pan-American International Women's Committee, Library of Congress.

32. Miller, *Latin American Women*, 98. This happened long before it did in Argentina, where feminist activism did flourish but political leaders did not support the vote as actively as in Uruguay.

33. Connections that Luisi had with Mary Sheepshanks, a British woman who lived for a time in Uruguay, would later facilitate Luisi's connections with the IWSA in Europe. Mary Sheepshanks to Luisi, November 22, 1921, carpeta "S," PL-BN; Ehrick, "Madrinas and Missionaries," 413.

34. Luisi, "Alianza Uruguaya para el sufragio femenino," *Acción Femenina*, 120; Ehrick, "Madrinas and Missionaries," 408.

35. Brum, *Los derechos de la Mujer*, 29, 31. It also reasoned that women's active involvement in the First World War proved their worthiness of equal rights. Brum also consulted Luisi on a 1921 proposed amendment for women's equal rights. In speeches and articles, Brum also praised the suffrage movements in the United States and Uruguay. "Palabras de aliento del doctor Brum, ex-Presidente del Uruguaya y paladín de la causa feminista," undated newspaper clipping, December 27, 1918, caja 257, carpeta 5, PL-AGN.

36. Sara Justo to Luisi, July 26, 1919, carpeta "J," PL-BN. Alicia Moreau wrote to Luisi, "If we have support of the North Americans, [the Pan-American women's conference] will go well." Alicia Moreau to Luisi, March 30, 1919, carpeta "M," PL-BN. In December 1919 the organ of the National American Woman Suffrage Association, the *Woman's Journal*, wrote of the planned congress, as did Katherine Dreier, a U.S. artist traveling

in Buenos Aires who served as a liaison between the Argentinian feminists and Catt in organizing the conference. Dreier, *Five Months in the Argentine*, 257; "How Latin American Women are Gaining," *Woman's Journal* 4, no. 22 (December 20, 1919): 601, 603; "Pan-American Feminism," *St. Albans (Vt.) Daily Messenger*, June 25, 1919, 2.

37. Connolly, *World More Concrete*, 109.

38. If slavery was mentioned at all, it was in reference to its abolition in Brazil, Cuba, and the United States, upheld as evidence of a progressive common destiny of the Americas. U.S. promotion of "liberal internationalism" and "democracy" emerged at the high noon of imperialism and of racism and racial violence in the United States. At the same time, many countries in South America, especially in the A.B.C. nations that promoted Pan-Americanism, emphasized increased immigration of European people to "whiten" their populations. It was the effort to write these countries into the discourse of civilization, on the same rung as the United States and western Europe, upon which many Latin American–led definitions of Pan-Americanism often hinged. For more on race in Latin America and politics of whitening, see Stepan, *"Hour of Eugenics"*; and Loveman, *National Colors*.

39. Loveman, *National Colors*, 165, 229–30, 245–47.

40. Brum, *La paz de América*, 13.

41. Christine Ehrick has explored how Luisi's soon-to-be close friend Elena Arizmendi protested the denigration of the "Latin" race by Anglo-American culture while simultaneously articulating racist ideas about Jewish people. Ehrick, "Il femminismi ispanici." On the significant neoimperial and conservative strains of Pan-Hispanism, see Pike, *Hispanismo*.

42. Nancy Stepan has argued that French neo-Lamarckian notions of heredity produced a brand of eugenics in Latin America that was less harsh than the Mendelian, "negative" eugenics of Britain and the United States that included sterilizing the unfit. Stepan, *"Hour of Eugenics."* Christine Ehrick explains that Luisi initially embraced a "negative" form of eugenics, although she directed her early sterilization proposals toward men, not women. Her turn toward a French, environmentalist form of eugenics in 1919 occurred alongside her turn toward socialist politics. Luisi also advocated for women's frank discussion of sex and for sexual education as part of her eugenic and feminist platforms. See Ehrick, *Shield of the Weak*, 98–105.

43. Andrews, *Blackness in a White Nation*, 3–7. On politics of antiblack erasure and violence as constitutive of nationalism elsewhere in the Americas, see García-Peña, *Borders of Dominicanidad*.

44. Burton, *Burdens of History*; Sinha, *Specters of Mother India*; Sreenivas, "Birth Control in the Shadow of Empire"; de Haan, "Continuing Cold War Paradigms," 551–52.

45. Moreau expressed these ideas at the 1920 Pan American Physicians Congress; see A. S. B., "Women of the Argentine," *Woman Citizen*, February 14, 1920, 867–68. As Stephanie Smith has shown, feminists at Mexico's First Feminist Congress in the Yucután in 1916 expressed similar sentiments about the differences between themselves and "traditional" and "backward" Maya women, whom they excluded from the congress. S. Smith, *Gender and the Mexican Revolution*, 29–31. For more on the influence of evolutionary theory on U.S. feminism, see Hamlin, *From Eve to Evolution*; and Newman, *White Women's Rights*.

46. "Congreso de la Alianza I. para el Sufragio Femenino: Informe presentado por la Dra Paulina Luisi sobre su realización, 1920," caja 257, carpeta 3, PL-AGN. See more on Catt and Jacobs's trip in Bosch, "Colonial Dimensions of Dutch Women's Suffrage."

47. Rupp, *Worlds of Women*, 23.

48. The countries that now had women's suffrage included New Zealand (1893), Australia (1902), Finland (1906), Norway (1913), Denmark (1915), Iceland (1915), Russia (1917), Austria (1918), Canada (1918), Germany (1918), Hungary (1918), Latvia (1918), Lithuania (1918), Poland (1918), the United Kingdom (1918), Belgium (1919), Kenya (1919), Luxembourg (1919), the Netherlands (1919), Rhodesia (1919), Albania (1920), Czechoslovakia (1920), and the United States (1920). Of those countries, members of the IWSA included representatives from Australia, Finland, Norway, Denmark, Iceland, Russia, Austria, Canada, Germany, Hungary, Poland, Great Britain, Belgium, Luxembourg, the Netherlands, South Africa, and the United States.

49. Celia Paladino de Vitale to Luisi, from Montevideo, September 11, 1923, caja 257, carpeta 4, PL-AGN.

50. Argentina and Uruguay were the only Latin American representatives of the IWSA at this time. See Rupp, *Worlds of Women*, table 1, 16.

51. Emphasis in original. "Congreso de la Alianza I. para el Sufragio Femenino: Informe presentado por la Dra Paulna Luisi sobre su realización, 1920," caja 257, carpeta 3, PL-AGN. Ultimately, the IWSA decided to maintain the fight for suffrage where it did not exist while also broadening its goals to equal nationality of married women, the civil status of women, the protection of infancy, the equal moral standard, the traffic of women, women's work, and equality of salary. See also Ehrick, "*Madrinas* and Missionaries," 418.

52. Sheepshanks to Luisi, June 12, 1919, and September 19, 1919, carpeta "S," PL-BN.

53. Upon her return to Montevideo, Luisi shared news widely that Uruguay had been considered inferior to other places because women in Uruguay did not have the right to vote and that Luisi herself had been treated as a second-class citizen by women from "enfranchised" countries. A mention of this incident was even included in the introductory comments to the 1925 revised edition of Brum, *Los derechos de la mujer*.

54. "Congreso de la Alianza I. para el Sufragio Femenino: Informe presentado por la Dra Paulina Luisi sobre su realización, 1920," caja 257, carpeta 3, PL-AGN.

55. Sheepshanks to Hubert, December 21, 1921, 2:17, and Luisi to Sheepshanks, December 20, 1922, 2:17, LWV. Catt to Luisi, November 21, 1921, caja 253, carpeta 7, PL-AGN. Catt did write to Luisi personally to invite her to the conference in late November, though because of the mail's slowness, her letter only arrived at the beginning of January.

56. Luisi to Catt, January 16, 1922, caja 253, carpeta 7, PL-AGN.

57. Celia Paladino de Vitale would represent Uruguay alongside the wife of Uruguayan Ambassador to the U.S. Jacobo Varela, Olga Capurro de Varela. Uruguayan Deputy of Exterior to Luisi, January 28, 1922; Uruguayan Minister of Exterior to Luisi, February 14, 1922; Uruguayan Minister of Foreign Relations to Luisi, February 25, 1922, all in caja 253, carpeta 7, PL-AGN.

58. "Proposición de la Alianza Uruguay para el Sufragio Femenino sometida a la consideración de la conferencia Panamericana de Mujeres," undated, 2:17, LWV. Her proposal noted that women's emancipation in North America served as a "high example and a rich lesson for the women of the Americas."

59. Luisi to Paladino, March 1922, caja 257, carpeta 4, PL-AGN.

60. Catt to Alicia Moreau, November 2, 1921, reel 5, Carrie Chapman Catt Papers, Library of Congress, Washington, D.C., microfilm collection; Statement of Plan for proposed Pan-American Conference of Women, 2:16, LWV. Not only would such an event carry commercial benefit during a postwar economic recession in the United States, but the State Department also hoped that it would help repair the worsening image of the United States in Latin America.

61. See Threlkeld, *Pan American Women*, chapter 2.

62. Lavinia Engle to Maud Wood Park, [1921], 2:16, LWV; Threlkeld, "Pan American Conference," 805.

63. Luisi to Don Jacobo Varela Acevedo, March 1922, carpeta "V," PL-BN.

64. She also sent her proposal to Uruguayan Ambassador Jacobo Varela, and she sent English translations of Brum's publication to the League of Women Voters and to the U.S. Ambassador in Uruguay. "Proposición de la Alianza Uruguay para el Sufragio Femenino sometida a la consideración de la conferencia Panamericana de Mujeres," undated, caja 257, carpeta 4, PL-AGN; Luisi to Don Jacobo Varela Acevedo, March 1922, carpeta "V," PL-BN; Luisi to Norman Armour, March 1922, and Luisi to Maud Wood Park, undated, both in 2:17, LWV.

65. Luisi to Paladino, March [?], 1922, caja 257, carpeta 4, PL-AGN.

66. Luisi to Paladino, March 17, 1922, caja 257, carpeta 4, PL-AGN.

67. Lutz to Luisi, October 3, 1921, carpeta "L," PL-BN. Luisi noted in the margins of this letter that Lutz was slow to respond and sometimes did not respond to her.

68. Luisi to Lutz, January 14, 1922, Qo.ADM, COR.1922.2, AFBPF.

69. Roy F. Nash, "The Brains of Brazil's Woman's Movement," *Woman Citizen*, March 25, 1922, 9, 16.

70. Lutz also earned a law degree in Rio de Janeiro, writing her thesis in support of equal citizenship rights for women internationally. Lutz, *Nationality of Married Women*.

71. Lutz, "Seção Cartas de Mulher," *Revista da Semana*, December 28, 1918; Hahner, *Emancipating the Female Sex*, 134.

72. Bertha Lutz, "The Limits Imposed upon the Individual Activity of Woman by Biologic Factors," *A Folha Médica* (Rio de Janeiro), December 1920, in 2:6, LWV. Lutz believed that the biological effects of motherhood atrophied women's potential in other areas: "The pregnant organism carrying the parasitic egg feels the influence of this parasitism upon all the functions."

73. Lutz, "Limits Imposed upon the Individual Activity of Woman by Biologic Factors."

74. Draft of letter from Lutz to Heloise Brainerd, undated, 1930, Qo.BLZ, COR.A930, TXT.18, AFBPF. On her fluency in those languages, see Esther Van Dresser Kralick, "Brazil Woman at S.F. Meet," *Salt Lake Tribune*, June 3, 1945, 17.

75. Luisi to Lutz, July 14, 1921, Qo.ADM, COR.1921, pp. 12–16, AFBPF.

76. Lutz to "Madam" [Emmeline Pankhurst], March 17, 1921, Qo.ADM, COR.1921.13, p. 7; Margery Corbett Ashby to Lutz, April 24, 1921, Qo.ADM, COR.1921.11, p. 8, AFBPF.

77. Bertha Lutz, *A Noite*, October 11, 1921, in Blachman, "Eve in Adamocracy," 122.

78. Lutz quoted in "The Latin Point of View," *National Business Woman*, October 1922, 21.

79. Lutz to Belle Sherwin, May 27, 1926, 2:156, LWV.

80. Bethell, "Brazil and 'Latin America,'" 465; J. Smith, *Unequal Giants*.

81. "Address of Bertha Lutz before the Final Session of the Pan-American Conference of Women at a Mass Meeting Held in Continental Hall, Washington, D.C., 29 April, 1922," Qo.ADM, EVE.CNF, TXT.1, VOL 2, AFBPF.

82. "Address of Bertha Lutz before the Final Session."

83. Amanda Finch to Mary Anderson, August 5, 1936, box 8 "Inter-American Commission," RG 86.

84. Lutz to Catt, February 1, 1933, Qo.ADM, COR.1933, p. 15, AFBPF.

85. League member Harriet Chalmers Adams recommended the LWV contact Lutz about the conference. Adams, whose husband worked in the Pan-American Union, had

met Lutz on a trip to Rio de Janeiro in 1921 and credited her with "revolution[izing] the status of women in Brazil." "Notes on Interview with Mrs. Harriet Chalmers Adams, Pan American Conference," 2:16, LWV. Adams took an active role in planning the 1922 conference, recommending Lutz before other Latin American feminists when she met with League members in Washington, D.C.

86. Maud Wood Park to Belle Sherwin, February 18, 1922; "Payments Made to Official Delegates to the Pan American Conference of Women to date May 2nd," 2:16, LWV. The amounts of $500 and $1,000 were significant in 1922, roughly equivalent to $7,377 and $14,754, respectively, in 2018 (see http://www.usinflationcalculator.com, accessed March 9, 2018).

87. Lutz to Carrie Chapman Catt, July 7, 1922, reel 4, Carrie Chapman Catt Papers, Library of Congress, Washington, D.C., microfilm collection.

88. Draft letter to Ambassadors, Ministers, and Chargés d'Affaires [undated], 2:16, LWV. Many Latin American invitees to the conference were wives of diplomats in the United States.

89. Each session had a keynote speaker from the United States and one or two speakers from Latin America.

90. Threlkeld, Pan American Women, chapter 2, and "Pan American Conference," 822–23.

91. The French Napoleonic tradition, while influential regarding property, economic, and commercial law, was not, in fact, as influential concerning married women's property rights in Latin America as the colonial Luso-Hispanic legal tradition. Deere and León, "Liberalism and Married Women's Property Rights."

92. Minutes of the Congress, 2:16, LWV; "Life in Uruguay Is Pictured as Really Utopian," undated newspaper article, box 1a, ENC. On Uruguayan law see also Ehrick, The Shield of the Weak; and Alanis, Altieri, and Otegui Carrasco, Family Law in Uruguay, 128.

93. "Congreso de la Alianza I. para el Sufragio Femenino: Informe presentado por la Dra Paulina Luisi sobre su realización, 1920," caja 257, carpeta 3, PL-AGN. These accomplishments included equal nationality rights, rights of illegitimate children, equality of salary in public jobs, and investigation of paternity.

94. "Latin American Women to Extend Conference," Baltimore Sun, April 22, 1922.

95. "Proposición de la Alianza Uruguay para el Sufragio Femenino sometida a la consideración de la conferencia Panamericana de Mujeres," undated, caja 257, carpeta 4, PL-AGN.

96. Celia Paladino de Vitale, "Discurso Ante la Conferencia Pan-Americana de Mujeres en Baltimore," April 1922, caja 257, carpeta 4, PL-AGN.

97. Paladino, "Discurso."

98. Paladino.

99. Mildred Adams, "All the Americas Meet at Baltimore," Woman Citizen, May 6, 1922, 10, 12.

100. The other positions would be filled by Esther Neira de Calvo of Panama, vice president for Central America; Elena Torres of Mexico, vice president for North America; María Suarez de Coronado of Colombia, secretary; and Olga Capurro de Varela of Uruguay, treasurer. "Acta de la Tricesima Sesion de la Conferencia Feminista Pan-Americana," April 24, 1922, and "Feminismo Triunfante," January 1923 (newspaper article clippings), box 6, folder 1, ENC.

101. "Brazil Sends Brilliant Woman to Conference," WP, March 9, 1922, 42; Rodney Dutcher, "Here's Free Adv. for Ships Bound to Brazil Ports," Atlanta Constitution, June 13, 1922, 1; "Women Voters to Welcome Brazilian Suffragist To-day," New York Tribune, April 8,

1922, 9. In 1923, a *Boston Daily Globe* article called Lutz "South America's Most Prominent 'New Woman'": Margaret Bell, "Six Great Feminists, V. Dona Bertha Lutz," *Boston Daily Globe*, September 7, 1923, 16.

102. John Barrett, "Women's Big Conference," NYT, April 16, 1922, 6.

103. Florence Kelley to Bertha Lutz, May 9, 1922, Q0.ADM, COR.1922.54, and Grace Abbott to Lutz, May 18, 1922, Q0.ADM, COR.1922.137, p. 1, AFBPF.

104. The Illinois League of Women Voters also hosted Lutz for two days in Chicago. "Rio's Leader in Woman's Sphere Due Here Today," *Chicago Daily Tribune*, June 11, 1922, 14. W. E. B. Du Bois to Lutz, May 24, 1922, Q0.ADM, COR.1922.122, and Woodrow Wilson to Lutz, June 21, 1922, Q0.ADM, COR.1922.133, AFBPF.

105. "U.S. Declared Teacher for All America," *San Francisco Chronicle*, June 11, 1922, 1. The *Wichita Beacon* reported that "the League of Women Voters frankly fell in love with Dona Bertha and the rest of America, wherever she speaks, follows their example." "Brazil Orator Coming Friday; Public Address," *Wichita (Kans.) Beacon*, May 24, 1922, 8; "Donna Lutz Honored by Detroit Officials," *Detroit Free Press*, May 7, 1922, 70.

106. Lutz quoted in "The Latin Point of View," 21. In *The Salvaging of Civilization*, H. G. Wells wrote, "America is still a hopeful laboratory of world-unifying thought. A long string of arbitration treaties stands to the credit of America, and a series of developing Pan-American projects, pointing clearly to at least a continental synthesis within a measurable time. There has been, and there still is, a better understanding of, and a greater receptivity to, ideas of international synthesis in America than in any European state" (21).

107. Lutz said that although she had "been in Europe and learned" what she could there, "the League of Women Voters presented to me something so tremendous that I find it hard to define this wonderful force." She believed it was up to the United States to lead and to the women of Central and South America to "follow" in order "to make of this wonderful gathering of women that has meant so much to all of us . . . the glorious beginning of a movement that shall bring gladness to all lives." "Woman Delegate from Brazil to Give Talk Here," *Chicago Daily Tribune*, June 8, 1922, 21; "Rio's Leader in Woman's Sphere Due Here Today," *Chicago Daily Tribune*, June 11, 1922, 14. Lutz in *Proceedings and Report of the Columbus Day Conferences*, 29.

108. Palmer and Chaves, "Democrats and Feminists," 158; "Homenaje del feminismo costarricense a sus abanderadas de América," *La Opinión*, November 2, 1924, caja 257, carpeta 5, PL-AGN. Costa Rican delegate Sara Casal de Quirós launched the Liga Feminista Costarricense that remained a crucial engine for organizing for decades to come. Panamanian delegate Esther Neira de Calvo founded the Sociedad Nacional para el Progreso de la Mujer as the group's Panamanian branch. Chilean delegate Graciela Mandujano also threw herself into organizing when she returned home. Elcira R. de Vergara and Clara de Vásquez to Doris Stevens, December 1, 1938, box 75, folder 8, DSP; Esther Neira de Calvo to Georgina Fletcher, March 6, 1959, ENC; Pernet, "Chilean Feminists," 674.

109. Cano, "México 1923."

110. Elena Torres to Lutz, June 25, 1922, Q0.ADM, COR.1922.88,301, p. 1, AFBPF. Specifically Torres referred to Panamanian delegate Esther Neira de Calvo and Mexican feminist Elena Landázuri.

111. Torres to Lutz, June 25, 1923, Q0.ADM, COR.1923, p. 1–2, AFBPF. Torres explained that they had had a successful Pan-American congress in Mexico that year and that they had received animosity from the press.

112. "Diaries, 1922–23, Tour of Europe and South America," reel 2, Carrie Chapman

Catt Papers, Library of Congress, microfilm collection; Catt to Lutz, August 24, 1923, Qo.ADM, COR.1923.10, p. 7, AFBPF.

113. Carrie Chapman Catt, "Anti-feminism in South America," *Current History* 18, no. 6 (September 1923): 1028–36. Ehrick, "Madrinas and Missionaries."

114. Elena Torres, "Canales interocéanoicos: Panamá, Nicaragua," *Repertorio Americano*, October 10, 1931, 224. See also Federico Henríquez y Carvajal, "Feminismo i Sufragismo," *Fémina*, July 30, 1923, 1–4.

115. Sara de Quirós to Luisi, April 30, 1922, folder "P–Q," PL-BN.

116. Paladino to Lutz (undated), Qo.ADM, COR.1923, p. 3, AFBPF. Lutz responded with a brief note insisting that she had written to Luisi, although record of that letter does not exist in the archives. Lutz to Paladino, September 2, 1923, Qo.ADM, COR.1923, p. 2, AFBPF.

117. Prof. Miguel Rodriguez y Coss c/o Mrs. Elena Arizmendi to Julia Abbott, May 3, 1922, with attached English translation of an article in *La Prensa* about Arizmendi, April 15, 1922, 2:15, LWV; Elena Arizmendi, "Una entrevista con Mrs. Carrie Chapman Catt," *Feminismo Internacional*, September 1923, 1, 9.

118. "Liga Internacional de Mujeres Ibéricas e Hispanoamericanas," August 6, 1938, box 3, folder 19, Gabriela Mistral Collection, UCLA, Charles Young Research Library, Los Angeles; L. Cohen, *Colombianas en la vanguardia*, chapter 3; Manley, *Paradox of Paternalism*, 35–36; González-Rivera, *Before the Revolution*, 35.

119. *Actas de las sesiones plenarias*, 288–89, 292–94. Soto Hall announced that "to my way of thinking, the cardinal points of the tendency of humanity at the present moment are only four, to wit: the educational problem, the working problem, the problem of peace, and the feminine problem." It was their "duty as Latin Americans" to confront this issue of women's rights, he said, "seeing that the Americans of the North have already frankly solved it and have placed womanhood in the position to which she has full right." *Actas de las sesiones plenaries*, 292. On similar civilizational arguments for women's suffrage, see Towns, *Women and States*, 104–14.

120. *Actas de las sesiones plenarias*, 287–88.

121. *Actas de las sesiones plenarias*, 291.

122. *Actas de las sesiones plenarias*, 295.

123. Chilean feminists influenced by the Baltimore conference resolutions pressured Chilean delegate Rivas Vicuña to forward it; at the 1923 conference he declared the resolution "answers an aspiration of American women." *Actas de las sesiones plenarias*, 287–88.

124. Greg Grandin notes that Soto Hall's anti-imperialist writings "blended Enlightenment liberalism with a diffuse Spanish antipathy toward Anglo-Protestant 'individualism.'" Grandin, "Your Americanism and Mine," 1048.

125. McPherson, *Invaded*, 208. Many of these same delegates, including Soto Hall and Rivas Vicuña, threw their support behind Baltasar Brum's unsuccessful proposal to restructure the Monroe Doctrine along multilateral lines and reorganize the Pan-American Union into a more multilateral body.

126. Labarca, *Feminismo contemporaneo*, 50.

127. Bertha Lutz telegram to Rivas Vicuña, Qo.ADM, EVE.CNF, TXT.3, AFBPF.

128. Bertha Lutz, untitled manuscript in Portuguese, 1924, Qo.ADM, CPA.DCV, TXT.1, AFBPF.

129. Minutes and reports, meetings of the International Committee and Board of Officers of the International Woman Suffrage Alliance at Rome, May 11, 13, 19, 20, 1923, caja 253, carpeta 7, PL-AGN.

130. The Spanish-speaking women with whom Lutz did correspond regularly were usually those in Argentina and Chile attached to the International Council of Women.

131. Catt to Lutz, January 11, 1924, Qo.ADM, COR.1924.12, p. 5, AFBPF.

132. Catt to Lutz, February 4, 1924, Qo.ADM, COR.1924.12, p. 23, AFBPF.

133. Lutz to Catt, March 19, 1924, Qo.ADM, COR.1924.12, p. 24, AFBPF.

134. Ehrick, *Shield of the Weak*, 106. For more on Luisi's role in the Advisory Committee on the Traffic of Women and Children, see Limoncelli, *Politics of Trafficking*, 80–81, 84.

135. Lutz, *D. Bertha Lutz*, 7, 9, 19–20.

136. "Novos despachos," *Jornal de Recife*, August 8, 1922, 2.

137. Catt to Lutz, April 24, 1924, Qo.ADM, COR.1924.12, p. 29, AFBPF. Catt urged Lutz not to repeat this information.

CHAPTER 2

1. González, "La mujer latin-americana," 893.

2. Esther Neira de Calvo to Carrie Chapman Catt, November 25, 1925, 2:50, LWV.

3. Neira de Calvo called Catt the "spiritual force" for women of the Americas. Esther Neira de Calvo, "Historia de mi Viaje a los Estados Unidos como Delegada official a la convención de Baltimore—1922," November 21, 1989, box 6, folder 3, ENC; Esther Neira de Calvo to Catt, November 25, 1925, 2:50, LWV; Bertha Lutz to Esther Neira de Calvo, April 6, 1926, Qo.ADM, EVE.CNG.TXT.5, p. 15, and Catt to Lutz, December 17, 1926, Qo.ADM, COR.1926.12, p. 2, AFBPF. Since Neira de Calvo had not gained participation from feminists from Brazil, Argentina, Chile, and Uruguay, Lutz suggested calling the event a "Central American" or "Caribbean" rather than an "inter-American" congress, which reflected Lutz's desire to separate it from what she conceived of as her own "Pan-American" purview. Lutz to Neira de Calvo, May 24, 1926, Qo.ADM, EVE.CNG, TXT.5, p. 23, AFBPF; Catt to Neira de Calvo, February 15, 1926, series 2, box 50, ENC; Neira de Calvo to Sherwin, April 26, 1926, 2:54, LWV. Neira de Calvo was only somewhat mollified when Emma Bain Swiggett, executive secretary of the Pan American International Women's Committee, agreed to attend as a League of Women Voters representative.

4. List of delegates to Panama conference, undated, box 3, Records of the Pan-American International Women's Committee, Library of Congress.

5. Clara González, *Cuaderno amarillo*, ACG; Marco Serra, *Clara González de Behringer*, 82–86.

6. Marco Serra, *Clara González de Behringer*, 49. She gained a scholarship to the Instituto de Derecho in Panama.

7. González wrote to Porras in one letter: "It is unfair that I have spent the past four years in law school to satisfy a legitimate aspiration of mine on my own time and . . . sacrificed more than anyone imagines to find myself at the end of the day in the situation I'm in . . . with doors closed to me." González to Porras, March 28, 1923. See other letters between González and Porras from January to March, 1923, serie. 2-11, tomo 14, 1923, letra "G," Archivo Belisario Porras, Universidad de Panamá, Panama City; Marco Serra, *Clara González de Behringer*, 73–74.

8. Marco Serra, *Clara González de Behringer*, 70–72, 75; Clara González, "La mujer ante el derecho panameño," 1922, ACG.

9. Marco Serra, "El movimiento sufragista," 69, 86–99.

10. Its leaders included Afro-Panamanian Felicia Santizo and West Indian–descended Panamanian Linda Smart. Bareiro and Soto, *Ciudadanas*, 69; Linda Smart, "Disertación," *Nuevos Horizontes* (Panama City), October 12, 1923, 5–7.

11. Marco Serra, *Clara González de Behringer*, 88.

12. González, "La mujer latin-Americana," 892–93.

13. Marco Serra, *Clara González de Behringer*, 79, 83–84.

14. Greene, *Canal Builders*, 270–71.

15. Elizabeth Manley describes a similar nationalist feminism in the Dominican Republic during and after the U.S. occupation. Manley, *Paradox of Paternalism*, 34–37.

16. Clara González, "El Congreso Inter-americano de Mujeres," *Orientación Feminista* 3, no. 6 (May 1926): 5–7, ACG. González selected the topic of political rights of women to discuss at the conference. Esther Neira de Calvo to González, May 10, 1926, ACG.

17. Marco Serra, *Clara González de Behringer*, 95. Catt's comments caused J. D. Moscote to assert that Panamanian women should work for their emancipation "alone, by their own initiative, and by their own inspiration." *El Nuevo Tiempo*, October 21, 1923, quoted in Morgan, "Role of North American Women," 152.

18. González, "El Congreso Inter-americano de Mujeres," 6.

19. González, "La mujer latin-americana, 887."

20. She was born in the town of Manicaragua, near the town Santa Clara in the Las Villas province.

21. Domínguez, *50 años de una vida*, 49; Stoner, "Ofelia Domínguez Navarro."

22. Stoner, *From the House to the Streets*, 67; Domínguez, *50 años de una vida*, 79. The Club Femenino president was Hortensia Lamar.

23. Her Cuban suffrage group, Club Femenino, had received an invitation from Esther Neira de Calvo. Esther N. de Calvo to Hortensia Lamar, January 14, 1926, box 673, no. 3; Hortensia Lamar to Domínguez, May 26, 1926, caja 673, no. 1, ODN-AN.

24. "Mrs. Chapman Catt con sus colegas de Cuba," *El Mundo* (Havana), January 30, 1924, Maria Collado, Donativos y Remisiones, Archivo Nacional, Havana. Emma López Seña, who had attended the 1922 conference in Baltimore, later told Jane Norman Smith that Catt "talked down" to Club Femenino women on that visit. Jane Norman Smith to Alva Belmont, January 20, 1929, folder 102, Jane Norman Smith Papers, Schlesinger Library, Radcliffe Institute, Harvard University, Cambridge, Mass.

25. R. A. Catalá, "Motivos de la semana," *El Fígaro*, April 19, 1925, reprinted in *Repertorio Americano*, May 25, 1925, 182.

26. Marinello and Báez, *Conversaciones con Juan Marinello*, 33.

27. Domínguez, "La mujer ante el código civil que rige en Cuba, Tema para el Congreso de Mujeres en la República de PANAMA," caja 675, no. 18, ODN-AN.

28. Lamar to Domínguez, June 2, 1926, caja 673, no. 1, ODN-AN.

29. Domínguez, "La mujer ante el código civil que rige en Cuba."

30. Domínguez, "La mujer ante el código civil que rige en Cuba". On Cuba's 1917 property law and 1918 divorce law, see Stoner, *From the House to the Streets*, 45–53.

31. In the United States at the time, less than 2 percent of lawyers were women and many law schools did not admit women. Solomon, *In the Company of Educated Women*, 127, 131.

32. González, "La mujer latin-americana," 873–74. The one Western European *precursora* she mentioned was eighteenth-century French political activist Olympe de Gouges.

33. González, 892–93.

34. González, 892–93.

35. "'Ecos del Congreso Interamericano de Mujeres,' Las dos últimas sesiones del Congreso Interamericano de Mujeres," caja 675, no. 18, ODN-AN; K. P. P., "The Woman's Page," *Panama Times*, June 26, 1926. Ana Rosa Tornero from Bolivia was the delegate who raised this issue.

36. "Congreso Inter-Americano de Mujeres, Delegadas de la Zona del Canal," ACG.

37. K. P. P., "The Woman's Page"; Domínguez, 50 años de una vida, 89.

38. K.P.P., "The Woman's Page," Panama Times, June 27, 1926. On the Panama Canal Treaty negotiations in 1926, see Woolsey, "Sovereignty of the Panama Canal Zone" and Major, Prize Possession, 184–87.

39. K. P. P., "The Woman's Page," June 27, 1926.

40. Domínguez, 50 años de una vida, 90.

41. Domínguez, 90; "'Ecos del Congreso Interamericano de Mujeres.'"

42. Domínguez, 50 años de una vida, 91. A number of delegates, including U.S. women from the Canal Zone, supported this interpretation.

43. Domínguez quoted in "'Ecos del Congreso Interamericano de Mujeres.'"

44. Domínguez, 50 años de una vida, 90–91. On the role of the United States in promoting the idea that Cuba should show it "gratitude" and on the power of this idea, see Pérez, "Incurring a Debt of Gratitude."

45. "La Lcda. Clara González responde a las opiniones de la Señora Emma López Seña," Diario de Panamá, July 16, 1926, 2.

46. "La Lcda. Clara González," 2.

47. "Emma López Seña critica a las delegadas de Sur América," Diario de Panamá, July 14, 1926, 1.

48. "La Lcda. Clara González," 1–2.

49. González to Domínguez, July 22, 1926, caja 673, no. 1, ODN-AN.

50. González founded the Partido Nacional Feminista with Afro-Panamanian educators and feminists Sara Sotillo and Felicia Santizo and West Indian feminist Linda Smart. On Felicia Santizo see Barrera, Felicia Santizo. In 1929, Ofelia Domínguez Navarro and other founding members of the Alianza Nacional Feminista in Cuba actively sought to include Afro-Cuban women. They directed their founding call to "Compañera of all races, of all social classes, you white like Martí and Agramonte, you black like Moncada and Maceo." Domínguez, 50 años de una vida, 120; González-Pagés, En busca de un espacio, 86; Brunson, "Constructing Afro-Cuban Womanhood," 211.

51. González to Domínguez, July 22, 1926, caja 673, no. 1, ODN-AN.

52. Domínguez, 50 años de una vida, 91.

53. This conference was organized by the Partido Femenino Democrático in Santiago, Chile, September 9–17, 1926. Domínguez, 50 años de una vida, 80–81.

54. Stoner, From the House to the Streets, 72, 109, 111.

55. The 1906 Third International Conference of American States in Rio de Janeiro created an International Committee of Jurists to work on codification of international law in the Americas. The commission met in Rio de Janeiro in 1927 and drafted the "General Convention of Private International Law" that included fifty-three articles relating to women's civil status but none relating to political rights. Jane Norman Smith, "For the Equal Rights Treaty," Equal Rights, February 25, 1928, 21.

56. Clara González to Eduardo Chiari, Ricardo J. Alfaro, Secretaría Gral. De la Conferencia Panamericana, Havana, Cuba, January 18, 1928, folleto "Sexto Conferencia Internacional Americana, La Habana, Cuba," Archivo del Ministerio de Relaciones Exteriores, República de Panamá, Panama City. On González's law school teachers, see Marco Serra, Clara González de Behringer, 71.

57. New York World article quoted in "Can Coolidge Win Latin America?," Literary Digest, January 28, 1928, 1.

58. This 1927 Marine action in Nicaragua was one of the first uses of aerial dive-bombing. Jiménez-Muñoz, "Deconstructing Colonialist Discourse," 14. In order to quell

anti-American sentiment, President Coolidge was planning to travel to the conference, an unprecedented move for a U.S. president.

59. Stevens, *Jailed for Freedom*. For more on Doris Stevens, see Trigg, *Feminism as Life's Work*; and Rupp, "Feminism and the Sexual Revolution."

60. Untitled speeches by Pilar Jorge de Tella, January 24, 1928, box 94, folder 3, DSP.

61. Untitled speeches by Pilar Jorge de Tella.

62. Stevens to Jonathan Mitchell, January 25, 1928, box 24, folder 3, DSP.

63. Stevens, "International Feminism Is Born," and Stevens, "Support of Cuban Women," box 70, folder 1, DSP.

64. Stoner, *From the House to the Streets*, 111.

65. The U.S. woman was Pilar Houston, who represented the Woman's Party at the 1923 National Congress of Women in Havana and supplied the party with information about Club Femenino. In 1924, *Equal Rights* noted that the Cuban "feminist movement … is assuming large and important proportions" and that a number of women in Cuba were "enthusiastic readers" of *Equal Rights*. Edith B. Newman, a U.S. Woman's Party member who lived in Havana as a translator, also served as a conduit. Between 1924 and 1928, *Equal Rights* published information sent by Newman about the growth of suffrage and feminist organizations in Cuba. See the following articles in *Equal Rights*: Newman, "Appreciation from Cuba," May 31, 1924, 123; "Feminist Notes: the Womans Suffrage Party of Cuba," September 13, 1924, 242; "Cuba Now on International Council," July 17, 1926, 184. Cuban feminists knew about the party's antecedent, the Congressional Union for Woman Suffrage, the "militant wing" of the U.S. suffrage movement. Pilar Houston to Woman's Party, February 27, 1928, series 1, reel 38, NWP.

66. Cott, "Feminist Politics in the 1920s."

67. "Feminism in Cuba," *Equal Rights*, June 18, 1927, 147.

68. [Margaret Lambie] to Jane Norman Smith, December 16, 1927, series 1, reel 38, NWP. Díaz Parrado also conveyed this information to Katharine Ward Fisher.

69. [Lambie] to Smith, December 16, 1927. Díaz Parrado explained that she was not in favor of her government and had no influence with it.

70. Alice Paul quoted in Jane Norman Smith to Mabel Vernon, December 26, 1927, and Katharine Ward Fisher to Jane Norman Smith, December 30, 1927, series 1, reel 38, NWP.

71. "Interparliamentary Union for Equality," *Equal Rights*, September 26, 1925, 261; "Equality for Women of All Nations," *Equal Rights*, October 3, 1925, 269; "The Interparliamentary Union," *Editorial Research Reports* 3, no. 529 (1925) http://library.cqpress.com /cqresearcher/cqresrre1925090400 (accessed September 16, 2015). Belle Sherwin to Ella M. Thorburn, November 10, 1925, 2:50, LWV. Since one of the Interparliamentary Union tenets was "equality among peoples, regardless of race, religion, color and sex," the organization had long interested Alice Paul. The Interparliamentary Union may have in part inspired the international organization of the National Woman's Party. As Nancy Cott writes, "Paul, studying international law in the 1920s, framed her aims more and more abstractly and legalistically; her interest in international organization was spurred by Belmont's grandiose visions of an 'international parliament of women.'" Cott, "Feminist Politics in the 1920s," 65.

72. Emmeline Pethick Lawrence, "A Living Center of Union," *Equal Rights*, October 24, 1925, 291.

73. Alice Paul to Anita Pollitzer, December 28, 1927, box 126, folder 7, DSP; Margaret Lambie to Jane Norman Smith, December 22, 1927, Katharine Fisher to Jane Norman

Smith, December 22, 1927, and Katharine Ward Fisher to Jane Norman Smith, January 6, 1928, series 1, reel 38, NWP.

74. Alice Paul quoted in Jane Norman Smith to Mabel Vernon, December 26, 1927, series 1, reel 38, NWP.

75. Stevens secured a $5,000 contribution from the son of Alva Belmont, William K. Vanderbilt II, to cover their travel and lodging expenses. "Transcription of taped narrative re: IACW from February–October 1928," box 126, folder 5, DSP; Stevens to Alma Lutz, April 28, 1942, box 32, folder 11, DSP.

76. Paul also had an M.A. and a Ph.D. from the University of Pennsylvania, where her doctoral dissertation examined the legal status of women in Pennsylvania. In 1927 she had begun studying law again at American University, where she would receive law degrees in 1927 and 1928. Boxes 22 and 23, Alice Paul Papers, Schlesinger Library, Radcliffe Institute, Harvard University, Cambridge, Mass.; Alice Paul to Anita Pollitzer, December 28, 1927, box 126, folder 7, DSP.

77. Jane Norman Smith referred to many of these inter-American inspirations in "For the Equal Rights Treaty," Equal Rights, February 25, 1928, 21–22; Muna Lee, "Report of the Work Done by Committee on International Action of the National Woman's Party, U.S.A. at Pan-American Conference on Behalf of Rights of Women," February 21, 1928, series 1, reel 38, NWP.

78. Missouri v. Holland (1920), 252 U.S. 416. Although international lawyers like James Brown Scott, founder of the American Institute for International Law, would later be extremely influential in helping the IACW push its treaties, at this point Paul had no contact with Scott. In fact, Scott, who attended the Havana conference, would not be helpful to the Woman's Party there, telling Stevens that a treaty was not the "proper method." "Transcription of taped narrative re: IACW from February–October 1928," box 126, folder 5, DSP.

79. Paul to Stevens and Smith, January 27, 1928, box 70, folder 15, DSP.

80. Doris Stevens quoted in Muna Lee, "Report of the Work Done by Committee on International Action of the National Woman's Party, U.S.A."

81. Jane Norman Smith to Katharine W. Fisher, December 31, 1927; Jane Norman Smith to Margaret Lambie, January 2, 1928, series 1, reel 38, NWP.

82. Katharine Ward Fisher to Jane Norman Smith, January 6, 1928, series 1, reel 38, NWP. Earlier, in a speech Díaz Parrado gave at NWP headquarters during her visit, she traced a history of Cuban feminists, writers, and artists, and emphasized the need for mutual understanding of different cultures if successful collaboration was to happen. She also wrote letters of introduction and gave the NWP women advice on where to stay and whom to contact when they reached Havana. Flora Díaz Parrado, "The Women of the Americas," Equal Rights, January 14, 1928, 389; [Margaret Lambie] to Jane Norman Smith, December 22, 1927, series 1, reel 38, NWP; Jane Norman Smith to Katharine W. Fisher, December 22, 1927, series 1, reel 38, NWP.

83. They emphasized that they came "not to instruct the women of Cuba but to seek their cooperation." National Woman's Party press release, January 26, 1928, box 94, folder 1, DSP.

84. In one speech, Smith stated that women in the United States "have equal political rights, but that is all we have. We are in the same boat." She asked that Cuban women "aid us in securing our civil rights." National Woman's Party press release, January 26, 1928; Stevens, Winters, and Smith, "The Pan-American Conference and Equal Rights for Women," [undated], box 94, folder 3, DSP.

85. Cuban feminist María Cabrera de Fernández de Espinosa translated the article

into "¡Ahora, o Quizás Nunca!," Havana, January 18, 1928, caja 663, no. 17, María Collado, Donativos y Remisiones, Archivo Nacional, Havana. Because their planning of the trip was so rushed, Stevens and Smith decided not to contact their Cuban counterparts before going to Havana so that they could explain their position in person. Pilar Houston had alerted the club of their arrival, but Emma López Seña, who had recently replaced Lamar as president, was ill, and Smith was told that the Club Femenino members "preferred to wait until we arrived and told them what we wanted." Jane Norman Smith to [Margaret] Lambie, January 18, 1928, series 1, reel 38, NWP.

86. Jane Norman Smith, untitled memo about meeting with Charles Evan Hughes, January 19, 1928, box 84, folder 3, DSP.

87. The United States delegation was not the only one that believed a women's rights treaty would violate national sovereignty. In 1926, while deliberating on plans for the 1928 Havana conference, Argentinean diplomats disputed consideration of "social problems" such as the eight-hour day and prohibition on night work for women on the grounds that these were national and not international issues. "Informe de la Comisión del Programa de la Sexta Conferencia Internacional Americana," November 3, 1926, Eduardo Racedo to Ángel Gallardo, May 18, 1926, and Ministerio de Relaciones Exteriores, "Memorandum sobre la lista de temas para la sexta conferencia panamericana," August 24, 1926, caja 0026, Asuntos Políticos, Conferencias Panamericanas, Archivo del Ministerio de Relaciones Exteriores y Culto, Buenos Aires. I am grateful to Max Paul Friedman for sharing this material with me.

88. See Baldez, *Defying Convention*.

89. Grandin, "Your Americanism and Mine," 1051.

90. Alice Park gave several speeches in Palo Alto and San Francisco upon her return from the 1928 conference in which she discussed Hughes's hypocrisy. John D. Barry, "What a Woman Noted at Havana Conference," *San Francisco News*, April 9, 1928; "Socialist Symposium: Alice Park and Her Havana Experiences," *San Francisco Labor World*, March 30, 1928, box 25, APH. Also a representative of the WILPF, Park hand-delivered letters opposing the U.S. intervention in Nicaragua and reported for the All-America Anti-Imperialist League, a transnational group originally formed in response to the Spanish-American War and resuscitated in response to U.S. intervention in Nicaragua. See All-America Anti-Imperialist League press release dated February 5, 1928, and letter dated May 9, 1928 in box 12, APH. Alice Park went to Havana as a reporter for "a syndicated press service out of Chicago serving 115 labor and radical papers in the U.S." Alice Park autobiography, unpublished, box 29, and "Women's League Asks Coolidge to End Fighting," *New York World*, January 27, 1928, box 24, APH.

91. Stevens to William K. Vanderbilt, December 29, 1927, box 36, folder 13, DSP.

92. Alice Paul to Stevens and Smith, January 27, 1928, box 70, folder 15, DSP. Scott and Bustamante were both in the American Institute for Law and promoted the international codification of private law in the Americas.

93. Vergara, *Memorias*, 80.

94. Alice Paul to Stevens and Smith, January 27, 1928, box 70, folder 15, DSP.

95. "La vanguardia intelectual de mujeres norteamericanas esté segura de que su voz será escuchada en el seno de conferencia," *La Prensa* (Havana) January 22, 1928.

96. "En la Conferencia Panamericana será estudiada la IGUALDAD de DERECHOS para la MUJER," *La Prensa* (Havana), January 21, 1928, 2; "La vanguardia intelectual de mujeres norteamericanas," *La Prensa* (Havana), January 22, 1928; Maria Collado, "Por la mujer y para la mujer," *La Discusión*, January 20, 1928.

97. "En la Conferencia Panamericana," *La Prensa* (Havana), January 21, 1928, 3. Julia L.

Mickenberg argues that the U.S. militant suffrage movement was linked to Russia at least in the imagination and thus was perceived by others internationally to be radical and "anti-American." This perception may have helped the image of Doris Stevens and other NWP feminists in Havana. Mickenberg, "Suffragettes and Soviets."

98. Jane Norman Smith recalled that "the sitting room was usually crowded with people and no work could be done there." "Memorandum Attached to Statement of Jane Norman Smith in re Receipts and Expenditures for Pan American Conference," New York, March 24, 1928, series 1, reel 38, NWP. Stevens's bedroom was also used as an office for a stenographer and a few other clerical workers. Doris Stevens, "Support of Cuban Women," and Stevens to Miss Isabel K. MacDermott, March 29, 1928, DSP.

99. "'Hasta para el amor es necesaria la igualdad política—Miss Stevens,'" El País, January 29, 1928.

100. Stevens to Jonathan Mitchell, January 16, 1928, box 24, folder 3, DSP.

101. Lantern slide, "Gran Asamblea de Mujeres," from Teatro "Fausto," Havana, Cuba, box 71, folder 14, PD.97z, DSP; Doris Stevens speech, January 24, 1928, DSP.

102. Ofelia Domínguez Navarro, "Harán valer sus derechos en la sexta conferencia las mujeres de Cuba," La Prensa (Havana), January 22, 1928. Domínguez lobbied Antonio Sánchez de Bustamante, president of the conference; see lobbying log, undated, box 93, folder 20, DSP.

103. Domínguez, "Harán valer sus derechos," 3, 31.

104. On Martí's vision, see Keller, "Building 'Nuestra América.'"

105. Alice Park diary, January 28, 1928, box 12, APH; Dr. Margarita López, secretary of Federación Nacional de Asociaciones Femeninas de Cuba, "A Significant Note in the Tribute to Martí," [undated], box 93, folder 19, DSP; Doris Stevens, "Support of Cuban Women," March 29, 1928, Stevens to Miss Isabel K. MacDermott, undated, Jane Norman Smith to Mabel Vernon, January 28, 1928, series 1, reel 38, NWP; Smith to Clarence Smith, January 29/30, 1928, folder 66, box 2, Jane Norman Smith Papers, 1913–53, Schlesinger Library, Radcliffe Institute, Harvard University, Cambridge, Mass.

106. Supporters included Dr. Enrique Olaya Herrera, Colombian minister in Washington; Dr. Bustamante, the Cuban president of the conference; Dr. Ferrara of Cuba; Dr. Amézaga of Uruguay; Dr. Alfaro of Panama; Dr. Guerrero of Salvador; Dr. Garcia of Mexico.

107. Quoted in Sheinin, Argentina and the United States, 1.

108. Muna Lee de Muñoz Marín, "Correspondence, Pan-American Women," The Nation, March 14, 1928, 295.

109. Jonathan Mitchell to Stevens, February 4, 1928, box 24, folder 3, DSP.

110. "Address Made by Miss Doris Stevens, Chairman Committee of International Action, National Woman's Party (U.S.A.) in Behalf of Equal Rights Treaty before Unofficial Plenary Session of Sixth Pan American Conference," February 7, 1928, box 61, folder 11, DSP. Benjamin Cohen was her translator.

111. "Address Made by Miss Doris Stevens," February 7, 1928, box 61, folder 11, DSP.

112. Jane Norman Smith to Mabel Vernon, February 28, 1928, series 1, reel 38, NWP. Stevens, Smith, Lee, Pilar Jorge de Tella, Maria Montalvo de Soto Navarro, Dr. Julia Martínez, Dr. Angela Mariana Zaldivar, and Plintha Woss Y Gil from the Dominican Republic spoke.

113. Dra. Julia Martínez speech, Havana, February 1928, box 71, folder 4, DSP.

114. Muna Lee's speech to delegates, series 1, reel 38, NWP. The Puerto Rican newspaper El Mundo noted that "for the first time the status of Puerto Rico was mentioned in a plenary session of the Pan-American conference." "El 'status' de Puerto Rico planteado incidentalmente ante la Conferencia Pan-americana," El Mundo (Puerto Rico), February 9,

1928, 1. For more on Muna Lee, see Lee and Cohen, *A Pan-American Life*. For an analysis of how the 1928 Havana conference fits into a longer history of U.S. and Puerto Rican suffrage activism and colonialist exchanges, see Jiménez-Muñoz, "Deconstructing Colonialist Discourse" and "'A Storm Dressed in Skirts.'"

115. "Representadas las obreras en la Conferencia," *El País*, February 7, 1928. The tobacco stemmers' union was led by Afro-Cuban women Eudosia Lara and Inocente Valdés. González-Pagés, *En busca de un espacio*, 86.

116. Diane Hill notes of this moment, "Never before had women formally addressed an inter-governmental conference to speak on behalf of the rights of women as human beings and not in a specific capacity as mothers or workers." Hill, "International Law for Women's Rights," 44.

117. "Memo from Miss Stevens," [undated] box 70, folder 15, DSP.

118. Stevens, "Showing Solidarity of American Women," box 70, folder 15, DSP.

119. Stevens to Paul, February 10, 1928, box 70, folder 15, DSP.

120. Muna Lee de Munoz Marin, "Correspondence, Pan-American Women," *The Nation*, March 14, 1928, 295.

121. Stevens, "International Feminism Is Born," draft for *Time and Tide*, 1928, box 71, folder 5, DSP.

122. Elena Mederos de González speech at the 1930 meeting in Havana, box 11, folder 13, and Lillian Mederos de Baralt to Doris Stevens, November 13, 1928, box 60, folder 5, DSP; Stoner, *From the House to the Streets*, 73. In founding the Alianza, Domínguez worked closely with Pilar Jorge de Tella.

123. Discurso de la Dra. Ofelia Domínguez Navarro en el Salón de Recepción del Palacio Presidencial in 1929, caja 675, no. 4, ODN-AN.

CHAPTER 3

1. Stevens to González, September 5, 1928, box 84, folder 7, DSP; Muna Lee, "Woman's Place in the Sun: An Inter-American Commission Will Seek It by Developing Uniform Laws for Women in this Hemisphere," *Independent Woman*, October 1928, 434; "Sufragio Femenina," *Gráfico* (New York), July 29, 1928, 5; "El Feminismo Avance!," *Gráfico* (Panama City), July 29 1928; "Feminismo," *Revista da Semana*, September 29, 1928, 31.

2. "Doris Stevens Heads Pan-American Women's Committee," *Equal Rights*, April 14, 1928, 77.

3. Domínguez to Paulina Luisi, April 6, 1931, carpeta "D," PL-BN.

4. Stevens to James Brown Scott, February 3, 1929, box 48, folder 1, JBSP; "Memorandum to the State Department Submitted by the Inter-American Commission of Women, 1929," February 18, 1929, 710.F IACW/1, D.F., RG 59.

5. Stevens to González, June 7, 1928, box 70, folder 17, and Stevens to González, June 9, 1928, box 84, folder 7, DSP.

6. Stevens to González, June 16, 1928, box 84, folder 7, DSP. While Stevens was away in Europe in the summer of 1928, González was handling the volunteer helpers at their Pan-American Union headquarters. "Takes Up Latin Legal Work," *Washington Times*, July 17, 1928; "Panama's Only Portia," *WP*, July 17, 1928; "Visiting Here," *Washington Daily News*, July 17, 1928.

7. Shields also spoke fluent Spanish and French. Lee, "Woman's Place in the Sun," 436; Fanny S. Chipman oral history, 30.

8. González to Stevens, December 27, 1929, box 84, folder 7; Clara González, "The Inter American Commission of Women Honored. Latin American Federation Praises Its Work and Offers Fullest Support," undated memo, box 84, folder 7; "Message Received

from the Latin American Federation by the Inter American Commission of Women on Their First Conference in Havana, February 23, 1930," February 12, 1930, box 71, folder 11, DSP.

9. Memo from Francis White to Wilbur J. Carr, February 15, 1929, and Francis White to Stevens, March 8, 1929, 710.F IACW/6 and IACW/3, D.F., RG 59.

10. The Pan-American Union would often describe the commission as "created by the 1928 Pan American conference" but never as "part of the Pan-American Union." Doris Stevens to Jonathan Mitchell, June 20, 1928, box 24, folder 4, and Stevens to Betty Archdale, February 14, 1929, box 60, folder 14, DSP; Stevens to James Brown Scott, February 3, 1929, box 48, folder 1, JBSP.

11. Vergara, *Memorias*, 95. Vergara's metaphor of the "illegitimate child" would have been redolent with meaning for readers familiar with early twentieth-century Latin American feminist arguments for "equality for legitimate and illegitimate children" and determination of paternity of illegitimate children.

12. Stevens to Helen Archdale, 1929, box 27, folder 12, DSP.

13. "Briand-Kellogg Pact Renouncing Warfare Signed by 15 Nations," *WP*, August 28, 1928, 1; "15 Nations Sign Treaty Written by Briand-Kellogg Renouncing Aggression," *Atlanta Constitution*, August 28, 1928. Others, however, like Missouri senator James Reed called it an "international kiss," which became a much-quoted description of Kellogg-Briand. Steiner, *Lights That Failed*, 572–74. Stevens's soon-to-be husband, James Mitchell, later ridiculed the Kellogg-Briand peace pact writing that it "assum[ed] . . . a make-believe world, in which governments are not nationalistic, greedy for power and economically selfish." Mitchell, *Goose Steps to Peace*, 271; Mitchell to Stevens, August 26, 1928, box 24, folder 4, DSP.

14. Alice Paul encouraged Stevens to do this. Stevens to Lady Rhondda, August 16, 1928, box 89, folder 2, and Alva Belmont to Alice Paul, October 23, 1928, box 84, folder 16, DSP; Jane Norman Smith, "Excerpts from letter, Mrs. Belmont to Miss Paul," August 29, 1928, box 39, folder 139, Alice Paul Papers, Schlesinger Library.

15. "Doris Stevens Seized during Palace Riot," *New York American*, August 29, 1928. A selection of the press surrounding the event includes "10 Women Arrested at Dinner to Envoys," *NYT*, August 29, 1928, 1; "Feminist Leaders Storm Presidential Palace in France—U.S. Trio Arrested," *New York Telegram*, August 28, 1928, 1; "Feminists Raid Pact Envoys and Doris Stevens Is Jailed," *New York Evening Post*, August 28, 1928, 1; "Algunas feministas han sido arrestadas ayer cerca de París," *La Prensa* (New York), August 29, 1928; "Arrests Ten Feminists in Riot," *Los Angeles Herald*, August 28, 1928, 1; "U.S. Feminists Jailed Trying to Invade Peace Pact Treaty," *WP*, August 29, 1928; "Doris Stevens Loses Fight with Paris Cops," *New York World*, August 28, 1928, 1; "Women's 'Equal Rights' Storm," *Daily Mail* (London), August 29, 1928; "Votes for Women," *The Argus* (Melbourne), August 29, 1928; "Equal Rights Scene in Paris," *The Courier* (Brisbane), August 29, 1928; "Women Advance Equality Rights," *Paris Times*, August 28, 1928; "Los derechos de la mujer," *La Nación* (Buenos Aires), August 28, 1928, 1; "Numerosas sufragistas fueron arrestadas ayer en Rambouillet, Francia," *La Prensa* (Buenos Aires), August 29, 1928; and "Domergue agasajo a los delegados," *La Nación* (Buenos Aires), August 29, 1928. For more on the French protest, see Sara L. Kimble, "Politics, Money, and Distrust: French-American Alliances in the International Campaign for Women's Equal Rights, 1925–1930," forthcoming in *Practiced Citizenship*, ed., Barton and Hopkins, draft in author's possession.

16. "Mrs. Kellogg Criticizes Women's Tactics in Paris," *New York Sun*, August 27, 1928; "Mrs. Kellogg Raps Plan of Feminists," *New York Evening Post*, August 27, 1928; "Femi-

nists' Plea in Paris Rebuked by Mrs. Kellogg," *New York American*, August 28, 1928; "Mrs. Kellogg's Rebuke Angers Feminists," *New York Herald Tribune*, August 28, 1928.

17. Clotilde Betances Jaeger quoted in Sabas Alomá, *Feminismo*, 172.

18. Transcription of untitled *New York Worker* article, September 3, 1928, by Alice Park, in letter from Alice Park to IACW, September 28, 1928, box 84, folder 16, DSP; "Police of Paris Out in Force to Curb Reds," *New York Herald Tribune*, August 29, 1928.

19. "Memorandum for Miss Muna Lee," November 3, 1931, box 79, folder 7, DSP.

20. Clara González quoted in "Votes for Women, Paris Demonstration," *The Argus* (Melbourne), August 30, 1928. González also quoted in "Doris Stevens Jailed in France for Rights Protest," *Washington Herald*, August 29, 1928, 3.

21. Stevens to González, September 5, 1928, box 84, folder 7, DSP.

22. Stevens to Elsie Ross Shields, September 20, 1928, box 90, folder 13, DSP. Ferrara earlier praised Stevens's speech in Havana as "daring and comprehensive" and the women's action there "like a cyclone." He now ardently championed her mission to include women as plenipotentiaries in future international conferences. "Excerpts from the preliminary remarks made by Ambassador Ferrara," March 22, 1928, box 70, folder 11, DSP.

23. Cott, "Feminist Politics in the 1920s," 67.

24. The treaty read, "there will be no distinction based on sex as regards nationality, in the legislation [of state parties] or in their practice." James Brown Scott, "The Seventh International Conference of American States," 219.

25. "Women Win at Geneva," NYT, September 14, 1928.

26. Stevens to González, September 5, 1928, box 84, folder 7, DSP.

27. See Bredbenner, *Nationality of Her Own*; and Cott, "Marriage and Women's Citizenship."

28. "La cubana no perderá nunca su nacionalidad," *La Opinión*, August 4, 1929. Part of the reason a number of Western Hemisphere countries did not distinguish nationality laws based on sex was because many of these countries determined nationality by the rule of jus soli, or place of birth. Hill, "International Law for Women's Rights," 118.

29. Clara González, "La Comisión Inter-Americana de Mujeres y el estudio de la nacionalidad," *Diario de Panamá*, September 5, 1928, 1–2. González described the *Gráfico* article.

30. "List of Inter-American Commission of Women delegates with descriptions, from *Equal Rights*, July 14, 1928," 2:50, LWV. Stevens to González, September 5, 1928, box 84, folder 7, DSP; "Memorandum to the State Department Submitted by the Inter-American Commission of Women, 1929." The delegates were María Elena de Hinestrosa from Colombia, María Álvarez de Guillén-Rivas from El Salvador, and Alice Téligny Mathon from Haiti. The appointments also included Ernestina López, a former professor at the University of La Plata in Argentina and president of the charitable organization Club de Madres in Buenos Aires, and Lucila Luciani de Pérez Díaz, Venezuelan magazine editor and journalist. Some, like Alice Téligny Mathon, became significant feminist leaders. On Mathon as cofounder of the Ligue Féminine d'Action Sociale in Haiti, see G. Sanders, "La Voix des Femmes," 94, 109–10.

31. González to Domínguez Navarro, February 1, 1930, ODN-IH.

32. Arizmendi to Stevens, January 29, 1929, box 61, folder 10, DSP.

33. Arizmendi to Muna Lee, July 24, 1928, box 32, folder 11, DSP.

34. Stevens to Adelaida Artola de Allen, February 12, 1929, box 61, folder 10, DSP.

35. Stevens to James Brown Scott, February 3, 1929, box 48, folder 1, JBSP; Betty Archdale, "The Inter American Commission of Women," undated, box 60, folder 14, DSP.

36. Of sleeping "side by side with Negro prostitutes," she wrote, "not that we shrank from these women on account of their color, but how terrible to know that the institution had gone out of its way to bring the prisoners from their own wing to the white wing in an attempt to humiliate us. There was plenty of room in the Negro wing. But prison must be made so unbearable that no more women would face it." Stevens, *Jailed for Freedom*, 99–121. See also Terborg-Penn, "Enfranchising Women of Color," 45.

37. Pike, *FDR's Good Neighbor Policy*, chapter 12.

38. See chapter 7.

39. Rupp and Taylor, *Survival in Doldrums*, 102.

40. Mitchell to Stevens, February 5, 1928, and Mitchell to Stevens, August 22, 1928, box 24, folder 4, DSP.

41. Viscountess Rhondda to Doris Stevens, August 27, 1928, box 5, folder 154, DSP.

42. Arizmendi to Paulina Luisi, August 15, 1928, carpeta "A," PL-BN.

43. Luisi to Arizmendi, November 26, 1930, carpeta "de P. Luisi," PL-BN.

44. S. Gurgel do Amaral to Senhor Ministro de Estado, April 5, 1928, lata 128, 1048, Archivo Histórico do Itamaraty, Rio de Janeiro; "Dr. Manoel D. Lima, Diplomat, Dies," *NYT*, March 25, 1928, 32; "Inter-America Commission Holds Conference," *Equal Rights*, March 1, 1930, 28; "Memorial to Dr. Lima," *Equal Rights*, December 5, 1931, 352. For Stevens's long correspondence with Oliveira Lima, see box 62, folders 11, 12, 13, DSP. See also Leo Rowe to James Brown Scott about her appointment, February 12, 1930, box 48, folder 2, JBSP.

45. Stevens to Paul, February 10, 1928, box 70, folder 15, DSP.

46. Luisi to Stevens, August 15, 1932, and Stevens to Luisi, June 20, 1934, box 76, folder 13; Stevens to Paul, March 16, 1932, box 92, folder 5, DSP.

47. Paulina Luisi to Margarita Robles de Mendoza, May 2, 1935, caja 252, carpeta 6, PL-AGN. Her phrase "All America for the North Americans" is a reference to the Monroe Doctrine's "America for the Americans" clause, which many Latin Americans interpreted as Luisi did. Grandin, "Why Stop at Two?"

48. Stevens to Paul, March 16, 1932, and Stevens to Marta Vergara, May 25, 1932, box 92, folder 5, DSP.

49. Paul to Stevens, April 2, 1932, box 92, folder 5, DSP.

50. Stevens to Paul, April 22, 1932, box 60, folder 11; and Luisi to Stevens, August 25, 1932, box 76, folder 13, DSP.

51. "Panama Has 27-Year-Old Portia," *Baltimore Sun*, July 22, 1928; "Panama's Only Portia," *WP*, July 17, 1928; "Visiting Here," *Washington Daily News*, July 17, 1928; "Only Woman Lawyer in Panama Working to Get Suffrage There," *Christian Science Monitor*, July 25, 1928. Since the late nineteenth century, "Portia" was a common moniker for the first generation of female U.S. and European jurists and lawyers. Kimble, "The Rise of 'Modern Portias,'" 55.

52. IACW cash books, 1929–1931, box 98, folder 1, DSP; statements of receipts and disbursements, February 17, 1929–October 15, 1933, box 99, folder 4, DSP. See Stevens to James Brown Scott, December 1, 1934, box 48, folder 4, JBSP. Sizable gifts from James Brown Scott, on the founding board of the Carnegie Endowment for International Peace, kept the commission afloat for nearly a decade.

53. "Women Labor without Pay to Help Sex," *New York Telegram*, July 30, 1928, 1. In 1929, Stevens offered a salary to Fanny Bunand-Sevastos, a French woman who became a Woman's Party member and worked for the Commission from 1929 to 1935. Fanny S. Chipman oral history, Association for Diplomatic Studies and Training, Foreign Affairs Oral History Program, Foreign Spouse Series, July 22, 1987, 28, 30. Stevens offered to

pay Vergara's travel expenses to go to Montevideo and other conferences. Vergara, *Memorias*, 95.

54. Stevens to González, June 16, 1928, and González to Stevens, June 21, 1928, box 84, folder 7, DSP.

55. Rupp, *Worlds of Women*, 70–73.

56. Elena Torres, "Canales interocéanoicos: Panamá, Nicaragua," *Repertorio Americano*, October 10, 1931, 224.

57. Stevens had secured the invitation from Cuba through close relationships with James Brown Scott and Cuban jurist Antonio Sánchez de Bustamante. This meeting would coincide with a celebration of the University of Havana and a meeting of the International Institute of American Law, of which Brown Scott and Sánchez de Bustamante were leaders.

58. "Agreement between the Director General, the Assistant Director of the Pan-American Union and the Chairman of the Inter American Commission of Women — May 9, 1929," box 65, folder 16; Stevens, "Inter American Commission of Women," memorandum, May 9, 1929, and attachment from Stevens to James Brown Scott, memorandum, November 30, 1929, box 90, folder 6; and minutes of February 17, 1930, meeting in Havana, box 71, folder 12, DSP.

59. "Experimental Schools in Santiago, Chile," *Bulletin of the Pan American Union*, December 1939, 743.

60. González to Stevens, December 27, 1929, box 84, folder 7, DSP.

61. This feminist was Elena Mederos de González.

62. González to Domínguez Navarro, February 1, 1930, ODN-IH.

63. González, "Antecedentes Personales y Políticos, ACG.

64. Whitney, *State and Revolution in Cuba*, 58. By 1930, as McGillivray explains, "almost everyone on the island began to resent Cuba's combined state of depression and dictatorship." McGillivray, *Blazing Cane*, 190.

65. Domínguez, *50 años de una vida*, 132–34.

66. By the time of the meeting, only eleven of the twenty-one commissioners had been named. "Business Meeting of the Inter American Commission of Women, held Feb 20, 1930," box 71, folder 12, DSP.

67. "Business Session of the Inter-American Commission of Women on Tuesday, February 18, 1930 at 11:00 am," box 71, folder 11, DSP.

68. "Business Meeting of the Inter American Commission of Women, February 20, 1930," box 71, folder 11, DSP.

69. Minutes of the Executive Meeting of Officers, February 17, 1930, box 71, folder 11, DSP.

70. "Business Meeting of the Inter American Commission of Women, February 20, 1930."

71. Amalia M. Mallén de Ostolaza to [Alice Paul], January 3, 1929; Mallén de Ostolaza to "Secretary of National Woman's Party," January 31, 1929; and Mallén de Ostolaza to [Alice Paul], March 2, 1929, box 82, folder 9, DSP.

72. Cuban feminists' fears were prescient; several months after the Havana conference, the U.S. government passed the Hawley-Smoot Tariff Act, which increased the duty on Cuban sugar to favor producers in U.S. states and territories and further damaged the Cuban economy. Gott, *Cuba*, 134–35; McGillivray, *Blazing Cane*, vi; Pérez, *Cuba*, 190–91.

73. Sabas Alomá, *Feminismo*, 171. In the same chapter, she decried a denigrating comment that Catt had made about Latin American women threatening inter-American "peace" and called Catt's brand of imperial feminism "*feminismo* 'made in U.S.A.'" (170).

74. James Brown Scott to Stevens, May 14, 1929, and Scott to Stevens, May 27, 1929, box 90, folder 6, DSP.

75. "Congreso de mujeres, opiniones sobre el alcance de la conferencia," El País, February 18, 1930, 1; "Labor de hoy del congreso de mujeres," El País, February 18, 1930; "No debe perder nunca la mujer su nacionalidad," El Heraldo de Cuba, February 19, 1930; "La Comisión Inter-Americana de Mujeres desarolló ayer una labor muy fecunda durante sus 2 sesiones," Diario de la Marina, February 19, 1930.

76. Stevens believed that a firm line should be drawn between "feminism" and "politics." As she wrote to Adelaida Artola de Allen, a Mexican feminist and international lawyer who lived in New York City, "As you know I am strictly nonpartisan and have no political affiliations. All my affiliations are purely feminist. The moment a feminist allows herself to be drawn from one side to another in a controversy which is temporary, her usefulness to feminism, it seems to me, is impaired." Stevens to Artola de Allen, May 9, 1929, box 61, folder 10, DSP. See also Stevens to Emma Boehm Oller, May 9, 1929, box 61, folder 10, DSP.

77. Aída Parada to Domínguez, March 23, 1930, box 673, no. 2, ODN-AN; González to Domínguez, February 1 and March 3, 1930, ODN-IH. Parada was inspired by Will Durant's The Story of Philosophy, in which he included "feminism" along with "monarchy, aristocracy, democracy, socialism, [and] anarchism" as the "dramatis personae of political philosophy." From Durant, The Story of Philosophy, 4.

78. "'Las latinoamericanas disfrutaron el papel de comparsas en la reciente conferencia de mujeres,'" El País (Havana), February 28, 1930.

79. "'Las latinoamericanas.'"

80. "'Las latinoamericanas."

81. Stevens to Mederos, March 8, 1930, box 65, folder 5, DSP. Stevens received a copy of the article from Elena Mederos de González, an Alianza member who was now the Cuban commissioner.

82. The term González used was "la aludía," which she underlined. The verb aludir means to refer to someone without naming them, or to allude to. Given the emphasis González placed on the word and given that she did not mention Stevens by name, "she-who-shall-not-be-named" seems to best capture González's meaning here.

83. González to Domínguez, March 3, 1930, ODN-IH.

84. Stevens to González, March 6, 1930, box 84, folder 7, DSP. I have not found evidence in the archives to support Stevens's statement about the Pan-American Union's withholding of support.

85. González to Stevens, March 10, 1930, box 84, folder 7, DSP.

86. They were Florence Bayard Hilles, Ella Riegel, Margaret Whittemore, and Mary Caroline Taylor. "Emma Wold Named Adviser at The Hague," Equal Rights, March 8, 1930, 35. Lucy Branham also joined. Fanny Bunand-Sevastos, the executive secretary, also joined. "Two Million Dollar Fund," Equal Rights, June 29, 1929, 168.

87. Mildred Reeves to Clara González, March 10, 1930, ACG.

88. González later noted that the conclusion of her time working for the commission in D.C. coincided with its failure to provide funding for her to go to The Hague. Clara González, "La mujer panameña en la conquista de sus derechos," ACG.

89. González was one of a number of Latin American feminists who sought to preserve a cordial relationship with Stevens, regardless of their opinion of her, because of Stevens's and the commission's influence. A number of them appealed to Stevens for letters of recommendation to the Latin American Fellowship offered by the American

Association of University Women and others that would enable them to study in the United States.

90. Clara González to Ricardo Alfaro, March 11, 1930, ARA. Alfaro had helped secure money to send González to the Havana conference. In April she wrote, in Spanish, to Rosalmiro Colomo, assistant in the IACW D.C. office, asking if Colomo could send González's diplomas to her and saying she would send Stevens a note of explanation from Panama. González to Colomo, April 1930, box 84, folder 7, DSP. This note is not in the archives, but González and Stevens remained in touch.

91. Domínguez, *50 años de una vida*, 159.

92. Stoner, "Ofelia Domínguez Navarro," 129.

93. Letterhead of Unión Laborista de Mujeres, January 1, 1930, caja 675, no. 7, ODN-AN.

94. Domínguez, *50 años de una vida*, 297.

95. Domínguez to Luisi, June 4, 1930, carpeta "D," PL-BN.

96. Luisi to Domínguez, August 27, 1930, caja 673, no. 16, ODN-AN.

97. Luisi to Domínguez, August 29, 1930, caja 673, no. 16, ODN-AN.

98. Domínguez and her group formed part of this opposition, and on January 3, 1931, the *porra* arrested Domínguez and a number of her cohort for recruiting students from the normal school to their revolutionary cause. Stoner, "Ofelia Domínguez Navarro," 132; "Cuban Cane Fires Increasingly Huge," NYT, January 24, 1931, 8. Released after a short term, Domínguez was arrested and jailed again on charges of conspiracy against the government on March 4, 1931. Secret Service raided her law office. "Woman Lawyer Arrested," NYT, March 6, 1931, 5. On the Machado dictatorship in 1930 see McGillivray, *Blazing Cane*, 191.

99. Domínguez to Luisi, April 6, 1931, carpeta "D," PL-BN.

100. Domínguez to Luisi, April 6, 1931, carpeta "D," PL-BN. Domínguez was released a few days later, on April 8, 1931. "Cuba President Frees Political Prisoner Group," LAT, April 9, 1931, 18. Domínguez published an account of her prison experiences in Domínguez, *De 6 a 6.*

101. Luisi to Domínguez, June 1931, caja 675, no. 8, ODN-AN.

102. Domínguez to Luisi, [undated], caja 673, no. 8 ODN-AN.

103. Domínguez to Luisi, June 10, 1931, carpeta "D," PL-BN.

104. On how Domínguez's imprisonment radicalized her, see Stoner, "Ofelia Domínguez Navarro," 133–34. Domínguez would reclaim the "feminist" mantle after the revolution and continue to promote women's equality along with other causes. Domínguez joined the Communist Party of Mexico in 1935. Domínguez Navarro, "Biografía de Ofelia Domínguez Navarro sus antecedentes y su hogar," 3/237.1/1-29, ODN-IH.

105. See Whitney, *State and Revolution in Cuba.* As Christine Ehrick has noted, the leftist groups in Uruguay in the 1920s "had problems organizing working-class women, due to an inability to bridge gender gaps and an overall conceptualization of the Communist vanguard in masculine terms." Ehrick, *Shield of the Weak*, 182.

106. Weaver, *Peruvian Rebel*, 22; García-Bryce, "Transnational Activist," 678, 684–85. The Aprista, or Alianza Popular Revolucionaria Americana (APRA) founding agenda included the five points: anti-imperialism, Pan-American unity, internationalization of the Panama Canal, nationalization of land and industries, and concern for Indo-America's indigenous heritage and solidarity with all oppressed peoples. Drawing on Marxist thought but not allying themselves with communism, Apristas believed that the nationalist middle classes of Latin America should lead the anti-imperialist movement.

107. Magda Portal, "Dos libros de mujeres," *Repertorio Americano*, September 20, 1930,

170. In this article she reviewed Cuban writer Mariblanca Sabas Alomá's book *Feminísmo* and argued that the book was about women, the defense of the woman worker, women's production, and commercial exploitation, but not about "feminism," which Portal defined as "liberal feminism"—a fight for equal civil and political rights. For more on Portal's relationship to feminism, see Wallace Fuentes, *Most Scandalous Woman*, 280–89.

108. Magda Portal, "Rol de la mujer revolucionaria. El voto femenino," *Repertorio Americano*, June 6, 1931, 332, 336. See also Cubillo Paniagua, *Mujeres e identidades*, 105–7.

109. Domínguez to Luisi, June 10, 1931, carpeta "D," PL-BN.

110. Although Luisi later joined the Socialist Party in Uruguay, she viewed communism as too extreme. Luisi to Lee, June 16, 1933, box 79, folder 7, DSP.

111. Stevens to Margarita de Aragón, Stevens Collection, September 18, 1931, box 65, folder 6, DSP.

112. "Militant Women in Brazil and Cuba," *Equal Rights*, January 17, 1931, 399. The NWP sent Mederos a copy. Fanny Bunand-Sevastos to Mederos, January 24, 1930, box 65, folder 5, DSP.

113. Mederos to Bunand-Sevastos, February 13, 1931, box 65, folder 5, DSP. While Stevens and other Woman's Party members apologized, they also responded that their policy as an organization was to take no stand on matters that did not involve equal rights for women. "Women's Actions in Recent Events in Cuba," *Equal Rights*, February 7, 1931, 5–6; and Muna Lee to Mederos, February 25, 1931, Bunand-Sevastos to Mederos, February 27, 1931, and Mederos to Bunand-Sevastos, March 1931, box 65, folder 5, DSP.

114. The secretary of the Unión Laborista wrote to Stevens first to announce the group's formation. Margarita de Aragón to Stevens, June 21, 1931, Stevens to Aragón, July 8, 1931, Aragón to Stevens, July 28, 1931, Stevens to Aragón, September 18, 1931, box 65, folder 6, DSP.

115. Domínguez and Aragón to Stevens, October 3, 1931, box 65, folder 6, DSP.

116. Stevens to Domínguez, November 16, 1931, box 65, folder 6, DSP.

117. Domínguez to Stevens, November 23, 1931, box 65, folder 6, DSP.

118. "Union Laborista de Mujeres, A la Conciencia Política de la Mujer Latino Americana, Carta de la Srta. Doris Stevens, Presidenta de la Inter American Commission of Woman a la Unión Laborista de Mujeres," caja 675, no. 8, ODN-AN.

119. Domínguez to Adelia di Carlo, November 5, 1933, caja 673, no. 9; Domínguez to "Compañeras," URM letter attached to the "Informe," September 8, 1933, caja 675, no. 11, ODN-AN. The Unión Laborista de Mujeres also provided a detailed account of its conflict with Stevens in its 1931 annual report. Ofelia Domínguez Navarro and Bertha Darder Babe, "Unión Laborsita de Mujeres, Informe de la Secretaría, 1931–1932," 6–7, caja 675, no, 10, ODN-AN.

120. "Se ha reconocido a la mujer uruguaya el derecho al voto activo y pasivo, tanto en materia nacional como municipal," *El Pueblo*, December 16, 1932, 1.

121. Luisi to Stevens, August 25, 1932, box 76, folder 13, DSP.

122. "Terra Repressing Foes," NYT, November 3, 1933, 10. On Luisi's response to the Terra dictatorship, see Sapriza, "Clivajes de memoria," 258–59.

123. Luisi to Muna Lee, June 16, 1933, box 79, folder 7; Luisi quoted by Stevens to Margarita Robles de Mendoza, November 4, 1933, box 77, folder 8, DSP.

124. Stoner, "Ofelia Domínguez Navarro," 137; Domínguez, *50 años de una vida*, 274–75.

125. Domínguez to Adelia di Carlo, November 5, 1933, caja 673, no. 9; Soto Hall to Excmo. Señor Presidente de la República, Havana, August 17, 1933, caja 673, no. 3, ODN-AN.

126. Domínguez to Adelia di Carlo, November 5, 1933, caja 673, no. 9, ODN-AN.

127. Mederos to Stevens, October 7, 1933, box 65, folder 5; Ricardo Hinestrosa D. to

Stevens, November 4, 1933, box 60, folder 10, DSP. Another commissioner who cited ill health as the reason for declining her was Chilean Aída Parada. Stevens to Parada, November 2, 1933, box 64, folder 6, DSP.

128. González to Stevens, December 22, 1931, box 84, folder 7, DSP. A serious illness had left her unable to work when she returned to Panama in 1930, but she had maintained a cordial though intermittent correspondence with Stevens.

129. Stevens to González, October 19, 1933, box 84, folder 8, DSP.

CHAPTER 4

1. Lutz later described the IACW this way. Lutz to Catt, June 3, 1945, reel 12, NAWSA.

2. Lutz and Catt blamed each other for not anticipating this turn of events. Lutz complained that Catt and LWV president Belle Sherwin failed to heed her advice to send women to the 1928 Havana conference to follow up on Soto Hall's 1923 women's rights resolution. From Brazil, Lutz had also urged the Cuban minister there to send women the conference, to no avail. See the following in Qo.ADM, COR.1927, AFBPF: Lutz to Belle Sherwin, October 26, 1927, p. 1; Lutz to Leo Rowe, October 26, 1927, p. 6; Rowe to Lutz, November 21, 1927, p. 35; Sherwin to Lutz, November 19, 1927, p. 16; Rowe to Lutz, May 21, 1927, p. 8; Rowe to Lutz, May 24, 1927, p. 22; Rowe to Sherwin, November 21, 1927. See also Lutz to Sherwin, October 26, 1927, 2:156; Sherwin to Leo Rowe, November 18, 1927, and Rowe to Sherwin, November 21, 1927, 2:111; Sherwin to Lutz, January 26, 1928, 2:156, LWV. In turn, Catt criticized Lutz for not having attended the 1926 congress in Panama, where Central American and Caribbean feminists paved the way for collaborations in Havana. Catt wrote that Lutz had "acted as contrary, jealous, and incompetent as a woman could" about the Panama conference. Catt to Sherwin, March 27, 1928, 2:155, LWV.

3. Sherwin to Lutz, October 17, 1929, 2:156, LWV. The Inter-American Union of Women did not officially dissolve until 1932. As soon as the IACW was formed, Lutz also asked the LWV to persuade the Pan-American Union to have the Inter-American Union of Women appoint women to the commission, to no avail. See Hill, "International Law for Women's Rights," 290–91; Sherwin to Lutz, February 11, 1930, Qo.ADM, COR.1930, p. 1, AFBPF.

4. Lutz studied Trotsky and other Marxist literature. Lutz to Catt, February 12, 1934, Qo.ADM, COR.1934.26, AFBPF.

5. Vargas enacted these measures between 1930 and 1937. Women's suffrage in Brazil was subject to the same literacy qualifications as men. These literacy requirements were not removed until 1985. Hahner, "The Beginnings of the Women's Suffrage Movement in Brazil," 200. Wolfe, Working Women, 51–45.

6. Mary Wilhelmine Williams to Alice Paul and Doris Stevens, September 25, 1933, box 85, folder 1, DSP.

7. Although women dominated some of Brazil's industries, like textiles, their union leadership was always male and did not make efforts to safeguard women's interests. Wolfe, Working Women, 58.

8. Besse, Restructuring Patriarchy, 140–48, 168, 170–71.

9. Besse, 171. Glaucia Fraccaro shows that in Brazil, working women had been making arguments for maternity legislation and equal pay for equal work before the formation of FBPF. On the influence of working women on Brazilian feminism, see her Os direitos das mulheres and "Uma história social do feminismo."

10. "Sugestões para as declarações de direitos," [1932], Qo.PIT.71, AFBPF.

11. Lutz, 13 princípios básicos, 24, 31, 38, 49, 51.

12. "Victory in Brazil: A Short Report on Fifteen Years of Work," *Boletim da FBPF*, February 1935, 3; Besse, *Restructuring Patriarchy*, 170.

13. She believed that "the essence of justice is in the equal application of the law to human beings independent of sex or civil status." "La Nacionalidad de la Mujer Casada," 1933, 23, Qo.ADM, CPA.NMC.3, AFBPF. (This was an unpublished Spanish translation of Lutz, *Nationality of Married Women*.) In 1933, she published an updated version of it, *A nacionalidade da mulher casada perante o direito internacional privado*.

14. Untitled notes from Lutz, "Tese a nacionalidade de mulher casada," Qo.ADM, CPA.NMC.3, AFBPF.

15. Lutz to Flora de Oliveira Lima, January 6, 1931, Qo.ADM, COR.1931, p. 27, AFBPF.

16. Lutz to Catt, December 1, 1934, reel 12, NAWSA.

17. Ware, *Beyond Suffrage*, 16.

18. Lutz had also met many of the groups' leaders during and after the 1922 Baltimore conference. The sisters Grace and Edith Abbott and Katharine Lenroot, all social workers with the Children's Bureau, had fostered epistolary connections between Lutz and members of the Women's Bureau, including Mary Anderson, Sophonisba Breckinridge, and Frieda Miller, who in turn put Lutz in touch with Women's Trade Union League members. Lutz to Mary Anderson, February 15, 1931, Qo.ADM, COR.1931, p. 52; Margaret Dreier Robins to Lutz, March 4, 1931, Qo.ADM, COR.1931, p. 108; Breckinridge to Lutz, June 18 and June 19, 1931, Qo.ADM, EVE.CNG.TXT.10,VOL.9, p. 99, 101; Amanda Finch to Sophonisba Breckinridge, September 15, 1931, Qo.ADM. EVE.CNG,TXT.10,VOL.9, p. 231; Finch to Frieda Miller, June 8, 1932, Qo.ADM, COR.1932, p. 3; E. B. Patton to Bertha Lutz, December 23, 1932, Qo.ADM, COR.1932, p. 3; Lutz's untitled notes in Portuguese on constitutional changes and on idea of a Women's Bureau in Brazil [1934], Qo.ADM, COR.1934, p. 1, AFBPF.

19. Lutz et al., *O trabalho feminino*.

20. These groups thus favored a "specific bills for specific ills" approach to remedy women's legal inequalities rather than the sweeping ERA promoted by the National Woman's Party.

21. Catt to Sherwin, March 27, 1928, 2:155, LWV.

22. For more on Lenroot's work at Pan-American Child Congresses, see Guy, "Pan American Child Congresses." Her engagement in Pan-American Child Congresses began in 1927.

23. Lenroot to Lutz, undated "Tuesday morning," 1932; Lutz to Lutz, "Wednesday eve," 1932; Lenroot to Lutz, July 17, 1932, Qo.ADM, COR.1932.87, AFBPF.

24. She told Lenroot that she pushed the League of Women Voters to send women to the 1928 Havana conference to little avail.

25. Grace Abbott, "Memorandum for the Secretary," October 9, 1933; Grace Abbott to Frances Perkins, September 30, 1933, folder "Conference Pan American, Montevideo, Dec 1933," box 50, MLR entry 20, RG 174.

26. Barr, "Profession for Women," 358–60. Particularly concerned about the hostility toward working women that the Great Depression had generated, Breckinridge had just published a significant study detailing women's rise in employment over the past two decades and critiquing the existing barriers to women's full employment. Breckinridge, *Women in the Twentieth Century*. Her work included detailed tables of women in employment and asserted that women's political involvement had brought about many social welfare gains in terms of mothers' pensions, child labor laws, and appropriations for the U.S. Children's Bureau. For more on Breckinridge see Jabour, "Relationship and Leadership."

27. Anita L. Pollitzer, "The New Deal for Women," *Equal Rights*, September 19, 1933,

260–61. The Economy Act, for instance, provided that when both a husband and wife were working, the wife would be the first discharged. The Woman's Party had begun campaigns to eliminate all discriminations against women in NRA codes. See the following in *Equal Rights*: "Press Comment: Demand Square Deal for Women," August 26, 1933, 239; "A New Deal for Married Women," October 7, 1933, 286–87; "Press Comment: New Deal Should Mean Square Deal," October 28, 1933, 304; Helena Hill Weed, "The New Deal that Women Want," December 15, 1934, 365–67.

28. "Miss Breckinridge Accepts," NYT, October 28, 1933, 16. For more on Roosevelt's relationship to the network of New Deal women and social legislation politics, see Ware, *Beyond Suffrage*, 44–58, 98–100. State Department press release, December 2, 1933, "Press Releases," MLR entry 210, U.S. Delegation to the Seventh International Conference of American States, General Records, 1933–1934, Records of International Conferences, Commissions, and Expositions, Record Group 43, National Archives and Records Administration, College Park, Md.

29. Specifically Lutz admired Breckinridge's "Survey of the Legal Status of Women in the 48 States." Lutz to Sherwin, September 3, 1930, 2:156, LWV; Breckinridge to Lutz, June 18 and June 19, 1931, Q0.ADM, EVE.CNG, TXT.10, VOL.9, p. 99, 101, AFBPF. Lutz also heard Breckinridge speak at a League of Women Voters convention in Washington, D.C., in the early 1930s. Amanda Finch to Sophonisba Breckinridge, September 15, 1931, Q0.ADM, EVE.CNG, TXT.10, VOL.9, p. 231, AFBPF.

30. Guy, "Politics of Pan-American Cooperation," 460.

31. E. Smith, *Toward Equal Rights for Men and Women*.

32. "Suggestions for Memorandum on Instructions, items 6, 8, 18, 19 of the Agenda," n.d., attachment to Perkins to Hull, October 30, 1933, folder "Conference Pan American, Montevideo, Dec 1933," box 50, MLR entry 20, RG 174. Initially their instructions acceded ground to the commission only on the Equal Nationality Treaty, which Perkins wrote the U.S. delegation could "support" as long as it "follow[ed] . . . the general principles of the Cable Act.'" Hull to Perkins, October 25, 1933, folder "Conference Pan American, Montevideo, December 1933," box 50, MLR entry 20, RG 174.

33. Cordell Hull, "Instructions to Delegates," in *Foreign Relations of the United States*, 84.

34. The official State Department instructions doubted the merit of an intergovernmental group whose U.S. representatives did not reflect the U.S. administration's position on women's labor or social concerns. *Foreign Relations of the United States*, 84–85.

35. Mary Wilhelmine Williams, also a member of the Women's International League for Peace and Freedom and historian of Latin America, visited Lutz in Rio de Janeiro late in 1932 and celebrated Lutz's change of position on protective labor legislation. On her return, Williams visited Doris Stevens in Washington, D.C., urging Lutz's appointment to Montevideo. Williams to Paul and Stevens, September 25, 1933, box 85, folder 1; Stevens to Lutz, September 23, 1933, box 62, folder 11; memorandum, attached to letter from Stevens to Oliveira Lima, box 62, folder 13, DSP. Lutz also wrote to James Brown Scott directly, but her greatest help came from Williams. For more on Lutz and Williams's friendship, see Marino, "Transnational Pan-American Feminism."

36. Lutz to Stevens, October 6, 1933, box 62, folder 11, DSP. As of October 2, Stevens was trying to fund Flora Oliveira's travel to Montevideo as the IACW delegate. Stevens to Maúrtua, October 2, 1933, box 62, folder 13, DSP.

37. Stevens to Smith, October 25, 1933, box 125, folder 6, Jane Norman Smith Papers, Schlesinger Library.

38. American University class notes, box 10, folders 6–8; Columbia University class notes, box 10, folder 9, box 11, folders 1–6, and box 12, folders 1–5, DSP.

39. "Report of the Inter-American Commission of Women to the Seventh International Conference of American States on the Civil and Political Rights of Women," box 78, folders 15–17, DSP. (The report included all countries except Canada.)

40. "Study of Women's Status: Pan-American Commission Will Take It to Montevideo," NYT, November 11, 1933, 16; "Laws Made for Women Assembled," LAT, November 11, 1933, 3.

41. "Hull, Optimistic, Sails for Uruguay," NYT, November 12, 1933, 1.

42. Untitled log of the IACW, box 96, folder 8, DSP. IACW member Ella Reigel would go ahead of them and meet them in Montevideo. Fanny Bunand-Sevastos and Anne Carter joined Stevens on the trip to Montevideo.

43. Robles de Mendoza to Stevens, October 13, 1933, box 77, folder 8, DSP. Robles de Mendoza had worked in the Washington, D.C., office of the IACW for three months in 1931 and 1932, during which time the IACW paid her transportation and living expenses. Stevens to Robles de Mendoza, May 20, 1935; Stevens to Robles de Mendoza, September 29, 1933, box 77, folder 8, DSP.

44. Carmen Portinho Lutz of Brazil and Ana Rosa Tornero of Bolivia would also attend the conference.

45. Stevens to Lutz, November 6, 1933, box 62, folder 11, DSP; "Miss Breckinridge Accepts," NYT, October 28, 1933, 16.

46. Bess Furman, [untitled], *Cincinnati Times-Star*, November 14, 1933, mentioned in Jane Norman Smith to Stevens, November 17, 1933, box 78, folder 7, DSP.

47. Montevideo conference: narrative and timeline, ca. 1933–1934, box 96, folder 8, DSP; Stevens's manuscript about the IACW, box 126, folder 13, DSP. Breckinridge to [Edith Abbott], November 25, 1933, reel 10, SBP.

48. Breckinridge to Abbott, November 28, 1933, reel 10, SBP.

49. Breckinridge to Sherwin, December 8, 1933, reel 10, SBP. Lutz explained to Breckinridge that she had urged the League of Women Voters to intervene in the 1928 Havana conference that had, in their absence, led to the Woman's Party leadership of the commission.

50. "Yanqui Imperialismo," *New Republic*, December 6, 1933, 89–90.

51. Telegram from Hull to Ambassador in Mexico (Daniels), September 28, 1933, *Foreign Relations of the United States*, 17; Gellman, *Secret Affairs*, 49.

52. "Hull, Optimistic, Sails for Uruguay," 1, 20; "Hull Sets Sail to Montevideo," LAT, November 12, 1933, 6.

53. Montevideo conference, box 96, folder 8, DSP.

54. The *New York Times* team consisted of John W. White, dean of the *New York Times* press corps in South America; Harold Hinton of the Washington Bureau; and Peter Khill. Both White and Hinton became close, lifelong friends of Stevens. Lutz also wrote to Katharine Lenroot that Stevens "chases the press and has a great sense of publicity." Lutz to Lenroot, December 1933, Q0.ADM, EVE.CNF, TXT.17, AFBPF.

55. The subcommittee delegates were Sofía Álvarez Vignoli de Demicheli from Uruguay, Neuhaus Uguarteche from Peru, Alberto Angel Giraudy from Cuba, Francisco da Silva Campos from Brazil, and Gustavo Rivera from Chile.

56. Montevideo conference, box 96, folder 8, DSP; Harold B. Hinton, "Rights of Women Bring Parley Rift," NYT, December 12, 1933, 20.

57. "Boletín de Prensa," no. 58, VII Conferencia Internacional Americana, Montevideo, December 12, 1933, box 78, folder 16; Informe de la subcomisión, C. III, N. 2, VII Conferencia Internacional Americana, box 78, folder 16; untitled document, box 78, folder 10; telegram from IACW, December 12, 1933, box 78, folder 14, DSP.

58. Telegram, Hull to Phillips, December 9, 1933, 710.G 1A/145, D.F., RG 59.

59. "Conference with the Secretary of the United States of America," December 11, 1933; "Memorandum for the Secretary of State," December 11, 1933, box 78, folder 10, DSP.

60. Telegram, Phillips to Hull, December 11, 1933, 710.G 1A/145, D.F., RG 59.

61. Memo attached to telegram, Phillips to Hull, December 11, 1933, 710.G 1A/145, D.F., RG 59.

62. Stevens had little inkling that Cordell Hull was worried about the commission. Unlike her chilly interviews with Alexander Weddell and Breckinridge, her talks with Hull had been congenial. "Doris Stevens at Montevideo," box 126, folder 13, DSP. When Stevens tried to tell Weddell about the IACW's work, he apparently interrupted her with "I know all about you" and told her that she had no right to make requests. Stevens's manuscript about the IACW, box 126, folder 13, DSP.

63. Untitled document, box 78, folder 10; untitled document, box 86, folder 8 DSP.

64. Untitled document, box 78, folder 10, DSP.

65. "Doris Stevens at Montevideo," box 126, folder 13, DSP.

66. "Minutes of the Fourth Session (December 16, 1933)," in Pan-American Union, Third Committee, 10–11; "VII International Conference of American States, Speech of Delegate Weddell at Plenary Session of Chapter III—Political and Civil Rights of Women," December 18, 1933, 710.G IACW/60, D.F., RG 59.

67. "Minutes of the Fourth Session (December 16, 1933)," 11.

68. "Minutes of the Fourth Session," 12; untitled document, box 78, folder 10, and "Doris Stevens at Montevideo," box 126, folder 13, DSP.

69. On December 16, the Third Committee had accepted the subcommittee's report.

70. Thomson, "The Montevideo Conference," 2.

71. One anti-ERA pamphlet, published by the League of Women Voters and written by the legislative secretary of the Women's Trade Union League, rued that Cuban feminists had signed onto the Equal Rights Treaty that would, unbeknownst to them, remove social and economic welfare goals, a claim that was not accurate. E. Smith, Toward Equal Rights for Men and Women, 125–27.

72. "Doris Stevens at Montevideo," box 126, folder 13, DSP.

73. "Doris Stevens at Montevideo."

74. Lutz to Catt, December 1, 1934, reel 12, NAWSA.

75. "Strictly Confidential Memorandum Commission No. III Political and Civil Rights of Women (Topic 8)," 710.G 1A/145, D.F., RG 59.

76. Soto Hall to Excmo. Señor Presidente de la Republica, Havana, August 17, 1933, caja 673, no. 3, ODN-AN. Ramón Grau San Martín was a friend of Domínguez, although she was ultimately disappointed with his government.

77. Gronbeck-Tedesco, Cuba, 93.

78. Lutz to Lenroot, December 1933, Qo.ADM, EVE.CNF, TXT.17, AFBPF. Lutz reported this information to Lenroot based on her conversation with Angel Giraudy.

79. "Proposal Made by Bertha Lutz, Technical Advisor to Brazilian Delegation to Subcommittee of III Commission, Seventh International Conference of American States, Montevideo, December 1933," box 78, folder 9, DSP.

80. "Tercera Comisión, Proposición de la Delegación del Brasil, C. III, No. 4," box 78, folder 16, DSP.

81. "Boletín de la Prensa, No. 61, III Comisión," December 15, 1933, box 78, folder 16, DSP.

82. Bertha Lutz, untitled document, undated, "Third Committee—Political & Civil

Rights of Women," MLR entry 203, U.S. Delegation to the Seventh International Conference of American States, General Records, 1933–1934, Records of International Conferences, Commissions, and Expositions, Record Group 43, National Archives and Records Administration, College Park, Md.

83. Among the purposes of such an organization would be the "defense of the work of women" and the education of working women. "Project for Women's Department in an Inter American Labor Institute Proposed by Bertha Lutz at the Montevideo Conference, 1933" (this became "Resolution XXIII" of the Conference Resolutions), box 8, "Inter-American Commission," RG 86; Bertha Lutz to Frieda Miller, February 18, 1936, reel 12, NAWSA.

84. "Civil and Political Rights of Women, Minimum Replevin, C. III, No. 5," in Pan-American Union, *Third Committee*, 28–29. Lutz also sent her proposal to the U.S. delegation.

85. "Proposición de las delegadas de Cuba y del Uruguay, C. III, No. 6," box 78, folder 16, DSP.

86. Cable, Doris Stevens to Alice Paul, December 22, 1933, box 85, folder 1, DSP.

87. Transcription of recorded narrative of IACW, box 126, folder 13; Stevens to Oliveira Lima, March 15, 1934, box 62, folder 13, DSP.

88. Stevens to Oliveira Lima, March 15, 1934, box 62, folder 13, DSP.

89. "Minutes of the Fifth Session (December 19, 1933)," "Minutes of the Sixth Session (December 20, 1933)," "Minutes of the Seventh Session, (December 21, 1933)," in Pan-American Union, *Third Committee*, 14–16.

90. Gustavo Rivera, "Report of Sub-committee," December 14, 1933, in Pan-American Union, *Third Committee*, 26.

91. Stevens, unpublished memoir, box 126, folder 13, DSP.

92. Untitled document, "Proposed to Initiatives Sunday, December 24," box 78, folder 9, DSP.

93. In legislative terms, a "ripper bill" is "a legislative bill or act for taking powers of appointment to and removal from office away from the usual holders of these powers and conferring them unrestrictedly on a chief executive, as a governor or mayor, or on a board of officials." See WordReference.com, http://www.wordreference.com/definition /ripper (accessed February 2, 2017).

94. Transcription of recorded narrative of IACW, box 126, folder 5, DSP.

95. Transcription of recorded narrative of IACW; "Conference Saves Women's Board," NYT, December 25, 1933.

96. Transcription of recorded narrative of IACW, box 126, folder 5, DSP.

97. "A Polite Conference," *The Nation*, December 27, 1933, 724.

98. "Inter American Commission of Women, Legislative Palace, Statement by Doris Stevens," December 26, 1933, box 79, folder 1, DSP.

99. Hill, "International Law for Women's Rights," 292; Alexander Weddell to Sumner Welles, August 20, 1936, box 38, folder 5, Sumner Welles Papers, Franklin D. Roosevelt Presidential Library and Museum, Hyde Park, N.Y.

100. Lutz to Breckinridge, January 1, 1934, reel 11, SBP.

101. Lutz to Catt, February 12, 1934, reel 12, NAWSA. By "French secretary," Lutz was referring to Fanny Bunand-Sevastos, a French woman who worked for the IACW and also was a member of the Haitian delegation at Montevideo. Fanny S. Chipman, oral history, July 22, 1987, 33.

102. Untitled play, undated, box 43, folder 11, DSP. The sketch ends with the delegate

caressing the face of the dazed, flattered, but ultimately resolute feminist who tells him that this idea would be "very difficult to realize."

103. Scott's $1,000 gift from the Carnegie Endowment enabled Stevens to send herself and other Woman's Party members to Montevideo. Teresa Cristina de Novaes Marques has pointed out the instrumental role the Carnegie Endowment for International Peace played in raising attention to women's rights as a matter of diplomatic importance in these years. Novaes Marques, "Entre o igualitarismo e a reforma dos direitos das mulheres," 930–31.

104. Scott to Stevens, [December?] 18, 1930, box 35, folder 8, DSP. Scott, "Miss Stevens' Thirty-Seven Beautiful Years," October 26, 1929, box 35, folder 8, DSP. I am grateful to Nancy Cott for telling me about the love letters from Scott to Stevens. Romantic letters from Stevens to him do not exist in either of their archives, possibly because he wanted to hide the affair and also possibly because, as Trigg relates, Stevens asked her lovers to burn her letters lest Alice Paul discovered them. Trigg, *Feminism as Life's Work*, 76.

105. On Stevens and Mitchell's approach to relationships, see Trigg, *Feminism as Life's Work*, 79–81.

106. Rupp, "Feminism and the Sexual Revolution."

107. "To Be a Bachelor Is an Art, Brazilian Feminist Explains," NYT, July 1, 1939, 16. Although Lutz never married, two letters from Catt in 1924 refer to a brief engagement Lutz had to be married. Catt to Lutz, July 23, 1924, Q0.ADM, COR.1924.12, p. 44, AFBPF. Lutz seems to have taken pains to remove from her archives her own correspondence to Catt discussing this relationship. In later letters to Catt, Lutz proposed they build a convent for an international "lay community" of feminists, inspired by St. Theresa of Spain and the *béguinage* at Bruges. Lutz to Catt, July 10, 1940, Q0.ADM, COR.A940.6, p. 22, AFBPF.

108. Lutz to Breckinridge, January 1, 1934, reel 11, SBP.

109. Lutz to Catt, February 1936, reel 12, NAWSA.

110. Lutz to Frieda Miller, February 18, 1936, reel 12, NAWSA.

111. Lutz to Breckinridge, January 1, 1934, reel 11, SBP.

112. Lutz to Breckinridge, February 10, 1934, Q0.ADM, COR.1934, p. 96, AFPBF.

113. Robles de Mendoza and Bernardino told Lutz that "they were going to put Miss Stevens out of the presidency at the [N]ew York banquet, thanking her and saying they want a Latin"—an event that never occurred. Lutz to Breckinridge, February 10, 1934.

114. The only proposal Lutz found viable was Máximo Soto Hall's idea to form a new commission composed of men and women. Lutz to Breckinridge, February 10, 1934.

115. Isabel Morel, "An Evaluation of International Feminism," undated, translated into English from an article from the Havana-based magazine *Social*, box 63, folder 4, DSP. She wrote another article on the same topic in an Ecuadorian periodical: Isabel Morel, "Sobremesa de la VII Conferencia Internacional," *Nuevos Horizontes*, March 1934, 8. Morel echoed Lutz's sentiments about social and economic justice. Equal rights under the law for women were important, she acknowledged, but this time of intense social and economic turmoil raised another question, too: "What has America done for her children?" Morel had written to Lutz earlier in 1933, asking her to write for her journal *Nosotras* "a message from Brazil to the women of all America." Morel to Lutz, August 29, 1933, BR.MN.BL.0.FEM.1/41, BLMN.

116. Morel, "Sobremesa de la VII Conferencia Internacional," 8.

117. Stevens to Jane Norman Smith, June 23, 1937, box 90, folder 17, DSP.

118. Portell Vilá urged readers to "look for contacts with liberal women's organizations in the United States, such as the Women's International League for Peace and Free-

dom," a group with which he had collaborated in protesting the Platt Amendment. He also supported the work of Paraguayan Felicida Gonzalez and Uruguayan Sofía de Demicheli. "Entrevista do delegado plenipotenciario de Cuba, Dr. Portell Vilá," Qo.ADM, EVE. CNF, TXT.17, AFBPF.

119. Robles de Mendoza, "La Comisión Interamericana de Mujeres debe cambiar sede," Mexico, April 1940, box 77, folder 3. Stevens to Mitchell, December 29, 1938, box 25, folder 5; Stevens to Robles de Mendoza, April 12, 1939, box 77, folder 9; Robles de Mendoza to Stevens, April 17, 1939, box 77, folder 3, DSP. On Robles de Mendoza's role in the Mexican feminist movement, see Olcott, *Revolutionary Women*, 159–66.

120. Robles de Mendoza wrote to Stevens, "I personnaly [sic] believe that it is rather shameful that this Commission has only existed through the generosity of AMERICAN PEOPLE, I mean North American people. When … is [it] going to be beneficial mainly to the … Spanish speaking women of this Continene [sic]?" Robles de Mendoza to Stevens, January 20, 1932, box 77, folder 3, DSP.

121. "Unión de Mujeres Americanas (UMA), Objetivos y Bases de Organización," June 1934, box 77, folder 8; "Recortes de la Revista Mensual 'UNO' organo del Partido Nacional Revolucionario, Número de Abril, 1935, Mexico, D.F.," box 77, folder 3, DSP. Its motto was "peace and equality." Robles de Mendoza credited the Cuban delegation for raising the rotation proposal at Montevideo. She also explained that women throughout the Americas wanted an inter-American feminist group that was not connected to the Pan American Union. Robles de Mendoza to Edelmira R. de Escudero, November 20, 1934, caja 144, exp. 26, Archivo Particular de Tomás Garrido Canabal, Archivo General de la Nación, Mexico City.

122. Robles de Mendoza, "La Comisión Interamericana de Mujeres debe cambiar sede."

123. Luisi to Robles de Mendoza, May 2, 1935, caja 252, carpeta 6, PL-AGN. Luisi, who received Robles de Mendoza's letter a few months later, had been planning to found a new international association of feminists from the Americas and Spain upon her return to Uruguay, but she now decided to desist because she was so hopeful about UMA. Luisi heard about Robles de Mendoza from her friends in the Alianza Uruguaya, where Robles de Mendoza had spoken at a mass meeting in Montevideo. Photographs of Robles de Mendoza speaking in Montevideo to the Alianza, MC 546-PD. 64f-19, DSP.

124. Luisi to Robles de Mendoza, May 2, 1935.

125. Luisi to Robles de Mendoza, May 2, 1935.

126. For more on this campaign, see McKenzie, "The Power of International Positioning."

127. "Debate at League of Nations," *Equal Rights*, October 15, 1935, 1–3.

128. "La Gran Batalla Feminista de Montevideo," *Todos*, July 20, 1935, DSP. Even Bertha Lutz acknowledged that although she found the analyses of women's rights "inadequate" at the Montevideo conference, the progress made with the Equal Nationality and Equal Rights treaties demonstrated the thriving of a "feminist movement." "Feminist Is Encouraged," NYT, January 7, 1934, 26.

CHAPTER 5

1. Stevens to Vergara, January 1, 1934, box 77, folder 11, DSP.

2. Telegrams, Stevens to Vergara, December 3, December 4, December 5, December 7, and December 10, 1933, box 77, folder 11, DSP.

3. Vergara to Stevens, December 7, 1933, box 77, folder 11.

4. Stevens openly complained about the "eleventh-hour tricks" against her in a news-

paper interview, "Parley to End Tomorrow Minus Chaco Peace Pact," *LAT*, December 25, 1933, 1.

5. "Feminist Leader Returns," NYT, January 25, 1934, 2.

6. Vergara, *Memorias*, 141; Vergara later referred to the idea proposed by Stevens of her becoming chair in her letter to Stevens, September 29, 1936, box 64, folder 7, DSP.

7. See Lambe, "Cuban Antifascism and the Spanish Civil War," and Ojeda Revah, *Mexico and the Spanish Civil War.* On the long-term influence of the Spanish Civil War in Latin America, see Weld, "The Spanish Civil War and the Construction of a Reactionary Historical Consciousness in Augusto Pinochet's Chile."

8. At that time, the small women's rights movement in Chile was led by educator Amanda Labarca, who was a family friend. Vergara, *Memorias*, 34, 242, and chapter 11.

9. Vergara, *Memorias*, 8–33, 66–76.

10. Vergara learned that a "committee of ladies" would pay these expenses. This was likely Alice Paul's Women's Consultative Committee of Nationality. Vergara, 66.

11. Vergara, 65.

12. Vergara, 67–69.

13. "Chilean Representative Pleads for Equality," *Equal Rights*, May 17, 1930, 117. Even though no international legislation resulted from the 1930 Hague conference, Ellen DuBois argues that the IACW campaign and Vergara's activism in it were central to "open[ing] up . . . a prolonged feminist presence in the League of Nations." DuBois, "Internationalizing Married Women's Nationality," 204. Marta Vergara, "The Women at The Hague," *Equal Rights*, August 9, 1930, 211.

14. Vergara, "Women Fight for Equal Economic Rights," *Equal Rights*, August 1, 1931, 203–5; "News from the Field: Chile Appoints Marta Vergara Technical Advisor," *Equal Rights*, September 19, 1931, 264; "Marta Vergara of Chile to Go to Geneva," *Equal Rights*, August 20, 1932, 227.

15. Vergara, *Memorias*, 67.

16. Vergara's journalistic work had put her in contact with many avant-garde leftist thinkers and activists in Paris, where she was also a close friend and roommate with leftist Chilean artist Laura Rodig. A meeting with French pacifist and socialist Henri Barbusse led her to read the *Communist Manifesto* and the works of Lenin and Trotsky. Vergara, *Memorias*, 53–54, 86–89.

17. Vergara, 53–54 and 79–80.

18. "Chilean Representative Pleads for Equality," 117. As she explained in her 1930 speech at The Hague, women should be allowed to flourish as equals with men, and these rights of the individual could be fully compatible with the "[rights] of society, whether [they] be represented by the family, the State, or humanity." In Chile, she explained, it was "the family" that "continues to be the fundamental unit of our social and political organization."

19. Vergara, *Memorias*, 80. For an insightful exploration of the racialist and imperialist dimensions of the World Woman's Party, see Zimmermann, "Night Work for White Women."

20. Vergara, *Memorias*, 70.

21. Stevens even offered for the IACW to pay Vergara to travel to its Washington, D.C., headquarters and then embark on an organizing tour of South American countries for equal rights. The Great Depression, however, made it difficult for Stevens to raise those funds. In early 1933 Vergara allied with Amanda Labarca and other feminists in the formation of the Comité Nacional pro Derechos de la Mujer, which in the following year secured ratification of an amendment that granted women suffrage in municipal elec-

tions in Chile. Stevens to Vergara, November 15, 1932; Vergara to Stevens, December 16, 1932; Stevens to Vergara, January 31, 1933; Vergara to Stevens, March 24, 1933; Stevens to Vergara, April 27, 1933; Stevens to Vergara, July 13, 1933; Vergara to Stevens, July 23, 1933, box 64, folder 7, DSP. On the Comité Nacional pro Derechos de la Mujer, see Lavrin, *Women, Feminism, and Social Change*, 302–3.

22. By 1936 Parada was a professor at the University of Chile in Santiago. Vergara later told Stevens that Parada had warned her about Stevens's dominance over the IACW. Vergara to Stevens, December 20, 1938, box 64, folder 5, DSP.

23. Vergara to Stevens, October 24, 1933, box 78, folder 3, DSP.

24. Barr-Melej, *Reforming Chile*, 110.

25. Vergara to Stevens, October 24, 1933; Vergara to Stevens, December 8, 1933, box 78, folder 3, DSP.

26. Vergara to Stevens, October 24, 1933, box 78, folder 3, DSP.

27. Vergara to Stevens, December 8, 1933, box 78, folder 3, DSP.

28. Vergara, *Memorias*, 95. Chamudes was the head of the Chilean Communist Party's Political Bureau. Vergara wrote that he was much more invested in her not going to the conference than she was interested in going, ultimately. It is important to note that the context in which Vergara's memoirs were written—a time when she was disenchanted with the Communist Party—influenced the way that she retrospectively recounted these 1930s events.

29. Vergara, 95; telegram, Stevens to Vergara, November 26, 1933, box 77, folder 11, DSP.

30. Vergara, *Memorias*, 141. Vergara noted that she not only refused Stevens's call to go to Uruguay but also wrote an article in *La Opinión* about her break with the commission.

31. Vergara, 93.

32. "Nazi Treatment of Women," *The Vote*, London, 9 June 1933, reprinted in *Equal Rights*, June 24, 1933, 167; "Hitler Derides Women's Rights," *Baltimore Sun*, September 9, 1934, reprinted in *Equal Rights*, September 22, 1934, 271.

33. De Grazia, *How Fascism Ruled Women*.

34. Vergara, *Memorias*, 93.

35. On the influence of the 1934 Paris conference on influential Argentinian anti-fascist women's organizing, see Deutsch, "New School Lecture 'An Army of Women.'" In 1932 and in 1933, communist intellectuals Romain Rolland and Henri Barbusse had created in Amsterdam and Paris the World Committee against Fascism and War. Coons, "Gabrielle Duchêne," 131.

36. Dimitrov, *United Front*.

37. "Congreso Internacional de Mujeres Contra la Guerra y el Fascismo," undated, caja 250, carpeta 3; "Congreso Internacional de Mujeres Contra la Guerra y el Fascismo, Principios Fundamentales," caja 256, carpeta 2, PL-AGN.

38. Several African American women were part of the delegation of forty women from the United States; they included Iquala McKeith and Capitola J. Tasker of the Alabama Sharecroppers Union; Rosa Rayside, member of the Domestic Workers' Union from Harlem; and Mabel Byrd, African American economist and former government worker on the NRA codes. Dorothy Chertak, "Peace Congress to Meet," NYT, May 26, 1934, 16; "Mable Byrd [sic] Heads Women's Anti-war, Fascist Committee," *Chicago Defender*, June 2, 1934, 3; "Anti-fascist Women Open Paris Congress," NYT, August 5, 1934, 5; "2 Negro Women Go to Anti-war Confab," *New York Amsterdam News*, August 4, 1934, 8; "Peace Confab 'Just Like a Bunch of Biddies,'" *New York Amsterdam News*, August 25, 1934, 1; "Women and Fascism," *Manchester Guardian*, July 30, 1934, 16; Davis, *Women, Race, and Class*, 156–59.

39. Women's World Committee against War and Fascism, *Rassemblement mondial des femmes!*, 15, 32, 50.

40. As historian Erik McDuffie has demonstrated, African American Communist women were at the vanguard of intersectional feminist demands in the 1930s. This Paris conference brought these demands to the attention of women around the world. McDuffie, *Sojourning for Freedom*.

41. Yusta, "Strained Courtship"; Yusta Rodrigo, *Madres coraje contra Franco*. On the influence of the 1934 Paris conference in Mexico, see S. Smith, *Power and Politics of Art*, 63. French feminist and pacifist Gabrielle Duchêne became the president of the World Committee of Women against War and Fascism.

42. Paulina Luisi had collaborated with Isabel Blume from Belgium, Margarita Nelken from Spain, Gabrielle Duchêne of France, and about a dozen other women in helping to organize the conference. "Congreso Internacional de Mujeres Contra la Guerra y el Fascismo," undated, caja 250, carpeta 3; "El Congreso Mundial de las Mujeres Contra la Guerra y el Fascismo," *La Correspondencia Internacional*, no. 43, 833–34; "Por una gran jornada femenina anti-guerrera el 1 de Agosto!," [undated], box 256, folder 7, PL-AGN. See also "Ha Dado un Manifiesto Contra la Guerra el C. Mundial de Mujeres," *El País* (Montevideo), July 5, 1934. On the importance of the Italian invasion of Ethiopia to the transnational Popular Front, see Fronczak, "Local People's Global Politics."

43. [Ofelia Domínguez Navarro] to María Dolores Machín de Huppman, November 7, 1934, caja 675, no. 2; "Informe del Frente Único de Mujeres," undated; Comité Mondial des Femmes Contre la Guerre et le Fascisme to Bertha Darder, November 16, 1934; "Frente Único de Mujeres Contra la Guerra," undated [1935?], caja 677, no. 5, ODN-AN. Domínguez's group, now called the Unión Radical de Mujeres, sent its support to the 1934 Paris congress. (It changed its name in 1933, in part to oppose the mediation of Sumner Welles in Cuba.) Domínguez, *50 años de una vida*, 282–83, 295; "5 Hurt in Cuban Riot," NYT, November 30, 1934, 20.

44. As a journalist in Paris, Vergara had interviewed a number of the French intellectuals who were starting the Amsterdam-Pleyal movement, including Romain Rolland. *La Mujer Nueva* reported on the World Congress of Women against War and Fascism and its subsequent meetings. "Conferencia del Comité Mundial de Mujeres contra la Guerra y el fascismo," *La Mujer Nueva*, March 1937, 5.

45. Vergara, *Memorias*, 92.

46. She cofounded MEMCh with lawyer Elena Caffarena. Antezana-Pernet, "Mobilizing Women"; Rosemblatt, *Gendered Compromises*, 3–4, 6, 101–3; Vergara, *Memorias*, 135–36.

47. Elena Pedraza quoted in Rosemblatt, *Gendered Compromises*, 100.

48. Rosemblatt, 100.

49. MEMCh Manifesto, *La Mujer Nueva*, November 1935.

50. "News from the Field: Against War and Fascism," *Equal Rights*, December 8, 1934, 360; "Resolution Unanimously Adopted August 7, 1934, by Women's International Congress against War and Fascism, Paris, France," *Equal Rights*, September 1, 1934, 244; Monica Whately, "Equality, Freedom and Peace," *Equal Rights*, September 8, 1934, 254–55.

51. Stevens to Vergara, November 25, 1935, box 72, folder 4, DSP. Stevens's letters to Vergara were most often translated into Spanish from English with the help of a translator in the Washington, D.C., IACW office.

52. From the beginning of its involvement in Pan-American feminism, the Woman's Party framed the Equal Rights Treaty as opposed to international resolutions for maternity legislation. See, for instance, "Press Comment, Women Ask Equal Rights before Havana Delegates," WP, February 8, 1928, reprinted in *Equal Rights*, February 25, 1928, 23.

53. Stevens to Vergara, November 25, 1935, box 72, folder 4, DSP.

54. Mink, *Wages of Motherhood*, 62–63; Gordon, "Social Insurance and Public Assistance"; Nelson, "The Origins of the Two-Channel Welfare State."

55. See chapter 7.

56. "Victory in Brazil: A Short Report on Fifteen Years of Work," *Boletim da FBPF*, February 1935, 3.

57. Frieda Miller, "Personal and Confidential Report to the Secretary of Labor on the First Pan-American Labor Conference of the International Labor Organization, Santiago, Chile, 2–14 January 1936," box 47, RG 174.

58. Vergara to Stevens, December 10, 1935, box 72, folder 4, DSP.

59. Vergara to Stevens, December 10, 1935; Felisa Vergara, "Tres Mujeres en la Conferencia Panamericana del Trabajo," *Acción Social* 46, 1936, 16–17; Maria Aracil, "Qué es la Conferencia Panamericana?" *La Mujer Nueva*, January 1936; "La Gran Concentración del MEMCh," *La Mujer Nueva*, January 1936.

60. Rosemblatt, *Gendered Compromises*, 276.

61. Black women spearheaded the first domestic workers' unions in the United States, Brazil, Uruguay, and elsewhere in the late 1930s. Many organizers were connected to communist and antifascist networks. It was at the 1936 meeting of Paulina Luisi's Unión Femenina that Afro-Uruguayan domestic workers Iris Cabral and Maruja Pereyra, representing the newly created Comité de la Raza Negra contra la Guerra y el Fascismo in Uruguay, proposed what became the first domestic workers' union in that country. "La mujer negra en la acción," *Nuestra Raza*, 1936, in Instituto Nacional de las Mujeres, *Mujeres afro uruguayas*; Gascue, "Un intento de organización política," 49. The first domestic workers' union was ultimately created in Uruguay in 1940. Similar goals were being launched elsewhere in the Americas. In Brazil in 1936, Laudelina de Campos Melo founded the first union for domestic workers in that country—the Associaçã de Trabalhadores Domésticos do Brasil. She also joined the Communist Party that year and was a member of the Black Brazilian Front. Pintó, "Etnicidade." In the United States, African American women created the Domestic Workers Union in New York in 1934, one of many similar unions throughout the country. In 1936 the DWU joined the Building Service Employees International Union (BSEIU), the predecessor to the Service Employees International Union (SEIU). Nadasen, *Household Workers Unite*, 16–17; Boris and Nadasen, "Domestic Workers Organize!," 417–18.

62. S. Becker, *Origins of the Equal Rights Amendment*, 178; Cott, "Historical Perspectives," 54.

63. Antezana-Pernet, "Peace in the World," 174.

64. Vergara to Stevens, December 30, 1935, box 72, folder 4, DSP; Aracil, "Qué es la Conferencia Panamericana?"; "La Gran Concentración del Memch"; "Una gran concentración feminina para ocuparse de la Conferencia Panamericana," *La Opinión* (Santiago), December 28, 1935; "Concentración feminina en el Teatro Balmeceda," *El Mercurio*, December 30, 1935.

65. "Informe de la señora Marta Vergara, representante chilena ante la C. I. de M. sobre las actividades de la Comisión junto a la Conf. Pan-Americana del Trabajo," undated, box 64, folder 7, DSP.

66. "Committee on Work of Women and Juveniles, Resolutions and recommendations at the I.L.O. Regional Conference, Habana, Cuba, November, 1939," box 72, folder 8, DSP.

67. "Informe de la señora Marta Vergara."

68. Vergara to Stevens, January 16, 1936, box 72, folder 4, DSP.

69. Vergara to Stevens, September 29, 1936, box 64, folder 7, and Vergara to Stevens, January 16, 1936, box 72, folder 4, DSP.

70. Vergara to Stevens, September 29, 1936, box 64, folder 7, DSP.

71. Stevens to Vergara, September 10, 1936, and October 19, 1936, box 64, folder 7, DSP; "Informe de la señora Marta Vergara"; "Report of Señora Marta Vergara, Member for Chile on the Inter-American Commission of Women," Equal Rights, March 15, 1936, 1–4. A complete Spanish-language version of Vergara's report, with her statements about maternity legislation, can be found in Marta Vergara, "Conclusiones que aprobara la Conferencia Pan-Americana del Trabajo en lo que al trabajo feminine se refiere," La Mujer Nueva, March 1936.

72. "Unequal Minimum Wage Level Attacked by Chilean Women," Chicago Daily Tribune, December 1, 1936, 8.

73. Stevens to Vergara, September 10, 1936, box 64, folder 7, DSP.

74. On MEMCh's lobbying for the inclusion of women's rights at the official conference see Elena Caffarena to Mabel Vernon, August 19, 1936, folder 3, Correspondencia de la Secretaría General del Movimiento Pro-Emancipación de las Mujeres de Chile (MEMCH), Elena Caffarena, Biblioteca Nacional de Chile, Santiago, Chile, http://www.memoriachilena.cl/602/w3-article-96049.html (accessed November 14, 2015).

75. Peterson, Argentina and the United States, 389; State Department Memo, "Inter-American Conference for the Maintenance of Peace," August 3, 1936, 710.PEACE-AGENDA/76, D.F., RG 59. Vergara's letters to Stevens of June 15 and August 17, 1936, refer to Stevens's requests, box 64, folder 7, DSP.

76. "La próxima Conferencia de Paz de Buenos Aires," La Mujer Nueva, July 1936, 6; Vergara to Stevens, August 17, 1936, box 64, folder 7, DSP.

77. Stevens to Vergara, September 10, 1936, box 64, folder 7, DSP.

78. "La próxima Conferencia de Paz de Buenos Aires," La Mujer Nueva, July 1936, 6.

79. Stevens to Vergara, October 19, 1936, box 64, folder 7, DSP.

80. Stevens to Edith Houghton Hooker, November 28, 1936, box 63, folder 3; untitled memo re: Buenos Aires Conference, box 62, folder 14; "Record of Main Events of the Trip to and from Buenos Aires and in Buenos Aires, 7 November 1936–13 January 1937," box 63, folder 6, DSP.

81. "Resolución propuesta sugerida para ser adoptada por el Congreso de Mujeres pro Paz en Buenos Aires," November 23, 1936; "La Conferencia Popular por la Paz de América," box 63, folder 3, DSP.

82. Dewson was the former director of the Women's Democratic National Committee. Musser was a League of Women Voters member and former Democratic state senator of Utah.

83. Lutz rued that Stevens had inserted her equal rights agenda into the official peace conference: "Doris Stevens is on the loose and it is very much on the loose too." Lutz to Catt, July 7, 1936, Qo.ADM, COR.1936.25, pp. 25–26, AFBPF.

84. "Record of Main Events," box 63, folder 6, DSP.

85. "Rough Notes on Equal Rights Battle—People's Conference for the Peace of America," November 25, 1936, box 63, folder 3, DSP.

86. "Rough Notes on Equal Rights Battle."

87. Stevens to Mitchell, November 28, 1936, box 25, folder 4, DSP.

88. Stevens to Flora Oliveira Lima, June 23, 1939, box 62, folder 12, DSP.

89. Stevens notes on CIA files, "Chile," dictated February 26, 1960, box 64, folder 5, DSP; John W. White, "U.S. Women Clash at Peace Meeting," NYT, November 26, 1936, 18.

90. "Record of Main Events," box 63, folder 6, DSP.

91. Alicia Moreau de Justo to Dr. Carlos Saavedra Lamas, December 1936, box 63, folder 1, DSP.

92. "Record of Main Events," box 63, folder 6, DSP.

93. Stevens to Fanny Bunand-Sevastos, April 19, 1937, box 29, folder 5, DSP.

94. Vergara, *Memorias*, 141; Stevens to Fanny Bunand-Sevastos, April 19, 1937, box 29, folder 5, DSP.

95. Vergara, *Memorias*, 141.

96. Vergara, 141.

97. Vergara, 141–42. For other descriptions of Liborio Justo's outcry at the conference, see Dorothy McConnell, "The Americas," *The Fight*, January 1937, 22. In the mid-1930s the raised fist became the antifascist act in opposition to the straight-arm salute of fascists. See Vergnon, "Le *poing levé*."

98. Vergara, *Memorias*, 142.

99. Vergara, 143.

100. Stevens to Fanny Bunand-Sevastos, April 19, 1937, box 29, folder 5, DSP.

101. Vergara, *Memorias*, 142.

102. Vergara, 142. Argentinian feminist and president of the UAM Santa Fe chapter Marta Samatán would be a strong link between UAM and MEMCh. Thanks to Sandra McGee Deutsch for this insight. For more on Samatán see Deutsch, "New School Lecture 'An Army of Women,'" 113–114; and Valobra, "Formación de cuadros y frentes populares," 139.

103. Guy, *Women Build the Welfare State*, 153–54; Carlson, *¡Feminismo!*, 172. On the connections between the UAM and antifascist solidarity movements in Argentina and transnationally, see Deutsch, chapter 1 of her forthcoming *Engendering Antifascism*, "New School Lecture 'An Army of Women,'" "Argentine Women against Fascism," and "Hands across the Río de la Plata."

104. Roosevelt and Hardman, *Rendezvous with Destiny*, 143–45.

105. "Memo for Dr. Feis," December 12, 1936, box 62, folder 1, DSP.

106. "Record of Main Events," box 63, folder 6; "Points for the Ambassador," December 12, 1936, box 62, folder 16, DSP. Brazilian delegate Rosalina Coelho Lisboa Miller formally introduced the resolution with signatures of thirteen heads of delegations. Harold B. Hinton, "Compromise Made on Women's Rights," NYT, December 18, 1936, 16.

107. John W. White, "Equal Rights Fight at Peak at Parley," NYT, December 9, 1936, 19; "Statement of Mrs. Elise F. Musser," December 8, 1936, and "Statement Made to *New York Times* by Doris Stevens," December 14, 1936, box 62, folder 16, DSP.

108. "Statement of Hispanic Organization of Women and Other Feminist Individual Leaders Concerning Women's Rights in the Peace Conference," box 62, folder 16, DSP.

109. "Statement Made to *New York Times* by Doris Stevens," December 14, 1936, box 62, folder 16, DSP.

110. "Equal Rights at the Inter American Conference for Peace," box 62, folder 16; "Verbatim Translation of Debate in Sixth Commission, Tuesday, 15 December 1936," box 63, folder 2, DSP.

111. "Declaración de la mujer Argentina," box 62, folder 16, DSP.

112. Vergara, *Memorias*, 144.

113. "Conferencia Argentina de Mujeres por la Paz," box 63, folder 3; "Declaración de la Mujer Argentina," box 63, folder 2, DSP. The police disrupted the November 1936 meeting. Deutsch, "New School Lecture 'An Army of Women,'" 109.

114. Domínguez to Adelia di Carlo, November 5, 1933, caja 673, no. 9, ODN-AN. In 1935, Adelia di Carlo publicized an adulatory account of Domínguez, praising her inter-

American feminism. Adelia di Carlo, "Los grandes valores femeninos de América: Ofelia Domínguez Navarro," *Caras y Caretas* (Buenos Aires), March 30, 1935.

115. Lutz conveyed this information to YWCA worker Mary Corbett in Brazil, who then told Carrie Chapman Catt and Josephine Schain. Mary Corbett to Josephine Schain, July 13, 1936, box 6, folder 18, JSP.

116. Susana G. de Lapacó to Bertha Lutz, July 9, 1938, Qo.ADM, COR.1938.29, AFBPF. Adelia di Carlo de Carimati represented the Asociacón Clorinda Matto de Turner. Susana G. de Lapacó was affiliated with the Biblioteca Theosofica Argentina. "Conferencia Argentina de Mujeres por la Paz," box 63, folder 3; "Declaración de la Mujer Argentina," box 62, folder 3, DSP.

117. Vergara, "Ecos y resultados de la Conferencia Popular por la Paz de Buenos Aires," *La Mujer Nueva*, December 1936, 5. Delia Rojas de White told Heloise Brainerd that Vergara did not want the Confederación, what Rojas called a "*Liga Continental Pacifista*," to include women from the U.S. because Vergara believed "the problems of the South American nations are different from those of other countries." Delia Rojas de White to Heloise Brainerd, March 25, 1937, box 24, part 3, series A,4, Part 1, WILPF.

118. "Las empleadas tendrán salario minimo igual al hombre," *La Mujer Nueva*, December 1936, 1.

119. Stevens to Smith, April 11, 1938, box 90, folder 17, DSP.

120. The commission inserted a study of maternity legislation throughout the Americas into its comprehensive research on women's civil and political rights, reporting on "pregnancy, maternity and other social benefits to the end that better conditions for mothers, and especially working mothers be consummated in industry, commerce, and agriculture." IACW report to Lima Conference, 1938, DSP.

121. Emphasis mine. Luisi, *Condiciones del trabajo femenino*, 11. See also *Women and Social Movements International*, http://wasi.alexanderstreet.com/, (accessed November 5, 2015).

122. Luisi, *Condiciones del trabajo femenino*, 11–12.

CHAPTER 6

1. Evelyn Rigby Moore to Doris Stevens, October 3, 1937, box 84, folder 5, DSP. In 1936, after learning of González's plans to travel to Mexico, Panamanian President Juan Demostenes Arosemena, believing that she intended "to make contacts with... Bolsheviks," removed González from her recently appointed position granted her by the Chamber of Deputies, to be secretary of a committee that would study legislation and propose reforms for the 1938 assembly. Arosemena replaced her with the brother of the secretary of the government. The following year the government reduced her teaching hours by half at the National Institute, resulting in a halving of her salary. González suspected this punishment was retaliation for support she gave Diógenes de la Rosa, a trade union leader and Trotskyist who in 1934 had established the Marxist-Leninist Workers' Party (that in 1935 merged with the Socialist Party of Panama) and had been arrested in 1937 for his energetic leadership of the Popular Front. Alexander, *International Trotskyism*, 636. Marco Serra, *Clara González de Behringer*, 125. In these years, the Socialist Party in Panama was also supporting West Indian workers against the xenophobia and racism of the Acción Comunal. Lasso, "Race and Ethnicity in the Formation of Panamanian National Identity," 72–74.

2. Moore to Stevens, October 3, 1937, box 84, folder 5, DSP. On Mexico as an international haven for leftists escaping political persecution, see S. Smith, *Power and Politics of Revolutionary Mexico*, 15.

3. The FUPDM women with whom she met were Mathilde Rodríguez Cabo, Isabel de Cossío, and Esther Chapa, all of whom were Ofelia Domínguez Navarro's friends.

They were professional women, reformers, and members of the Communist Party. Clara González to Doris Stevens, July 11, 1938, box 84, folder 8, DSP.

4. Domínguez Navarro, "Biografía de Ofelia Domínguez Navarro sus ascendientes y su hogar," 3/237.1/1–29, ODN-IH. For a brief time in 1935, Domínguez also lived in New York City, where she organized with other exiled Cubans and with Mexicans, Puerto Ricans, and Italians in protest of the Cuban government under Carlos Mendieta. Domínguez Navarro, 50 años, 284–85, 353–61; Gronbeck-Tedesco, 251. On the FUPDM, see Olcott, *Revolutionary Women*; and Tuñón Pablos, *Mujeres que se organizan*. For more on Domínguez's collaborations with Mexican feminists, see Olcott, "Center Cannot Hold," 230; and Cano, "Una perspectiva."

5. Domínguez was rallying support for Cárdenas's plans to nationalize the oil industry. In 1936 Domínguez also became a member of the Liga de Escritores y Artistas Revolucionarios and of the Frente Socialista de Abogados in Mexico. Report by Clark D. Anderson on "Dr. Ofelia Dominguez Navarro," Federal Bureau of Investigation, 8/31/50, 24 pp. (obtained under the Freedom of Information Act from U.S. Federal Bureau of Investigation, requested as "Ofelia Domínguez Navarro" June 2015, received August 2016).

6. Jane Eads, "Liberty Lies in Cooperation, Feminist Warns Conference," *Washington Herald*, January 19, 1938; "Feminist Move Shifts," *Washington Evening Star*, January 19, 1938; "Thanks Sent Mexico for Suffrage Bill," *WP*, January 19, 1938; Mildred Kahler Geare, "Women Support Mexican Bill for Suffrage," *Baltimore News-Post*, January 19, 1938.

7. Waltz, *Nationality of Married Women*. The Women's Consultative Committee had worked closely with the IACW and Latin American delegates to introduce the Equal Rights and Equal Nationality Treaties into the League of Nations Assembly in 1935 and 1937. Alexandra Kollontai, a member of the Soviet delegation, was one of the most avid supporters of these equal rights resolutions. In 1938 the League of Nations created the "Committee of Experts on the Status of Women" to study women's rights internationally. "Debate at League of Nations," *Equal Rights*, October 15, 1935, 1–3; Pfeffer, "'A Whisper in the Assembly of Nations.'"

8. Margarita Robles de Mendoza, "La igualdad de derechos para la mujer," 1937, box 661, no. 22, María Collado, Donativos y Remisiones, Archivo Nacional, Havana. "Discurso pronunciado por la Sra. Z. Evangelina A. de Vaughan Presidenta de la Union de Mujeres Americanas," March 5, 1937, box 92, folder 1, DSP.

9. Robles de Mendoza to Lázaro Cárdenas, February 16, 1939, 702.2–11130, Lázaro Cárdenas, Archivo General de la Nación, Mexico City; on the Nicaraguan UMA branch, see González-Rivera, *Before the Revolution*, 35.

10. Vaughan to Stevens, November 23, 1936, box 92, folder 1, DSP. Although the UMA did not ally with the World Committee of Women against War and Fascism or the Communist Party, it did ally with the Spanish Republic, identifying communist Spanish Civil War fighter Dolores Ibárruri as its heroine. The UMA also decried the Anti-Comintern Pact and Japan's invasion of China.

11. "Hermoso ejemplo de solidaridad," *La Mujer Nueva*, March 1937, 6. "The interests of the woman are inextricably linked," Argentine feminist Victoria Ocampo wrote. "The legislation of one country usually has repercussions in another, which justifies our international fight for our rights."

12. Chapa, *El derecho de voto para la mujer*, 4, quoted in Olcott, *Revolutionary Women*, 164. FUPDM leaders sought the vote as a tool to achieve multiple goals for women, including legalized abortion. Cano, "Una perspectiva del aborto en los años treinta"; Ofelia Domínguez Navarro, "El aborto por causas sociales y económicas," *Futuro*, June 1939, 19.

13. Felicia Santizo, untitled speech, April 6, 1938, box 84, folder 6, DSP. The organ of

Marta Vergara's MEMCh reproduced Santizo's words verbatim, though did not credit her in "Por qué pedimos el derecho al voto politico," *La Mujer Nueva*, July 1939, 4.

14. Due to feminist pressure, President Cárdenas conceded in a November 1937 speech before Congress that women's suffrage fulfilled the promises of the Mexican Revolution and urged Congress to pass an amendment granting women the right to vote and to be elected to office. Soon after, the Senate voted to adopt woman suffrage and the constitutional amendment was awaiting action by the Mexican Chamber of Deputies. Olcott, *Revolutionary Women*, 181.

15. Fanny Bunand-Sevastos to Doris Stevens, June 24, 1937, box 29, folder 5; Stevens to John White, August 14, 1937, box 73, folder 6; Stevens to Bunand-Sevastos, December 15, 1937, box 29, folder 5, DSP. Stevens shared the sentiments of her good friend writer Max Eastman, who in 1937 condemned Stalin's totalitarian dictatorship. Eastman, *End of Socialism in Russia*.

16. Stevens to González, July 15, 1935, box 84, folder 8; Stevens to Helen Robbins Bitterman, October 29, 1938, box 62, folder 1, DSP.

17. Stevens to González, September 25, 1936, box 85, folder 5, DSP. Stevens told González that the Liaison Committee was partially inspired by a proposal González had made at the 1930 Havana conference for the commission to work more actively and directly with feminist groups.

18. Stevens also utilized the new Liaison Committee to protest a plan by Ecuador's military dictator Federico Páez to revoke women's suffrage from the constitution, which ultimately did not happen. "Memorandum re: women's suffrage in Ecuador," box 66, folder 13; Stevens to González, September 25, 1936, box 84, folder 5; "Draft letter to the Commissioners," sent to Minerva Bernardino, August 5, 1937, box 74, folder 16, DSP; Lauderbaugh, *History of Ecuador*, 104.

19. Stevens to González, September 25, 1936, box 85, folder 5, DSP.

20. "Una mujer norteamericana reclama los derechos de la mujer hondureña," *Alma Latina*, 5, no. 53, March 1936, 1–2, quoted in Villars, *Para la casa más que para el mundo*, 298–301.

21. "Mulheres," *Correio da Manhã* (Rio de Janeiro), October 6, 1938. The article said the vote was a dead letter in so many countries like Peru where dictatorships reigned.

22. Morton, *Woman Suffrage in Mexico*, 21. See also speech by Cuca García in American League for Peace and Democracy, *Proceedings*.

23. The FUPDM insisted that "to eliminate the right of suffrage ... would ... place [Ecuador] at the rear of the social and political movement of America." "La Mujer Ecuatoriana en Peligro de perder sus DERECHOS," *La Mujer Nueva* (Mexico), June 1937. DSP.

24. For more on Robles de Mendoza, see Olcott, *Revolutionary Women*, 165, 172; Threlkeld, *Pan American Women*, 144, 165–70, 175, 183–91, 196–99; and Lau Javien, "Entre ambas fronteras."

25. The U.S. woman was Anna Kelton Wiley. "Mrs. Wiley Addresses Women of Mexico" and "Message of Cuca García to Women of North America," *Equal Rights*, July 15, 1937, 102. See also Olcott, *Revolutionary Women*, 176–77.

26. See *Rules and Regulations*. After protracted debates, the conference ultimately adopted resolutions endorsing suffrage and equal pay for equal work for male and female teachers and congratulating President Cárdenas on his recent declarations for women's suffrage in Mexico. "Equality for Women Scores Another Victory," *Equal Rights*, October 1, 1937, 141. The Inter-American Conference on Education took place August 22–29, 1937, in Mexico City. As Margarita Robles de Mendoza later speculated, perhaps FUPDM leaders "consider that there are things of more importance [than suffrage] to be dis-

cussed, or may be [sic] [their objections were] because all we Mexicans are inborn rebels and do not like to be bossed by any one." Robles Mendoza to Stevens, August 25, 1937, box 77, folder 9, DSP. The union that Vicente Lombardo Toledano led was the Confederación de Trabajadores Mexicanos.

27. L. Meyer, *Mexico and the United States*, chapter 8. Even U.S. Ambassador to Mexico Josephus Daniels admitted the oil companies' labor practices were "unscrupulous." L. Meyer, 165.

28. María del Refugio García to Doris Stevens, April 21, 1938, box 77, folder 2, DSP.

29. Stevens to García, May 2, 1938, box 77, folder 2, DSP.

30. The group seems to have gone by several names. In 1938 Susana G. de Lapacó described the group as "una Liga de mujeres americanas de Norte a Sud" (a League of American women from North to South). Lapacó to Brainerd, May 25, 1938, box 22, part 3, series A, 4, part 1, WILPF. I am using the name that Vergara gave the group: "Confederación Continental de Mujeres por la Paz."

31. Carta Circular No. 4, Internacional Femenina Por Paz y Libertad, Comité de las Américas, May 14, 1938, box 85, folder 2, DSP.

32. "Sólo aspiro a que la Luz de la Libertad y de la Paz nos Ilumine," *La Mujer Nueva*, November 1937, 7. According to U.S. YWCA leader Helen Hayes Weed, who led the Buenos Aires YWCA at this time, the Federación Argentina de Mujeres por la Paz, which was the seedbed for the Confederación Continental de Mujeres por la Paz, included in Argentina the Unión Argentina de Mujeres, the Partido Socialista Obrero, the Federacíon Obrera del Vestido, the Liga Argentina Contra Alcoholismo, and the Unión de Mujeres Argentinas. She noted all of these groups were "leftist" peace groups that also supported women's rights; the nonleftist (and U.S.-led) YWCA was not involved. Helen Hayes to Josephine Schain, June 12, 1939, box 60, folder 20, JSP.

33. Delia Rojas de White to Brainerd, March 25, 1937, box 24 and Lapacó to Brainerd, May 25, 1938, part 3, box 22, series A,4, part 1, WILPF.34. Carta Circular No 4, Internacional Femenina Por Paz y Libertad, Comité de las Américas, May 14, 1938, box 85, folder 2, DSP.

35. Lapacó to Bertha Lutz, July 9, 1938, Qo.ADM, COR.1938.29, AFBPF.

36. "Se ha iniciadio en nuestro país los preparativos para el II Congreso Mundial de la Juventud," *Claridad*, May 1938; "El II Congreso Mundial de la Juventud por la Paz (Valiosa aportación del Grupo Universitario 'América'),'" *Claridad*, September 1938.

37. *Youth Demands a Peaceful World*. Future civil rights leader Dorothy Height was one of the ten youths whom Eleanor Roosevelt invited to spend a weekend in Hyde Park to prepare for the World Youth Conference. "Dorothy Height," in Huock and Dixon, *Women and the Civil Rights Movement*, 220.

38. *Youth Demands a Peaceful World*. For more on the conference, see R. Cohen, *When the Old Left Was Young*, 184–87.

39. Vaughan to González, September 6, 1938, ACG. The PNF member was Mélida Maciá, a lawyer, treasurer of the PNF, and editor of its new news bulletin *Nosotras*. González to Stevens, August 7, 1938; González to Stevens, September 25, 1938, box 84, folder 8, DSP. The Mexican feminists were Josefina Rivera Torres, secretary of the Federation of State Workers, and Emma Sánchez Montalvo of the Autonomous University of Mexico.

40. UMA had been planning such a gathering at Lima since 1936. Robles de Mendoza, Memorandum Para el General de División Lázaro Cárdenas, November 12, 1936, Presidente de la República, L-E-270, GE-SRE.

41. Helen Hayes to Josephine Schain, June 12, 1939, box 60, folder 20, JSP; Lapacó to Brainerd, November 23, 1938, box 22, part 3, series A,4, part 1, WILPF.

42. A Bahá'í history reports that "Mrs. Frances Benedict Stewart was entrusted with the task of opening the doors of South America." Khan, *Heritage of Light*, 171. Stewart explained to WILPF president Dorothy Detzer: "I am myself da Bahai, affiliated, therefore, with no orthodox church . . . I work in and with Jewish temples, Catholic churches, etc. and they all know I have no religious bias, but am solely interested in human justice and Peace. I am so very busy corresponding with women all over S. America who want material for Peace study and action." Stewart to Detzer, October 20, 1937, box 31, part 3, series C, WILPF.

43. Frances Benedict Stewart, "The People's Conference," *World Order*, vol. 3, 1938, 126; Hayes to Schain, June 12, 1939, series 4: Organizations, Inter-American Conf. for Peace, JSP.

44. Stewart lived for a time with Marxist feminist and dentist Rosa Scheiner, who was a member of Partido Socialista Obrero in Argentina. Hayes to Schain, January 12, 1937, box 6, folder 20, JSP. In November 1938, Stewart was staying as a guest in Lapacó's home. Lapacó to Brainerd, November 23, 1938, box 22, part 3, series A,4, part 1, WILPF.

45. Stewart to Stevens, July 22, 1937, box 67, folder 2, DSP; Stewart to Detzer, February 3, 1938, box 31, WILPF.

46. Lapacó reached out to U.S. WILPF leader Heloise Brainerd informally as well. At this time, WILPF was forging connections with the growing numbers of antifascist feminists in the Americas. Stewart was a member of the WILPF's "Inter-American Committee" created in 1935 and led by Brainerd, former head of the Pan-American Union's inter-American intellectual committee, but Stewart was dismayed that Brainerd did not take a principled stand against what Stewart called the U.S. "war against Mexico" during the oil crisis. Stewart wrote to WILPF president Dorothy Detzer, urging a direct response to the Mexican oil crisis. Stewart to Detzer, March 28, 1938, WILPF; "500 Represent 57 Nations at Congress Here," *Vassar Miscellany News*, October 1, 1938, 4.

47. Stewart was likely a bridge between these two groups, conveying to FUPDM feminists the Confederación plans to gather at the Pan-American conference in Lima and organize a continental antifascist feminist conference to take place in Mexico the following year. The Mexican feminists at the World Youth Congress also likely helped forge these collaborations.

48. Balmaceda later told Stevens that she had consulted with Robles de Mendoza on plans for the Lima conference, although Robles de Mendoza denied this. Robles de Mendoza told Stevens that FUPDM's interest in in the IACW had been piqued by a speech she had given at the dinner and rally but insisted that, although Balmaceda had reached out to her, they had not communicated. Robles de Mendoza and Balmaceda were both present, however, at the rally and dinner honoring Nelken, and it seems probable that they did collaborate, as Balmaceda indicated to Stevens. Their plans to organize an extra-official women's conference in Lima resonated with Robles de Mendoza's long-standing plan to gather a UMA conference there. "Spanish Socialist Woman Deputy Here for Mexico Parley," *Daily Worker*, September 2, 1938; Morton, *Woman Suffrage in Mexico*, 36–37; Robles de Mendoza to Stevens, April 17, 1939; and Stevens to Robles de Mendoza, May 17, 1939, box 77, folder 3, DSP.

49. The key FUPDM leader who facilitated this was Mathilde Rodríguez Cabo Guzmán, head of the Social Security Department in the Cárdenas government, wife of one of the ministers of state, and close friend of the wife of Lázaro Cárdenas. Balmaceda was

appointed October 18, 1838. Acuerdo a la Secretaría de Relaciones Exteriores, October 18, 1938, L-E-276, 104, GE-SRE. The Mexican delegation was made official by October 21, 1938. Ernesto Hidalgo to C. Encargado de Negocios a.i. de México, October 21, 1938, SRE L-E-276, GE-SRE.

50. Robles de Mendoza to Stevens, April 17, 1939, box 77, folder 3, DSP.

51. They also reflected a list of requests that Margarita Robles de Mendoza sent to Leo Rowe of the Pan American Union following the Montevideo conference. Robles de Mendoza to Leo Rowe, translation of undated letter, box 77, folder 9, DSP.

52. Srta. Profesora Carlota de Gortari Carbajal, "Nuestra Delegada a la VIII Conferencia en Lima," *Vida Femenina*, December 15, 1938, 10–11. *Vida Femenina* began in 1933 by Socialist Party leaders and feminists Alicia Moreau de Justo and Maria Berrodondo and in 1938 was published by Moreau de Justo and Josefina Marpons.

53. Gortari Carbajal, 11. A recent Latin American Labor Congress in Mexico City had established a Latin American labor union federation to include all Latin American countries in a fight against fascism.

54. These women, in Mexico for the 5th Congress of the Confederación Americana del Magisterio, told then-Mexican IACW representative Amalia de Castillo Ledón about Balmaceda's plans. Castillo Ledón to Bernardino, July 17, 1946, caja 11, exp. 172, AGC-SRE.

55. The number of ethnic Haitians killed was roughly 15,000. Turtis, "World Destroyed," 590. Stevens, *Red International and Black Caribbean*, 255. Margaret Stevens explains that the Communist Party in the U.S. failed to effectively rally in solidarity around this event.

56. "Trujillo Promises Rights for Women," NYT, August 15, 1938, 8.

57. She added that she hoped he would add to this list "one more immortal act— the granting to [women] . . . the right to elect and be elected, a fundamental right in democracy." Doris Stevens speech given and broadcast over station HIN in the Palacio del Consejo Administrativo of Santo Domingo, August 12, 1938, box 66, folder 6, DSP. Trujillo pledged that he would recommend Congress pass a constitutional revision granting women suffrage, but he did not follow through with a suffrage amendment. For more on Stevens's visit to the Dominican Republic, see Manley, *Paradox of Paternalism*, 52–54.

58. This information was conveyed to the State Department by U.S. ambassador in the Dominican Republic R. Henry Norweb to Secretary of State Cordell Hull, August 17, 1938, 710.F IACW/17, D.F. RG 59.

59. Stevens to Evangelina Vaughan, September 16, 1938, box 92, folder 1, DSP. She told Vaughan that she was "getting some abuse by mail and otherwise for having gone to confer with such a 'cruel dictator, etc, etc.'"

60. "Minutes of Committee Meeting of Inter American Commission of Women Held in Pan-American Union, Washington, D.C., June 25, 1938, 11 a.m.," box 75, folder 7, DSP.

61. González to Stevens, October 26, 1938, box 75, folder 14, DSP.

62. Stevens to John White, November 16, 1938, box 74, folder 17, DSP.

63. Stevens to Mitchell, November 29, 1938, box 25, folder 4, DSP.

64. Elise Musser to Molly Dewson (and Mary Anderson), March 17, 1938, box 8, folder "Equal Rights Amendment, 1937–46," Mary (Molly) Dewson Papers, Franklin D. Roosevelt Presidential Library and Museum, Hyde Park, N.Y.

65. Elise Musser to Mary Anderson, December 18, 1937; Musser to Mary Dewson, March 3, 1938, "Equal Rights—1939," box 18, RG 86; Musser to Welles, August 3, 1938, 710.F IACW/15, D.F., RG 59.

66. "Doris Stevens Leaves Today for Dominica," WP, August 9, 1938; Molly Dewson to Sumner Welles, August 11, 1938, 710.F IACW/18, D.F., RG 59; Dewson to Welles,

March 9, 1938, Mary (Molly) Dewson Papers, Franklin D. Roosevelt Presidential Library and Museum.

67. Sophonisba Breckinridge also encouraged Mary Anderson to write to Lutz in 1935. Anderson to Lutz, January 5, 1935, Qo.ADM, COR.1935, p. 1; Lutz to Perkins, December 24, 1935, Qo.ADM, COR.1935, p. 10; Lutz to Catt, May 14, 1936, Qo.ADM, COR.1936.25, p. 13; Miller to Lutz, August 3, 1937, Qo.ADM, COR.1937.28, p. 1; Breckinridge to Lutz, March 10, 1934, Qo.ADM, COR.1934, p. 1, AFBPF.

68. Lutz to Berle, November 27, 1936, and FBPF Bulletin, box 60, folder "Inter-American Conference for the Maintenance of Peace," Buenos Aires, 1936–37, Adolf A. Berle Papers, Franklin De. Roosevelt Presidential Library and Museum, Hyde Park, N.Y.

69. The Buenos Aires Conference, record of main events, box 63, folder 3, DSP.

70. Roorda, *Dictator Next Door*. Roosevelt famously called a number of dictatorships in the Caribbean and Central America—Anastasio Somoza in Nicaragua, Trujillo in the Dominican Republic, and Fulgencio Batista in Cuba—"S.O.B.s . . . [but] our S.O.B.s." Schnitz, *Thank God They're on Our Side*. On divides among State Department officials in the FDR administration, see M. Friedman, *Nazis and Good Neighbors*, 75, 78–79. Years later, Senator McCarthy would make the infamous declaration that the State Department was "infested" with communists. Duggan would fall to his death from his New York office window in 1948, ten days after the FBI questioned him about contacts with Soviet intelligence. See Storrs, *Second Red Scare*, 123 and Stevens, "Welles after Lima," draft of book manuscript, box 127, folder 5, DSP.

71. Memo from Warren Kelchner to Duggan and Welles, June 18, 1938, 710.F IACW/13, D.F. RG 59.

72. Welles to Duggan, memorandum, March 9, 1938; Kelchner, "Inter-American Commission of Women," memorandum, March 15, 1938; Kelchner, IACW memo, June 18, 1938; Elise Musser to Sumner Welles, August 20, 1938; Henry Norweb, "Visit of Miss Doris Stevens . . . ," Dispatch No. 412, August 17, 1938; Musser to Welles, August 20, 1938, 710.F IACW/19-23, 20, 17, D.F. RG 59.

73. Mary Anderson to Perkins, September 19, 1938; Anderson to Perkins, November 19, 1938; Anderson memo to Perkins on Louise Leonard Wright, November 12, 1938, box 45, Office of the Secretary Frances Perkins, General Subject File, 1933–1941, RG 174.

74. This resolution was based on the Women's Charter, a document drawn up by the Women's Bureau and communist labor organizer Mary van Kleeck, which would take a "positive" and leftist approach to international women's rights. Mary Anderson to Frances Perkins, September 19, 1938; Mary Anderson to Perkins, May 13, 1937, box 107, Office of the Secretary Frances Perkins, General Subject File, 1933–1941, RG 174. For more on the Women's Charter, see Lynn, "Women's Charter."

75. "Instructions to the Delegates of the Eighth International Conference of American States, Lima, Peru," State Department Subject File, 1938–45, Latin American Republics: Conferences, 1936–40, Adolf A. Berle Papers, Franklin D. Roosevelt Presidential Library and Museum.

76. This woman was Elisabeth Shirley Enochs, and Anderson and Winslow used funds from the Women's Bureau and National Woman's Trade Union League to pay her. Mary Anderson to Frances Perkins, November 19, 1938, box 45, Office of the Secretary Frances Perkins, General Subject File, 1933–1941, RG 174. They told Perkins about hiring Enochs but said that they were not going to make this fact known more broadly.

77. "Every person I was seen lunching with . . . man or woman, was straightaway approached." Stevens to Mitchell, December 29, 1938, box 25, folder 5; "Lima—Another example of preemptory attitude, Duggan," box 127, folder 3, DSP.

78. "Lima—Another example of preemptory attitude, Duggan," box 127, folder 3, DSP.

79. "Lima—Enroute—Mrs. Wright," box 127, folder 3, DSP. The assistant was Louise Leonard Wright.

80. Stevens to Mercedes Gallagher de Parks, January 27, 1939, box 85, folder 5, DSP.

81. 1938 Eighth International Conference of American States book notes, box 127, folder 3; Stevens to Vergara, November 7, 1938, box 64, folder 7; Stevens to Mitchell, December 29, 1938, box 25, folder 5, DSP.

82. Vergara to Stevens, undated handwritten note, box 64, folder 5, DSP. Graciela Mandujano, a founding member of MEMCh, had attended the 1922 Pan-American conference in Baltimore.

83. Rosa Maria Martínez-Guerrero, "A Message to the Women of the Americas," *World Order*, vol. 4, 1938, 212. This was a "Pan-American Day" address. Frances Benedict Stewart had translated this article into English. Larguía and Schlieper were friends with Frances B. Stewart and Susana G. de Lapacó. Lapacó had given Larguía and Schlieper a pamphlet outlining the goals of the Confederación Continental to bring to the Lima conference. Lapacó to Brainerd, November 23, 1938, box 22, part 3, series A,4, part 1, WILPF. For more on Schlieper's background and activism around the Lima conference, see Deutsch, chapter 1 of *Engendering Antifascism*, 26–28.

84. Elena Caffarena de Jiles, "Las Mujeres y la Octava Conferencia Panamericana," undated, without place of publication, A1, 2, Archivo de Elena Caffarena, Santiago, Chile. I am very grateful to Karin Rosemblatt for sharing this source with me.

85. "Significado de la 8a Conf Panamericana," *La Mujer Nueva*, December 1938.

86. *New York Times* correspondent Jonathan White quoted in "Accusing Lima Hosts—a Problem Remaining," *New Orleans Item*, January 8, 1939. The same article noted that at the outset of the conference, Lima itself "appeared to be the site of a great Nazi rally rather than of a Pan-American conference [with] . . . literally thousands of swastika flags all over the city."

87. Notes on 1938 Eighth International Conference of American States, 1951–1960, box 127, folder 3, DSP.

88. Notes on 1938 Eighth International Conference of American States, 1951–1960, box 127, folders 3 and 4; Stevens to Mitchell, December 29, 1938, box 25, folder 5, DSP.

89. Emphasis Vergara's. Vergara to Stevens, December 20, 1938, box 64, folder 5, DSP.

90. Book notes: narrative pieces and notes, 1949–1962, box 127, folder 7, DSP.

91. Domínguez, "Las latinoamericanas disfrutaron el papel de comparsas," El País (Havana), February 28, 1930.

92. Mitchell to Stevens, December 16, 1938, box 25, folder 5, DSP. The "pukka" or "pukha sahib" refers to the English gentleman in the British Empire, particularly the posture of British administrators: "the aloof, impartial, incorruptible arbiter of the political fate of a large part of the earth's surface." M. Freedman, "Race against Time." Stevens and Mitchell had married in 1935.

93. Stevens to Mitchell, December 29, 1938, box 25, folder 5, DSP.

94. In the years after she was dethroned as commission chair, racist discourse more frequently punctuated Stevens's correspondence. In a letter to her friend Rebecca West she wrote, "The little dark ones keep writing for instructions on this and that," by whom she meant Minerva Bernardino and Marta Vergara, who continued to seek her advice. Stevens to Rebecca West, September 11, 1941, Rebecca West Papers, Beinecke Rare Book and Manuscript Library, Yale University, New Haven, Conn.

95. Typed notes on U.S. State Department's confidential file on Doris Stevens and IACW, 1960, with Jonathan Mitchell notes, box 26, folder 5, DSP.

96. Lic. Ramón Beteta to C. Subsecretario de la Asistencia Pública, November 5, 1938, L-E-280, GE-SRE.

97. Stevens observed Balmaceda was the "conspicuous leader" at these meetings and called her a "'propagandist' rather than the worker type" of communist. 1938 Eighth International Conference of American States, 1951–1960, box 127, folder 3, DSP.

98. Enochs, "Women at Lima Won Solidarity," NYT, January 8, 1939.

99. Enochs, "Women at Lima Won Solidarity"; "Women's Interests at the Lima Conference," Woman Worker, March 1939; reports on newsclippings from Universal in "Summary of News Items Referring to the Conference in the Lima Newspapers," December 16, 1938, box 38, folder 7, JBSP.

100. Pruneda, Departamento de Salubridad Pública, Memoria del VII Congreso Panamericano del Niño. Ofelia Domínguez Navarro also participated in this conference, which was later celebrated by socialist Argentinian feminists for its resolutions supporting maternity legislation and day-care centers for working women. Marpons, La mujer en el trabajo, 138.

101. Notes on 1938 Eighth International Conference of American States, 1951–1960, box 127, folders 3 and 4, DSP. Although Stevens enlisted the head of the Cuban delegation, Juan J. Remos, to serve as the chairman of the Fourth Committee, he had to leave the conference after the first full day, making Musser its chair.

102. This Pan-American conference passed resolutions rather than treaties.

103. Stevens to Mitchell, box 25, folder 5, DSP.

104. "Apoyo a moción sobre derechos de las mujeres," La Nación (Santiago), December 18, 1938; Lic. Pablo Campos Ortíz to C. Secreatrio General de la Delegación de México a la Octava Conferencia Internacional Americana, Lima, Perú, December 19, 1938, L-E-280, GE-SRE. See also "Chile apoyara en Lima moción de Mejico sobre derechos de la mujer," newspaper article undated and without publication information, box 64, folder 5, DSP.

105. Diario de sesiones, December 15, 1938, 540.

106. Diario de sesiones, December 15, 1938, 540.

107. Diario de sesiones, December 20, 1938, 567.

108. Diario de sesiones, December 20, 1938, 562.

109. As a delegate in the 1936 Buenos Aires conference, Coelho Lisboa, working with Doris Stevens, had introduced the commission resolution for civil and political rights into the proceedings. Bertha Lutz had sent Coelho Lisboa instructions for reorganizing the IACW at the conference, but Coelho Lisboa ignored Lutz's orders. Clara Curtis to Mary Anderson, November 30, 1938, box 10 "International Labor Organization (1936–1939)," RG 86. For more on the feminism of the Ação Integralista Brasileira and other right-wing groups in Brazil, Argentina, and Chile, see Deutsch, Las Derechas, 288–89.

110. Coelho Lisboa stated that Brazil's progressiveness regarding women's rights would make Balmaceda's Inter-American Congress unnecessary there.

111. Stevens to Mitchell, December 29, 1938, box 25, folder 5, DSP. After the 1936 Buenos Aires conference, Marta Vergara had published an article calling out Coelho Lisboa's fascism in La Mujer Nueva—"Una mujer defiende las dictaduras," La Mujer Nueva, March 1937, 5. When U.S. delegation members questioned Stevens about her close relationship with the Dominican delegate Cestero, who was "against feminism," Stevens later replied, "He's my friend and so is his boss [Trujillo]. In a cabal of this kind, I pick a friend." Stevens to Mitchell, December 29, 1938, box 25, folder 5, DSP.

112. *Diario de sesiones*, December 22, 1938, 572; "El día de hoy es un día histórico para las mujeres de América—declaró la Sra. Balmaceda de Josefé," *La Crónica*, December 23, 1938.

113. John W. White, "Betrayal by U.S. Is Charged at Lima," NYT, December 21, 1938.

114. Her insistence that the conference not be stymied by "censorship" alluded not only to attempts to quell her feminist resolutions but also the Cuban and Mexican resolutions. "We insist on our right to study, discuss, and debate all problems before this conference—not only the question now before this committee, but all other matters on the agenda." *Diario de sesiones*, December 20, 1938, 562.

115. "American Nations Adopt Unity Plan; Bar Persecution," NYT, December 12, 1938.

116. "A Program for All," *New Orleans Times Picayune*, January 11, 1939.

117. In the "Declaration in the Defense of Human Rights," the governments of the Americas expressed concern over humanitarian consequences of the impending armed conflict. When war broke out "in any other region of the world," the statement averred, "respect [should] be given to those human rights not necessarily involved in the conflict, to humanitarian sentiments, and to the spiritual and material inheritance of civilization.'" One newspaper article noted of Lima, "The American republics . . . have made a most valuable contribution to a system of international relations based upon law and upon respect for the rights of all nations and of all individuals regardless of race or religion." "Program for All."

118. García Montes and Alonso Avila, *Historia del Partido Comunista de Cuba*, 223.

119. "Resoluciones de la II Asamblea Nacional del Partido 'Unión Revolucionaria,' Celebrada en la Habana, los dias 14 y 15 de enero de 1939," ODN-AN. See de la Fuente, *Nation for All.*

120. María Sabas Alomá called Jim Crow segregation a "monstrosity." Sabas, Alomá, *Feminismo*, 165. When Eleanor Roosevelt resigned from the Daughters of the American Revolution in 1939 when it barred African American singer Marian Anderson from performing at its Constitution Hall in Washington, D.C., the FUPDM celebrated Roosevelt's stand against racism. Otilia Zambrano, "Mrs. Roosevelt y la Revolución," *Cauce* [undated], 23, caja 1, sección Revistas, exp. 6, Grupo Otilia Zambrano, Archivo General de la Nación, Mexico City. Many thanks to Jocelyn Olcott for sharing this finding with me.

121. Josefina Sapena Pastos de Grand, "A nadie como a la mujer debe interesar la conquista de la paz universal," box 24, part 3, series A,4, part 1, WILPF; "La mujer india en Peru," *La Mujer Nueva*, February 1936, 2. On black communist feminism, see McDuffie, *Sojourning for Freedom*. On the power of women's Pan-African organizing in these years, Blain, *Set the World on Fire*. On Caribbean migration and Pan-Africanism in the Americas see Putnam, *Radical Moves.*

122. "Temario del Tercer Congreso Nacional de Mujeres," 1939, caja 675, no. 17, ODN-AN.

123. Ofelia Domínguez Navarro, "La mujer y los prejuicios raciales," 3/28.1/1–29, ODN-IH. This concept of "triple discrimination" had been introduced by earlier Afro-Cuban labor women in the 1920s who were active in fights for reform. Brunson, "Constructing Afro-Cuban Womanhood," 209–10, 221–23.

124. Robles de Mendoza to Stevens, April 17, 1939, box 77, folder 3; Robles de Mendoza to Stevens, March 15, 1939, box 77, folder 9, DSP; Edith García Buchanan to Lázaro Cárdenas, exp 433/391, Lázaro Cárdenas, Archivo General de la Nación, Mexico City. Cuban feminists explicitly reached out to Balmaceda and other FUPDM members attending the conference to promote their Popular Front goals.

125. Vergara told Stevens that Balmaceda had visited her in the hospital. Vergara to Stevens, April 5, 1939, and Stevens to Vergara, June 25, 1939, box 64, folder 5, DSP.

126. Book notes: Eleanor Roosevelt and IACW, 1945–1959, box 127, folder 8, DSP; Frank R. Kent, "The Great Game of Politics," LAT, February 22, 1939, 7; Pfeffer, "Eleanor Roosevelt," 50.

127. Transcription of recorded narrative of IACW, ca. 1960, box 126, folder 5, DSP.

128. Luisi to Balmaceda, August 24, 1939; Luisi to Josefa Vidaurreta de Marinello, June 15, 1939, caja 253, carpeta 2, PL-AGN.

129. Instituto Uruguayo de Investigación y Lucha Contra el Fascismo, el Racismo, y el Antisemitismo, Estatutos del Instituto Uruguayo.

130. "Democracies of the West Are Urged to Ban Fascism," Christian Science Monitor, March 20, 1939, 3; César Vilar, "The Unity of the American Democracies," The Communist 18, no. 7 (1939): 624–33; Manuel Seoane, "El Congreso Continental de las Democracias," Claridad, June 1939; Paulina Luisi, "Congreso de las Democracias de América: Derechos de la mujer y tratado de derechos iguales," Temario B, Sección V, N° 40 – 41, doc. 50, sección 3, serie 3.2, PL-ACRE; Declaraciones de Montevideo, 3–12; Luisi to Heloise Brainerd, September 16, 1941, box 30, part 3, series A,4, part 1, WILPF. MEMCh was also invited to the Montevideo meeting. "El MEMCh es invitado al Congreso de la Democracia," La Mujer Nueva, December 1938, 7.

131. Robles de Mendoza told Stevens that the Cuba congress was postponed because of lack of money. Robles de Mendoza to Stevens, April 17, 1939, box 77, folder 3, DSP.

132. Ibárruri, Women Want a People's Peace, 58.

133. Paulina Luisi, "Por la Paz y la Libertad, Congreso Mundial de Mujeres," caja 252, carpeta 5, PL-AGN.

134. Comité Femenina Paz y Libertad, Congreso Mundial de Mujeres, October 1939, caja 252, carpeta 5, PL-AGN.

CHAPTER 7

1. Domínguez to Luisi, October 21, 1942, carpeta "L," PL-BN.

2. Luisi to Domínguez, January 19, 1943, carpeta "L," PL-BN.

3. Luisi ran in 1942 for the House of Representatives on the Socialist ticket, although she withdrew her candidacy and resigned from the Socialist Party because its leaders did not appreciate her feminist politics. Sapriza, Clivajes de la memoria, 259; Ehrick, Radio and the Gendered Soundscape, 112–13.

4. The Popular Front also saw an alliance between the Batista government and the Communist Party of Cuba, which was legalized in 1938. After its legalization, Domínguez returned to Cuba. Later in 1940 Domínguez officially withdrew from the Communist Party, called the Partido Socialista Popular.

5. Cuba entered the war shortly after the U.S., with other countries in Latin America following suit. In January 1942, Uruguay broke its long-standing neutrality and joined the Allied war effort.

6. Luisi to Heloise Brainerd, January 14, 1942, box 30, part 3, series A,4, part 1, WILPF. Shortly after the bombing of Pearl Harbor, Luisi also wrote to Eleanor Roosevelt on behalf of her antifascist feminist group to "invite all the women of the Americas to join together . . . in a movement of unanimous condemnation of . . . totalitarianism [and in] . . . continental solidarity." "A las mujeres de los Estados Unidos de America en nombre del Comité Femenino de Afirmación Democrática contra la Agresión Japonesa," December 18, 1941, sección 1, serie 1.12, doc. 2, PL-ACRE.

7. Norman Armour to Secretary of State, October 24, 1939, State Department, 710.F IACW/139, D.F. RG 59. As Laurence Duggan, head of South American affairs in the State Department, penned in an internal memo, "The Argentine Ambassador informs me that she is a woman of talent and beauty not affiliated with any group." Duggan to Kelchner, Welles, and Hull, June 1, 1939, State Department, 710.F IACW/99, D.F., RG 59.

8. On the Junta de la Victoria, see the following by Deutsch: "Argentine Women against Fascism" "New School Lecture: 'An Army of Women,'" 117–24; and *Engendering Antifascism*. Valobra, "Partidos, tradiciones y estrategias de movilización social."

9. Leo Rowe, the president of the Pan-American Union, warned that "were she to be elected, [she] would merely be a rubber stamp for Miss Stevens." Telephone conversation memo between Dr. L. S. Rowe and Mr. Duggan, May 22, 1939, 710.F IACW/109-110. Bernardino wrote a letter to Cordell Hull vehemently denying that she would "be a mere instrument of Miss Stevens" and insisting that the fierce debates over the Equal Rights Amendment in the United States had little relevance to her or to other Latin American delegates. Minerva Bernardino to Cordell Hull, October 28, 1939, 710.F IACW/138, D.F., RG 59.

10. Lutz to Catt, June 3, 1945, NAWSA. For commentary on Schlieper's appearance, see "Changed Status Seen for Argentine Women," NYT, November 24, 1943, 14; Genevieve Reynolds, "Buenos Aires Women Work for Democracy," WP, November 7, 1942, B4. Jessie Ash Arndt, untitled article, WP, November 2, 1940, 15.

11. *Pan American: Magazine of the Americas*, November–December 1940, 27, 30. Schlieper was described as a "'harmonious composite of the Nordic and Latin types.' . . . She is blonde and has extremely arched eyebrows, well chiseled nose and large eyes." Carolyn Bell, "Argentine Visitor Arrives," WP, November 3, 1940, S3; Ubelaker, "Impossible Americas," 148.

12. "A Rockefeller Swings into Action," *Pan American: Magazine of the Americas*, November–December 1940, 3. The precursor to this group was the Office of the Coordinator of Commercial and Cultural Relations, founded in 1940.

13. The CIAA grew out of earlier efforts at "cultural exchange" starting with the creation at the 1938 Lima conference of the Division of Cultural Relations and Division of International Communications. See also Ubelaker, "Impossible Americas." The goal was to create commercial, economic, and cultural programs "in such fields as the arts and sciences, education and travel, the radio, the press and cinema, that will further the national defense and strengthen the bonds between the nations of the Western Hemisphere." *Program of the Department of State Office of Cultural Relations*, 2.

14. "Miss Mary E. Winslow," WP, March 7, 1941, 17. "Pan American Women Add to Exchange of Information," *New York Times*, October 26, 1941, D5. During the war, the popular sentiment increased that women's groups were key to Pan-Americanism. "Women Seen Aiding Hem Pan-Americanism," *New York Times*, April 15, 1943, 12.

15. "Women Representing 29 Clubs Meet with Nelson Rockefeller," WP, April 2, 1941, 14; Rebecca Stiles Taylor, "Activities of Women's National Organizations," *Chicago Defender*, April 19, 1941, 17.

16. "First Lady Invited to Tour Americas," NYT, December 2, 1941, 27.

17. Mary "Molly" Dewson had written to Eleanor Roosevelt supporting Winslow as the new U.S. commissioner: "*Because* the fight has been to get rid of Doris Stevens, the Natl Woman's Party, and those opposed to protective legislation . . . the PRIME REQUIREMENT is for someone who understands." Mary Dewson to Eleanor Roosevelt, January 27, 1939, box 685, "100. Personal Letters 1939 Da–Di," Eleanor Roosevelt Papers, Franklin D. Roosevelt Presidential Library and Museum, Hyde Park, N.Y. Numerous women's groups,

including the National Women's Trade Union League, the YWCA, the National Council of Catholic Women, and the National Consumers' League, and prominent individuals like Rose Schneiderman, Sophonisba Breckinridge, Carrie Chapman Catt, Mary Dewson, Mary Anderson, and Mary van Kleeck all wrote to Sumner Welles to support her endorsement. Ruth Shipley to Sumner Welles, January 13, 1939 (and other letters), 710.F IACW/32–38, D.F., RG 59.

18. "Gist of Miss Mary Winslow's Remarks at Meeting of Legislative Department, League of Women Voters, at the Y.W.C.A.," January 9, 1940, box 127, folder 3, DSP.

19. "First Lady Links Women to Amity," NYT, October 11, 1941, 7. "Miss Mary E. Winslow," WP, March 7, 1941, 17.

20. Winslow had obtained funds to fly Mexican commissioner Castillo Ledón to the U.S. as early as 1940. Telegram, Winslow to Castillo Ledón, October 31, 1940, caja 5, exp. 88, AGC-SRE. Other recipients of Rockefeller funding for "Good Neighbor" tours included Esther Neira de Calvo, Graciela Mandujano, and Maria Rosa Oliver. See "1942 Report to Mr. Nelson Rockefeller, Coordinator of Inter-American Affairs," box 1a, ENC; "Gira de Conferencias, 12 mayo–5 de julio 1946," box 5, folder 57, María Rosa Oliver Papers, Princeton University Library, Manuscripts Division, Princeton, N.J. Oliver worked in the Office of the Coordinator of Inter-American Affairs in Washington, D.C., during World War II. Rapoport, "Argentina," 113; Iber, Neither Peace nor Freedom, 66.

21. "First Lady Links Women to Amity," 7.

22. Quote from Roosevelt and Beasley, White House Press Conferences of Eleanor Roosevelt, 330.

23. Although the ERA gained some new adherents in the 1940s and was reintroduced into Congress in 1941, the Eleanor Roosevelt–Molly Dewson political network still maintained a powerful opposition for fear it would eliminate protective labor legislation. They also opposed the ERA on the basis of their assumption that women's rights were already intact in the United States. In these years, organizations like the LWV now actively moved away from women's rights and toward a more general support of women's "civil duties," "civil defense," and role in securing friendship and Pan-American understanding. See Rymph, "Exporting Civic Womanhood," 66–67; and Ware, "American Women in the 1950s," 291.

24. Acción Femenina Peruana reached out to Clara González in Panama for support and leadership. Acción Femenina Peruana to Clara González, April 15, 1940, ACG; Mary M. Cannon, "Women's Organizations in Ecuador, Paraguay, and Peru," Bulletin of the Pan American Union, 1943, 601–7; Miller, Latin American Women, 115; E. Friedman, Unfinished Transitions, 87; "Carta de la mujer venezolana a sus hermanas de las americas" and "La II conferencia de mujeres venezolanas," March 9, 1945, caja 9, exp. 151; "Informe de la Delegada de Nicaragua, Dr. Olga Nuñez Abaúnza a la 5a Asamblea de la Comisión Interamericana de Mujeres," November 4, 1946, caja 11, exp. 178, AGC-SRE; Coker Gonzalez, "Agitating for Their Rights," 699–700.

25. Argentinian feminist Alicia Moreau de Justo admitted that the IACW "no longer had, perhaps because of its official character, the full freedom of expression and action that it had under the presidency of Miss Doris Stevens." She believed that the primary focus of the commission should still be "awakening interest" among women "in countries where women have not achieved their civil and political rights." Moreau de Justo, La mujer en la democracia, 74. Marta Vergara later concurred: "With the departure of Doris Steven [from the commission]," she wrote, "left the last [U.S.] feminist of importance." She expressed frustration that the U.S. women now at its helm were "all . . . in positions of [government] responsibility" and not feminists. "There was the secretary of Labor,

Frances Perkins; the head of the Women's Bureau, Mary Anderson; and a delegate of the U.S. for our Commission, Mary N. Winslow. All were friends with Mrs. Roosevelt. All wanted to be considered distinguished human beings in this or that profession of work . . . beyond the fact of being a woman." Vergara, *Memorias*, 190.

26. Her friends included Carrie Chapman Catt and other women in the League of Women Voters, along with Katharine Lenroot, Mary Anderson, Frances Perkins, and Mary Winslow. See also Paulina Luisi's "Encuesta de Josefina Marpons para El *Hogar*," July 1940, sección 3, serie 3.2, doc. 39, PL-ACRE.

27. Bertha Lutz to Carrie Chapman Catt, [July?] 1940, Qo.ADM, COR.A940.6, p. 20, AFBPF.

28. Lutz to [Marquerite Wells], January 13, 1940, 3:120, LWV; Lutz to Winslow, March 30, 1942, AFBPF.

29. Wells to Lutz, February 9, 1940, 3:120, LWV; Lutz to Catt, [July?] 1940, Qo.ADM, COR.A940.6, p. 20, AFBPF.

30. Lutz quoted in "Await Suffrage in Latin America," NYT, March 23, 1941, D4.

31. Women's Bureau member Mary M. Cannon, in Argentina at the time, reported on FDR's Four Freedoms speech, "I don't believe a pronouncement by the Pope could have had as much publicity as Roosevelt's speech. It was re-broadcast here in Spanish and English, the big papers carried the text, and of course all the papers commented." Cannon to Nienburg, June 28, 1941, box 1, "Cannon, Mary (1932–1941)," RG 86.

32. Roosevelt, "Four Freedoms."

33. See Leonard and Bratzel, *Latin America during World War II*, 47–48.

34. Freda Kirchwey, "Program of Action," *The Nation*, March 11, 1944, 300–305.

35. Lauren, *Evolution of International Human Rights*, 137.

36. Frens-String, "Pan-America's Quarry."

37. Borgwardt, *A New Deal for the World*, chapter 1.

38. Frens-String, "Pan-America's Quarry," 15.

39. Frens-String. This was the case, for example, of the powerful Chilean Socialist Party.

40. Since the Nazi-Stalin Pact in 1939 and resulting dislocations in the Communist Party in Chile, Vergara's husband, Marcos Chamudes, had been ousted from his position as Communist Party leader. The two had moved to New York City in 1941, and Chamudes enrolled in the army, became a U.S. citizen, and ultimately decamped to train in Texas, while Vergara taught Spanish first at Middlebury College in Vermont and then at Tulane University in Louisiana. Vergara, *Memorias*, part 2, chapter 10; part 3, chapters 1–3.

41. In August 1942, after Brazil became one of the first countries in the Americas to declare war on Germany and Italy, President Getulio Vargas moved Rosalina Coelho Lisboa, the former Brazilian IACW delegate, into a wartime position in his cabinet. As her replacement on the IACW, he appointed Carneiro de Mendonça, Lutz's friend and long-time colleague, vice president of the Federação Brasileira pelo Progresso Feminino, and well-known poet. Lutz to Margery Corbett Ashby, November 24, 1942, Qo.ADM, COR. A942.22, p. 77, AFBPF.

42. This group included Mexican commissioner Amalia de Castillo Ledón, who was the assistant director of the Department of Civic Action in Mexico. Amalia de Castillo Ledón, "Servicio Civil Femenino de Defenso (1942)," in Castillo Ledón and Cano, *Amalia de Castillo Ledón*, 95–97.

43. "Hemisphere Group Hails Africa Coup," NYT, November 14, 1942, 6.

44. "Hemisphere Group Hails Africa Coup," 6.

45. "Hemisphere Group Hails Africa Coup," 6. In October 1942, the month before

the IACW meeting, Lutz and Carneiro de Mendonça planned a three-day women's conference in Rio de Janeiro, the Fourth National Women's Convention, that drew on the participation of thirty-seven women's groups in Brazil. It opened at the Palacio de Itamaraty, the Ministry of Foreign Relations. Calling for the "victory of the United Nations," the meeting drew up resolutions on women's work in Brazil, women's contribution to the war effort, and "women of the Americas in the reconstruction of peace" that Carneiro de Mendonça then brought to the IACW meeting in D.C. Lutz to "Associações," October 13, 1942, Qo.ADM, COR.A942.22, p. 53, AFBPF; "'A Pax americana das repúblicas deste continente é uma associação de nações livres e irmãs,'" A Manhã (Rio de Janeiro), October 27, 1942, 3.

46. "Argentina, Chile Urged to Break," NYT, November 13, 1942, 8.

47. "Argentina, Chile Urged to Break," 8; Susana Larguía to Paulina Luisi, November 24, 1942, box "L," PL-BN.

48. Winslow to Eleanor Roosevelt, December 10, 1942, box 514, White House Correspondence, 1933–1945, "90. Congrats. & Greetings 1942 Hou–Ly," Eleanor Roosevelt Papers, Franklin D. Roosevelt Presidential Library and Museum.

49. Marpons, La mujer y su lucha con el ambiente, 185. Marpons hoped the Atlantic Charter would promote a "full-blooded internationalism" of workers and the global proletariat in contrast to what she called the "anemic" internationalism of the League of Nations and the International Labor Organization. Bertha Lutz also referred to the "individual and collective freedom" that would emerge from the war. Lutz to Welles, January 24, 1942, Qo.ADM, COR.A942.22, p. 14, AFBPF.

50. Josefina Marpons, "La Mujer Norte Americana Pide Su Place en el Sol," El Hogar, February 27, 1942. On the Women's Bureau during the war, see Anderson and Winslow, Woman at Work; and Hartmann, The Home Front and Beyond, 20, 53, 55, 65–66. Hartmann explains that one of "the greatest effects of the war" was the "attention it focused on . . . equal pay" for women. The Women's Bureau and the NWP both played a key role in promoting equal pay for women during the war, influencing provision for equal pay in eleven state legislatures in the United States (137–38).

51. The Women's Bureau had facilitated "all the new aspects of . . . the adaptation of women workers to war production." Marta Vergara, "Mujeres y pantalones," September 1942, unidentified Chilean newspaper clipping, box 2 "Cannon, Mary (1942–1943)," RG 86.

52. The Women's Bureau formed part of the Interdepartmental Committee on Cooperation with the American Republics, founded in 1938. It was renamed the Interdepartmental Committee on Scientific and Cultural Cooperation in 1946. Under the charge of the State Department, it administered scientific and cultural exchanges with Latin America. Sealander, "In the Shadow of Good Neighbor Diplomacy," 239–40.

53. Antezana-Pernet, "Mobilizing Women," 244–45. At the Pan-American and regional ILO conferences from 1936 to 1939, leftist Pan-American feminists pushed maternity legislation as a "right."

54. Notes from the Second Labor Conference of the American States Which Are Members of the International Organization, Havana, 1939, Committee on Work of Women and Juveniles, Mary N. Winslow Papers, 1923–1951, A-53, Schlesinger Library, Radcliffe Institute, Harvard University, Cambridge, Mass; Friedman, Unfinished Transitions, 59.

55. Cannon's notes on maternity legislation in Chile, Cannon to Anderson, October 3, 1941, box 1 "Cannon, Mary," RG 86.

56. Eileen Boris underscores this point in Boris, "'No Right to Layettes or Nursing Time.'" Karin Rosemblatt has also pointed out that in Chile, enforcement of these poli-

cies was minimal, which was why these women mobilized around them. Rosemblatt, *Gendered Compromises*, 81–82.

57. While some U.S. Women's Bureau members did support maternity legislation in the 1930s, as Dorothy Sue Cobble explains, their support of maternity leave became more robust after the start of the Second World War, when female workers also increasingly pushed unions to implement maternity leave plans. Cobble, *Other Women's Movement*, 57, 128–29.

58. Women's Bureau members who had lived through the conservative push-back against earlier experiments with state-sponsored maternity legislation, like the Sheppard-Towner Act, recognized the resistance of the U.S. federal government to any-thing resembling "family legislation." See Katharine Lenroot oral history, Katharine F. Lenroot Papers, Columbia University Special Collections, New York. I am grateful to Donna Guy for sharing her copy of this microform with me.

59. See Gordon, *Pitied but Not Entitled*.

60. *Record of Proceedings [of the] Second Labour Conference*, 140.

61. *Record of Proceedings [of the] Second Labour Conference*, 142.

62. "To Report on Women Working in Americas," NYT, November 28, 1942, 9; Mary Cannon to Winnifred Fisher, January 23, 1942, box 2 "Cannon, Mary (1942–1943)," RG 86. On Cannon's trip to Brazil, see Fraccaro, "O trabalho feminino sob o olhar estran-geiro."

63. Cannon would hold the position of international bureau chief at the Women's Bureau until 1965. She was born in Ohio in 1900, had gone to Miami University of Ohio, and had done graduate work in social work at Ohio State University and the University of Chicago. She was a member of the Women's National Democratic Club. Significantly, she was also a founding member of the National Council of Negro Women and an adviser to the women's affairs committee of the African American Institute. Her commitment to antiracism likely influenced her ability to gain the trust and friendship of many Latin American women. "Mary M. Cannon," WP, July 29, 1988.

64. "Second rate pianists" quote, Cannon to Anderson, April 28, 1941; Cannon to Nienburg, June 28, 1941, box 1 "Cannon, Mary," RG 86. She also wrote that there was a group "afraid that the U.S. is building up to take over as much of the commerce and in-dustry of Argentina as they can get, not the government itself, but the U.S. interest." "We wanted them on our side" quote, Judith Sealander interview with Mary Cannon, January 15, 1976, cited in Sealander, "In the Shadow of Good Neighbor Diplomacy," 243.

65. Cannon made this point in talks to U.S. audiences and stated that the Chilean Pan-American feminist Graciela Mandujano had told her this. Mary M. Cannon, "'Outline of Speech—on South America,' to be given at Summit, New Jersey, and Hartford, Connecti-cut, March 9 and March 10, 1942," box 2 "Cannon, Mary," RG 86.

66. Mary M. Cannon, "Influencia de la mujer en la sociedad y en la economía de los Estados Unidos del Norte," *Finanzas* (Buenos Aires), January–February, 1942, 6–8; also in box 2 "Cannon, Mary," RG 86.

67. Genevieve Reynolds, "Women's Club News," WP, September 2, 1943, B7; Sea-lander, "In the Shadow of Good Neighbor Diplomacy," 245–46.

68. A São Paulo newspaper recounted Cannon's meeting with the director of the Na-tional Department of Labor in Brazil, Luiz Augusto Rego Monteiro, who regaled her with many legislative features that promoted women's equality under Brazil's labor laws: "Mary Cannon . . . could not hide her pleasure when she learned that the same rights that the law assures the male worker are extended to women who enter industrial and com-

mercial establishments." "Empolgada com a regulamentação do trabalho da mulher Brasileira," *Correio Paulistano*, December 12, 1942.

69. Cannon's notes on maternity legislation in Chile, Cannon to Anderson, October 3, 1941, box 1 "Cannon, Mary," RG 86.

70. Cannon to Anderson, September 2, 1941, box 1 "Cannon, Mary," RG 86.

71. Cannon to Anderson, September 2, 1941; Cannon to Anderson, October 2, 1941, box 1 "Cannon, Mary," RG 86.

72. Cannon to Anderson, October 2, 1941, box 1 "Cannon, Mary," RG 86.

73. Bertha M. Nienburg memo and "Amendment to Mrs. Nyswander's letter on Day Nurseries and Maternity Leave," October 8, 1941, box 1 "Cannon, Mary," RG 86.

74. Bertha M. Nienburg memo and "Amendment to Mrs. Nyswander's letter on Day Nurseries and Maternity Leave," October 8, 1941, box 1 "Cannon, Mary," RG 86.

75. "Employment of Women in War Industries (Prepared for Mary Winslow)," May 25, 1942. It was "expected that 2½ to 3 million women will be in war industries by the end of 1942, and 4 million in 1943." Susan Hartmann has shown that this ambivalence carried well into the war. In 1944, the Women's Bureau sent women's employers a statement of their "opposition to the employment of mothers of children under fourteen, and urged that such applicants be questioned closely about their provisions for their children's care." During the war, some employers would establish day-care centers on site. Hartmann, *Home Front and Beyond*, 58.

76. Hartmann, *Home Front and Beyond*, 53. As Elizabeth More has explained, the war "represented the first time in U.S. history that married women and mothers who sought jobs outside their own homes were widely perceived as working for the good of the nation at large rather than providing desperately needed support to their poverty-stricken families or selfishly pursuing riches and self-aggrandizement." More, "Best Interests," 23. By the end of the war, the number of women working outside the home in the United States had grown by 60 percent, and one-third of these women were mothers with young children. May, *Homeward Bound*, chapter 3.

77. After the start of the war, under Mary Anderson's leadership, the Women's Bureau focused on labor standards for women working in factories and on publicly encouraging women to take jobs, reassuring the public that women's work would not upset the family order, and planning for reconversion after the war had been won.

78. The Children's Bureau announced in promotional material for the Emergency Maternity and Infant Care Act, "The service of your husband to our country gives you and your baby the right to this care wherever it can be provided." Quotes from Hoffman, *Health Care for Some*, 50.

79. Michel, *Children's Interests/Mother's Rights*, 132.

80. As Alice Kessler-Harris has explained, "Even as the Second World War drew to a close it attracted only marginal attention. Despite a good deal of support from women in the federal Children's Bureau and Women's Bureau, most Americans dismissed it." Kessler-Harris, *In Pursuit of Equity*, 209. Michel, *Children's Interests/Mother's Rights*, 141–46.

81. Emphasis mine. Lenroot to Lutz, December 15, 1943, Q0.ADM, COR.1943.20, AFBPF.

82. Cannon to Ana Rosa Schlieper de Martínez Guerrero, July 1942, box 2 "Cannon, Mary," RG 86.

83. Mary M. Cannon, "Women of Latin American Countries," *Woman's Press*, November 1942, 468–69.

84. "Break Tradition in South America," NYT, June 30, 1943, 18.

85. "Latin American Women Called Better Off Than Many in Industrial Pursuits Here," NYT, April 10, 1944.

86. Paulina Luisi, "Peligro de una Guerra Mundial, entretelones de las guerras," Congreso de Mujeres contra la Guerra y el Fascismo, Montevideo, Abril 17–23–25–1936, sección 1, serie 1.9, doc. 7, PL-ACRE.

87. Sandra McGee Deutsch has explained that the Agrupación Femenina Antiguerrera in Argentina espoused these same beliefs. Deutsch, "New School Lecture 'An Army of Women,'" 103–10.

88. Rosenberg, *Spreading the American Dream*, 195.

89. "II° Cuestionario del Bureau of Latin America Research," Montevideo, May, 1943. sección 1, serie 1.12, doc. 5, PL-ACRE. Luisi also believed that production of war materials should be submitted to the regulatory control of international organizations.

90. "II° Cuestionario del Bureau of Latin America Research."

91. Thanks to Sandra McGee Deutsch for pointing out that the Argentinian military dictatorship fired Schlieper as the Argentinian representative to the commission. It considered her a communist, but she was really a Radical.

92. "Good Neighbor Aid in War Is Praised," NYT, April 13, 1944.

93. "Good Neighbor Aid in War Is Praised"; *Bulletin of the Inter-American Commission of Women* (Pan-American Union, Washington, D.C., July, 1944), Inter-American Commission of Women Records, Sophia Smith Collection, Smith College, Northampton, Mass.

94. *Bulletin of the Inter-American Commission of Women*; Maria Currea de Aya was the Colombian commissioner. "The low wages that prevail in Latin America are determined in part by prices paid for commodities," she explained, "and if higher prices are paid for Latin American products, the producers could increase their wage scale."

95. Rock, "War and Postwar Intersections," 29; Fitzgerald, "ECLA and the Formation of Latin American Economic Doctrine," 91.

96. "Fund Pact Gives Veto on Exchange Rates to the United States," NYT, July 23, 1944, 27.

97. Memorandum to Sumner Welles, February 1945, box 179, folder 8, Sumner Welles Papers, Franklin D. Roosevelt Presidential Library and Museum.

98. Borgwardt, *New Deal for the World*, 172.

99. On the 1944 Dumbarton Oaks proposals and their lack of human rights language, see C. Anderson, *Eyes off the Prize*, 35–36; and Hilderbrand, *Dumbarton Oaks*, 92. They included a brief note that the responsibilities of the Economic and Social Council would include "promoting respect for and observance of human rights and fundamental freedoms for all."

100. Portal to Luisi, December 13, 1944, folder "P," PL-BN.

101. Luisi to Domínguez, January 1943, ODN-AN; Domínguez to Luisi, January 27, 1945, carpeta "D," PL-BN. The letter from Domínguez to Luisi is also reproduced in Domínguez, *50 años de una vida*, 424–26.

102. Amalia de Castillo Ledón to Marta Vergara, January 30, 1945, caja 7, exp. 130, AGC-SRE. On Amalia de Castillo Ledón, see Castillo Ledón and Cano, *Amalia de Castillo Ledón*; Cano, "El 'feminismo de estado' de Amalia de Castillo Ledón"; and Rodríguez de Ita, "La Comisión Interamericana de Mujeres durante la presidencia de Amalia de Castillo Ledón."

103. Untitled list of demands (1945), caja 7, exp. 130, AGC-SRE.

104. Cannon's "Notes from a conversation with Miss Miller," February 15, 1945, box 5 "Cannon, Mary," RG 86.

105. Inter-American Conference on Problems of War and Peace, Motion of the Dele-

gation of Mexico on a Charter for Women and Children, Records Relating to the Inter-American Conference on Problems of War and Peace, Mexico, Committee and Commission Files, 1945, Records of International Conferences, Commissions, and Expositions, Record Group 43, National Archives and Records Administration, College Park, Md.

106. *Diario de la Conferencia Interamericana*, 1, no. 6, February 27, 1945, 92.

107. *Diario de la Conferencia Interamericana*, 84.

108. On LULAC's use of the Chapultepec antiracism resolutions to fight discrimination against Mexican immigrants in the United States, see Zamora, *Claiming Rights*, 105, 112–16.

109. Telegram, "Organización Femenil Nuevo Leon Represento, Solidarizase Ponencias Presentadas Conferencia Cancilleres Senora Castillo Ledón, Atte Secretaría Acción Femenil," 481(23) L-E-492, GE-SRE. Castillo Ledón and Bernardino emphasized that these resolutions drew from the long movement of Pan-American feminism. Amalia de Castillo Ledón, "Deberes y Derechos de la Mujer Ante los problemas de la Paz," August 2, 1944, caja 7, exp. 115, AGC-SRE. The CIM would also publish a pamphlet about their work at Chapultepec.

110. *Diario de la Conferencia Interamericana*, 1, no. 4, February 24, 1945, 43, 46.

111. Eleanor Roosevelt had suggested that the U.S. delegation include Lenroot as a technical adviser to "represent women and children." Lenroot oral history.

112. Lenroot, "Report on the Work of Committee IV-B, Social Questions," March 7, 1945, Records Relating to the Inter-American Conference on Problems of War and Peace, Mexico, Committee and Commission Files, 1945, Records of International Conferences, Commissions, and Expositions, Record Group 43, National Archives and Records Administration, College Park, Md.; Genevieve Reynolds, "Latin Only Voting Woman Delegate at Chapultepec," *Washington Post* clipping, box 21, RG 86.

113. Reynolds, "Latin Only Voting Woman Delegate at Chapultepec."

114. These affirmations helped reinforce the value of many of the inter-American efforts that the U.S. Women's Bureau, Children's Bureau, and CIAA had made in their outreach to Latin America during the war, focusing on governmental bureaucracies for women and labor. After the conference, Nelson Rockefeller wrote to Katharine Lenroot praising her for her work at Chapultepec. Nelson Rockefeller to Lenroot, March 13, 1945, box 20, folder 8, series 2:3, Katharine F. Lenroot Papers, Colombia University Special Collections.

115. *Diario de la Conferencia Interamericana*, 1, no. 14, March 8, 1945, 232.

116. Bases de la Unión Nacional de Mujeres, December 31, 1944, ACG.

117. Gaeta Wold Boyer to Esther Neira de Calvo, May 8, 1939, box 60, folder 11; "Replies from Foreign Office of American Republics to Scott and Bustamante, Opinion of June 12, 1939," box 127, folder 5, DSP. Neira de Calvo was appointed in May 1939 as the Panamanian representative of the IACW. After being banned from teaching at the National Institute, González moved to Costa Rica in 1939 in "voluntary exile" and to recuperate from ill health. She may have collaborated there with Panamanian opposition forces planning an armed overthrow of the Acción Comunal, which never materialized. After the National Police deposed Arias in 1941, González returned to Panama. Moore to Stevens, November 18, 1939, box 84, folder 4, DSP. Marco Serra, *Clara González de Behringer*, 125.

118. Antezana-Pernet, "Peace in the World," 175.

119. Quoted in Pernet, "Chilean Feminists," 684. In Cuba, Ofelia Domínguez Navarro also organized a large International Women's Day celebration on March 8, 1944, to bring "homage and fraternal good will" to the "millions of women who work in the enormous

camp of war production," and to demand that women have a seat at the peace table after the war. Domínguez Navarro, "Memo para Día Internacional de la Mujer," March 8, 1944, caja 673, no. 13, ODN-AN.

120. See Leslie, "United for a Better World," chapter 1.

121. "Hemisphere Security," WP, March 4, 1945, B4; Robert C. Albright, "Mexico Treaty Held Guide for San Francisco: Security," WP, March 13, 1945, 1; "P.S. to Chapultepec," WP, March 14, 1945, 8; James B. Reston, "Delegates of U.S. Map Plan to Keep Regional Powers," NYT, May 13,1945, 1; Sumner Welles, "Chapultepec: Unity of Americas," WP, March 21, 1945, 8.

122. Marion Parks, "That Women May Share," Bulletin of the Department of State, July 22, 1945, 112.

123. Tuñon, ¡Por fin . . . ya podemos elegir y electas!, 59.

CHAPTER 8

1. Bertha Lutz, "Reminiscences of the San Francisco Conference That Founded [the] United Nations," Qo.ADM, EVE.CNF, TXT.27, VOL 6; Lutz to "Amigas," April 30, 1945, Qo.ADM, EVE.CNF, TXT.27, VOL 7, AFBPF. Adolf Berle, the U.S. consul in Brazil and a friend of Lutz, had recommended this course. She might have been seeing the Irazu volcano.

2. "Viajantes," Correio da Manhã (Rio de Janeiro), April 19, 1945, 13; "Latin Diplomat Tells Confidence," LAT, April 24, 1945, 7.

3. Lutz was at that time the chief of the Department of Natural History and Geology and the chief pro tem of the Department of Botany at the National Museum of Rio de Janeiro. Bertha Lutz, "Reminiscences of the San Francisco Conference That Founded [the] United Nations"; Lutz to "Amigas," April 30, 1945.

4. "35 Women's Groups Fete Bertha Lutz," NYT, August 3, 1944, 22.

5. Lutz, "Reactions to Events in Brazil," March 1–15, 1945, Qo.ADM, p. 1; Lutz, "Revolution Its Aftermath" (1932), Qo.BLZ, PIN, TXT 29, AFBPF. Lutz's notion of international collaboration, steeped in paternalism, coexisted comfortably with liberal Christianity and racism. But these particular views were unique even among her white middle-class feminist collaborators in the FBPF, many of whom supported Gandhi's nationalist movement and the notion of Brazilian "racial democracy" recently espoused by Gilberto Freyre.

6. Vargas Garcia, O sexto membro permanente, 192–93.

7. Lutz, "Reactions to Events in Brazil," March 1–15, 1945. Lutz was disappointed by the omission of "human rights" from the Dumbarton Oaks conference and by the consolidation of Great Power hegemony over the United Nations.

8. The FBPF had lobbied the Brazilian government to appoint a woman to the San Francisco delegation and had invoked the Chapultepec resolution. Lutz to Donald Gainer, April 2, 1945, MN.BL.o.FEM 6/19, BLMN.

9. Adela Formoso de Obregón Santacilia was head of the Universidad Femenina de México, founder of a women's symphony orchestra, and director of the Mexican Association for the Prevention of Blindness. Edith Bristol, "Noted, Conference Women in S.F. Program," San Francisco News clipping (undated), part 1, reel 9, MMB. Isabel Pinto de Vidal, though not an IACW commissioner, had nonetheless been involved in inter-American women's organizing ever since she was president of the National Council of Women in Uruguay in the 1920s and affiliated with the Pan-American International Women's Committee, founded in 1915, alongside Paulina Luisi.

10. Catt had advised Lutz to seek out the help of Gildersleeve, whom she described as a "very important woman." Catt to Lutz, April 10, 1945.

11. Lutz to Catt, May 21, 1945, reel 12, NAWSA. Interestingly, in Gildersleeve's account of this meeting, she says that Wilkinson was not in attendance. Gildersleeve, *Making of the United Nations Charter*, 350.

12. Lutz to Margaret Corbett Ashby, August 11, 1945, BR.MN.BL.0.FEM.03/11, BLMN.

13. Lutz, "Notes on the San Francisco Conference, as Seen by Bertha Lutz, Plenipotentiary Brazilian Delegate," Qo.ADM, EVE.CNF, TXT.27, VOL 6, AFBPF.

14. Lutz, "Notes on the San Francisco Conference"; Lutz to Catt, May 21, 1945, reel 12, NAWSA.

15. Lutz, "Notes on the San Francisco Conference."

16. Lucy Somerville Horworth, "Women's Responsibility in World Affairs." *Journal of the American Association of University Women* (Summer 1994): 195–98, reprinted in Litoff and Smith, *What Kind of World Do We Want?*, 111.

17. "Women Playing Important Roles in UNCIO," *San Francisco News*, April 26, 1945; Gildersleeve, "Women Must Help Stop Wars," *Women's Home Companion*, May 1945, 32.

18. Roosevelt and Beasley, *White House Press Conferences of Eleanor Roosevelt*, 330.

19. Litoff, "Southern Women in a World at War," 56–59. See also Leslie, "United for a Better World."

20. Zilfa Estcourt, "Women at Conference Table," *San Francisco Chronicle*, April 22, 1945, 25; Edith Efron, "Portrait of a Dean and Delegate," *New York Times Magazine*, April 1, 1945.

21. Gildersleeve later opined in her memoirs that for women in the United States, "The best policy for them is to *not talk too much* about the abstract principles of women's rights, but to do good in any job they get." Gildersleeve, *Many a Good Crusade*, 350–51.

22. Gildersleeve, 349–50.

23. Gildersleeve, 349–50.

24. Gildersleeve, 353.

25. Lutz to Catt, May 21, 1945, reel 12, NAWSA.

26. Lutz to "Amigas," April 30, 1945.

27. Paulina Luisi, "Homage a la Dra. Pinto de Vidal," sección 3, serie 3.2, doc. 44, PL-ACRE.

28. Edith Goode to Alice Paul, May 2, 1945, series 7, reel 174, NWP.

29. They had also consulted with each other afterward over their shared dislike for Stevens's rule. Lutz to Sophonisba Breckinridge, February 1, 1934, reel 11, SBP.

30. Lutz to Catt, June 3, 1945, NAWSA. In 1939, when Lutz tried to assuage Elise Musser's fears that if appointed the new chair of the commission, Bernardino would reproduce Doris Stevens's strict focus for "equal rights," she wrote that Bernardino would probably be barred from the presidency because of "the undoubted race prejudice against African blood found in most [L]atin American countries, though it does not mean that we would endorse such a prejudice." Lutz to Musser, August 9, 1939, Qo.ADM, COR.1939.5, p. 25, AFBPF.

31. In 1942 Bernardino heartily supported resolutions Lutz sent to the commission meeting. At Chapultepec the two had supported nearly identical demands: equal political, civil, economic, and social rights for women and also for the inclusion of women in international conferences.

32. Minerva Bernardino's relationship with the notorious Trujillo dictatorship was closer and more complicated than Lutz's with Vargas. Bernardino's brother was one of Trujillo's overseas operatives, and Bernardino's position as IACW president was paid for

by Trujillo. Yet Bernardino's sinecure as the D.C.-based president of the IACW enabled her to escape from Trujillo. For an insightful analysis of Bernardino in the IACW, see DuBois and Derby, "The Strange Case of Minerva Bernardino."

33. Bernardino, *Lucha, agonía y esperanza*, xxviii.

34. Jessie Street, part of the Australian delegation, Canadian Cora Casselman, and Wu Yi-Fang from China attended. The U.S. women's groups that had gained "consultant status" were part of what historians later called an "experiment of democracy." In a public relations move, the State Department invited forty-two U.S. civic, business, labor, and nongovernmental organizations to the conference to periodically meet with the U.S. delegation in an effort to gain public support for and Senate ratification of the United Nations. The People's Mandate was a group of women that pushed ratification of the inter-American peace treaties. Representing the American Association of University Women were Helen D. Reid (international relations representative for the association) as consultant and Mrs. Malbone W. Graham and Aurelia Henry Reinhardt as associates; representing the General Federation of Women's Clubs were Lucy Dickinson as consultant and Constance Sporborg and Mrs. Earl Shoesmith as associates; the National Federation of Business and Professional Women had Margaret Hickey as consultant and Josephine Schain as associate; the National League of Women Voters had Mrs. William Johnson as consultant and Mrs. George H. Engels and Mrs. Anne Hartwell Johnson as associates. Other women there were Dorothy McConnell, Mary McLeod Bethune with the NAACP, and Vera Michaels Dean in the Foreign Policy consultant group. Robins, *Experiment in Democracy*, 206–9. "Assurances Given to Consultants," NYT, April 27, 1945, 14.

35. Lutz upheld Brazilian legislation as a model, with its equal pay laws and national maternity legislation. Lutz to Margery Corbett Ashby, August 11, 1945, BLMN. These arguments did not persuade most of the U.S. women, who ultimately believed that gender-neutral issues of peace, welfare, and humanitarian assistance should take precedence over women's rights. Katharine Bompas, British leader of the International Alliance of Women, also did not think "issues of men and women" should concern the conference, although she did wire her support for the idea of equal representation of men and women in all UN bodies. Telegram, Bompas to Lutz, undated, Qo.ADM, EVE.CNF, TXT.27, VOL 8; Bompas to Lutz, April 30, 1945, Qo.ADM, COR.1945.14, p. 2, AFBPF.

36. Quoted in Lutz to Alice Morgan Wright, March 1, 1950, box 3, folder 10, Alice Morgan Wright Papers, Sophia Smith Collection, Smith College, Northampton, Mass.

37. Margaret Hickey became a key collaborator of Lutz and Bernardino. Clotilde Grunsky to Lutz, May 8, 1945, Qo.ADM, EVE.CNF.27, VOL 7, AFBPF.

38. Ethel Bogardus, "'Nation Great as Its Women,'" *San Francisco* newspaper clipping, MMB. Hickey favored the ERA on principle, but, like Lutz, opposed the controversial style of the National Woman's Party and believed in a more "feminine" feminism that emphasized working for the common good. At a New York City meeting months before the conference, she advocated writing women into the UN Charter: "What is to be woman's role in the world women want? It is as yet an 'unchartered' one. There is no great platform of principles to which women over the world can turn. The world needs such a charter, just as it needs the creative, invigorating faith women would bring to a great declaration of interdependence of people and nations. Let us write such a world charter." Margaret A. Hickey, "The World Women Want," statement at International Federation Day Meeting, Hotel Biltmore, New York City, February 5, 1945, box 1, folder 10, addenda, Margaret Hickey Papers, State Historical Society of Missouri, St. Louis.

39. Edith Goode to Alice Paul, May 2, 1945, series 7, reel 174, NWP.

40. Before the UN conference, Jessie Street's organization had sent the FBPF a copy of the Australian Women's Charter which called for "abolish[ing] sex discrimination and provid[ing] working women free access to daycare." Street to secretary, Brazilian Federation for the Advancement of Women, April 17, 1944, Qo.ADM, COR.A944.4, p.vi, AFBPF. At Lutz's meeting, Street cited that charter.

41. Edith Goode to Laura E. W. Kendall, May 23, 1945, series 7, reel 174, NWP.

42. Edith Goode to Alice Paul, May 4, 1945, series 7, reel 174, NWP; Lutz to the Right Honourable Anthony Eden, May 11, 1945, Qo.ADM, EVE.CNF.27, VOL.7, AFBPF.

43. These groups included the Commission to Study the Organization of Peace, the American Jewish Committee, and the NAACP. They were also deeply disappointed by the cursory mention of human rights in the 1944 Dumbarton Oaks agreement. Loeffler, "'Conscience of America.'"

44. Octavio Méndez Pereira to Ricardo J. Alfaro, May 16, 1945. Alfaro argued that the charter should include a "Declaration of the Rights and Duties of Nations" and a "Declaration of the Essential Rights of Man," but he found that such commitments were "taboo" for the Great Powers, and his appeals lost by two-thirds of a vote. His resolutions found favor, however, with many Latin American delegates. The Mexican and Salvadorean delegations congratulated and thanked Alfaro for his efforts regarding human rights. See memos, May 14, 1945, ARA. See also Sikkink, "Latin American Countries as Norm Protagonists," 395–96.

45. "Haiti: Collaboration is Necessary," *San Francisco News* (undated clipping), part 1, reel 9, MMB.

46. At the 1945 meeting at Chapultepec only a few months before the UN conference, the Mexican foreign minister Ezequiel Padilla had demanded that some promises of the wartime Four Freedoms be accomplished. There, the twenty-one nations of the Americas had signed the Act of Chapultepec, including a resolution that proclaimed their support of principles of international law that safeguard essential human rights and favored a system of international protection of the rights of man.

47. "Libertades y Derechos Esenciales del Hombre," *El Mundo* (Havana), undated, 1945, 6.121.C13.1, ARA.

48. Lutz speech to the Bar Association of Courts of California, undated [1945], Qo.ADM, EVE.CNF, TXT.27, VOL 6, AFBPF.

49. Stettinius diary, week of April 23 to May 1, 1945, box 29, State Department Records of Harley A. Notter, National Archives and Records Administration, College Park, Md. Their demands were these: (1) human rights must be identified as a "purpose" of the UN, (2) all member states of the UN must assume the obligation of guaranteeing human rights, and (3) establishment of a human rights commission must be stipulated by name in the charter. Korey, *NGOs and the Universal Declaration of Human Rights*, 36. Walter White also insisted that human rights include the rights of colonial and other dependent people. Anderson, *Eyes Off the Prize*, 43. On May 5, the Great Powers jointly submitted their amendments that included acknowledgment of human rights in the preamble and purposes.

50. Doc. 2, G/25, May 5, 1945, United Nations Conference on International Organization, United Nations Archives, New York.

51. Edith Goode to Alice Paul, May 4, 1945, reel 86, NWP.

52. They called for the inclusion of women's rights in the purposes of the UN and in the "Arrangements for International Economic and Social Cooperation" of the General Assembly, as well as for inclusion of women on equal terms with men in the UN itself and in the secretariat. Doc. 2, G/25, May 5, 1945, United Nations Conference on International

Organization. See also "Amendments to the Dumbarton Oaks Proposals Submitted by the Delegations of Brazil, the Dominican Republic, and the United States of Mexico"; Lutz to the Right Honourable Anthony Eden, May 11, 1945, AFBPF.

53. As Alice Morgan Wright put it, "We put our demands in the hands of Bertha Lutz . . . and Miss Bernardino." Alice Morgan Wright, "Summary of Situation at San Francisco," [May 1945], reel 86, NWP.

54. Frances Lee McGillicuddy, "Sex at San Francisco," December 1970, typewritten manuscript, Qo.PIT.39; transcript of Lutz's speech at concluding plenary session, Qo.ADM, EVE.CNF.27, VOL.7; Lutz, "Notes on the San Francisco Conference," AFBPF.

55. Vierdag, *Concept of Discrimination*, 87.

56. "Pan-American Plan Studied by Big Five," LAT, May 9, 1945, 1; H. H. Shackford, "Pan Americanism Becomes the Hottest Potato at UNCIO," *Washington Daily News*, May 15, 1945, 4.

57. Russell Porter, "Latin American Back Argentina to Make for Unity of Hemisphere," NYT, May 12, 1945, 9. Lutz wrote, "At first the Russians tried to overrule the people, but the unexpected gesture of the 20 Latin American countries rising in defense of Argentina made them see that one cannot bully anyone." Lutz to Alston, May 6, 1945, Qo.ADM, EVE.CNF.27, VOL.7, AFBPF.

58. Telegram to "Senoritas Bertha Lutz delegada Brasilena, Isabel Urdaneta . . . ," May 5, 1945, Qo.ADM, EVE.CNF.TEXT. 27, VOL.8, AFBPF. Ironically, many outside the conference were protesting the Argentine government's violations of human rights.

59. Alonso S. Perales to Lutz, September 6, 1945, Qo.ADM, EVE.CNF, TXT.27, VOL.8, AFBPF. He also wrote to Ricardo Alfaro in support.

60. Edith Goode to Alice Paul, May 12, 1945, reel 174, NWP. Goode met with White and NAACP lawyers periodically throughout the conference to apprise him of the women's rights resolutions and seek his advice. On the NAACP at the UN conference, see C. Anderson, *Eyes Off the Prize*, 8–57.

61. Leslie, "United for a Better World," 154–55. White and Du Bois had begrudgingly accepted Bethune as a fellow NAACP consultant. Plummer, *Rising Wind*, 135–43; "Vijaya Lakshmi Pandit at San Francisco," *Voice of India*, June 1945; Letter, Mary McLeod Bethune to Dear Friends, May 10, 1945; and Bethune, "Our Stake in Tomorrrow's World," *Aframerican Woman's Journal* (June 1945): 2, reprinted in *What Kind of World Do We Want?*, 216–22. African American anticolonial activist Eslanda Robeson also served in San Francisco as an unofficial delegate of the Council on African Affairs. Ransby, *Eslanda*, 146–49.

62. Bethune's scrapbook is full of articles relating to the women's rights resolutions at the conference.

63. Esthela Jiménez Esponda, Esther Chapa, and Consuelo Hernández, Bloque Nacional de Mujeres Revolucionarias to Comité Interamericano de Mujeres, April 1945, caja 9, exp. 149, AGC-SRE. For more on the Bloque Nacional de Mujeres Revolucionarias, see S. Smith, *Power and Politics of Art*, 139.

64. "Palabras a tu oido," [undated radio address by Castillo Ledón], caja 11, exp. 174, AGC-SRE.

65. On Smuts's role in the UN, see Mazower, *No Enchanted Palace*, 28–65. The NAACP, the National Negro Council, and Indian organizations vociferously challenged Smuts's definition of "human rights," mobilizing around antiracist and anticolonial definitions. See von Eschen, *Race against Empire*, 201. Although Lutz was not on the committee discussing the trusteeship system, she supported this system on the assumption that it would gradually give way to "self-government" at some time in the future.

66. Quoted in Tuñón, *¡Por fin . . . ya podemos elegir y ser electas!*, 62–63.

67. Street, *Jessie Street*, 182; Lutz to the Right Honourable Anthony Eden, May 11, 1945, AFBPF.

68. Summary Report of Fifth Meeting of Committee I/2, May 11, 1945, doc. 244, I/2/12, United Nations Conference on International Organization.

69. Lutz to Representative Charles A. Eaton, May 14, 1945, AFBPF. There were roughly 8 women and 800 men on delegations.

70. Quote from Sekuless, *Jessie Street*, 135.

71. Street, *Jessie Street*, 181–83. Lutz noted, "We worked to obtain rights for women in Brazil for twenty-five years, women in the United States worked for sixty years and women in Great Britain for seventy years. Why should women have had to do all this work if it was unnecessary?"

72. Quoted in Street, 183. Lutz also pointed out to delegates that Germany and other countries had revoked women's political rights after the rise of Hitler and that "the text of an International Charter should be above vicissitudes of interpretation. It should be a real bill of rights." Lutz to the Right Hon. William Mabane, May 14, 1945, and their hand-written notes, Qo.ADM, EVE.CNF.27, VOL 7, AFBPF.

73. C. Anderson, *Eyes Off the Prize*, 8. In addition, the United States did not want "international human rights law . . . [to] develop in ways antithetical to U.S. conceptions of rights [for fear] . . . that it would be used by the Soviet bloc in its ideological campaign against the United States." Bradley, "The United States and Human Rights Treaties," 326.

74. Street, *Truth or Repose*, 281; Jessie Street, "United Nations Decision on the Status of Women Commission at the San Francisco Conference 1945," *Jessie Street: Documents and Essays*, 195.

75. Lutz to the Representative of the Netherlands in Committee 2 of Commission 1, May 15, 1945, Qo.ADM, EVE.CNF, TXT.27, VOL.8, AFBPF.

76. Lutz to Representative Sol Bloom, May 14, 1945: "Why not practice it, by including it in a paragraph permitting it?," AFBPF; Lutz to Representative Charles A. Eaton, May 14, 1945, AFBPF. See also Lutz's handwritten notes on meeting Sol Bloom, AFBPF.

77. Jessie Street, letter from San Francisco to the United Associations, June 10, 1945, in *Jessie Street: Documents and Essays*, 197. A newspaper article explained somewhat derisively, "no less than 28 speeches 'approving of women' were made, the list having grown so large that any country keeping a dignified silence would have been regarded as anti-woman." The article explained Lutz's mission was "to assert her sex's position in nearly every chapter" of the charter. I. Norman Smith, "I. N. S. Diary of a Week at San Francisco," *Ottowa Journal*, June 16, 1945, 8.

78. "Charter Grants Sex Equality," *San Francisco News* (undated clipping); "Latins Win Feminine Rights," *San Francisco News* (undated clipping), part 1, reel 9, MMB.

79. Lutz to "Amigas," April 30, 1945.

80. Lutz to Catt, May 21, 1945, reel 12, NAWSA. "The pace at which the telephone keeps going and the hundreds of people who want all sorts of things from you . . . the loud speeches, the irritating voices all drive me nearly mad." Lutz to Alston, May 6, 1945, AFBPF.

81. Alice Morgan Wright to Lutz, May 22, 1945, Qo.ADM, EVE.CNF.27, VOL.7, AFBPF.

82. United Women's Conference, *Women's Share in Implementing the Peace*, 63–64, in *Women and Social Movements International 1840 to the Present*. Katherine Hanrahan to Bertha Lutz, May 25, 1945, Qo.ADM, EVE.CNF.27, VOL.7, AFBPF.

83. The women were Josephine Schain, Anne Hartwell Johnson, Lucy Dickinson, Mary

McLeod Bethune, Helen Dwight Reid, Emily Hickman, Constance Sporberg, and Margaret Hickey. Letter to Edward R. Stettinius Jr., May 21, 1945, box 10, folder 12, JSP.

84. Lutz to Catt, May 21, 1945, reel 12, NAWSA.

85. Lutz to Catt, May 21, 1945.

86. Lutz to Catt, May 21, 1945.

87. Quotes from Borgwardt, *New Deal for the World*, 183.

88. Borgwardt, 183. Philippine delegate Carlos Romulo recalled that the Latin American delegates took offense and "became anti-Russian to a man."

89. Lutz to Catt, May 21, 1945, reel 12, NAWSA.

90. Lutz once effusively praised all of the Roosevelts, including Theodore. Lutz to Eleanor Roosevelt, [undated letter, 1937], Qo.BLZ, PIN, TXT.31, AFBPF.

91. In 1948, Lutz wrote to British IWSA leader Katherine Bompas, "Only those who live in the tropics have a real knowledge of the white man's burden. I still hope tho to see the day when . . . Mr. Attlee will leave the government into more competent hands. It hurts me to see the Empire disintegrating as all these peoples now released are too unformed to understand democracy and will eventually land themselves into a mess." Lutz to Bompas, February 19, 1948, Qo.ADM, COR.A948.4, 3–4, AFBPF.

92. Lutz to Catt, June 3, 1945, reel 12, NAWSA. On the committee discussing the veto, Lutz had been instructed as part of the Brazilian delegation to work for revision of the charter application without the right to veto, and she faced stiff opposition from Tom Connally, chairman of the Senate Foreign Relations Committee.

93. Lutz was one of the authors of a "Brazil-Canadian amendment" that called "for total revision [to the veto power] within a definite period of years." According to Lutz, this proposal "had such wide approval that, if two absent Latin American states had been present to vote, it would have won the necessary two-thirds majority." Lutz quoted in Nancy Barr Mavity, "United Nations Bar Franco," *Oakland Tribune*, June 20, 1945, 3.

94. Mazower, *Governing the World*, 210.

95. Mazower, 210–11; Glendon, *World Made New*, 14. The United States and Great Britain opposed proposals by Latin American delegates "to include a bill of rights in the Charter and also rejected their suggestion that the Charter should contain a commitment to set up special commissions for education, culture, and human rights."

96. Lutz to Catt, June 3, 1945, reel 12, NAWSA.

97. The ECOSOC was created at the Dumbarton Oaks conference with limited jurisdiction, and its powers grew at the UNCIO.

98. Glendon, *World Made New*, 14.

99. Lutz to Mudaliar, President Committee II/3 [undated, June 1945], Qo.ADM, EVE. CNF, TXT.27, VOL 8, AFBPF.

100. Sir Ramaswami Mudaliar, "The United Nations and the World," *Pakistan Horizon* 13, no. 4 (Fourth Quarter, 1960): 300; Lutz to Catt, June 3, 1945, reel 12, NAWSA.

101. Lutz to Peter Fraser, May 4, 1945, Qo.ADM, EVE.CNF, TXT.27, VOL 7, AFBPF.

102. Lutz, "Reminiscences of the San Francisco Conference that Founded [the] United Nations."

103. Street, *Jessie Street*, 188.

104. Lutz to Mudaliar [undated, June 1945], AFBPF.

105. "Women at the Conference in San Francisco, Report by Bertha Lutz, Delegate from Brazil," Qo.ADM, EVE.CNF, TXT.27, VOL.6, AFBPF.

106. Lutz to Catt, June 3, 1945, reel 12, NAWSA; Oral history with Bertha Lutz, January 2, 1975.

107. Brazilian Declaration, Journal No. 38, June 7, 1945, A-37, folder 143, Frieda S.

Miller Papers, Schlesinger Library, Radcliffe Institute, Harvard University, Cambridge, Mass.; Lutz, "Notes on the San Francisco Conference."

108. UNCIO report of daily proceedings; "Declaration Made on Equal Rights," *San Francisco Chronicle*, June 11, 1945.

109. Lutz wrote in a hand-scribbled note ιο Mudaliar, "The British women have gone home, thank God!" Lutz to Mudaliar, June 5, 1945, Qo.ADM, EVE.CNF, TXT.27, VOL 8, AFBPF. Street, *Jessie Street*, 181.

110. Gildersleeve, *Many a Good Crusade*, 349–50, 352. She also explained that a Commission on the Status of Women already existed in the League of Nations.

111. "Statement on Behalf of the United States Delegation In Committee II/3, on the Role of the United Nations in Promoting Equality of Rights and Opportunity for Women," June 6, 1945, Qo.ADM, EVE.CNF, TXT.07, VOL.3, AFBPF.

112. Interview with Lutz, January 2, 1975, Society of Women Geographers; Lutz's list of attendance and support, Qo.ADM, EVE.CNF, TXT.27, VOL.6, AFBPF. They included Mudaliar, Antonio Espinosa de los Monteros from Mexico, O. Méndez from Panama, and Allah Yar Saleh from Iran.

113. Alonso S. Perales to Bertha Lutz, September 6, 1945, AFBPF.

114. Street, *Jessie Street*, 183.

115. Mudaliar to Lutz, undated, Qo.ADM, EVE.CNF, TXT.27, VOL 6, AFBPF.

116. Manuel Noriega Morales to Lutz, June 6, 1945, Qo.ADM, EVE.CNF, TXT.27, VOL 8, AFBPF.

117. Lutz to Catt, June 7, 1945, Qo.ADM, EVE.CNF.27, VOL 7, AFBPF.

118. Gildersleeve, *Many a Good Crusade*, 353. NWP members also noted the "Lutzwaffe" nickname. E. Witt to "Olive," February 7, 1946, box 41, folder 564, Alice Paul Papers, Schlesinger Library.

119. Octavio Méndez Pereira statement, ARA.

120. Lutz to Veloso, New York, July 20, 1945, Ministério das Relações Exteriores, Brasilia, Brazil.

121. Nancy Barr Mavity, "United Nations Bar Franco," *Oakland Tribune*, June 20, 1945, 3. Mabel Vernon of the Women's Charter also held a luncheon after the conference, distinguishing the work of Lutz, Bernardino, and Pinto de Vidal. "Pan-American Work Seen Strengthened by World Charter," *News Journal* (Wilmington, Del.), July 5, 1945, B.

122. Lutz recalled, "It was the first time a woman addressed the Plenary Assembly. At the closing session only the Great Powers spoke." Lutz, "Notes on the San Francisco Conference."

123. "The UNCIO Ladies Have Their Say," *San Francisco News*. The press paid more attention to her physical appearance than her words, noting that "in her middle forties, Dr. Lutz retains much of the beauty that brought her fame two decades ago," and commenting on her "black hat and half veil that perched itself sassily atop her black hair" and "her dark, form-fitting dress topped with a yoke of red and yellow [that] was by far the most colorful." Mavity, "United Nations Bar Franco," 3.

124. National Broadcasting Company sound recording of the proceedings of the second session of commission 1, committees 1 and 2, on June 19, 1945, box 4, Register of the United Nations Conference on International Organization proceedings, Hoover Institution, Stanford, Calif.

125. Lutz also announced, "The gods of war feed on the blood of their children, and someday the mothers of human beings will put a stop to this bloodshed." National Broadcasting Company sound recording of the proceedings, June 19, 1945, box 4, Register of the United Nations Conference on International Organization proceedings.

126. National Broadcasting Company sound recordings of proceedings, NBC sound recording of the proceedings of commission 2, committee 3, on June 11, 1945, box 5, Register of the United Nations Conference on International Organization proceedings.

127. Lutz to Catt, June 3, 1945, reel 12, NAWSA.

128. Edith Goode to Laura E. W. Kendall, May 23, 1945, series 7, reel 174, NWP.

129. In the meetings drafting the declaration, Eleanor Roosevelt repeatedly insisted that the word "men" was inclusive of "men and women." Glendon, *World Made New*, 68, 90. Roosevelt also believed that a separate Commission on the Status of Women was not necessary.

130. Lutz remained in close touch with Margaret Hickey, Edith Goode, and Alice Morgan Wright, as well as with Isabel Pinto de Vidal and Minerva Bernardino, continuing to work with them for many years on the Inter-American Commission of Women and the Commission on the Status of Women.

131. On Mehta, see Glendon, *A World Made New*, 35, 38, 40–41, 46, 84, 87, 90, 92.

132. Untitled speech by Castillo Ledón, proceedings of 1948 Lake Success meeting, caja 9, exp. 150, AGC-SRE.

EPILOGUE

1. Domínguez Navarro, *50 años de una vida*, 427. She noted this constituted a dramatic contrast with the League of Nations covenant—a "pompous" agreement of the "high contracting parties" of governments.

2. *Congrès international des femmes: compte rendu des travaux du congrès qui s'est tenu à Paris du 26 novembre au 1er décembre 1945* (Paris: Fédération démocratique internationale des femmes, 1946), 218–19. On the WIDF see de Haan, "Women's International Democratic Federation" de Haan, "Continuing Cold War Paradigms," and de Haan, "Eugénie Cotton, Pak Chong-ae, and Claudia Jones." On the WIDF in Latin America, see Soihet, "A conquista do espaço público," 230–31; Pieper Mooney, "Fighting Fascism"; de Haan, "La Federación Democrática Internacional de Mujeres (FDIM) y América Latina"; and Chase, "La Federación Democrática de Mujeres Cubanas." In Mexico the Bloque Nacional de Mujeres Revolucionarias drew on both the Atlantic Charter and the UN Charter to promote their feminist goals to the administration of President Alemán. Bloque Nacional de Mujeres Revolucionarias, "Puntos que deberan ser incluidos en el programa del Lic. Miguel Alemán en relación con la mujer," January 18, 1946, caja 10, exp. 163, AGC-SRE.

3. Robles de Mendoza to Stevens, July 24, 1945, box 77, folder 3, DSP. In an article, she also connected the UN Charter to its origins in the 1923 Santiago resolution of Máximo Soto Hall. Margarita Robles de Mendoza, "La carta de San Francisco," *La Nueva democracia*, July 1945, 12–13;

4. Hughitt, "International Federation of Women Lawyers."

5. "La Educación del Niño y de la Juventud como Garantía de una paz duradera, trabajo pesentado por la Dra Ofelia Domínguez Navarro a la Primera Conferencia Internacional de Abogadas celebrada en la Habana," August 31–September 5, 1945, ODN-AN. The following year at its annual meeting, the Federación Internacional de Abogadas resolved to fight for the equal rights resolutions promoted by Pan-American feminists at the 1938 Lima and 1945 San Francisco conferences. Bertha Lutz was the fifth vice president and Clara González the third vice president of the organization. "Se prepara un agasajo para la Lic. González," September 14, 1945, newspaper clipping, ACG.

6. Resolutions that Bernardino and Castillo Ledón had secured at the 1945 Chapultepec conference put the IACW on firmer financial footing with the Pan-American Union, which now paid Vergara a sinecure. Inter-American Commission of Women, Informe de

la Comisión Interamericana de Mujeres a la Novena Conferencia Internacional Americana, Sobre Derechos Civiles y Políticos de la Mujer (1948), p. 227 (accessed on Women and Social Movements International, 1840 to Present, http://wasi.alexanderstreet.com .proxy.lib.ohio-state.edu/view/1664781, October 12, 2015); Vergara, *Memorias*, 246, 259.

7. Vergara to Stevens, August 22, 1945, box 64, folder 5, DSP. Letters from Vergara to Bernardino, 1946, caja 11, exp. 174, AGC-SRE. See Vergara's criticisms of Bernardino as IACW chair in *Memorias*, part 2, chapter 11.

8. Luisi to Brainerd, June 30, 1947, carpeta "de P. Luisi," PL-BN; Eloísa Garcia Etchegoyen to Luisi, July 1947, PL-BN. In her letter, Uruguayan feminist Garcia Etchegoyen relayed to Luisi the points that she would promote as a vice secretary of the conference. "Derechos humanos" were on the top of her list.

9. Participants included Amalia de Castillo Ledón and representatives from the Alianza in Uruguay. Clara González was invited though she did not attend. Heloise Brainerd wrote to a WILPF member that she was "glad some of the known leaders like [Bertha] Lutz and [Amanda] Labarca did not come." Heloise Brainerd to Esther Crooks, August 21, 1947 and Brained to Stewart, June 12, 1947, box 15, part 3, series A,4, part 1, WILPF. From Chile, MEMCh could not afford to send a delegate, but it sent a speech about peace, and María Rivera Urquieta, a founding member of MEMCh, attended on behalf of several other Chilean women's groups. A1 10, Comité Ejecutivo Nacional, Circular N° 4 a los Comités Provinciales y Locales, Archivo de Elena Caffarena, Memoria de Chilena; *Memoria del primer congreso*, 12. See also Matilde Elena López, Delegada por El Salvador, "Balance del primer congreso interamericano de mujeres," *Revista de Guatemala*, October 1, 1948.

10. Patricia Harms notes that the 1947 conference attracted the attention of antirevolutionary forces and increased allegations of communism toward the regime of democratically elected Juan José Arévalo. Harms, "Imagining a Place for Themselves," 253. In 1954, the Jacobo Arbenz regime led a CIA-backed coup that overthrew Arévalo.

11. *Memoria del primer congreso*, 6, 13, 25–50; Batista Guevara, *Gumersinda Páez*. For a rich account of this conference, see Harms, chapter 7. See also Leslie, "United for a Better World," 264–69.

12. López, "Balance del primer congreso interamericano de mujeres." Rodríguez de Ita, "El Primer"; and Resoluciones, El Congreso Interamericano de Mujeres, 1947, caja 252, carpeta 2, PL-AGN. The conference also emphasized compliance "with the international agreements subscribed to in Chapultepec and in the Charter of the UN" for women's political, civil, and social rights. One resolution connected the statement of women's rights in the UN charter with "promoting true democracy in our Hemisphere." *Memoria del primer congreso*, 25–50. Ana Rosa Tornero had helped found one of the first feminist organizations in Bolivia in 1923, El Ateneo Femenino, and had directed its organ, *Eco Femenino*. Coordinadora de la Mujer, *La participación de las mujeres en la historia de Bolivia*, 35.

13. *Memoria del primer congreso*, 136–37.

14. Stewart to Luisi, June 5, 1945, carpeta "S," PL-BN.

15. Luisi to Domínguez Navarro, January 4, 1945; Domínguez Navarro to Luisi, January 27, 1945, in *50 años de una vida*, 423–24.

16. Even at the 1947 Inter-American Congress of Women in Guatemala, calls for women's social rights had led to charges by some that the conference was "communist." President of the Congress Gumersinda Paez retorted, "If this Congress is communist, so is the Atlantic Charter [and] the Charter of Chapultepec [and] the United Nations." Paez quoted in Leslie, "United for a Better World," 267.

17. Francisca de Haan makes a compelling case for the relationship between the long legacy of the Cold War and our historical memories of feminism today in "Continuing Cold War Paradigms."

18. On the influence of the 1945 UN Charter, 1948 Bogotá conventions, and subsequent IACW resolutions on married women's civil rights in Brazil, see Novaes Marques and Pereira de Melo, "Os direitos civis das mulheres casadas no Brasil," 464–65, 478–80; and Caulfield and Schettini, "Gender and Sexuality in Brazil," 24.

19. M. Becker, "Anticolonial and Anticommunist Resolutions." In 1947, the Treaty of Reciprocal Assistance, or Rio Pact, also augured the Cold War militarization of the Americas.

20. Guy, *White Slavery*, 34.

21. M. Meyer, "Negotiating International Norms." The CIM also worked with the Comisión Interamericana de Derechos Humanos (CIDH), created in 1959. On the inter-American human rights work in these years, see Sikkink, *Evidence for Hope*.

22. Grandin, "Human Rights and Empire's Embrace." See also Grandin, *Last Colonial Massacre* and *Empire's Workshop*. As political scientist Niamh Reilly has argued, the international human rights agenda was at this time still constructed around "limited models of representative democracy, the non-commission of egregious violations by states, and free-market capitalism." Reilly, *Women's Human Rights*, 26.

23. In 1948 Luisi published *Otra voz clamando en el desierto* [Another voice crying in the wilderness]. It was a collection of her writing about sex education, prostitution, and the traffic in women, but as historian Christine Ehrick notes, "its title could be Luisi's autobiography. . . . It suggests a voice without listeners." Ehrick, *Radio and the Gendered Soundscape*, 114.

24. Domínguez left the Partido Socialista Popular in 1940. The FBI began to trace Domínguez in 1944, when she was the director of the Office of War Propaganda of the Cuban Ministry of Defense. (Documents obtained under the Freedom of Information Act from U.S. Federal Bureau of Investigation, requested as "Ofelia Domínguez Navarro" June 2015, received August 2016.)

25. Jesús González Scarpetta, "Derechos humanos," *Bohemia*, July 1, 1950.

26. Domínguez, *50 años de una vida*, 439–44. See also FBI documents on Ofelia Domínguez Navarro from FOIA.

27. Ofelia Domínguez Navarro application to the Communist Party in Cuba, ODN-AN. On the changes in feminism in this period, see Chase, *Revolution within the Revolution*. In her memoirs, Domínguez lauded the Federación de Mujeres Cubanas and asserted that early twentieth-century efforts for women's equal rights had helped pave the way for the Cuban Revolution. Domínguez Navarro, *50 años de una vida*, 451–55.

28. Domínguez Navarro, *50 años de una vida*, 153; Miller, *Latin American Women*, 96.

29. She ran on a ticket with José Isaac Fábrega as presidential candidate and Ricardo Arias Espinosa as first vice presidential candidate in the alliance formed by the Partido Liberal Renovador and the Partido Nacional Revolucionario. Marco Serra, *Clara González de Behringer*, 153.

30. "La delincuencia como fenómeno de desorganización familiar" by Clara González de Behringer and others, for the 10th Pan-American Child Congress, 1955, ACG.

31. González was the legal adviser to the Panamanian Committee of Cooperation to the Comsión Interamericana de Mujeres, Cecilia de la G. de Fábrega to Clara González, June 3, 1959; "Informe del Comite Panameño de Cooperación a La Comisión Interamericana de Mujeres," May 29, 1959. She went to a meeting of the Federación Internacional de Abogadas in Havana in 1956, ACG.

32. Emphasis in original. Untitled and undated document outlining her activities, ACG.

33. González to Don J. E. Lefevre, February 17, 1960, ACG.

34. Beauvoir, *Second Sex*, 145. The book was first published in English in 1952.

35. "Clara de Behringer y el movimiento feminista," *La Prensa* (Panama City), March 9, 1990, 15, ACG.

36. Vergara to Stevens, August 16, 1962, box 36, folder 13, DSP.

37. Vergara, *Memorias*, 279–82.

38. Vidal, "Marta Vergara la irreverente."

39. Stevens's manuscript about the IACW, 1945–1962, subseries H, boxes 126–27, DSP.

40. The Princeton chair was created in 1986. Mary K. Trigg notes that before she died, Stevens sought to create a Lucy Stone Chair of Feminism at Radcliffe College, without success. Trigg, *Feminism as Life's Work*, 194. Jonathan Mitchell to Rebecca West, December 22, 1967, box 13, folder 575, Rebecca West Papers, Beinecke Rare Book and Manuscript Library, Yale University, New Haven, Conn.; Rupp, "Feminism and the Sexual Revolution," 292.

41. Cott, *Grounding of Modern Feminism*; Rupp and Taylor, *Survival in the Doldrums*; Ford, *Iron-Jawed Angels*.

42. On Lutz's retreat to her scientific work, see Soihet, *O feminismo tático*; and Novaes Marques and Pereira de Melo, "Os direitos civis das mulheres casadas no Brasil," 476.

43. Interview with Bertha Lutz, January 2, 1975, Society of Women Geographers.

44. Lutz's notes on pages of Gildersleeve's book, Qo.PIT.96/100, AFBPF.

45. Gildersleeve also inaccurately explained that women at the UN conference were only involved in committees related to "women's work." Lutz was on the committee that discussed the veto power and Security Council. Histories of the United Nations that have utilized Virginia Gildersleeve's accounts to describe women's participation in the San Francisco conference include Schlesinger, *Act of Creation*; Gaddis, *United States and the Origins of the Cold War*; and Moyn, *Last Utopia*, to name only a few.

46. Lutz was pleased by the attention paid her at the end of her life, though she believed the conference focused too much on international development and not enough on "equal rights." "Para Diretrizes do Congresso ou mesa rodonda," Qo.PIT.136; Lutz to Dr. Kennedy, July 13, 1975, Lutz to Dr. Blair, July 13, 1975, Qo.BLZ, COR.1975, TXT.3, AFBPF; Lutz notes on the 1975 conference BR.MN.BL.0.FEM.1/256, BLMN.

47. For the definitive history of the IWY Conference, see Olcott, *International Women's Year*. On the influence of the IWY, see E. Freedman, *No Turning Back*, 110, 336–37; Stansell, *Feminist Promise*, chapter 11. On transnational feminisim based on the Indochinese Women's Conferences in these years, see Wu, *Radicals on the Road*, chapters 7–9. On the influence of feminism on international development, see Meyerowitz, "Developing Women."

48. Kelly, "1973 Chilean Coup"; Kelly, *Sovereign Emergencies*; Moyn and Eckel, *Breakthrough*; Moyn, *Last Utopia*; Keys, *Reclaiming American Virtue*.

49. The sisters, Patria Mercedes, María Argentina Minerva, and Antonia María Teresa Mirabal Reyes, were murdered on November 25, 1960. In 1999, the day became the UN-designated "International Day for the Elimination of Violence against Women." "International Day for the Elimination of Violence against Women" (http://www.un.org/womenwatch/daw/news/vawd.html, accessed July 10, 2016). For more on the *Encuentros*, see Sternbach et al., "Feminisms in Latin America"; Alvarez et al., "Encountering Latin American and Caribbean Feminism"; and Friedman, *Interpreting the Internet*.

50. Bunch, "Women's Rights as Human Rights"; MacKinnon, *Are Women Human?*; Keck and Sikkink, *Activists beyond Borders*, 165–98; M. Meyer, "Negotiating International Norms"; Fregoso and Bejarano, *Terrorizing Women*, 18.

51. Clinton, "Remarks to the U.N. 4th World Conference on Women." On the 1995 conference, see Levenstein, "Faxing Feminism" and "U.S. Women in Beijing"; and Zheng and Zhang, "Global Concepts."

52. Lao-Montes and Buggs, "Translocal Space of Afro-Latinidad"; Falcón, *Power Interrupted*.

53. See Encarnación, *Out in the Periphery*.

54. See, for example, Grewal, *Transnational America*; Mohanty, *Feminism without Borders*; Suchland, *Economies of Violence*; Edwards, *Violence against Women*.

BIBLIOGRAPHY

ARCHIVES

Argentina

- Archivo del Ministerio de Relaciones Exteriores y Culto, Buenos Aires

Brazil

- Arquivo Histórico do Itamaraty, Rio de Janeiro
- Arquivo Nacional, Rio de Janeiro
    - Fundo Federação Brasileira pelo Progresso Feminino
- Ministério das Relações Exteriores, Brasilia
- Museu Nacional, Rio de Janeiro
    - Fundo Bertha Lutz

Cuba

- Archivo Instituto de Historia de Cuba, Havana
    - Fondo Ofelia Domínguez Navarro
- Archivo Nacional de Cuba, Havana
    - Archivo María Collado, Donativos y Remisiones
    - Archivo Ofelia Domínguez Navarro, Donativos y Remisiones

Mexico

- Archivo General de la Nación, Mexico City
    - Archivo Particular de Tomás Garrido Canabal
    - Grupo Lázaro Cárdenas del Rio
    - Grupo Otilia Zambrano
- Secretaría de Relaciones Exteriores, Mexico City
    - Archivo Histórico Genaro Estrada
    - Archivo Particular Amalia González Caballero de Castillo Ledón

Panama

- Archivo Belisario Porras, Universidad de Panamá, Panama City
- Archivo Personal de Clara González, Panama City
- Archivo Ricardo J. Alfaro, Panama City
- Hemeroteca, Biblioteca Nacional, Panama City
- Archivo del Ministerio de Relaciones Exteriores, República de Panamá, Panama City

United States

- Beinecke Rare Book and Manuscript Library, Yale University, New Haven, Conn.
    - Rebecca West Papers
- Columbia University Special Collections, Columbia University, New York
    - Virginia Crocheron Gildersleeve Papers
    - Katharine F. Lenroot Papers
- Franklin D. Roosevelt Presidential Library and Museum, Hyde Park, N.Y.
    - Adolf A. Berle Papers
    - Mary (Molly) Dewson Papers

Eleanor Roosevelt Papers
Sumner Welles Papers
Georgetown University Library Booth Family Center for Special Collections,
Georgetown University, Washington, D.C.
Esther Neira de Calvo Papers
James Brown Scott Papers
Hoover Institution, Stanford University, Stanford, Calif.
Alice Park Papers
Register of the United Nations Conference on International Organization
proceedings
Library of Congress, Manuscripts Division, Washington, D.C.
Records of the League of Women Voters (U.S.)
Records of the National Woman's Party
Records of the Pan American International Women's Committee
Records of the Society of Women Geographers
National Archives and Records Administration, College Park, Md.
RG 43, Records of International Conferences, Commissions, and Expositions
RG 59, General Records of the Department of State
RG 86, Records of the Women's Bureau
RG 174, General Records of the Department of Labor
New York Public Library, New York
Carrie Chapman Catt Papers
Princeton University Library, Manuscripts Division, Princeton, N.J.
María Rosa Oliver Papers
Schlesinger Library, Radcliffe Institute, Harvard University, Cambridge, Mass.
Alma Lutz Papers
Frieda S. Miller Papers
Alice Paul Papers
Jane Norman Smith Papers
Doris Stevens Papers
Mary N. Winslow Papers
Louise Leonard Wright Papers
Sophia Smith Collection, Smith College, Northampton, Mass.
Dorothy Kenyon Papers
Inter-American Commission of Women Records
Josephine Schain Papers
Alice Morgan Wright Papers
Stanford University Special Collections, Stanford, Calif.
Mary Wilhelmine Williams Collection
State Historical Society of Missouri, St. Louis, Mo.
Margaret Hickey Papers
Swarthmore College Peace Collection, Swarthmore, Pa.
Heloise Brainerd Collected Papers
Ellen Starr Brinton Papers
People's Mandate Records
Women's International League for Peace and Freedom Records
UCLA, Charles Young Research Library, Los Angeles, Calif.
Gabriela Mistral Collection

United Nations Archives, New York
  United Nations Conference on International Organization (UNCIO)
Utah State Historical Society, Salt Lake City
  Elise Furer Musser Papers
Uruguay
  Archivo del Centro Republicano Español, Facultad de Humanidades y Ciencias de la
  Educación, Montevideo
    Fondo Paulina Luisi
  Archivo General de la Nación, Montevideo
    Archivo Paulina Luisi
  Biblioteca Nacional de Uruguay, Montevideo
    Archivo Paulina Luisi

ARCHIVES ACCESSIBLE ONLINE

Biblioteca Nacional de Chile, Santiago, Chile
  Gabriela Mistral, Archivo de Escritor, Manuscritos
  Correspondencia de la Secretaría General del Movimiento Pro-Emancipación de las
  Mujeres de Chile (MEMCH), Elena Caffarena

MICROFILM COLLECTIONS

Sophonisba Preston Breckinridge Papers, Library of Congress, Washington, D.C.
Carrie Chapman Catt Papers, Library of Congress, Washington, D.C.
Anna Melissa Graves Papers, Swarthmore College Peace Collection, Swarthmore,
  Pennsylvania.
League of Women Voters Records, Library of Congress, Washington, D.C.
Gabriela Mistral Papers, Organization of American States, Department of Cultural
  Affairs, Washington, D.C.
Mary McLeod Bethune Papers: The Bethune Foundation Collection.
National American Woman Suffrage Association Records, Library of Congress,
  Washington, D.C.
National Woman's Party Records, Library of Congress, Washington, D.C.
The Women's Movement in Cuba, 1898–1958: The Stoner Collection on Cuban
  Feminism, Scholarly Resources, Wilmington, Delaware.

ORAL HISTORY SOURCES

Chipman, Fanny S. Oral history, July 22, 1987, interviewed by Hope Meyers. Association
  for Diplomatic Studies and Training, Foreign Affairs Oral History Program, Foreign
  Spouse Series. Accessed May 19, 2018, https://adst.org/wp-content/uploads/2013/12
  /Chipman-Fanny-S.pdf.
Lutz, Bertha. Interview, January 2, 1975, Rio de Janeiro, Brazil, interviewed by Eleanor
  Mitchell, Society of Women Geographers. Cassette tape of the interview from
  Society of Women Geographers, Washington, D.C., in author's possession.
Suffragists Oral History Project, Bancroft Library, University of California, Berkeley.

U.S. FEDERAL BUREAU OF INVESTIGATION FILES

Documents, 1944–1957. Obtained under the Freedom of Information Act.
  "Ofelia Domínguez Navarro." June 2015, received August 2016.

NEWSPAPERS, MAGAZINES, AND JOURNALS

Argentina
  Caras y Caretas
  Claridad
  Finanzas
  El Hogar
  El País
  La Nación
  La Prensa
  Vida Femenina
Australia
  The Argus
  The Courier
Brazil
  Boletim da FBPF
  Correio da Manhã
  Correio Paulistano
  A Folha Médica
  Jornal de Recife
  A Manhã
  A Noite
  Revista da Semana
Canada
  Ottowa Journal
Chile
  Acción Social
  El Mercurio
  La Nación
  La Mujer Nueva
  La Opinión
Costa Rica
  Repertorio Americano
Cuba
  Bohemia
  Diario de la Marina
  El Fígaro
  El Heraldo de Cuba
  El Mundo
  El País
  La Discusión
  La Prensa
Dominican Republic
  Fémina
Ecuador
  Nuevos Horizontes
France
  Paris Times
Guatemala
  Revista de Guatemala

Mexico
  Futuro
  La Mujer Nueva
  Todos
Pakistan
  Pakistan Horizon
Panama
  Diario de Panamá
  Gráfico
  La Ley
  El Nuevo Tiempo
  Nuevos Horizontes
  Panama Times
  La Prensa
Peru
  La Crónica
Puerto Rico
  El Mundo
  La Opinión
United States
  Atlanta Constitution
  Baltimore News-Post
  Baltimore Sun
  Bluefield (W.Va.) Daily Telegraph
  Boston Daily Globe
  Bulletin of the Department of State
  Bulletin of the Pan American Union
  Chicago Daily Tribune
  Chicago Defender
  Christian Science Monitor
  Cincinnati Times-Star
  The Communist
  Current History
  Daily Worker
  Detroit Free Press
  Equal Rights
  Feminismo Internacional
  The Fight
  Foreign Policy Association
  Gráfico (New York)
  Independent Woman
  Literary Digest
  Los Angeles Herald
  Los Angeles Times
  The Nation
  National Business Woman
  New Orleans Item
  New Orleans Times Picayune

New Republic
News Journal (Wilmington, Del.)
New York American
New York Amsterdam News
New York Evening Post
New York Herald Tribune
New York Sun
New York Telegram
New York Times
New York Times Magazine
New York Tribune
New York World
La Nueva democracia
Oakland Tribune
Pan American: Magazine of the Americas
La Prensa (New York)
Salt Lake Tribune
San Francisco Chronicle
San Francisco Labor World
San Francisco News
South American

St. Albans (Vt.) Daily Messenger
Vassar Miscellany News
Washington Daily News
Washington Evening Star
Washington Herald
Washington Post
Washington Times
Wichita (Kans.) Beacon
Woman Citizen
Woman Worker
Woman's Journal
Woman's Press
Women's Home Companion
World Order
United Kingdom
    Manchester Guardian
Uruguay
    Acción Femenina
    El País
    El Pueblo

PRIMARY SOURCES

Actas de las sesiones plenarias de la quinta Conferencia Internacional Americana. Vol. 1. Santiago: Imprenta Universitaria, 1923.

Addams, Jane, Emily Greene Balch, and Alice Hamilton. Women at The Hague: The International Congress of Women and Its Results. New York: Macmillan, 1915.

Álvarez, Alejandro. "Latin America and International Law." American Journal of International Law 3, no. 2 (April 1909): 269–353.

American League for Peace and Democracy. Proceedings: Fourth National Congress, People's Congress for Democracy and Peace, Pittsburgh, Pennsylvania, Nov. 26–28, 1937. New York: The League, 1938. https://archive.org/stream/proceedooamer/proceedooamer_djvu.txt. Accessed September 20, 2015.

Anderson, Mary, and Mary N. Winslow. Woman at Work: The Autobiography of Mary Anderson, as Told to Mary N. Winslow. Minneapolis: University of Minnesota Press, 1951.

Andrade Coelle, Alejandro. "Esthetic Education." Inter-America 5–6 (1922): 393–95.

Beauvoir, Simone de. The Second Sex. Translated by Constance Borde and Sheila Malovany-Chevallier, with introduction by Judith Thurman. New York: Knopf, 2010.

Bernardino, Minerva. Lucha, agonía y esperanza: trayectoria triunfal de mi vida. Santo Domingo, República Dominicana: Editora Corripio, 1993.

Borja de Icaza, Rosa. Hacia la vida. [Guayaquil, Ecua.]: Imprenta i Talleres Municipales, 1936.

Breckinridge, Sophonisba. Women in the Twentieth Century. New York: McGraw-Hill, 1933.

Brum, Baltasar. Los derechos de la Mujer: Reforma a la legislación civil y política del Uruguay. 2nd ed. Montevideo, Urug.: Peña Hnos., 1925.

———. La paz de América: Solidaridad americana, Solidaridad mundial. Montevideo, Urug.: Imprenta Nacional, 1923.

Bunch, Charlotte. "Women's Rights as Human Rights: Toward a Re-vision of Human Rights." Human Rights Quarterly 23, no. 4 (November 1990): 486–98.

Castillo Ledón, Amalia, and Gabriela Cano, eds. *Amalia de Castillo Ledón: Mujer de letras, mujer de poder: antología*. Mexico City: Consejo National para la Cultural y las Artes, 2011.

Chapa, Esther. *El derecho de voto para la mujer*. Mexico: Frente Único pro Derechos de la Mujer, 1936.

Clinton, Hillary Rodham. "Remarks to the U.N. 4th World Conference on Women." Delivered September 5, 1995, Beijing, P.R. China. http://5wcw.org/docs/Clinton _Speech.html. Accessed September 15, 2015.

Congrès international des femmes: compte rendu des travaux du congrès qui s'est tenu à Paris du 26 novembre au 1er décembre 1945. Paris: Fédération démocratique internationale des femmes, 1946.

Declaraciones de Montevideo, Confederación de las Democracias de América. Montevideo, Urug.: Tipografía Atlántida, 1939.

Diario de la Conferencia Interamericana sobre Problemas de la Guerra y de la Paz. Mexico, 1945.

Diario de sesiones [de la] octava Conferencia Internacional Americana (versions taquigráficas) Lima, diciembre de 1938. Lima: Imp. Torres Aguirre, [1939].

Dimitrov, Georgi. *The United Front: The Struggle against Fascism and War*. New York: International Publishers, 1938.

Domínguez Navarro, Ofelia. *50 años de una vida*. Havana: Instituto Cubano del Libro, 1971.

———. *De 6 a 6: La vida en las prisones*. Mexico City: s.n., 1937.

Dreier, Katherine. *Five Months in the Argentine from a Woman's Point of View, 1918–1919*. New York: F. F. Sherman, 1920.

Durant, Will. *The Story of Philosophy: The Lives and Opinions of the Greater Philosophers*. New York: Simon and Schuster, 1930.

Eastman, Max. *The End of Socialism in Russia*. New York: Little, Brown, 1937.

Espinosa, Doña María. *Influencia del feminismo en la legislación contemporanea*. Madrid: Editorial Reus, 1920.

Foreign Relations of the United States, Diplomatic Papers, 1933. Vol. 4, *The American Republics*. Washington, D.C.: U.S. Government Printing Office, 1950.

Gildersleeve, Virginia. *The Making of the United Nations Charter, San Francisco, 1945, by a Member of the United States Delegation*. New York: Macmillan, 1954.

———. *Many a Good Crusade*. New York: Macmillan, 1954.

González, Clara. "La mujer latin-americana ante la conquista de sus derechos políticos." *La Ley* 2, nos. 16, 17, 18 (1926): 865–93.

González, Clara, and Anayasi Y. Turner, eds. *Clara González: La mujer del siglo, selección de escritos*. Panama: Imprenta Articsa, 2006.

Horworth, Lucy Sumerville. "Women's Responsibility in World Affairs." *Journal of the American Association of University Women* 37 (Summer 1944): 195–98.

Hughitt, Dorothy. "The International Federation of Women Lawyers." *Women Lawyers Journal* 32, no. 1 (March 1946): 19–20.

Ibárruri, Dolores. *The Women Want a People's Peace*. New York: Workers Library, 1941.

Instituto Uruguayo de Investigación y Lucha Contra el Fascismo, el Racismo, y el Antisemitismo. *Estatutos del Instituto Uruguayo de Investigación y Lucha Contra el Fascismo, el Racismo, y el Antisemitismo*. Montevideo, Urug.: El Instituto, 1938.

Labarca, Amanda. *Actividades femeninas en los Estados Unidos*. Santiago: Imprenta Universitaria, 1914.

———. *Feminismo contemporáneo*. Santiago: Zig-zag, 1947.

Lauderbaugh, George M. *The History of Ecuador*. Santa Barbara, Calif.: ABC-CLIO, 2012.

Lee, Muna, and Jonathan Cohen. *A Pan-American Life: Selected Poetry and Prose of Muna Lee*. Madison: University of Wisconsin Press, 2004.

López, Elvira V. *El movimiento feminista*. Buenos Aires: Impr. Marian Moreno, 1901.

López, Ernestina A. "Keynote Speech Presented at the First International Women's Congress of the Republic of Argentina (Buenos Aires), May 18, 1910." In *Women and Gender in Modern Latin America: Historical Sources and Interpretations*, edited by Pamela S. Murray, 124–29. New York: Routledge, 2014.

Luisi, Paulina. *Condiciones del trabajo femenino*. Montevideo, Urug.: [Open Door International], 1936.

———. *Movimiento sufragista: Conferencia leída en el Augusteo de Buenos Aires, el 21 de febrero 1919, a pedido de la Unión Feminista Nacional Argentina*. Montevideo, Urug.: Imp. "El Siglo Ilustrado," de Gregorio V. Mariño, 1919.

Lutz, Bertha. D. *Bertha Lutz: Homenagem das senhoras brasileiras a illustre presidente da União inter-americana de mulheres*. Rio de Janeiro: Typ. do Jornal do Commercio, de Rodrigues & C., 1925.

———. *A nacionalidade da mulher casada perante o direito internacional privado*. Rio de Janeiro: I. Pongetti, 1933.

———. *Nationality of Married Women in the American Republics*. Washington, D.C.: Pan-American Union, 1926.

———. *13 princípios básicos: Suggestões ao ante-projecto da constituição*. Rio de Janeiro: Publição da Federação Brasileira Pelo Progresso Feminino, 1933.

Lutz, Bertha, Congresso Nacional, Câmara dos Deputados, Comimissão especial do estatute da mulher. *O trabalho feminino: A mulher na ordem econômica e social, Documentação organizada*. Rio de Janeiro: Imprensa nacional, Industria do jornal, 1937.

Marinello, Juan, and Luis Báez. *Conversaciones con Juan Marinello*. Havana: Casa Editorial Abril, 2006.

Marpons, Josefina. *La mujer en el trabajo*. Santiago: Ediciones Ercilla, 1938.

———. *La mujer y su lucha con el ambiente*. Buenos Aires: El Ateneo, 1947.

Memoria del primer congreso interamericano de mujeres, celebrado en la capital de Guatemala, del 21 al 27 de Agosto de 1947. Guatemala: [Nacional,] [1948].

Mitchell, Jonathan. *Goose Steps to Peace*. Boston: Little, Brown, 1931.

Moreau de Justo, Alicia. *La mujer en la democracia*. Buenos Aires: El Ateneo, 1945.

Ocampo, Victoria, and Patricia Owen Steiner, trans. and eds. *Victoria Ocampo: Writer, Feminist, Woman of the World*. Albuquerque: University of New Mexico Press, 1999.

Pan-American Union. *Third Committee: Civil and Political Rights of Women: Minutes and Antecedents*. Montevideo, Urug.: Imprenta Nacional, 1933.

Parker, William Belmont. *Uruguayans of Today*. London: Hispanic Society of America, 1921.

Proceedings and Report of the Columbus Day Conferences Held in Twelve American Countries on October 12, 1923. New York: Inter-America Press, 1926.

The Program of the Department of State Office of Cultural Relations. Washington, D.C.: U.S. Government Printing Office, 1940.

Pruneda, Alfonso, Departamento de Salubridad Pública. *Memoria del VII Congreso Panamericano del Niño reunido en la Ciudad de México del 12 al 19 de octubre de 1935*. Mexico: Talleres gráficos de la Nación, 1937.

Record of Proceedings [of the] Second Labour Conference of the American States Which Are Members of the International Labour Organisation. Havana, November 21–December 2, 1939. Montreal: International Labour Office, 1941.

Rodó, José Enrique. *Ariel*. 3rd ed. Montevideo, Urug.: Libreria Cervantes de J. M. Serrano, 1910 .

Roosevelt, Eleanor, and Maurine Hoffman Beasley. *The White House Press Conferences of Eleanor Roosevelt*. New York: Garland, 1983.

Roosevelt, Franklin D. "The Four Freedoms." Address to Congress, January 6, 1941. *Congressional Record*, 1941, vol. 87, pt. 1., 46–47.

Roosevelt, Franklin D., and J. B. S. Hardman. *Rendezvous with Destiny: Addresses and Opinions of Franklin Delano Roosevelt*. New York: Dryden Press, 1944.

Rules and Regulations: August 22 to 29, 1937, Mexico D.F., Mexican Republic. [Mexico City], [Talleres gráficos de la nación], [1937].

Sabas Alomá, Mariblanca. *Feminismo: Cuestiones sociales y crítica literaria*. 1930. Santiago de Cuba: Editorial Oriente, 2003.

Scott, James Brown. "The Seventh International Conference of American States." *American Journal of International Law* 28, no. 2 (April 1934): 219–30.

Smith, Ethel M. *Toward Equal Rights for Men and Women*. Washington, D.C.: Committee on the Legal Status of Women, National League of Women Voters, 1929.

Stevens, Doris. *Jailed for Freedom*. New York: Boni and Liveright, 1920.

Street, Jessie M. G. *Jessie Street: A Revised Autobiography*. Edited by Lenore Coltheart. Annandale, N.S.W.: Federation Press, 2004.

———. *Truth or Repose*. Sydney: Australian Book Society, 1966.

Street, Jessie M. G., and Lady Heather Radi. *Jessie Street: Documents and Essays*. Broadway, N.S.W.: Women's Redress Press, 1990.

Swiggett, Mrs. Glen Levin. *Report on the Women's Auxiliary Conference Held in the City of Washington, U.S.A., in Connection with the Second Pan American Scientific Congress, December 28, 1915–January 7, 1916*. Washington, D.C.: U.S. Government Printing Office, 1916.

Third Committee: Civil and Political Rights of Women: Minutes and Antecedents. Montevideo, Urug.: Imprenta Nacional, 1933.

Thomson, Charles A. "The Montevideo Conference." *Foreign Policy Bulletin*, December 22, 1933, 1–2.

United Women's Conference. *Women's Share in Implementing the Peace: United Women's Conference, San Francisco, 19 May 1945*. San Francisco, Calif.: United Women's Conference, 1945. In *Women and Social Movements International 1840 to the Present*, edited by Thomas Dublin and Kathryn Kish Sklar. Alexandria, Va.: Alexander Street Press, 2013.

Uruguay, Ministerio de Relaciones Exteriores. *Memoria del Ministerio de relaciones exteriors*. Montevideo: Imprenta "El Siglo Ilusrado," Vol. 2, September 1916–February 15, 1918.

Vergara, Marta. *Memorias de una mujer irreverente*. Santiago: Zig-zag, 1961.

Waltz, Waldo Emerson. *The Nationality of Married Women: A Study of Domestic Policies and International Legislation*. Urbana: University of Illinois Press, 1937.

Wells, H. G. *The Salvaging of Civilization*. New York: Macmillan, 1921.

Women's World Committee against War and Fascism. *Rassemblement mondial des femmes! Contre la guerre et le fascisme: Compte rendu des travaux du congrès* [Paris]: Comité mondial des femmes contre la guerre et el fascism, 1934.

Woolsey, L. H. "The Sovereignty of the Panama Canal Zone." *American Journal of International Law* 20, no. 1 (January 1926): 117–24.

Youth Demands a Peaceful World: Report on 2nd World Youth Congress, Vassar College, Poughkeepsie, New York, August 16–23, 1938. New York: World Youth Congress, 1938.

SECONDARY SOURCES

Alanis, Walter Howard, Santiago Altieri, and Mercedes Otegui Carrasco. *Family Law in Uruguay*. Alphen aan den Rijn, Neth.: Kluwer Law International, 2011.

Alexander, Robert Jackson. *International Trotskyism, 1929–1985: A Documented Analysis of the Movement*. Durham: Duke University Press, 1991.

Alonso, Harriet Hyman. *Peace as a Woman's Issue: A History of the U.S. Movement for World Peace and Women's Rights*. Syracuse: Syracuse University Press, 1993.

Alvarez, Sonia E., Elisabeth Jay Friedman, Ericka Beckman, Maylei Blackwell, Norma Stoltz Chinchilla, Nathalie Lebon, Marissa Navarro, and Marcela Ríos Tobar. "Encountering Latin American and Caribbean Feminisms." *Signs: Journal of Women in Culture and Society* 28, no. 2 (Winter 2003): 537–79.

Anderson, Bonnie. *Joyous Greetings: The First International Women's Movement, 1830–1860*. New York: Oxford University Press, 2000.

Anderson, Carol. *Eyes Off the Prize: The United Nations and the African American Struggle for Human Rights, 1944–1955*. Cambridge: Cambridge University Press, 2003.

Andrews, George Reid. *Blackness in a White Nation: A History of Afro-Uruguay*. Chapel Hill: University of North Carolina Press, 2010.

Antezana-Pernet, Corinne A. "Mobilizing Women in the Popular Front Era: Feminism, Class, and Politics in the Movimiento Pro-Emancipación de la Mujer Chilena (MEMCh), 1935–1950." Ph.D. diss., University of California, Irvine, 1996.

———. "Peace in the World and Democracy at Home: The Chilean Women's Movement in the 1940s." In *Latin American in the 1940s: War and Postwar Transitions*, edited by David Rock, 166–86. Berkeley: University of California Press, 1994.

Baldez, Lisa. *Defying Convention: U.S. Resistance to the UN Treaty on Women's Rights*. New York: Cambridge University Press, 2014.

Bareiro, Line, and Clyde Soto. *Ciudadanas: Una memoria inconstante*. Asunción, Paraguay: Centro de Documentación y Estudios, 1997.

Barr, Nancy Ellen. "A Profession for Women: Education, Social Service Administration, and Feminism in the Life of Sophonisba Preston Breckinridge, 1886–1948." Ph.D. diss., Emory University, 1993.

Barrera, Eugenio. *Felicia Santizo: Una educadora al servicio de su pueblo*. Panama: Centro de Estudios Latinoamericanos Justo Arosemena, 1980.

Barr-Melej, Patrick. *Reforming Chile: Cultural Politics, Nationalism, and the Rise of the Middle Class*. Durham: University of North Carolina Press, 2001.

Batista Guevara, Dania Betzy. *Gumersinda Páez: Pensamiento y proyección*. Panama: Universidad de Panamá, 2011.

Becker, Marc. "Anticolonial and Anticommunist Resolutions at the Ninth Pan American Conference." American Historical Association Annual Meeting, Atlanta, Ga., 2016.

Becker, Susan D. *The Origins of the Equal Rights Amendment: American Feminism between the Wars*. New York: Greenwood Press, 1981.

Berlant, Lauren. "Intimacy: A Special Issue." *Critical Inquiry* 24, no. 2 (Winter 1998): 281–88.

———, ed. *Intimacy*. Chicago: Chicago University Press, 2000.

Besse, Susan K. *Restructuring Patriarchy: The Modernization of Gender Inequality in Brazil, 1914–1940*. Chapel Hill: University of North Carolina Press, 1996.

Bethell, Leslie. "Brazil and 'Latin America.'" *Journal of Latin American Studies* 42, no. 3 (August 2010): 457–85.

Blachman, Morris J. "Eve in Adamocracy: The Politics of Women in Brazil." B.A. thesis, Brandeis University, 1976.

Blain, Keisha N. *Set the World on Fire: Black Nationalist Women and the Global Struggle for Freedom.* Philadelphia: University of Pennsylvania Press, 2018.

Borgwardt, Elizabeth. *A New Deal for the World: America's Vision for Human Rights.* Cambridge, Mass.: Harvard University Press, 2005.

Boris, Eileen. "'No Right to Layettes or Nursing Time': Maternity Leave and the Question of U.S. Exceptionalism." In *Workers across the Americas: The Transnational Turn in Labor History*, edited by Leon Fink, 171–93. Oxford: Oxford University Press, 2011.

Boris, Eileen, and Jill Jensen. "The ILO: Women's Networks and the Making of the Woman Worker." In *Women and Social Movements International 1840 to the Present*, edited by Thomas Dublin and Kathryn Kish Sklar. Alexandria, Va.: Alexander Street Press, 2013. http://wasi.alexanderstreet.com/View/1879476. Accessed September 12, 2015.

Boris, Eileen, and Premilla Nadasen. "Domestic Workers Organize!" *WorkingUSA: The Journal of Labor and Society* 11 no. 4 (December 2009): 413–37.

Bosch, Mineke. "Colonial Dimensions of Dutch Women's Suffrage: Aletta Jacobs's Travel Letters from Africa and Asia, 1911–1912." *Journal of Women's History* 11, no. 2 (1999): 8–34.

Bradley, Curtis A. "The United States and Human Rights Treaties: Race Relations, the Cold War, and Constitutionalism." *Chinese Journal of International Law* 9, no. 2 (2010): 321–44.

Bredbenner, Candice Lewis. *A Nationality of Her Own: Women, Marriage, and the Law of Citizenship.* Berkeley: University of California Press, 1998.

Briggs, Laura. *How All Politics Became Reproductive Politics.* Oakland: University of California Press, 2017.

———. *Reproducing Empire: Race, Sex, Science, and U.S. Imperialism in Puerto Rico.* Berkeley: University of California Press, 2002.

Brunson, Takkara Keosha. "Constructing Afro-Cuban Womanhood: Race, Gender, and Citizenship in Republican-Era Cuba, 1902–1958." Ph.D. diss., University of Texas at Austin, 2011.

Burke, Roland. *Decolonization and the Evolution of International Human Rights.* Philadelphia: University of Pennsylvania Press, 2013.

Burnett, Christina Duffy. "Contingent Constitutions: Empire and Law in the Americas." Ph.D. diss., Princeton University, 2010.

Burton, Antoinette. *Burdens of History: British Feminists, Indian Women, and Imperial Culture, 1865–1915.* Chapel Hill: University of North Carolina Press, 1994.

Cano, Gabriela. "El 'feminismo de estado' e Amalia de Castillo Ledón durante los gobiernos de Emilio Portes Gil y Lázaro Cárdenas." *Relaciones Estudios de Historia y Sociedad* 149 (Winter 2017): 39–69.

———. "México 1923: Primer Congreso Feminista Panamericano." *Debate Feminista* 1 (March 1990): 303–18.

———. *Se llamaba Elena Arizmendi.* Mexico: Tusquets Editores, 2010.

———. "Una perspectiva del aborto en los años treinta: La propuesta marxista." *Debate Feminista* 2 (1990): 362–72.

Cano, Gabriela, and Patricia Vega. *Amalia González Caballero de Castillo Ledón: Entre las letras, el poder y la diplomacia.* [Ciudad Victoria, Mex.]: Instituto Tamaulipeco para la Cultura y las Artes, 2016.

Capello, Ernesto. *City at the Center of the World: Space, History, and Modernity in Quito.* Pittsburgh: University of Pittsburgh Press, 2011.

Carlson, Marifran. *¡Feminismo! The Woman's Movement in Argentina from Its Beginnings to Eva Perón.* Chicago: Academy Chicago Publishers, 1988.

Carozza, Paolo G. "From Conquest to Constitutions: Retrieving a Latin American Tradition of the Idea of Human Rights." *Human Rights Quarterly* 25 (2008): 281–313.

Caulfield, Sueann. *In Defense of Honor: Sexual Morality, Modernity, and Nation in Early Twentieth-Century Brazil.* Durham: Duke University Press, 2000.

Caulfield, Sueann, and Cristina Schettini. "Gender and Sexuality in Brazil since Independence." In *The Oxford Research Encyclopedia of Latin American History*, edited by William Beezley. New York: Oxford University Press, 2017. Accessed online September 5, 2017.

Chaney, Elsa M. *Supermadre: Women in Politics in Latin America.* Austin: University of Texas Press, 1970.

Chase, Michelle. "La Federación Democrática de Mujeres Cubanas: de la República a la Revolución." In *Queridas camaradas: Historias iberoamericanas de mujeres comunistas*, edited by Adriana Valobra and Mercedes Yusta, 193–214. Buenos Aires: Miño y Dávila Editores, 2017.

———. *Revolution within the Revolution: Women and Gender Politics in Cuba, 1952–1962.* Chapel Hill: University of North Carolina Press, 2016.

Cobble, Dorothy Sue. "A Higher 'Standard of Life' for the World: U.S. Labor Women's Reform Internationalism and the Legacies of 1919." *Journal of American History* 100 (March 2014): 1052–85.

———. *The Other Women's Movement: Workplace Justice and Social Rights in Modern America.* Princeton: Princeton University Press, 2005.

Cobble, Dorothy Sue, Linda Gordon, and Astrid Henry. *Feminism Unfinished: A Short, Surprising History of American Women's Movements.* New York: Liveright, 2015.

Cohen, Lucy M. *Colombianas en la vanguardia.* Medellín: Col. Ed. Univ. de Antioquia, 2001.

Cohen, Robert. *When the Old Left Was Young: Student Radicals and America's First Mass Student Movement, 1929–1941.* New York: Oxford University Press, 1993.

Coker Gonzalez, Charity. "Agitating for Their Rights: The Colombian Women's Movement, 1930–1957." *Pacific Historical Review* 69, no. 4 (November 2000): 689–706.

Connolly, N. D. B. *A World More Concrete: Real Estate and the Remaking of Jim Crow South Florida.* Chicago: University of Chicago Press, 2014.

Coons, Lorraine. "Gabrielle Duchêne: Feminist, Pacifist, Reluctant Bourgeois." *Peace and Change* 24, no. 2 (April 1999): 121–47.

Coordinadora de la Mujer. *La participación de las mujeres en la historia de Bolivia.* La Paz, Bolivia: Coordinadora de la Mujer, 2006.

Costigliola, Frank. "Reading for Emotion." In *Explaining the History of American Foreign Relations*, edited by Frank Costigliola and Michael Hoganson, 356–74. New York: Cambridge University Press, 2016.

———. *Roosevelt's Lost Alliances: How Personal Politics Helped Start the Cold War.* Princeton: Princeton University Press, 2012.

Cott, Nancy F. "Feminist Politics in the 1920s: The National Woman's Party." *Journal of American History* 71, no. 1 (June 1984): 43–68.

———. *The Grounding of Modern Feminism.* New Haven: Yale University Press, 1987.

———. "Historical Perspectives: The Equal Rights Amendment in the 1920s." In *Conflicts in Feminism*, edited by Marianne Hirsch and Evelyn Fox Keller, 44–59. New York: Routledge, 1990.

———. "Marriage and Women's Citizenship in the United States, 1830–1934." *American Historical Review* 103, no. 5 (December 1998): 1440–74.

Cubillo Paniagua, Ruth. *Mujeres e identidades: Las escritoras del "Repertorio Americano" (1919–1959).* San José: Editorial de la Universidad de Costa Rica, 2001.

Davis, Angela Y. *Women, Race, and Class*. New York: Vintage Books, 1981.

Dawley, Alan. *Changing the World: American Progressives in War and Revolution*. Princeton: Princeton University Press, 2003.

Deere, Carmen Diane, and Magdalena León. "Liberalism and Married Women's Property Rights in Nineteenth-Century Latin America." *Hispanic American Historical Review* 85, no. 4 (2005): 627–78.

De Grazia, Victoria. *How Fascism Ruled Women: Italy, 1922–1945*. Berkeley: University of California Press, 1992.

de Haan, Francisca. "Continuing Cold War Paradigms in Western Historiography of Transnational Women's Organisations: The Case of the Women's International Democratic Federation (WIDF)." *Women's History Review* 19, no. 4 (2010): 547–73.

———. "Eugénie Cotton, Pak Chong-ae, and Claudia Jones: Rethinking Transnational Feminism and International Politics." *Journal of Women's History* 25, no. 4 (Winter 2013): 174–89.

———. "La Federación Democrática Internacional de Mujeres (FDIM) y América Latina, de 1945 a los años setenta." In *Queridas camaradas: Historias iberoamericanas de mujeres comunistas*, edited by Adriana Valobra and Mercedes Yusta, 17–44. Buenos Aires: Miño y Dávila Editores, 2017.

———. "The Women's International Democratic Federation (WIDF): History, Main Agenda, and Contributions, 1945–1991." *Women and Social Movements International 1840 to Present*, edited by Thomas Dublin and Kathryn Kish Sklar. Alexandria, Va.: Alexander Street Press, 2012. http://wasi.alexanderstreet.com/help/view/the _womens_international_democratic_federation_widf_main_agenda_and _contributions_19451991. Accessed February 2, 2017.

de la Fuente, Alejandro. *A Nation for All: Race, Inequality, and Politics in Twentieth-Century Cuba*. Chapel Hill: University of North Carolina Press, 2001.

Delap, Lucy. *The Feminist Avant-Garde: Transatlantic Encounters of the Early Twentieth Century*. Cambridge: Cambridge University Press, 2007.

Denning, Michael. *The Cultural Front: The Laboring of American Culture in the Twentieth Century*. New York: Verso, 1998.

Deutsch, Sandra McGee. "Argentine Women against Fascism: The Junta de la Victoria, 1941–1947." *Politics, Religion, and Ideology* 13, no. 2 (2012): 221–36.

———. *Crossing Borders, Claiming a Nation: A History of Argentine Jewish Women, 1880–1955*. Durham: Duke University Press, 2010.

———. "Engendering Antifascism: The Rise of the Argentine Victory Board in Transnational Perspective, 1930–1947." Unpublished book manuscript.

———. *Las Derechas: The Extreme Right in Argentina, Brazil, and Chile, 1890–1939*. Stanford: Stanford University Press, 1999.

———. "Hands across the Río de la Plata: Argentine and Uruguayan Antifascist Women, 1941–1947." *Contemporánea: Historia y problemas del siglo XX* 8, no. 8 (2017): 29–53.

———. "The New School Lecture 'An Army of Women': Communist-Linked Solidarity Movements, Maternalism, and Political Consciousness in 1930s and 1940s Argentina." *The Americas* 75, no. 1 (January 2018): 95–125.

DuBois, Ellen. "Internationalizing Married Women's Nationality: The Hague Campaign of 1930." In *Globalizing Feminisms, 1789–1945*, edited by Karen Offen, 204–16. London: Routledge, 2010.

———. "Woman Suffrage: The View from the Pacific." *Pacific Historical Review* 69 (2000): 539–51.

———. "Woman Suffrage and the Left: An International Socialist-Feminist Perspective." *New Left Review* 186 (1991): 20–45.

DuBois, Ellen, and Kate Oliviero. "Circling the Globe: International Feminism Reconsidered, 1920 to 1975." *Women's Studies International Forum* 32 (2009): 1–3.

DuBois, Ellen, and Lauren Derby. "The Strange Case of Minerva Bernardino: Pan American and United Nations Women's Right Activist." *Women's Studies International Forum* 32 (2009): 43–50.

Dubois, Laurent. "An Enslaved Enlightenment: Rethinking the Intellectual History of the French Atlantic." *Social History* 31, no. 1 (February 2006): 1–14.

Edwards, Alice. *Violence against Women under International Human Rights Law*. Cambridge: Cambridge University Press, 2010.

Ehrick, Christine. "Il femminismi ispanici, pan-americani e atlantici, fra le due guerre." *Genesis: rivista della Società italiana della storiche* 8, no. 2 (2009): 41–64.

———. "Madrinas and Missionaries: Uruguay and the Pan-American Women's Movement." *Gender and History* 10 (1998): 406–24.

———. *Radio and the Gendered Soundscape: Women and Broadcasting in Argentina and Uruguay, 1930–1950*. New York: Cambridge University Press, 2015.

———. *The Shield of the Weak: Feminism and the State in Uruguay, 1903–1933*. Albuquerque: University of New Mexico Press, 2005.

Eltit, Diamela. *Crónica del sufragio femenino en Chile*. Santiago: Chile Servicio Nacional de la Mujer SERNAM, 1994.

Encarnación, Omar G. *Out in the Periphery: Latin America's Gay Rights Revolution*. New York: Oxford University Press, 2016.

Esquirol, Jorge L. "Alejandro Álvarez's Latin American Law: A Question of Identity." *Leiden Journal of International Law* 19 (2006): 931–56.

Eustace, Nicole, Eugenia Lean, Julie Livingston, Jan Plamper, William M. Reddy, and Barbara H. Rosenwein. "AHR Conversation: The Historical Study of Emotions." *American Historical Review* 119 (2012): 1487–1531.

Evans, Richard J. *The Feminists: Women's Emancipation Movements in Europe, America and Australia, 1840–1920*. London: Routledge, 1977.

Falcón, Sylvanna M. *Power Interrupted: Antiracist and Feminist Activism inside the United Nations*. Seattle: University of Washington Press, 2016.

Fitzgerald, E. V. K. "ECLA and the Formation of Latin American Economic Doctrine." In *Latin America in the 1940s: War and Postwar Transitions*, edited by David Rock, 89–108. Berkeley: University of California Press, 1994.

Ford, Linda. *Iron-Jawed Angels: The Suffrage Militancy of the National Woman's Party, 1912–1920*. Lanham, Md.: University Press of America, 1991.

Foster, Carrie Ann. *The Women and the Warriors: The U.S. Section of the Women's International League for Peace and Freedom, 1915–1946*. Syracuse: Syracuse University Press, 1995.

Fraccaro, Glaucia Cristina Candian. *Os direitos das mulheres: organização social e legislação trabalhista no entreguerras brasileiro (1917–1937)*. Campinas: UNICAMP, 2016.

———. "O trabalho feminino sob o olhar estrangeiro: Relatório de Mary M. Cannon ao Departamento do Trabalho dos Estados Unidos, 1943," *Revista Mundos do Trabalho* 2, no. 4 (August-December, 2010): 336–52.

———. "Uma história social do feminismo: diálogos de um campo politico brasileiro (1917–1932)." *Estudos Históricos* 31, no. 63 (January-April 2018): 7–26.

Freedman, Estelle B. *No Turning Back: The History of Feminism and the Future of Women*. New York: Ballantine Books, 2002.

Freedman, Maurice. "Race against Time." *Phylon* 14, no. 4 (1953): 401–9.

Fregoso, Rosa-Linda and Cynthia L. Bejarano, eds. *Terrorizing Women: Feminicide in the Americas.* Durham: Duke University Press, 2010.

Frens-String, Joshua. "Pan-America's Quarry: World War II, Latin American Commodities, and Some Roots of the Postwar Order." Latin American Studies Association Congress, San Francisco, Calif., May 23–26, 2012.

Friedman, Elisabeth Jay. *Interpreting the Internet: Feminist and Queer Counterpublics in Latin America.* Oakland: University of California Press, 2016.

———. *Unfinished Transitions: Women and the Gendered Development of Democracy in Venezuela, 1936–1996.* University Park: Penn State University Press, 2000.

Friedman, Max Paul. *Nazis and Good Neighbors: The United States Campaign against the Germans of Latin America in World War II.* Cambridge: Cambridge University Press, 2005.

Fronczak, Joseph. "Local People's Global Politics: A Transnational History of the Hands Off Ethiopia Movement of 1935." *Diplomatic History* 39, no. 2 (2015): 245–74.

Gaddis, John Lewis. *The United States and the Origins of the Cold War, 1941–1947.* New York: Columbia University Press, 1972.

García Montes, Jorge, and Antonio Alonso Avila. *Historia del Partido Comunista de Cuba.* Miami: Rema Press, 1970.

García-Bryce, Iñigo. "Transnational Activist: Magda Portal and the American Popular Revolutionary Alliance (APRA), 1926–1950." *The Americas* 70, no. 4 (2014): 677–706.

García-Peña, Lorgia. *The Borders of Dominicanidad: Race, Nation, and Archives of Contradiction.* Durham: Duke University Press, 2016.

Gascue, Alvarado. "Un intento de organización política de la raza negra en Uruguay— Partido Autócono Negro." *Hoy es historia* 5, no. 27 (June 1988): 47–54.

Gellman, Irwin F. *Secret Affairs: Franklin Roosevelt, Cordell Hull, and Sumner Welles.* Baltimore: Johns Hopkins University Press, 1995.

Gilderhaus, Mark T. *Pan American Visions: Woodrow Wilson in the Western Hemisphere, 1913–1921.* Tucson: University of Arizona Press, 1986.

Glendon, Mary Ann. "The Forgotten Crucible: The Latin American Influence on the Universal Human Rights Idea." *Harvard Human Rights Journal* 16, no. 27 (2003): 27–40.

———. *A World Made New: Eleanor Roosevelt and the Universal Declaration of Human Rights.* New York: Random House, 2001.

Gobat, Michael. "The Invention of Latin America: A Transnational History of Anti-imperialism, Democracy, and Race." *American Historical Review* 118, no. 5 (December 2013): 1345–75.

Goebbel, Michael. *Anti-imperial Metropolis: Paris and the Seeds of Third World Nationalism.* Cambridge: Cambridge University Press, 2015.

González, Victoria, and Karen Kampwirth, eds. *Radical Women in Latin America: Left and Right.* University Park: Penn State University Press, 2001.

González-Pagés, Julio César. *En busca de un espacio: Historia de mujeres en Cuba.* Havana: Editorial de Ciencias Sociales, 2003.

González-Rivera, Victoria. *Before the Revolution: Women's Rights and Right-Wing Politics in Nicaragua, 1821–1979.* University Park: Pennsylvania State University Press, 2011.

Gordon, Linda. *Pitied but Not Entitled: Single Mothers and the History of Welfare, 1890–1935.* New York: Free Press, 1994.

———. "Social Insurance and Public Assistance: The Influence of Gender in Welfare Thought in the United States, 1890–1935." *American Historical Review* 97 (1992): 19–54.

Gore, Dayo F. *Radicalism at the Crossroads: African American Women Activists in the Cold War.* New York: New York University Press, 2011.

Gott, Richard. *Cuba: A New History.* New Haven: Yale Nota Bene, 2005.

Gottlieb, Julie. *"Guilty Women," Foreign Policy, and Appeasement in Inter-war Britain.* London: Palgrave Macmillan, 2015.

Gould, Deborah B. *Moving Politics: Emotion and ACT UP's Fight against AIDS.* Chicago: University of Chicago Press, 2009.

Grandin, Greg. *Empire's Workshop: Latin America, the United States, and the Rise of the New Imperialism.* New York: Holt, 2006.

———. "Human Rights and Empire's Embrace: A Latin American Counterpoint." In *Human Rights and Revolutions,* edited by Lynn Hunt, Greg Grandin, and Jeffrey N. Wasserstrom, 191–222. New York: Rowman and Littlefield, 2007.

———. *The Last Colonial Massacre: Latin America in the Cold War.* Chicago: University of Chicago Press, 2004.

———. "The Liberal Traditions in the Americas: Rights, Sovereignty, and the Origins of Liberal Multilateralism." *American Historical Review* 117, no. 1 (February 2012): 68–91.

———. "Why Stop at Two?" *London Review of Books,* October 29, 2009, 33–35.

———. "Your Americanism and Mine: Americanism and Anti-Americanism in the Americas." *American Historical Review* 111, no. 4 (October 2006): 1042–66.

Greene, Julie. *The Canal Builders: Making America's Empire at the Panama Canal.* New York: Penguin, 2009.

Grewal, Inderpal. *Transnational America: Feminisms, Diasporas, Neoliberalisms.* Durham: Duke University Press, 2005.

Gronbeck-Tedesco, John A. *Cuba, the United States, and Cultures of the Transnational Left, 1930–1975.* Cambridge: Cambridge University Press, 2015.

Guy, Donna J. "The Pan American Child Congresses, 1916–1942: Pan Americanism, Child Reform, and the Welfare State in Latin America." *Journal of Family History* 23, no. 3 (1998): 272–91.

———. "The Politics of Pan-American Cooperation: Maternalist Feminism and the Child Rights Movement, 1913–1960." *Gender and History* 10, no. 3 (November 1998): 449–69.

———. *Sex and Danger in Buenos Aires: Prostitution, Family, and Nation in Argentina.* Lincoln: University of Nebraska Press, 1991.

———. *White Slavery and Mothers Alive and Dead: The Troubled Meeting of Sex, Gender, Public Health, and Progress in Latin America.* Lincoln: University of Nebraska Press, 2000.

———. *Women Build the Welfare State: Performing Charity and Creating Rights in Argentina, 1880–1955.* Durham: Duke University Press, 2009.

Hahner, June E. *Emancipating the Female Sex: The Struggle for Women's Rights in Brazil, 1850–1940.* Durham: Duke University Press, 1990.

———. "The Beginnings of the Women's Suffrage Movement in Brazil." *Signs* 5, no. 1 (Autumn 1979): 200–204.

Hamlin, Kimberly A. *From Eve to Evolution: Darwin, Science, and Women's Rights in Gilded Age America.* Chicago: University of Chicago Press, 2014.

Harms, Patricia Faith. "Imagining a Place for Themselves: The Social and Political Roles of Guatemalan Women, 1871–1954." Ph.D. diss., Arizona State University, 2007.

Hartmann, Susan. *The Home Front and Beyond: American Women in the 1940s.* Boston: Twayne, 1982.

Hennessy, Rosemary. *Fires on the Border: The Passionate Politics of Labor Organizing on the Mexican Frontera*. Minneapolis: University of Minnesota Press, 2013.

Henry, Linda J. "Promoting Historical Consciousness: The Early Archives Committee of the National Council of Negro Women." *Signs* 7, no. 1 (1981): 251–59.

Hilderbrand, Robert C. *Dumbarton Oaks: The Origins of the United Nations and the Search for Postwar Security*. Chapel Hill: University of North Carolina Press, 1990.

Hill, Diane Elizabeth. "International Law for Women's Rights: The Equality Treaties Campaigns of the National Woman's Party and Reactions of the U.S. State Department and the National League of Women Voters (1928–1938)." Ph.D. diss., University of California, Berkeley, 1999.

Hobson, Emily K. *Lavendar and Red: Liberation and Solidarity in the Gay and Lesbian Left*. Oakland: University of California Press, 2016.

Hoffman, Beatrix. *Health Care for Some: Rights and Rationing in the United States since 1930*. Chicago: University of Chicago Press, 2012.

Hoganson, Kristin L. *Fighting for American Manhood: How Gender Politics Provoked the Spanish-American and Philippine-American Wars*. New Haven: Yale University Press, 1998.

Huock, Davis W., and David E. Dixon, eds. *Women and the Civil Rights Movement, 1954–1965*. Jackson: University Press of Mississippi, 2009.

Iber, Patrick. *Neither Peace Nor Freedom: The Cultural Cold War in Latin America*. Cambridge: Harvard University Press, 2015.

Instituto Nacional de las Mujeres, *Mujeres afro uruguayas: Raíz y sostén de la identidad*. Montevideo, Urug.: AECID, 2011.

Jabour, Anya. "Relationship and Leadership: Sophonsiba Breckinridge and Women in Social Work." *Affilia: Journal of Women and Social Work* 27, no. 1 (2012): 22–37.

Jensen, Steven L. B. *The Making of International Human Rights: The 1960s, Decolonization, and the Reconstruction of Global Values*. Cambridge: Cambridge University Press, 2017.

Jiménez-Muñoz, Gladys. "Deconstructing Colonialist Discourse: Links between the Women's Suffrage Movement in the United States and Puerto Rico." *Phoebe* 5, no. 1 (1993): 9–34.

———. "'A Storm Dressed in Skirts': Ambivalence in the Debate on Women's Suffrage in Puerto Rico, 1927–1929." Ph.D. diss., State University of New York at Binghamton, 1994.

Karr, James C. *Uruguay and the United States, 1903–1929: Diplomacy in the Progressive Era*. Kent, Ohio: Kent State University Press, 2012.

Keck, Margaret E., and Kathryn Sikkink. *Activists beyond Borders: Advocacy Networks in International Politics*. Ithaca: Cornell University Press, 1998.

Keller, Renata. "Building 'Nuestra América': National Sovereignty and Regional Integration in the Americas." *Contexto Internacional* 35, no. 2 (July/December 2013): 537–64.

Kelly, Patrick William. "The 1973 Chilean Coup and the Origins of Transnational Human Rights Activism." *Journal of Global History* 8, no. 1 (March 2013): 165–86.

———. *Sovereign Emergencies: Latin America and the Making of Global Human Rights Politics*. New York: Cambridge University Press, 2018.

Kelly-Gadol, Joan. "Did Women Have a Renaissance?" In *Becoming Visible: Women in European History*, edited by Renate Blumenthal and Claudia Koonz, 137–64. Boston: Houghton Mifflin, 1977.

Kessler-Harris, Alice. *In Pursuit of Equity: Women, Men, and the Quest for Economic Citizenship in 20th-Century America*. Oxford: Oxford University Press, 2003.

Keys, Barbara J. *Reclaiming American Virtue: The Human Rights Revolution of the 1970s.* Cambridge, Mass.: Harvard University Press, 2014.

Khan, Janet A. *Heritage of Light: The Spiritual Destiny of America.* Wilmette, Ill.: Baha'i Publishing Trust, 2009.

Kimble, Sara L. "Politics, Money, and Distrust: French-American Alliances in the International Campaign for Women's Equal Rights, 1925–1930." Forthcoming in *Practiced Citizenship: Women, Gender, and the State in Modern France,* edited by Nimisha Barton and Richard S. Hopkins. Lincoln: University of Nebraska Press, 2019.

———. "The Rise of 'Modern Portias': Feminist Legal Activism in Republican France, 1890s–1940s." In *New Perspectives on European Women's Legal History,* edited by Sara L. Kimble and Marion Röwekamp, 125–50. New York: Routledge, 2017.

Korey, William. *NGOs and the Universal Declaration of Human Rights: "A Curious Grapevine."* New York: Palgrave Macmillan, 2001.

Koskenniemi, Martii. *The Gentle Civilizer of Nations: The Rise and Fall of International Law, 1870–1960.* Cambridge: Cambridge University Press, 2001.

Lambe, Ariel Mae. "Cuban Antifascism and the Spanish Civil War: Transnational Activism, Networks, and Solidarity in the 1930s." Ph.D. diss., Columbia University, 2014.

Lao-Montes, Agustin, and Mirangela Buggs, "Translocal Space of Afro-Latinidad/ Critical Feminist Visions for Diasporic Bridge-Building." In *Translocalities/ Translocalidades: Feminist Politics of Translation in the Latin/a Américas,* edited by Sonia E. Alvarez, Claudia de Lima Costa, Verónica Feliu, Rebecca Hester, Norma Klahn, and Millie Thayer. Durham: Duke University Press, 2014.

Lasso De Paulis, Marixa. "Race and Ethnicity in the Formation of Panamanian National Identity: Panamanian Discrimination against Chinese and West Indians in the Thirties." *Revista Panameña de Política* 4 (July–December 2007): 61–92.

Lau Javien, Ana. "Entre ambas fronteras: la búsqueda de la igualdad de derechos para las mujeres." *Política y cultura* 31 (spring 2009): 235–55.

Lauren, Paul Gordon. *The Evolution of International Human Rights: Visions Seen.* Philadelphia: University of Pennsylvania Press, 1998.

Lavrin, Asunción. "International Feminisms: Latin American Alternatives." *Gender and History* 10 (1998): 519–34.

———. "Paulina Luisi: Pensamiento y escritura feminist." In *Estudios sobre escritores hispanoaméricanas en honor de Georgina Sabán Rivero,* edited by Lou Charnon-Deutsch, 156–72. Madrid: Editorial Castalia, 1992.

———. *Women, Feminism, and Social Change in Argentina, Chile, and Uruguay, 1890–1940.* Lincoln: University of Nebraska Press, 1995.

Leonard, Thomas M., and John F. Bratzel, eds. *Latin America during World War II.* New York: Rowman and Littlefield, 2007.

Leslie, Grace. "United for a Better World: Internationalism in the U.S. Women's Movement, 1939–1964." Ph.D. diss., Yale University, 2011.

Levenstein, Lisa. "Faxing Feminism: The Global Women's Movement and the 1995 Controversy over Huairou." *Global Social Policy* 14, no. 2 (2014): 228–43.

———. *A Movement without Marches: African American Women and the Politics of Poverty in Postwar Philadelphia.* Chapel Hill: University of North Carolina Press, 2009.

———. "U.S. Women in Beijing: The Fourth World Conference on Women and the Global Politics of American Feminism." 2013. http://rockarch.org/publications /resrep/levenstein.pdf. Accessed March 5, 2016.

Limoncelli, Stephanie A. *The Politics of Trafficking: The First International Movement to Combat the Sexual Exploitation of Women.* Stanford: Stanford University Press, 2010.

Litoff, Judy Barrett. "Southern Women in a World at War." In *Remaking Dixie: The Impact of World War II on the American South,* edited by Neil R. McMillen, 56–69. 1997. Rev. ed. Jackson: University of Mississippi Press, 2007.

Litoff, Judy Barrett, and David C. Smith, eds. *What Kind of World Do We Want? American Women Plan for Peace.* Wilmington, Del.: SR Books, 2000.

Loeffler, James. "'The Conscience of America': Human Rights, Jewish Politics, and American Foreign Policy at the United Nations San Francisco Conference, 1945." *Journal of American History* 100, no. 2(September 2013): 405–12.

Loveman, Mara. *National Colors: Racial Classification and the State in Latin America.* New York: Oxford University Press, 2014.

Lynn, Denise. "The Women's Charter: American Communists and the Equal Rights Amendment Debate." *Women's History Review* 23, no. 5 (2014): 706–22.

Macías, Anna. *Against All Odds: The Feminist Movement in Mexico to 1940.* Westport, Conn.: Greenwood Press, 1982.

MacKinnon, Catharine A. *Are Women Human? And Other International Dialogues.* Cambridge, Mass.: Harvard University Press, 2007.

Major, John. *Prize Possession: The United States and the Panama Canal, 1903–1979.* Cambridge: Cambridge University Press, 1993.

Manley, Elizabeth S. *The Paradox of Paternalism: Women and the Politics of Authoritarianism in the Dominican Republic.* Gainesville: University Press of Florida, 2017.

Marco Serra, Yolanda. *Clara González de Behringer: Biografía.* Panama: Edición Hans Roeder, 2007.

———. "El movimiento sufragista en Panamá y la construcción de la mujer moderna." In *Historia de los movimientos de mujeres en Panamá en el siglo XX,* edited by Fernando Aparicio, Yolanda Marco Serra, Miriam Miranda, and Josefina Zurita, 45–132. Panama: Universidad de Panamá, 2002.

Marino, Katherine. "Transnational Pan-American Feminism: The Friendship of Bertha Lutz and Mary Wilhelmine Williams, 1926–1944." *Journal of Women's History* 26, no. 2 (Summer 2014): 63–87.

Markaria, Vania. *Left in Transformation: Uruguayan Exiles and the Latin American Human Rights Networks, 1967–1984.* New York: Routledge, 2005.

May, Elaine Tyler. *Homeward Bound: American Families in the Cold War Era.* New York: Basic Books, 1988.

Mazower, Mark. *Governing the World: The History of an Idea.* New York: Penguin Press, 2012.

———. *No Enchanted Palace: The End of Empire and the Ideological Origins of the United Nations.* Princeton: Princeton University Press, 2009.

McCarthy, Helen. *Women of the World: The Rise of the Female Diplomat.* London: Bloomsbury, 2014.

McDuffie, Erik. *Sojourning for Freedom: Black Women, American Communism, and the Making of Black Left Feminism.* Durham: Duke University Press, 2011.

McGillivray, Gillian. *Blazing Cane: Sugar Communities, Class, and State Formation in Cuba, 1868–1959.* Durham: Duke University Press, 2009.

McFadden, Margaret H. *Golden Cables of Sympathy: The Transatlantic Sources of Nineteenth-Century Feminism.* Lexington: University Press of Kentucky, 1999.

McKenzie, Beatrice. "The Power of International Positioning: The National Woman's Party, International Law, and Diplomacy, 1928–34." *Gender and History* 23, no. 1 (April 2011): 130–46.

McPherson, Alan. *The Invaded: How Latin Americans and Their Allies Fought and Ended U.S. Occupation*. New York: Oxford University Press, 2014.

———. "World War I and U.S. Empire in the Americas." In *Empires in World War I: Shifting Frontiers and Imperial Dynamics in a Global Conflict*, edited by Richard Fogarty and Andrew Jarboe, 328–50. London: I. B. Tauris, 2014.

Meyer, Lorenzo. *Mexico and the United States in the Oil Controversy, 1917–1942*. Austin: University of Texas Press, 2014.

Meyer, Mary K. "Negotiating International Norms: The Inter-American Commission of Women and the Convention on Violence against Women." In *Gender Politics in Global Governance*, edited by Mary K. Meyer and Elisabeth Prügl, 58–71. Lanham, Md.: Rowman and Littlefield, 1999.

Meyerowitz, Joanna. "Developing Women: Global Poverty, U.S. Foreign Aid, and the Politics of Productivity in the 1970s." Unpublished paper for the Boston Seminar on the History of Women, Gender, and Sexuality, September 26, 2016.

Michel, Sonya. *Children's Interests/Mother's Rights: The Shaping of America's Child Care Policy*. New Haven: Yale University Press, 1999.

Mickenberg, Julia L. "Suffragettes and Soviets: American Feminists and the Specter of Revolutionary Russia." *Journal of American History* 100, no. 4 (March 2014): 1021–51.

Miller, Francesca. "Feminisms and Transnationalism." *Gender and History* 10 (1998): 569–80.

———. "The International Relations of Women of the Americas, 1890–1928." *The Americas* 43 (1986): 171–82.

———. "Latin American Feminism and the Transnational Arena." In *Women, Culture, and Politics in Latin America*, edited by Emilie Bergmann, 10–26. Berkeley: University of California Press, 1990.

———. *Latin American Women and the Search for Social Justice*. Hanover, N.H.: University Press of New England, 1991.

Mink, Gwendolyn. *The Wages of Motherhood: Inequality in the Welfare State, 1917–1942*. Ithaca: Cornell University Press, 1995.

Mohanty, Chandra Talpade. *Feminism without Borders: Decolonizing Theory, Practicing Solidarity*. Durham: Duke University Press, 2003.

More, Elizabeth Singer. "Best Interests: Feminists, Social Science, and the Revaluing of Working Mothers in Modern America." Ph.D. diss., Harvard University, 2012.

Morgan, Paul. "The Role of North American Women in U.S. Cultural Chauvinism in the Panama Canal Zone, 1904–1945." Ph.D. diss., Florida State University, 2000.

Morton, Ward M. *Woman Suffrage in Mexico*. Orlando: University of Florida Press, 1962.

Moyn, Samuel. *The Last Utopia: Human Rights in History*. Cambridge, Mass.: Belknap Press of Harvard University Press, 2010.

———. *Not Enough: Human Rights in an Unequal World*. Cambridge, Mass.: Belknap Press of Harvard University Press, 2018.

Moyn, Samuel, and Jan Eckel, eds. *The Breakthrough: Human Rights in the 1970s*. Philadelphia: Pennsylvania Studies in Human Rights, 2015.

Nadasen, Premilla. *Household Workers Unite: The Untold Story of African American Women Who Built a Movement*. Boston: Beacon Press, 2015.

Nari, Marcela M. A. *Políticas de maternidad y maternalismo político: Buenos Aires, 1890–1940*. Buenos Aires: Biblos, 2004.

Nelson, Barbara J. "The Origins of the Two-Channel Welfare State: Workmen's Compensation and Mothers' Aid." In *Women, the State, and Welfare*, edited by Linda Gordon, 123–51. Madison: University of Wisconsin Press, 1990.

Newman, Louise Michele. *White Women's Rights: The Racial Origins of Feminism in the United States.* New York: Oxford University Press, 1999.

Niess, Frank. *A Hemisphere to Itself: A History of US–Latin American Relations.* London: Zed Books, 1990.

Novaes Marques, Teresa Cristina de. "Entre o igualitarismo e a reforma dos direitos das mulheres: Bertha Lutz na Conferência Interamericana de Montevidéu, 1933." *Estudos Feministas* 21, no. 3 (September–December 2013): 927–44.

Novaes Marques, Teresa Cristina de, and Hildete Pereira de Melo. "Os direitos civis das mulheres casadas no Brasil entre 1916 e 1962. Ou como são feitas as leis." *Estudos Feministas* 16, no. 2 (May–August, 2008): 463–88.

Offen, Karen. *European Feminisms, 1700–1950: A Political History.* Stanford: Stanford University Press, 2000.

Ojedah Revah, Mario. *Mexico and the Spanish Civil War: Political Repercussions for the Republican Cause.* Eastbourne, UK: Sussex Academic Press, 2015.

Olcott, Jocelyn. "The Center Cannot Hold: Women on Mexico's Popular Front." In *Sex in Revolution: Gender, Politics, and Power in Modern Mexico,* edited by Jocelyn Olcott, Mary Kay Vaughan, and Gabriela Cano, 223–40. Durham: Duke University Press, 2006.

———. "A Happier Marriage? Feminist History Takes the Transnational Turn." In *Making Women's Histories,* edited by Pamela S. Nadell and Kate Haulman, 237–58. New York: NYU Press, 2013.

———. *International Women's Year: The Greatest Consciousness-Raising Event in History.* New York: Oxford University Press, 2017.

———. *Revolutionary Women in Postrevolutionary Mexico.* Durham: Duke University Press, 2005.

Orleck, Annelise. *Rethinking American Women's Activism.* London: Routledge, 2016.

Palmer, Steven, and Gladys Rojas Chaves. "Democrats and Feminists." In *The Costa Rican Reader: History, Culture, Politics,* edited by Steven Paul Palmer and Iván Molina Jiménez, 155–59. Durham: Duke University Press, 2004.

Pérez, Louis A., Jr. *Cuba: Between Reform and Revolution.* 4th ed. New York: Oxford University Press, 2011.

———. "Incurring a Debt of Gratitude: 1898 and the Moral Sources of United States Hegemony in Cuba." *American Historical Review* 104, no. 2 (April 1999): 356–98.

Pernet, Corinne. "Chilean Feminists, the International Women's Movement, and Suffrage, 1915–1950." *Pacific Historical Review* 69 (2000): 663–88.

Petersen, Mark Jeffrey. "The 'Vanguard of Pan-Americanism': Chile and Inter-American Multilateralism in the Early Twentieth Century." In *Cooperation and Hegemony in U.S.–Latin American Relations: Revisiting the Western Hemisphere Idea,* edited by Juan Pablo Scarfi and Andrew Reid Tillman, 111–37. London: Palgrave Macmillan, 2016.

Peterson, Harold F. *Argentina and the United States, 1810–1960.* Albany: State University of New York Press, 1977.

Pfeffer, Paula F. "'A Whisper in the Assembly of Nations': United States' Participation in the International Movement for Women's Rights from the League of Nations to the United Nations." *Women's Studies International Forum* 8, no. 5 (1985): 459–71.

———. "Eleanor Roosevelt and the National and World Woman's Parties." *The Historian* 59, no. 1 (Fall 1996): 39–57.

Pieper Mooney, Jadwiga. "Fighting Fascism and Forging New Political Activism: The Women's International Democratic Federation (WIDF) in the Cold War." In *Decentering Cold War History: Local and Global Change,* edited by Jadwiga Pieper Mooney and Fabio Lanza, 52–72. London: Routledge, 2012.

Pike, Fredrick B. *FDR's Good Neighbor Policy: Sixty Years of Generally Gentle Chaos*. Austin: University of Texas Press, 1995.

———. *Hispanismo, 1898–1936: Spanish Conservatives and Liberals and Their Relations with Spanish America*. Notre Dame: University of Notre Dame Press, 1971.

Pintó, Elisabeth. "Etnicidade, gênero e educação: A trajetória de vida de Da Laudelina de Campos Mello (1904–1991)." Master's diss., Universidade Estadual de Campinas, 1993.

Plummer, Brenda Gayle. *Rising Wind: Black Americans and U.S. Foreign Affairs, 1935–1960*. Chapel Hill: University of North Carolina Press, 1996.

Putnam, Lara. *Radical Moves: Caribbean Migrants and the Politics of Race in the Jazz Age*. Chapel Hill: University of North Carolina Press, 2013.

Quataert, Jean H. *Advocating Dignity: Human Rights Mobilizations in Global Politics*. Philadelphia: University of Pennsylvania Press, 2009.

Ransby, Barbara. *Eslanda: The Large and Unconventional Life of Mrs. Paul Robeson*. New Haven: Yale University Press, 2013.

Rapoport, Mario. "Argentina." In *Latin America between the Second World War and the Cold War: Crisis and Containment, 1944–1948*, edited by Leslie Bethell and Ian Roxborough, 92–119.

Reilly, Niamh. *Women's Human Rights: Seeking Gender Justice in a Globalizing Age*. New York: John Wiley and Sons, 2013.

Rief, Michelle. "Thinking Locally, Acting Globally: The International Agenda of African American Clubwomen, 1880–1940." *Journal of African American History* 89, no. 3 (Summer 2004): 203–22.

Robins, Dorothy B. *Experiment in Democracy: The Story of U.S. Citizen Organizations in Forging the Charter of the United Nations*. New York: Parkside Press, 1971.

Rock, David. "War and Postwar Intersections: Latin America and the United States." In *Latin America in the 1940s: War and Postwar Transitions*, edited by David Rock, 15–26. Berkeley: University of California Press, 1994.

Rodríguez de Ita, Guadalupe. "El primer Congreso Interamericano de Mujeres Democráticas realizado en Guatemala." VII Congreso Centroamericano de Historia, Universidad Nacional Autónomo de Honduras, July 12–23, 2004.

———. "La Comisión Interamericana de Mujeres durante la presidencia de Amalia de Castillo Ledón, una mexicana talentosa (1949–1953)." *Clío* 6, no. 36 (2006): 95–116.

Roorda, Eric Paul. *The Dictator Next Door: The Good Neighbor Policy and the Trujillo Regime in the Dominican Republic*. Durham: Duke University Press, 1998.

Rosemblatt, Karin. *Gendered Compromises: Political Cultures and the State in Chile, 1920–1950*. Chapel Hill: University of North Carolina Press, 2000.

Rosenberg, Emily. *Spreading the American Dream: American Economic and Cultural Expansion, 1890–1945*. New York: Hill and Wang, 1982.

———. "World War I and 'Continental Solidarity.'" *The Americas* 31, no. 3 (January 1975): 313–34.

Ruiz, Vicki. *Cannery Women, Cannery Lives: Mexican Women, Unionization, and the California Food Processing Industry, 1930–1950*. Rev. ed. Albuquerque: University of New Mexico Press, 1992.

———. "Class Acts: Latina Feminist Traditions, 1900–1930." *American Historical Review* 121, no. 1 (February 2016): 1–16.

Rupp, Leila. "Constructing Internationalism: The Case of Transnational Women's Organizations, 1888–1945." *American Historical Review* 99 (1994): 1571–600.

———. "Feminism and the Sexual Revolution in the Early Twentieth Century: The Case of Doris Stevens." *Feminist Studies* 15, no. 2 (Summer 1989): 289–309.

———. *Worlds of Women: The Making of an International Women's Movement.* Princeton: Princeton University Press, 1997.

Rupp, Leila, and Verta Taylor. *Survival in the Doldrums: The American Women's Rights Movement, 1945 to the 1960s.* New York: Oxford University Press, 1987.

Rymph, Catherine E. "Exporting Civic Womanhood: Gender and Nation Building." In *Breaking the Wave: Women, Their Organizations, and Feminism, 1945–1985,* edited by Kathleen A. Laughlin and Jacqueline L. Castledine, 65–79. New York: Routledge, 2011.

Sanders, Grace Louise. "La Voix des Femmes: Haitian Women's Rights, National Politics, and Black Activism in Port-au-Prince and Montreal, 1934–1986." Ph.D. diss., University of Michigan, 2013.

Sanders, James E. *The Vanguard of the Atlantic World: Creating Modernity, Nation, and Democracy in Latin America.* Durham: Duke University Press, 2014.

Sapriza, Graciela. "Clivajes de la memoria: Para una biografía de Paulina Luisi." In *Uruguayos notables: 11 biografías,* edited by Juan Jorge Rivera, 257–56. Montevideo, Urug.: Fundación BankBoston, 1999.

———. *Memorias de rebeldía: 7 historias de vidas.* Montevideo, Urug.: Puntosur Editores, 1988.

Scarfi, Juan Pablo. *The Hidden History of International Law in the Americas: Empire and Legal Networks.* New York: Oxford University Press, 2017.

Schlesinger, Stephen C. *Act of Creation: The Founding of the United Nations: A Story of Superpowers, Secret Agents, Wartime Allies and Enemies, and Their Quest for a Peaceful World.* New York: Basic Books, 2003.

Schnitz, David F. *Thank God They're on Our Side: The United States and Right-Wing Dictatorships, 1921–1965.* Chapel Hill: University of North Carolina Press, 1999.

Schott, Linda K. *Reconstructing Women's Thoughts: The Women's International League for Peace and Freedom before World War II.* Stanford: Stanford University Press, 1997.

Schwartz, Stuart B. *All Can Be Saved: Religious Tolerance and Salvation in the Iberian Atlantic World.* New Haven: Yale University Press, 2008.

Sealander, Judith. "In the Shadow of Good Neighbor Diplomacy: The Women's Bureau and Latin America." *Prologue* 11, no. 4 (Winter 1979): 236–50.

Sekuless, Peter. *Jessie Street: A Rewarding but Unrewarded Life.* St. Lucia: University of Queensland Press, 1978.

Sheinin, David. *Argentina and the United States at the Sixth Pan American Conference (Havana 1928).* London: Institute of Latin American Studies, 1991.

Shepard, Alexandra, and Garthine Walker. "Gender, Change, and Periodisation." *Gender and History* 20, no. 3 (November 2008): 453–62.

Sikkink, Kathryn. *Evidence for Hope: Making Human Rights Work in the 21st Century.* Princeton: Princeton University Press, 2017.

———. "Latin American Countries as Norm Protagonists of the Idea of International Human Rights." *Global Governance* 20 (2014): 389–404.

———. "Reconceptualizing Sovereignty in the Americas: Historical Precursors and Current Practices." *Houston Journal of International Law* 19, no. 3 (1977): 705–29.

Sinha, Mrinalini. *Specters of Mother India: The Global Restructuring of an Empire.* Durham: Duke University Press, 2006.

Smith, Joseph. *Unequal Giants: Diplomatic Relations between the United States and Brazil, 1889–1930.* Pittsburgh: University of Pittsburgh Press, 1991.

Smith, Stephanie J. *Gender and the Mexican Revolution: Yucatan Women and the Realities of Patriarchy.* Chapel Hill: University of North Carolina Press, 2009.

————. *The Power and Politics of Art in Postrevolutionary Mexico*. Chapel Hill: University of North Carolina Press, 2017.

Sneider, Allison L. *Suffragists in an Imperial Age: U.S. Expansion and the Woman Question, 1870–1929*. New York: Oxford University Press, 2008.

Soihet, Rachel. "A conquista do espaço público." In *Nova História das mulheres*, edited by Carla Bassanezi Pinksy and Joana Maria Pedro, 218–37. São Paulo: Editora Contexto, 2012.

————. *O feminismo táctico de Bertha Lutz*. Florianópolis: Editora Mulheres, 2006.

Solomon, Barbara. *In the Company of Educated Women: A History of Women and Higher Education in America*. New Haven: Yale University Press, 1985.

Spruill, Marjorie J. *Divided We Stand: The Battle over Women's Rights and Family Values That Polarized American Politics*. New York: Bloomsbury, 2017.

Sreenivas, Mytheli. "Birth Control in the Shadow of Empire: The Trials of Annie Besant, 1877–1878." *Feminist Studies* 41, no. 3 (2015): 509–37.

Stansell, Christine. *The Feminist Promise: 1792 to the Present*. New York: Modern Library, 2010.

Steiner, Zara S. *The Lights That Failed: European International History, 1919–1933*. New York: Oxford University Press, 2005.

Stepan, Nancy Leys. *"The Hour of Eugenics": Race, Gender, and Nation in Latin America*. Ithaca: Cornell University Press, 1991.

Sternbach, Nancy Saporta, Marysa Navarro-Aranguren, Patricia Chuchryk, and Sonia E. Alvarez. "Feminisms in Latin America: From Bogotá to San Bernardo." *Signs* 17, no. 2 (Winter 1992): 393–434.

Stevens, Margaret. *Red International and Black Caribbean: Communists in New York City, Mexico, and the West Indies, 1919–1939*. London: Pluto Press, 2017.

Stoner, K. Lynn. *From the House to the Streets: The Cuban Women's Movement for Legal Reform, 1898–1940*. Durham: Duke University Press, 1991.

————. "In Four Languages but with One Voice: Division and Solidarity within Pan American Feminism, 1923–1933." In *Beyond the Ideal: Pan Americanism in Inter-American Affairs*, edited by David Sheinin, 79–94. Westport, Conn.: Praeger, 2000.

————. "Ofelia Domínguez Navarro." In *The Human Tradition in Latin America: The Twentieth Century*, edited by William H. Beezley and Judith Ewell, 119–40. Wilmington: Scholarly Resources, 1987.

Storrs, Landon. *Civilizing Capitalism: The National Consumer's League, Women's Activism and Labor Standards in the New Deal Era*. Chapel Hill: University of North Carolina Press, 2000.

————. *The Second Red Scare and the Unmaking of the New Deal Left*. Princeton: Princeton University Press, 2012.

Suchland, Jennifer. *Economies of Violence: Transnational Feminism, Postsocialism, and the Politics of Sex Trafficking*. Durham: Duke University Press, 2015.

Teele, Dawn Langan. *Forging the Franchise: The Political Origins of the Women's Vote*. Princeton: Princeton University Press, 2018.

Terborg-Penn, Rosalyn. "Enfranchising Women of Color: Woman Suffragists as Agents of Imperialism." In *Nation, Empire, Colony: Historicizing Gender and Race*, edited by Ruth Roach Pierson and Nupur Chaudhuri, 41–56. Bloomington: Indiana University Press, 1998.

Tetrault, Lisa. *The Myth of Seneca Falls: Memory and the Women's Suffrage Movement, 1848–1898*. Chapel Hill: University of North Carolina Press, 2014.

Threlkeld, Megan. "The Pan American Conference of Women, 1922: Successful

Suffragists Turn to International Relations." *Diplomatic History* 31, no. 5 (2007): 801–28.

———. *Pan American Women: U.S. Internationalists and Revolutionary Mexico.* Philadelphia: University of Pennsylvania Press, 2014.

Towns, Ann E. "The Inter-American Commission of Women and Women's Suffrage, 1920–1945." *Journal of Latin American Studies* 42, no. 4 (November 2010): 779–807.

———. *Women and States: Norms and Hierarchies in International Society.* Cambridge: Cambridge University Press, 2010.

Trigg, Mary K. *Feminism as Life's Work: Four Modern American Women through Two World Wars.* New Brunswick, N.J.: Rutgers University Press, 2014.

Tuñón, Enriqueta. *¡Por fin . . . ya podemos elegir y ser electas! El sufragio femenino en México, 1935–1953.* Mexico City: Plaza y Valdés, 2002.

Tuñón Pablos, Esperanza. *Mujeres que se organizan: El frente único pro derechos de la mujer, 1935–1938.* Mexico City: Universidad Nacional Autónoma de México, 1992.

Turtis, Richard Lee. "A World Destroyed, a Nation Imposed: The 1937 Haitian Massacre in the Dominican Republic." *Hispanic American Historical Review* 82, no. 3 (2002): 589–636.

Tyrrell, Ian. *Woman's World, Woman's Empire: The Woman's Christian Temperance Union in International Perspective, 1880–1930.* Chapel Hill: University of North Carolina Press, 1991.

Ubelaker, Lisa A. "The Impossible Americas: Argentina, Ecuador, and the Geography of U.S. Mass Media, 1938–1948." Ph.D. diss., Yale University, 2013.

Valobra, Adriana María. "Formación de cuadros y frentes populares: relaciones de clase y género en el Partido Comunista de Argentina, 1935–1951." *Revista Izquierdas*, no. 23 (April 2015): 127–56.

———. "Partidos, tradiciones y estrategias de movilización social: de la Junta de la Victoria a la Unión de Mujeres de la Argentina." *Revista Prohistoria* 9, no. 9 (2005): 67–82.

Valobra, Adriana María, and Mercedes Yusta Rodrigo. *Queridas camaradas: Historias iberoamericanas de mujeres comunistas.* Buenos Aires: Miño y Dávila Editores, 2017.

Vargas Garcia, Eugênio. *O sexto membro permanente: O Brasil e a criação da ONU.* Rio de Janeiro: Contraponto, 2012.

Vergnon, Gilles. "Le poing levé, du rite solidatique au rite de mass." *Le mouvement social* 212 (July–September 2005): 77–91.

Vidal, Virginia. "Marta Vergara la irreverente." In *Anaquel Austral*, edited by Virginia Vidal. Santiago: Editorial Poetas Antiimperialistas de América, 2013. http://virginia-vidal.com/actas/realidad/article_510.shtml. Accessed December 12, 2016.

Vierdag, E. W. *The Concept of Discrimination in International Law: With Special Reference to Human Rights.* The Hague: Martinus Nijoff, 1973.

Villars, Rina. *Para la casa más que para el mundo: Sufragismo y feminismo en la historia de Honduras.* Tegucigalpa, Honduras: Editorial Guaymuras, 2001.

von Eschen, Penny M. *Race against Empire: Black Americans and Anticolonialism, 1937–1957.* Ithaca: Cornell University Press, 1997.

Wallace Fuentes, Myrna Ivonne. *Most Scandalous Woman: Magda Portal and the Dream of Revolution in Peru.* Norman: University of Oklahoma Press, 2017.

Wamsley, Esther Sue. "A Hemisphere of Women: Latin American and U.S. Feminists in the IACW, 1915–1939." Ph.D. diss., Ohio State University, 1998.

Ware, Susan. "American Women in the 1950s: Nonpartisan Politics and Women's

Politicization." In *Women Politics and Change*, edited by Louise A. Tilly and Patricia Gurin, 281–99. New York: Russell Sage Foundation, 1990.

———. *Beyond Suffrage: Women in the New Deal*. Cambridge, Mass.: Harvard University Press, 1981.

Weaver, Kathleen. *Peruvian Rebel: The World of Magda Portal, with a Selection of Her Poetry*. University Park: Penn State University Press, 2009.

Weigand, Kate. *Red Feminism: American Communism and the Making of Women's Liberation*. Baltimore: Johns Hopkins University Press, 2002.

Weld, Kirsten. "The Spanish Civil War and the Construction of a Reactionary Historical Consciousness in Augusto Pinochet's Chile." *Hispanic American Historical Review* 98, no. 1 (2018): 77–115.

Wells, Brandy Thomas. "'She Pieced and Stitched and Quilted, Never Wavering nor Doubting': A Historical Tapestry of African American Women's Internationalism, 1890s–1960s." Ph.D. diss., Ohio State University, 2015.

Whitney, Robert. *State and Revolution in Cuba: Mass Mobilization and Political Change, 1920–1940*. Chapel Hill: University of North Carolina Press, 2001.

Wolfe, Joel. *Working Women, Working Men: São Paulo and the Rise of Brazil's Industrial Working Class, 1900–1955*. Durham: Duke University Press, 1993.

Woloch, Nancy. *A Class by Herself: Protective Laws for Women Workers, 1890s–1990s*. Princeton: Princeton University Press, 2015.

Wu, Judy Tzu-Chun. *Radicals on the Road: Internationalism, Orientalism, and Feminism during the Vietnam Era*. Ithaca: Cornell University Press, 2013.

Yusta Rodrigo, Mercedes. *Madres coraje contra Franco: La Unión de Mujeres Españoles en Francia: Del antifascism a la Guerra Fría (1941–1950)*. Madrid: Cátedra, 2009.

———. "The Strained Courtship between Antifascism and Feminism: From the Women's World Committee (1934) to the Women's International Democratic Federation (1945)." In *Rethinking Antifascism: History, Memory and Politics, 1922 to the Present*, edited by Hugo García, Mercedes Yusta, Xavier Tabet, and Cristina Clímaco, 167–86. New York: Berghahn Books, 2016.

Zamora, Emilio. *Claiming Rights and Righting Wrongs in Texas: Mexican Workers and Job Politics during World War II*. College Station: Texas A&M University Press, 2009.

Zeller, Neici. "The Appearance of All, the Reality of Nothing: Politics and Gender in the Dominican Republic, 1880–1961." Ph.D. diss., University of Illinois at Chicago, 2010.

Zhao, Xiaojan. *Holding Up More Than Half the Sky: Chinese Women Garment Workers in New York Chinatown*. Urbana: University of Illinois Press, 2001.

Zheng, Wang, and Ying Zhang. "Global Concepts, Local Practices: Chinese Feminisms since the Fourth UN Conference on Women." *Feminist Studies* 36 (2010): 40–70.

Zimmermann, Susan. "Night Work for White Women, Bonded Labour for Colored Women? The International Struggle on Labour Protection and Legal Equality, 1926 to 1944." In *New Perspectives on European Women's Legal History*, edited by Sara Kimble and Marion Röwenkamp, 394–427. New York: Routledge, 2016.

INDEX

✳ ✳ ✳

Page numbers in *italics* refer to illustrations.

341

Asociación de Emigradas Revolucionarias, 61
Atlantic Charter, 10, 199, 207; feminists inspired by, 6, 172, 180, 181–82, 189, 210n2; United Nations Declaration linked to, 179; U.S. retreat from, 190–91, 208
Auclert, Hubertine, 3
Australia, 21, 220
Austria, 21
Ávila Camacho, Manuel, 181

Balmaceda de Josefé, Esperanza, 146, 154–56, 162–68
Barrett, John, 22, 33
Batista, Fulgencio, 9, 170, 289n70
Batlle y Ordóñez, José, 16, 246n5
Beauvoir, Simone de, 231
Bebel, August, 44
Belmont, Alva, 56, 78
Benavides, Óscar R., 160
Berle, Adolf A., 157–58, 159, 302n1
Bernardino, Minerva: as chair of IACW, 190, 192–94, 195, 196, 207, 229; connections with Trujillo dictatorship, 156, 192, 206; as Dominican commissioner of IACW, 103, 107, 149, 156, 160–62, 177, 180–81; racism against, 174, 205–6, 290n94; and Stevens, 116, 149, 156, 160, 162, 174; at UNCIO (1945), 199–200, 202, 205–12, 214, 218–19, 223–25
Betancourt, Rómulo, 229
Bethune, Mary McLeod, 210–11, 304n34
birth control, 7, 129
Bloom, Sol, 213, 215
Bloque Nacional de Mujeres Revolucionarias, 211, 310n2
Board of Economic Warfare, 179
Bolívar, Simón, 18, 41, 45
Bolivia: in Chaco War, 5, 96, 104; feminism in, 42, 49, 227, 272n44, 311n12; women's suffrage in, 230
Bompas, Katharine, 304n35, 308n91
Borja de Icaza, Rosa, 1
Brainerd, Heloise, 226, 283n117, 287n46, 311n9
Brazil, 150; constitution of, 7, 98, 131, 137; feminism in, 13, 27, 28–29, 35, 37, 116, 180, 183, 195; labor law and unions in, 98, 100, 102, 132, 188; maternity legislation in, 98, 131, 137, 183, 187–88; military coup in, 229, 233; Pan-American diplomacy of, 76, 106, 140, 165, 110–12; as regional power, 18, 39, 40; revolution in, 96–97; during Second World War, 179; United Nations and, 190, 198, 201–3, 209, 216–23, 235; U.S. special relationship with, 28–29, 33–34, 83, 201; women's suffrage in, 8, 26–27, 97, 147
Brazilian Declaration (1945), 218–20, 223
Brazilian Resolution (2004), 235
Breckinridge, Sophonisba, 101, 103, 104–5, 109, 111–15, 270n18, 289n67, 294–95n17
Bretton Woods conference, 190–91
Briand, Aristide, 71, 73
Brum, Baltasar, 19–20, 21, 22, 24, 26, 32, 64, 92, 253n125
Bunand-Sevastos, Fanny, 105, 107, 264–65n53
Bunch, Charlotte, 235

Cable Act (1922), 74, 271n32
Caffarena, Elena, 279n46
Canada, 21, 153
Cannon, Mary M., 184–86, 187–88, 193, 296n31
Cárdenas del Rio, Lázaro, 145, 148, 151, 163, 287n49
Carías Andino, Tiburcio, 150
Carneiro de Mendonça, Amélia Querioz, 180–81, 296n41
Carnegie Endowment for International Peace, 78, 114
Carter, Jimmy, 234
Casselman, Cora, 202, 304n34
Castillo Ledón, Amalia González Caballero de, 177, 181, 190, 192–94, 195, 196, 225; at UNCIO, 199–200, 202, 205–12, 214, 223, 224
Catholicism, 6, 7, 23, 35, 51, 118, 148
Catt, Carrie Chapman, 22–25, 27, 33, 37–39, 41, 54, 58, 97, 136–37, 178, 294–95n17; Latin American tour of, 34–35; Lutz's friendship with, 29,

of, 178; ill health of, 156, 157; inter-American feminism of, 40–41, 44–45, 48–53, 57, 64, 66, 121, 122, 143–47, 153, 167–68, 172, 196, 225, 227, 230–32; as judge, 230–31; as Panamanian commissioners of the IACW, 67–71, 73–74, 78–87, 94, 103, 152; Pan-Hispanism of, 40–41, 44, 48; Stevens and, 70, 78–87, 94, 96, 117, 125, 152, 154; U.S. government investigation of, 231

Goode, Edith, 207, 210, 214, 223
Good Neighbor Policy, 10, 104, 109, 113, 121, 134, 160, 173, 185, 190
Gorriti, Juana Manuela, 49
Grau San Martín, Ramón, 93, 109–10
Great Britain, 153, 193; as colonial power, 161, 201–2, 211, 217; feminism in, 79, 128, 168, 203; South American oil production and, 151, 188; United Nations and, 6, 190, 198–99, 204, 205, 210, 212, 214, 215, 220; women's suffrage in, 21
Great Depression, 1, 5, 69, 81, 83, 85, 87–88, 90, 96, 97–98, 102, 121, 125, 132–33, 179, 270n26
Gremio de Despalilladoras, 65
Guantánamo Bay, Cuba, 45
Guatemala, 64, 93, 133, 220, 226–27, 229, 230

Hague Codification Conference. See Conference for the Codification of International Law (1930)
Haiti: feminism in, 74, 133, 149, 245n25; Pan-American diplomacy of, 69, 106, 109, 114; at UNCIO, 208, 220; U.S. intervention in, 10, 19, 73, 104; women's suffrage in, 230
Haya de la Torre, Victor Raúl, 90, 135, 152
Hay-Bunau-Varilla Treaty (1903), 44
health care, 4, 99, 139, 172
Hickey, Margaret A., 207, 208, 209, 304n34
Hitler, Adolf, 99, 115, 127, 307n73
Honduras, 51, 118, 220; women's suffrage in, 150, 230
Hoover, Herbert, 71
Horsbrugh, Frances, 202–3, 204–5, 220
Hudicourt, Pierre, 73

Hughes, Charles E., 59, 64
Hull, Cordell, 96, 101, 104–7, 110, 113, 158, 174
human rights, 2, 3, 7, 11, 61, 66, 225–27, 233–34; antifascist meanings of, 147, 165–67, 169, 178; during Cold War, 228–29 ; Latin American contributions to, 6, 10, 165–67, 194–96, 207–10, 216, 221, 225, 234–35; Lima conference as turning point in articulation of, 165–67, 172; maternity legislation framed as, 182–84; during Second World War, 11, 172–73, 178–79, 191–92, 194–96; in UN Charter, 6, 207–9, 213, 216–18, 221, 224–26; at UNCIO, 6, 197, 199–200, 204–23; in Universal Declaration of Human Rights, 223–24, 225, 229; U.S. resistance to treaties for, 58–59, 106, 140, 212–13, 235–36; women's rights treaties as early formulations of, 5, 10, 40, 47–49, 52, 57–58, 60, 99, 143, 168–69, 196, 207, 225, 235–37

Ibáñez del Campo, Carlos, 124, 125
Ibárruri, Dolores ("la Pasionaria"), 5, 129, 168
illegitimate children, 46, 47, 71, 87, 103, 224, 227, 251n93
imperial feminism, 4, 11, 34–39, 59, 76, 211, 265n73
India, 23, 201, 210, 217, 223
indigenous women, 11, 42, 51, 164, 166, 174, 194, 226
inheritance laws, 44, 48, 58
Instituto Uruguayo de Investigación y Lucha Contra el Fascismo, el Racismo, y el Antisemitismo, 168
Inter-American Commission of Women (IACW; Comisión Interamericana de Mujeres), 145, 153–54, 201; antifascism connected to, 121, 130, 134, 143, 147–49, 176–77; appointment of commissioners in, 67–70, 74–76, 78–80, 110–12, 116–17, 125, 154, 158, 163, 167, 173–76, 196; equal rights agenda of, 69, 73–74, 78, 83, 87, 91–92, 97, 101, 107, 114, 121, 122, 125, 134, 141, 142, 147–52, 175–76, 180–82, 194; financial workings of, 78–82, 85–86, 94,

53, 59–60, 73, 83; women's suffrage in, 177, 230
Nineteenth Amendment, 3, 73
Ninth International Conference of American States (Bogotá, 1948), 224, 226, 228–29, 230

Ocampo, Victoria, 11, 139, 226, 284n11
Oliveira Lima, Flora de, 76, 82, 99
Oliver, María Rosa, 139, 295n20
Open Door International, 78
Organization of American States (OAS), 229, 235
Orientación Feminista, 44
Otero Gama de Lombardo Toledano, Rosa María, 184

pacifism, 10, 13–14, 20, 99, 121–22, 134–36, 138, 140–42, 146–47, 152–53, 162, 168–69, 181, 204
Padilla, Ezequiel, 192, 305n46
Páez, Gumersinda, 226
Paladino de Vitale, Celia, 25, 26, 31, 32–33, 35
Pan-Africanism, 166
Panama, 34, 55, 57, 61, 66, 80, 87, 94; authoritarianism in, 145, 230; feminism in, 41–53, 133, 149, 153, 167–68, 183, 196, 225, 226, 227, 230–31; marriage law in, 44; Pan-American diplomacy of, 41, 64, 69; Popular Front in, 146, 148, 152; during Second World War, 179; at UNCIO, 208, 220–21; as U.S. protectorate, 9, 40; women's suffrage in, 230
Panama Canal, 10, 19, 44, 49–50, 83; Canal Zone, 44, 49
Pan-American Association for the Advancement of Women (Inter-American Union of Women), 25–26, 32–35, 37–39, 40–41, 79, 97
Pan-American Child Congresses, 14, 19, 36, 100, 101, 162, 182, 187
Pan-American Conferences. *See* Eighth International Conference of American States (Lima, 1938); Fifth International Conference of American States (Santiago, 1923); Inter-American Conference for the Maintenance of Peace

(Buenos Aires, 1936); Ninth International Conference of American States (Bogotá, 1948); Seventh International Conference of American States (Montevideo, 1933); Sixth International Conference of American States (Havana, 1928)
Pan-American International Women's Committee. *See* Pan-American Women's Auxiliary
Pan-American Scientific Congress, 20
Pan-American Union (Commercial Bureau of American Republics), 19, 22, 25, 29, 33, 36, 57, 93, 111; IACW and, 66–71, 82, 86, 94, 112, 127, 154, 158, 163, 174, 226, 229
Pan-American Women's Auxiliary, 20, 21, 24, 25
Pan-American Women's Conference (Baltimore, 1922), 24–26, 28–34, 36
Pandit, Vijaya Lakshmi, 210–11, 217
Pan-Hispanic feminism. *See* Pan-Hispanism
Pan-Hispanism, 41, 87, 92; Domínguez's view of, 47–48, 87–88, 92, 94; feminism influenced by, 4–6, 8, 9, 13, 35–36, 41–53, 87–88, 92, 117–19, 147; González's view of, 40, 44–45, 48, 92; inter-American law shaped by, 4–5, 18, 36; Luisi's view of, 13, 15, 27, 35–36, 88, 92; Luso-American exceptionalism vs., 8, 13–14; Rodó's view of, 15, 18; whiteness linked to, 22
Parada, Aída, 80–87, 125, 160
Paraguay, 64, 103, 109; in Chaco War, 5, 96, 104; marriage law in, 74; as signatory to the Equal Rights Treaty, 113, 118; women's suffrage in, 230
Park, Alice, 59
Park, Maud Wood, 26
Partido Nacional Feminista (PNF), 42, 44, 145, 153, 167–68, 226
Partido Nacional Sufragista, 61, 63
Paul, Alice, 55–60, 66, 85, 93, 112, 125, 232; Equal Nationality Treaty backed by, 73–74; Equal Rights Treaty formulated by, 57–58; League of Nations work of, 78, 124

Stewart, Frances Benedict, 153–54, 167, 168, 226, 227
Street, Jessie, 199, 207, 209, 212, 213–14, 218, 223, 224
Sucre, Antonio José de, 18
Swiggett, Emma Bain, 49, 254n3

Tenth Amendment, 58
Tercero, José, 112
Terra, Gabriel, 92–93, 143
tobacco, 81
Toledano, Vicente Lombardo, 151, 184
Tornero, Ana Rosa, 227
Torres, Elena, 31, 34, 35, 79, 251n100
Trotsky, Leon, 124
Trujillo, Rafael, 149, 156, 157–58, 159, 165, 206, 235

UN Commission on Human Rights, 223, 224
UN Commission on the Status of Women, 200, 215, 217–21, 223, 224, 233, 234
UN Conference against Racism, Racial Discrimination, Xenophobia, and Related Intolerances (2001), 235
UN Decade for Women (1975–85), 234
UN Economic and Social Council (ECOSOC), 200, 217–18, 220, 221, 223
UN Educational, Scientific and Cultural Organization (UNESCO), 231
Unión Argentina de Mujeres (UAM), 139, 142, 146, 149, 159, 168, 173
Unión de Mujeres Americanas (UMA), 117–19, 143, 146, 147, 149, 177
Unión Femenina contra la Guerra, 129
Unión Laborista de Mujeres (Unión Radical de Mujeres), 87, 88, 90, 93, 129
United Nations (UN), 3, 6, 10, 179, 189, 190, 195–96, 197; charter of (1945), 192, 198–224, 225, 226, 228, 230, 233
United Nations Conference on International Organization (UNCIO), 198–224, 233, 234
UN Resolution on Human Rights, Sexual orientation, and Gender Identity (2011), 235
UN Universal Declaration of Human Rights, 223–24, 225, 229
Uranga, Consuelo, 129

Urdaneta, Isabel Sánchez de, 202, 207, 210, 214
Uruguay, 34, 38, 39, 67, 87, 156, 184, 229; afro-Uruguayan population of, 23, 280n61; constitution of, 7, 21; feminism in, 8, 12, 13–18, 21–26, 31–33, 35, 37, 88, 89, 91, 129, 146, 152–53, 168–70, 174, 191, 202; Pan-American diplomacy of, 19–20, 24–26, 64, 76, 78, 103, 106, 109, 111, 112; Popular Front in, 146, 148, 168–70; racial discourse of, 22–23; as regional power, 18, 40; during Second World War, 170; Seventh International Conference of American States in, 96, 103, 104–13; as signatory to the Equal Rights Treaty, 113, 118, 143; Socialist Party in, 91, 171; Terra dictatorship in, 92–93, 103, 143; at UNCIO, 198, 202, 208–9, 213; welfare state in, 16, 31; women's nationality law in, 74; women's suffrage in, 14, 21, 23–24, 35, 37, 91–92, 148
U.S. Children's Bureau, 33, 96, 100, 101, 131, 158–59, 172, 182, 187, 201
U.S. Women's Bureau, 96, 100, 101, 131, 158, 172, 175, 182, 183–87, 201

van Kleeck, Mary, 289n74, 294–95n17
Varela, Jacobo, 64, 78
Vargas, Getulio, 96, 97–98, 99, 165, 206, 296n31
Veloso, Leão, 202, 221
Venezuela, 69, 190; feminism in, 176–77; maternity legislation in, 183; Pan-American diplomacy of, 113; at UNCIO, 202, 205, 220, 229; women's suffrage in, 176–77, 230
Vergara, Marta, 7–8, 11, 60; as Chilean commissioner of the IACW, 71, 120–44, 180, 225–26; as cofounder of the Confederación Continental de Mujeres por la Paz, 141–43, 146, 152, 153; as communist, 125, 138–39; as feminist leader in Chile, 121–22, 127–34, 142, 159; later years of, 229, 232; League of Nations work of, 78, 122–28; as Popular-Front Pan-American feminist leader, 121–22, 130–44, 172; during Second World War, 178, 180–82, 192;